King Charles I twice mobilized England in an attempt to enforce religious uniformity in Scotland, and both times he failed. The result was the resurgence of Parliament as a partner in the government of the realm. *The Bishops' Wars* is an essay in military history in a political context, which analyses the institutions of war, its financing, and above all the recruitment of forces.

The main purpose of the book is to explain why the King could not and did not reduce Scotland by force. The book is significant in that it demonstrates how the military failures of 1639 and 1640 were determined by Charles's hand. Moreover, it seeks to show how poor strategic and tactical operations, coupled with the political controversy surrounding the war, plagued the English army. In the final measure, it is concluded that the King must bear responsibility for defeat at the hands of the Scots.

Cambridge Studies in Early Modern British History

THE BISHOPS' WARS

Cambridge Studies in Early Modern British History

Series editors

ANTHONY FLETCHER
Professor of Modern History, University of Durham

JOHN GUY
Professor of Modern History, University of St Andrews

and JOHN MORRILL
Reader in Early Modern History, University of Cambridge, and Fellow and Tutor of Selwyn College

This is a series of monographs and studies covering many aspects of the history of the British Isles between the late fifteenth century and the early eighteenth century. It includes the work of established scholars and pioneering work by a new generation of scholars. It includes both reviews and revisions of major topics and books, which open up new historical terrain or which reveal startling new perspectives on familiar subjects. All the volumes set detailed research into our broader perspectives and the books are intended for the use of students as well as of their teachers.

For a list of titles in the series, see end of book.

THE
BISHOPS' WARS

Charles I's campaigns against Scotland, 1638–1640

MARK CHARLES FISSEL

**Director of the Center for Teaching and Learning
and Associate Professor of History, Ball State University**

CAMBRIDGE
UNIVERSITY PRESS

Published by the Press Syndicate of the University of Cambridge
The Pitt Building, Trumpington Street, Cambridge CB2 1RP
40 West 20th Street, New York, NY 10011–4211, USA
10 Stamford Road, Oakleigh, Melbourne 3166, Australia

First published 1994

Printed in Great Britain at the University Press, Cambridge

A catalogue record for this book is available from the British Library

Library of Congress cataloguing in publication data
Fissel, Mark Charles.
The Bishops' Wars: Charles I's campaigns against Scotland, 1638–1640 /
Mark Charles Fissel.
p.   cm. – (Cambridge studies in early modern British history)
Includes bibliographical references (p.) and index.
ISBN 0 521 34520 0
1. Great Britain – History – Charles I, 1625–1649.
2. Charles I, King of England, 1600–1649.
3. Scotland – History – Charles I, 1625–1649.
4. England – Church history – 17th century.
5. England – History, Military.   6. Covenanters.
I. Title.   II. Series
DA395.F57   1994
941.06′2–dc20   93–12950   CIP

ISBN 0 521 34520 0 hardback

CE

In memoriam

Carmen Alucha	(1882–1947)
Jaime Griño	(1877–1950)
Olive Irene Dodd	(1892–1965)
John Henry Fissel	(1875–1965)

CONTENTS

MAPS

PREFACE

The military failures of 1639 and 1640 occupy a central place in the most controversial century in British history. On the eve of the 1637 prayer book rebellion in Scotland Charles I was solvent, which was unusual for monarchs in the sixteenth and seventeenth centuries. His kingdoms enjoyed peace, also something of an anomaly during the period of the Thirty Years' War. And the furore of the 1620s was behind him, Parliament being no more than an unpleasant memory.

The King's decision to beat the drum of war in the cause of ecclesiastical uniformity made political stability impossible within Britain. England and Scotland certainly were not nations destined for political breakdown in the 1630s. Ireland, though not entirely pacified, had been tamed by Sir Thomas Wentworth, the Lord Deputy. The fateful decision to minimize religious diversity by force sparked division in all three realms. Neither Bishops' War caused civil war. But by demanding that some of his subjects take up arms to enforce royal policy upon another group of subjects, the King in effect invited referendum. The peace enforced by Charles's embarkation upon Personal Rule had been dictated by political considerations which were largely domestic. The King's war now sowed division, first between himself and his subjects, and by the end of 1640 (with the summoning of the Long Parliament), amongst his subjects as well. If the most profound results of the Bishops' Wars were essentially political, it is because political and ecclesiastical forces by 1639–40 were two aspects of the same thing: royal policy in pursuit of uniformity and obedience, even at risk of internecine war.

A major concern of this book is the English militia. It is essential to understand that militia service was in fact a political issue throughout English history. The Crown used its political influence to obtain infantry from the shires; when the Crown was politically weak, the military obligation of the shires was difficult to enforce. Military service developed as an issue between the King and his Parliament as each tried to define liability for service on its own terms. In spite of numerous precedents for mobilization against Scotland and the trend toward a centralized, nation-alized military administration during the 1500s and 1600s, the militia's obligation to the Crown remained defined by traditional political power relationships. The fluidity of this arrangement had a fatal consequence in the substitution clause which allowed the vaunted 'perfect militia' to escape Scottish service. To understand why Charles's demands were in fact not extraordinary (though badly conceived) one must trace the develop-ment of the militia obligation. Such an examination reveals the funda-mentally political nature of militia service.

Traditionally the interpretation of the events prior to the outbreak of the Civil War has alternated between 'material' and 'ideological' views of the reign of Charles I. Of late, the theory of royal institutional breakdown has been eclipsed by that of ideological incompatibility between government and governed. This book attempts to synthesize conflicting interpretations. The ideological divisions, namely the contradiction of Stuart absolutism by a theory of balanced monarchy tempered by the rule of law and the controversy as to whether Protestantism was better served by Calvinism or Arminianism, existed (in earlier incarnations) before Charles I became King. But it was Charles I who exacerbated these incongruities in the English polity and made them explicit and explosive, placing himself firmly at the centre of the breakdown of Caroline government. This is not to say that the troubles were mono-causal, rather, the King served as a catalytic agent. One must consider the *deus ex machina*, the unpredictable actions of an influential personality on a potentially volatile state of affairs. For example, looking at the institutional weakness of the Exchequer one also must consider how it was managed by a personality, Charles I. The doctoral dissertation from which this book evolved moved in that direction in a final chapter entitled 'The Exchequer and the Personality of the King'. However, the dissertation was markedly 'revisionist', and subsequent research and reflection has produced what is, I hope, a more balanced work.

I have been fortunate in the help that has been rendered along the way. The editors of the series, Anthony Fletcher, John Guy, and John Morrill, provided consistent, expert advice throughout the writing of the book. My debt to John Guy is particularly heavy as he helped in many ways, and his candid evaluations and great patience were critical elements in finishing the typescript.

The Earl Russell suggested in 1978 that I write a book upon this topic; he generously criticized the 1983 doctoral dissertation and provided citations. Buchanan Sharp introduced me to the study of British history and then, twenty years later, expended much effort in revising this typescript. Tom Barnes taught me how to write military history. Like a good commanding officer, however, he did not confine his leadership to a single facet of this enterprise. No acknowledgment can adequately describe the steady guidance that John Guy, Conrad Russell, Buchanan Sharp, and Tom Barnes have provided. Whatever is good in these pages owes much to their collective wisdom.

Many friends and colleagues provided useful information and advice: Simon Adams, Richard Aquila, Drew Cayton, Paul Christianson, Tom Cogswell, Peter Donald, Edward Furgol, Dan Goffman, Rachel Guy, Martin Havran, Caroline Hibbard, Tom Mason, Philip Norris, Jane Ohlmeyer, the Countess Russell, Victor Stater, Richard Stewart, Andrew Thrush, and Mike Young. Ralph Waller, Principal of Manchester College Oxford, made possible two terms of work in the Bodleian and Tate Libraries. Thanks are due to the fellows and students of Manchester College, particularly several of the tutors, Rowena Archer, Gillian Carey, Bill Mander, Ann Mann, and Francis Walsh.

The Public Record Office, the Bodleian Library, the Scottish Record Office, the British Library, the National Library of Scotland, the Corporation of London Records Office, the John Rylands Library, and the Henry E. Huntington Library provided the excellent service for which they are renowned in dredging up manuscript sources for this work. David Lee of the Public Record Office and David Brown of the Scottish Record Office were particularly resourceful in locating documents. Manuscripts housed in the latter archive were used with permission of the Keeper of the Records of Scotland. The Earl of Crawford and Balcarres granted permission for me to consult his family papers, then situated in the John Rylands Library and now in the National Library of Scotland. The Earl of Dartmouth allowed access to his manuscripts in the Staffordshire Record Office. The Viscount De L'Isle made available his family papers at the Centre for Kentish Studies. The Duke of Norfolk permitted access to the Arundel Castle collection.

Ball State University proved a safe haven in which to write; University College, the Department of History, and the Office of Applied Research and Sponsored Programs were especially helpful in their support of this project. Deserving particular mention are Barbara Weaver, Warren Vander Hill, John Worthen, and Jim Pyle. Four word-processing specialists helped out at various stages – Karmen McKillip, Lori Line, Doreen Morrow, and Tammy Brewington. The maps were prepared by Bob Brewer. I hope this book demonstrates that institutions which value teaching can also foster research.

One's family makes an inestimable contribution to a book written over a length of time. Charles and Vecenta Fissel never doubted that historical endeavour was worth the effort. Christina Maria Fissel shared her childhood with the composition of this book. And Jodi Lynn Noles Fissel has accommodated life to the pursuit of 'romantic facts of musketeers'. Finally, this book is dedicated to my grandparents and their ancestors from Ulster, Catalonia, and Essenheim.

ABBREVIATIONS

BIHR	*Bulletin of the Institute of Historical Research*
BL	British Library
CCSP	O. Ogle and W. Bliss (eds.), *Calendar of the Clarendon State Papers preserved in the Bodleian Library*, vol. 1 (Oxford, 1872)
CECW	Conrad Russell, *The Causes of the English Civil War* (Oxford, 1990)
CSP Venetian	*Calendar of State Papers, Venetian*
CSPD	*Calendar of State Papers, Domestic*
EconHR	*The Economic History Review*
EHR	*The English Historical Review*
FBM	Conrad Russell, *The Fall of the British Monarchies, 1637–1642* (Oxford, 1991)
HEH	Henry E. Huntington Library, San Marino, Calif.
HMC	Historical Manuscripts Commission
JBS	*Journal of British Studies*
JSAHR	*Journal of the Society for Army Historical Research*
NLS	National Library of Scotland, Edinburgh
PC	Privy Council
PRO	Public Record Office, Chancery Lane, London
RO	Record Office
SP	State Papers
SRO	Scottish Record Office
TRHS	*Transactions of the Royal Historical Society*
WO	War Office

1

The events of the Bishops' Wars and Caroline politics

In 1639–40 Charles I twice mobilized England and Wales to suppress a Scottish rebellion against his ecclesiastical and, by implication, his temporal policies. Between these campaigns the Short Parliament of April–May 1640 was convened, bringing into sharp focus the mistrust that had festered between Charles I and those he ruled. The Bishops' Wars, so-called because they were fought to uphold episcopacy in Scotland, demolished the myth of Caroline political consensus and revealed the gulf between King and country.

England's inability to crush Scotland or even to prevent the invasion of the north by the army of the Covenanters, this book argues, was essentially a political failure which demonstrated Charles's inability to manage government. It was the King's maladministration of the institutions at his disposal, rather than structural failure within the institutions themselves, which precipitated failure in a war that was entirely of the King's choosing. Charles expected institutions such as the Exchequer, the Ordnance Office, and the lieutenancy to perform at unreasonably high levels of efficiency despite shortages of personnel, precipitous decisions that gave insufficient notification to royal servants expected to perform difficult tasks, and a dearth of funding, all results of his Personal Rule. He could not fully mobilize the nation's might because his subjects did not entirely trust his motives and methods.[1] Lacking that trust Charles could only start wars; successfully finishing them lay beyond his grasp so long as he could not harness fully the kingdom's resources.

Circumstances certainly contributed to the King's dilemma: he governed diverse kingdoms with different religious and political traditions, waged war in the era of the 'military revolution,' and in England possessed a truly national assembly that presumed to speak on behalf of the country. Ultimately, it was Charles I who insisted not once but twice that he should prosecute an ill-advised and badly financed war against Covenanter

[1] On this process, see M. B. Young, 'Charles I and the Erosion of Trust, 1625–8', *Albion*, 22 (Summer 1990), no. 2, pp. 217–35.

Scotland. Insufficient counsel and lack of funds were direct results of the King's political decisions.

The campaigns of 1639 and 1640 were called 'Bishops' Wars,' but in fact they belonged to the King. Charles I's obsession with redefining orthodoxy and imposing uniformity within the churches of his kingdoms led to a grave political miscalculation. The British King could achieve imperial control over Scotland and Ireland only if the centre of his authority, England, lay firmly in his grasp. Since 1629 the national political consensus in England had been lessened by Charles's insistence upon ruling without consultation with a Parliament. Country and city voices did not intrude at court, and the King's policies appeared to violate custom and tradition. Since the 1620s Charles I had been accused of imposing illegal taxes and failing to uphold godly religion in the face of popish threats. No Parliament was convened in the 1630s to assist the King in sorting out these problems. The absence of Parliament meant that in an era when wars cost more than ever, the King involved himself in a conflict which would be waged without parliamentary taxes which traditionally had been the mainstay of campaigns against Scotland. In spite of under-assessment and declining yields, parliamentary subsidies could provide desperately needed money.

Since the reign of Edward I the English Crown had pursued risky and expensive military operations in Scotland because diplomacy designed to preserve English security had to be backed with the threat of violence. Political and dynastic ambitions prompted wars in the north, the 'rough wooing' of the 1540s being a notable instance. The co-existence of two dynasties upon a single island virtually guaranteed conflict. To check the wealthier and more populous southern kingdom, the northerners cultivated a French alliance which could assist them in safeguarding their autonomy. Thus Anglo-Scottish relations were complicated by the 'French card', played incessantly by successive Scottish rulers. The reassertion of an 'auld alliance' against Henry VIII and Protector Somerset in turn, and the intervention of the French in the Lowlands in 1560, brought in turn English counter-strokes. This constantly shifting triangular diplomatic and dynastic configuration placed border skirmishes in an international context. A series of raids could trigger retaliation from either kingdom, with European repercussions.

Until the accommodation reached between Elizabeth I and James VI in the 1580s the wider perspective often obscured the regional or even local nature of border violence. The Union of the Crowns in 1603 should have ended conflict between the realms by placing both under a single dynasty. But the Union brought division in the 1630s when that solitary ruler, Charles I, tried to impose rigid uniformity upon the churches of both kingdoms. When the St Giles's Cathedral riot of 23 July 1637 signalled Scottish rejection of Charles's 'ecclesiastical imperialism,' culminating in the mass signing of the national Covenant and organized resistance in the Glasgow Assembly, the King and his English council suspected French complicity.[2] They placed the prayer book rebellion in too broad a context, for it was in reality a spontaneous uprising. Charles's self-deception about the Scottish troubles made his government receptive to those such as the Spanish minister Olivares, who, fishing in troubled waters, insinuated French instigation behind the Covenanters' activities.[3] Whether he believed it or not, Charles strove to prove treasonous collaboration with Louis XIII as justification for dismissing the rhetoric of the Covenanters, and produced a letter to substantiate that charge before the Short Parliament in April 1640.[4]

Previous English wars against Scotland gave Charles I three models from which to draw. First, the centuries-old stratagem of a series of border raids might bludgeon the Scots into obedience. But the Union of the Crowns with its political and dynastic implications discouraged Charles from raiding his own territory. Second, the King could garrison Scotland, as had been done during the reign of Edward VI. But the cost had proved too great, and as the prices of provisions and military equipment had risen threefold since the 1540s, extensive garrisoning in 1638–40 would have proved an immense financial burden to a monarch chronically short of money. The third model was expensive also, a major campaign to take Edinburgh, but it had the advantage of bolstering the King's image and authority, if managed properly. It was this last response which Charles chose in 1638.

THE FIRST BISHOPS' WAR, MARCH–JUNE 1639

The genesis of the First Bishops' War was in confidential communications between Charles, the Earl of Nithisdale, the Marquis of Hamilton, and possibly secretary Henry Vane. None of these possessed much sense of the religious climate or political situation. Charles relied on men whose views were as narrow as his own. Wentworth and Laud concurred that Scotland needed to be humbled, but in 1637–8 the pair were not of the inner

---

[2] The term 'ecclesiastical imperialism' has been appropriated from John Morrill, about which he has an article forthcoming.

[3] In March 1639 Condé-Duke Olivares asked the British ambassador at Madrid about French encouragement of the prayer book rebellion, as he had heard that the Scots were receiving assistance in designating commanders and that the Duke of Longueville would be a general in the Covenanter army. Bodleian Library, Clarendon State Papers, XVI, f. 28v, Hopton to Cottington, 19 March 1639.

[4] E. Cope and W. Coates (eds.), *The Proceedings of the Short Parliament of 1640*, Camden Society (London, 1977), pp. 58, 96, 122, 244 and J. Maltby, ed., *The Short Parliament (1640) Diary of Sir Thomas Aston* (London, 1988) pp. 3, 7.

sanctum of Charles's counsels. It was observed that only Arundel and Vane shared Charles's deepest thoughts about the mobilization and that the King 'confers leetle with anie Privie Counsaller heerin', while Laud 'madles in noe busines conserning Scotland'. Charles, in fact, made a point of telling his English council that he was the architect of his own policies.[5] He formulated decisions on his own, conferring with a tiny, trusted circle; for example in 1639, Arundel, Hamilton, and Vane, and in 1640 Vane and Strafford (who disliked each other intensely). According to Peter Donald, the Catholic Nithisdale proposed the triple-pronged strategy of the First Bishops' War early in 1638. Charles considered it through the spring and then expressed his resolve to pursue it in letters to Hamilton in June 1638.[6]

Charles preferred an offensive strategy to a defensive one. He wanted an expeditionary force, not a Maginot Line. In his resolve he chose to minimize hindrances to mobilization (such as shortages of ready money and sluggish recruitment and deployment) and indulged in false hopes that a show of force might dishearten the Covenanters. He himself did not fear that Scotland would seize the initiative and invade England, for such aggression would contradict the Covenanters' claim that they were seeking solely to defend their religious practices.[7] The Scots dared not violate English territory unless provoked. The ravaging of the English countryside would only unite England against them, inflaming anti-Scottish animosities, to the King's advantage and the peril of the Covenant. Therefore, Charles would prepare the trained bands and schedule a rendezvous at York for spring 1639. Yorkshire became a staging-area for forces destined for the borders and beyond. Northumberland, Cumberland, and Westmorland would serve as a buffer zone, protecting the assembly points for his army, particularly Newcastle and York.

[5] SRO, Hamilton MSS., GD 406/1/544, f. 1, Patrick Maule to Hamilton, 28 November 1638. Laud did, however, receive briefings from Hamilton, i.e. GD 406/1/567, 14 October 1638. S. R. Gardiner, *History of England from the Accession of James I to the Outbreak of the Civil War 1603–1642*, vol. VIII, p. 335, citing *Calendar of State Papers, Venetian*. The intimacy of the relationship between Vane, Hamilton, and the King is alluded to in GD 406/1/1188/1, 2, where Vane closes a letter (23 May 1639) to Hamilton with reference to a private conversation held by the three in the long gallery at Whitehall over the matter of the selection of officers for the First Bishops' War. He mentioned their private consultation again on 4 June 1639: GD 406/1/1179, Vane to Hamilton, 'what passed in the gallerie betwixt his majesty: your lordship: and my selfe'. Charles transacted important business in this fashion on a number of occasions. See below pp. 65–73 on the Council of War, and L. J. Reeve, *Charles I and the Road to Personal Rule* (Cambridge, 1989), p. 199.

[6] SRO, GD 406/1/10453, Hamilton Red Book, 18 April 1639. The question of Caroline policy and decision-making is explored by P.H. Donald's *An Uncounselled King: Charles I and the Scottish Troubles (1637–1644)* (Cambridge, 1990), pp. 1–42, 320–7. See also note 71 below.

[7] For example, Hamilton's observation that the King doubted that his own subjects would attack his own towns, namely Carlisle and Berwick, SRO, GD 406/1/711, 3 February 1639.

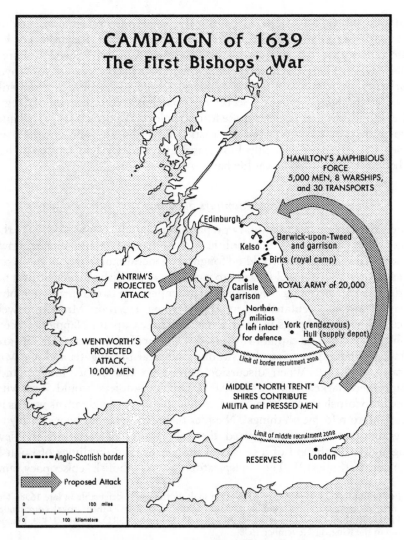

CAMPAIGN of 1639
The First Bishops' War

HAMILTON'S AMPHIBIOUS
FORCE
5,000 MEN, 8 WARSHIPS,
and 30 TRANSPORTS

Edinburgh

Berwick-upon-Tweed
and garrison

Kelso

Birks (royal camp)

ANTRIM'S
PROJECTED
ATTACK

Carlisle
garrison

ROYAL ARMY of 20,000

Northern
militias
left intact
for defence

York (rendezvous)
Hull (supply depot)

WENTWORTH'S
PROJECTED
ATTACK,
10,000 MEN

Limit of border recruitment zone

MIDDLE "NORTH TRENT"
SHIRES CONTRIBUTE
MILITIA and PRESSED MEN

Limit of middle recruitment zone

RESERVES

London

---- Anglo-Scottish border

Proposed Attack

0   100 miles
0   100 kilometers

1   Campaign of 1639: the First Bishops' War

Such was the grand strategy of King and council; but what seemed plausible in the second half of 1638 proved to be exceedingly difficult to achieve in the spring of 1639. The Union of the Crowns and a shared Protestant faith complicated Charles's strategic predicament. The Bishops' Wars were very different from earlier Anglo-Scottish conflicts. Sharing a common sovereign and Protestant beliefs, the Scots and the English did not manoeuvre to exact revenge, inflict maximum damage or deliver a lightning blow, but prepared cautiously, sometimes reluctantly, neither side wishing to fight unless forced to do so by the other. Regardless of his disclaimers that the war would be defensive, Charles knew Edinburgh Castle was the key, and that assailing it would be necessary to restore royal authority. A stronghold within Scotland served to encourage those still loyal to the King's regime.[8] Secretary Windebank described the strategy: 'the business was so layde as those forces sholde have bene transported into Scotlande, and have suprised the castle of Edinburgh; which wold have given the covenant a deadly blow, and His Majesty had mastered that rebellion by that time he sholde have arrived at Yorke'.[9]

Rumours of War

The Covenanters began military preparations quietly in late 1638. Like the King, they understood that political circumstance would dictate how, where and when a war would be fought. A general mobilization, the Scots reasoned, would compel Charles to summon an English Parliament; yet no writs were forthcoming.[10] Rumours of an impending Parliament and mobilization indeed circulated, as in August when a certain Mrs Cromewell received at her lodgings in Shire Lane, London, Captain Nappier, a Scottish gentleman. The captain conversed with three other guests: Dr Edward May, a London physician, Mr Swadlin, the vicar of Aldgate, and one Mrs Grace Southcott. When discussion turned to the events in Scotland, Nappier remarked that soon 40,000 English soldiers would join with 200,000 Scottish troops 'to have a Parliament, here in England, as well as in Scotland to reforme all things'. Nappier then divulged that he was privy to a grand plot that encompassed the deportation of recusants to New England (with the aid of a census of the wealth and dwellings of English Roman Catholics).[11] The conspirators would abolish episcopacy and

---

[8] For example, £2,000 was expended upon making the castle defensible in late 1638. The trick, though, was how Hamilton would manage 'to gett Ruthen [royal commander Patrick Ruthven] in with a few men and a lytell amunition', SRO, GD 406/1/400, Hamilton to the King, 11 November 1638.

[9] Bodleian Library, Clarendon SP, XVI, f. 20, Windebank to Hopton, 15 March 1639. For a description of the castle's condition in 1638, see SRO, GD 406/1/579, Hamilton to Laud, 11 December 1638 and S. R. Gardiner (ed.), *The Hamilton Papers*, Camden Society, new series, 28 (London, 1880), pp. 65–6. On the seizure of Edinburgh Castle on 21 March 1639 by Leslie and the musketeers see Traquair's description in GD 406/1/1001.

[10] See SRO, GD 112/39/738, Breadalbane Muniments, letter of Alexander Campbell, 3 August 1638.

[11] Public Record Office, SP 16/397/27, State Papers Domestic, Charles I, list of seditious statements made by Nappier compiled from the examinations of four witnesses, 8 August 1638. The original informations are in the Bodleian Library, Bankes MSS. 18/3; 58/1, 2; also, Nappier's examination 18/38, and a draft indictment 59/23. The captain was a likely candidate for the newly constructed rack in the Tower. See Rossingham's newsletter,

prevent ecclesiastics from meddling in affairs of state.[12] When asked about the King's reaction to all this, Nappier retorted, 'The king is deluded, and seduced, and made a Baby'; the man responsible for England's woes was William Laud, though it was Charles I who had made 'Coblers Sonnes, and the Sonnes of Meckanicks, to be privy Councellors and Bishops.' The King could no longer 'helpe himself', so the plotters took upon themselves the humbling of the prelates.[13] Struck by the confidence with which Nappier spoke his treasonous words, the vicar convinced his companions that the remarks should be reported to the authorities. The examinations came to the attention of Laud, and ultimately the King.[14] Nappier was either mad or drunk to suggest that such a plot was possible. But the episode is suggestive of the common currency of political and religious alienation in both kingdoms, and of the notion that what ailed Britain was largely political in nature.

Rumours regarding the Crown's strategy circulated throughout the summer and autumn of 1638 for two reasons. First, the Crown's plans for dealing with the Scots' revolt were veiled in secrecy. Apart from issuing proclamations, the government said little to dispel the rumours.[15] Second, the variety of strategies available to the Crown encouraged far-fetched speculation. Some observers felt that the matter would be settled through negotiation, while others believed Britain would plunge into the Thirty Years' War. The Crown had reason to conceal its designs, which might trigger a Scottish invasion of the north of England. The Venetian ambassador reported that: 'it is feared that if the king makes any demonstration of a desire to arm, the Scots will invade England to avoid being forestalled in their own country'.[16]

British Library, Additional MS. 11,045, ff. 3v–4. Andrew Thrush provided a transcript of the latter document.

[12] PRO, SP 16/397/28, statement of Thomas Swadlin. The vicar probably composed *The Soldier's Catechism*, circulated during the Civil War.

[13] PRO, SP 16/397/26, 27.

[14] PRO, SP 16/397/26, endorsed by Laud. The possibility that Nappier was involved in foreign, possibly French, conspiratorial activity brought the matter before Charles. See Bodleian Library, Clarendon SP, XVI, f. 100v, Windebank to the King, 30 April 1639. This was not the first time that Nappier's utterances had attracted government scrutiny. In December 1637 it was reported that a Captain 'Nepper' had conversed seditiously at the Cross Keys Tavern, talking of a plot and criticizing Laudian church policy. CSPD, Charles I (1637), XII, pp. 20–1.

[15] For example, PRO, SP 16/393/66, proclamation of 28 June 1638.

[16] *CSP Venetian* (1636–9), XXIV, p. 436, Zonca to the Doge and Senate, 16 July 1638; for example, the arms sent to Hull were rumoured to be headed for Berwick, which caused speculation in Edinburgh, SRO, GD 406/1/10793, Hamilton to Vane, 27 September 1638; also rumours of a Covenanter invasion of England, linked to reports of military preparations in England apparently, circulated according to Roxborough, SRO, GD 406/1/687, to Hamilton, 26 July 1638 – a significant date, for that day the English Privy Council

In November 1638 a Covenanter dominated General Assembly of the Church of Scotland convened at Glasgow and Charles's chief agent, Hamilton, probed all means by which the Covenant could be undermined or at least stalled. Musters were ordered in England and the rumblings prompted many Scots to stockpile arms and powder. With the new year came overt preparations: the English nobility received summonses to attend the King's standard at York on 1 April. An army of 30,000 would be pieced together from the nobles, the militia, and pressed men. Still no Parliament was summoned. The last time a monarch had declared a significant war without the assistance of Parliament was in 1323, and that particular ruler, Edward II, who had waged an expensive and unpopular Scottish war and harkened to the advice of 'evil counsellors', ultimately found himself deposed.[17] Precedents existed in Tudor military interventions launched without initial parliamentary sanction. The Earl of Surrey's French campaign of 1522 set forth without the blessing of Parliament, which did not meet until the following year. Elizabeth I's impressive repulse of the French from lowland Scotland in 1559–60 succeeded without parliamentary assistance. Elizabeth also engaged in the Le Havre campaign in 1562, though delayed calling a Parliament until 1563.

The Tudors, especially Henry VIII and Elizabeth during the earliest part of her reign, were adept at managing Parliament. Tudor campaigns had comparatively realizable goals: Elizabeth intended to dislodge the French in 1560, not to occupy Scotland. Le Havre was a single theatre in a larger struggle. The 1522 campaign was undertaken by a King who had the utmost confidence in his abilities to draw Parliament into the war effort once the conflict was under way. Charles I's relationship with Westminster was not as predictable. Having ruled without Parliament for a decade, Charles's distaste for that body persisted. In spite of rebellion and impending war, he refused to send out writs. With no extraordinary revenue from Parliament, Charles would have to suppress the Covenanter revolt with an improvised army. Hard currency could come from 'voluntary' contributions, loans based upon anticipation of future Crown revenues (a traditional Stuart fiscal expedient), and the sale of lands, offices, patents, and monopolies. However, there was little surplus money available from the Crown's annual income.

Why did Charles so adamantly oppose the summoning of a Parliament? By 1639 it was clear that the Personal Rule had not been a spectacular success, at least from the viewpoint of the ruled. Although local authorities

voted funds to go to war. There were plans to send a force against Scotland in July–August 1638: see SRO, GD 406/1/422.

[17] Conrad Russell, 'The Nature of a Parliament in Early Stuart England', in *Before the English Civil War*, ed. H. Tomlinson (New York, 1984), p. 129.

had performed their tasks, quarter sessions had been held, and rates collected, many grievances such as ship money and monopolies had arisen or become more burdensome. Some critics considered what Whig historians termed 'the Eleven Years' Tyranny' to be a grievance in itself. The ascendancy of Arminianism placed these concerns within a cosmic context, for the English and Scottish opponents of Charles I agreed that the church, even Christianity itself, was corrupted by his regime. Contemporaries were aware that the King might embark upon war without opening the Pandora's box of an unpredictable Parliament and refreshing memories of the administrative burdens, financial exactions, and human costs of the wars of the 1620s.[18] The longer the King delayed in summoning Parliament in 1639 and 1640, the more irrational and arbitrary his government appeared, which raised criticisms that had not been heard since the 1620s. Familiar complaints about coat-and-conduct money and billeting would shortly echo in the shires, in unison with grumblings over ship money, monopolies, and innovations in religion.

Charles I went about making war in the same way as he had governed during the Personal Rule. He made full use of local government (lieutenants, justices of the peace, and constables and mayors) and the feudal prerogatives of the Crown (enforcing scutage, summoning the lords to York, demanding that tenants perform feudal obligations for border service) to field an army. Improvisation and exploitation of traditional institutions characterized the King's military preparations. An expeditionary force pieced together from reluctant militiamen, conscripts, and a nobility no longer skilled in the practice of war was a pale imitation of the amalgamated armies which had proved effective in the Middle Ages. The efficacy of such improvised armies in the era of the military revolution was questionable because weapons and tactics had become more complex. Charles's strategies were limited by the political constraints involved in fighting one's subjects and the condition of existing institutions, namely the Exchequer, the lieutenancy, and the Ordnance.

The Personal Rule had not been popular, but it had worked; England was governed peacefully enough for a decade. It is illustrative, however, of Charles's thinking that he expected political acquiescence and an administrative machinery which had functioned less than spectacularly in peacetime to propel the kingdom into war with Scotland. The efficient operation of that administrative machinery in war depended upon a national political consensus embodied in Parliament's granting of extraordinary supply, and a local political consensus acted out in county and parish cooperation with

[18] HMC, Buccleuch, Montagu MSS. p. 276, Edward Montagu to Lord Montagu, February 1639. After listing contributors to the war effort, he states, 'so that the King will have no need of a Parliament'.

the mobilization. Charles shunned the former and took the latter for granted, failing to understand how his political and ecclesiastical policies affected his strategy. Most Covenanters feared Charles would pursue a strategy of conquest, for clearly the imposition of the prayer book could have been a foretaste of direct English rule.[19] In mid July 1638, when a strategy was only just being formulated, it was bruited in Scotland that Charles would mobilize 20,000 men supported by several score cannon; Arundel would secure Berwick and Carlisle and fortify Newcastle. The accuracy of this speculation was matched by its assessment of the temper of the southern kingdom: even when the King collected his weapons, few men would rush to shoulder them. The nobility, gentry, and commonalty of England sympathized with the religious concerns of the Covenant. The unpopularity of the war would hamper royal strategy, whatever it might be.[20]

Military Preparations in England

Sir Jacob Astley was entrusted with making the royal designs a reality. Having served the Danish King and in the Low Countries' Wars, Astley had spent much of 1638 inspecting the West country trained bands, and coastal fortifications and garrisons.[21] In late May or early June, Astley embarked for Holland to advise upon arms purchases. Probably he dwelt there for the entire summer; he wrote from The Hague on 6 October, when he and John Quarles discovered that 4,000 muskets were of smaller calibre than specified and returned them to the Dutch manufacturers.[22] He listed the arms and armour he would bring to Hull. By November Astley was

---

19 Contemporaries and historians are divided as to whether Charles intended a defensive or offensive strategy. Peter Donald suggests a more defensive posture, although the inclusion of scaling ladders in the ordnance account, PRO, Ordnance Office, bills and debentures, WO 49/68, ff. 22v–23, indicates that assaults on Scottish forts were a possibility. The strongest piece of evidence that Charles intended to storm Edinburgh Castle is Bodleian Library, Clarendon SP, XVI, f. 20, Secretary Windebank to ambassador Arthur Hopton, 15 March 1639.

20 National Library of Scotland, Wodrow MSS., Church and State papers, 1618–85, LXVI, no. 53, ff. 109–10, anonymous letter of intelligence, 11 July 1638.

21 PRO, SP 16/407/25, Astley to Nicholas, regarding the Devonshire trained bands; Astley's commission making him Sergeant-Major of the Field is recorded in the Council of War Entry Book, SP 16/396, f. 547, and printed in Thomas Rymer (ed.), *Foedera, Conventiones Literae et cujuscurque generis acta publica, inter reges angliae* (The Hague, 1744), p. 190, 19 December 1638; PRO, SP 16/404/88, Charles to Astley, 18 December 1638. See also SP 16/1/199. Astley also benefited the royal war effort in that he was a good friend of the Marquis of Hamilton, another old soldier with continental experience. See for example SRO, GD 406/1/199.

22 BL, Coke MS. C 59/11a for the letter and C 59/11b for the list. Andrew Thrush transcribed this reference; see also SRO, GD 406/1/10795, Vane to Hamilton, 24 September 1638.

back in England, overseeing border defences. He conferred with Essex and Newport and seems to have had at least one audience with the King in London.[23] He also met with the Ordnance officers, as well as Sir Thomas Morton, who shared the responsibility of coordinating northern defences. By early December, he had left London for Hull.[24] Captain Thomas Ballard and Leonard Pinkney were stationed at Hull, where they helped Captain William Legge position the town's cannon and disburse weapons and powder.[25]

From Hull Astley journeyed to York, which was to be his chief place of residence. The vice president of York and the deputy lieutenants who served as colonels met with Astley to schedule the mustering that had been neglected that year. Regiments of 1,000 men were increased by 500. The colonels were to see that the Yorkshire captains provided 'themselves with a Waggon or Cart for their owne and their Companies accomodacion'. Every soldier was 'to have with him a Knapsack wherein to carry certaine daies Victualls'. As had been the case in 1547, troops would carry their own foodstuffs between Berwick and Edinburgh. Companies lacking able officers were to notify Astley so that suitable men could be appointed (assuming that they could be found). Above all, the colonels were to prevent soldiers 'hired to carry Armes for any Township' from being absent without leave or deserting their colours.[26]

At Newcastle, Astley improved fortifications and established supply depots. Arms for 1,500 infantry, including fifteen lasts of gunpowder, awaited distribution or storage. Tynemouth Castle was surveyed and declared indefensible, and abandoned in favour of ground to the west, near Shields.[27] Newcastle's 500 militiamen were reviewed and organized into companies, with the selection of officers left to the discretion of the mayor and aldermen. Finally, Astley surveyed the banks of the Tyne in search of locations for the 'making of Stages for the Supply of Victualls for sustayning of an Army', and provided estimates of the local market price of foodstuffs.[28] After putting Newcastle in order, Astley turned his attention to the

---

[23] PRO, SP 16/396, f. 30; SP 16/40 1/76, Smith to Pennington, 14 November 1638. For Astley's instructions see BL, Coke MS. C 59/25, Coke's letter of 5 November 1638.

[24] SRO, GD 406/1/10799 f. 3, Vane to Hamilton, 3 December 1638 and Henry Oxinden, *The Oxinden Letters 1607–1642 being the Correspondence of Henry Oxinden of Barham and his Circle*, ed. Dorothy Gardiner (London, 1933), pp. 141–3, Peyton to Oxinden, 26 November 1638.

[25] PRO, SP 16/396, ff. 36–42, the King's instructions to Astley, 18 December 1639; SP 16/404/88, 89. Legge and his officers were not entirely welcome. See E. Gillett and K. MacMahon, *A History of Hull* (London, 1980), p. 166.

[26] PRO, SP 16/396, f. 39.

[27] PRO, MPF 287, map of fortifications at Newcastle-upon-Tyne.

[28] PRO, SP 16/396, f. 41.

garrison on Holy Island, located fifteen miles south of Berwick. Under the Tudors, bulwarks had been erected in erratic fashion. Holy Island's harbour and proximity to the borders made it a strategic outpost, but despite its utility, the works had fallen into decay.[29] By 1638, two decades of obsolescence had rendered the island useless. The Northumbrian lieutenants and the Admiralty commissioners surveyed the fort periodically. A skeleton garrison guarded the cannon, fourteen powder barrels and twenty muskets. The buildings required renovation if the island was to be used as a relay point. Since the fleet as well as expeditionary forces might draw on its stores, major repairs needed to be undertaken. The commander, Robert Rugge, mustered his troops quarterly, documented by a muster roll sent up to the auditors and receivers of York, though their pay remained in arrears. To keep the few troops in good morale, Sir Jacob was invited to suggest improvements regarding the garrison's pay. Even during the war years of the 1620s, the fort had been manned solely by Rugge, a master gunner (now eighty years old!) and whomever else he could persuade to help.[30] The Lieutenant of the Ordnance, Sir John Heydon, supplied Holy Island with food and ammunition throughout 1638 and greater use was to be made of it in early 1639.[31] Astley was to devise a means to strengthen the garrison clandestinely.[32] One begins to see how the royal strategy rested upon the performance of a few trusted men.

Sir Thomas Morton shouldered the responsibility of organizing those northern counties not under Astley's jurisdiction, namely Cheshire, Lancashire, Cumberland, Westmorland, the Bishopric of Durham, and the East and North Ridings of Yorkshire. Morton established his headquarters at Durham, and assisted the bishop in mustering the militia and organizing defences.[33] Morton and his captains, Gibson, Thelwell, and Waites, paid particular attention to the preparedness of the trained bands, since the northern militias would be expected to fight alongside Charles's expeditionary force.[34] Morton and Astley were not the only royal servants stiffening the border defences. Arundel, the Earl Marshal, who would be soon appointed Lord General, secured the garrison of Carlisle with the aid of the ageing Sir James Bagg. Victuals for 800 men, along with arms from either Bristol or the King's magazines at Hull or Newcastle, were to be laid up

[29] PRO, SP 16/396, f. 32.
[30] H. Colvin, O. Ransome, and J. Summerson, *The History of the King's Works*, vol. IV, pt. 2, pp. 674–9.
[31] SRO, GD 406/1/626, Rugge to Hamilton, 9 July 1638.
[32] Ibid., f. 42.
[33] Ibid., ff. 33–4, the King to the Bishop of Durham regarding the arrival of Morton, 13 December 1638; PRO, SP 16/404/61; Morton's formal instructions are SP 16/396, ff. 43–7; SP 16/404/99, 100.
[34] Gardiner, *History*, vol. VIII, pp. 384–5.

there. Seven hundred Welshmen were to be pressed and transported under the pretence that they were destined for Ireland. Arundel directed that bows and arrows be 'powred' into Cumberland, Westmorland, and Northumberland, because the inhabitants were 'allready used to Archerye'. The traditional 'olde armes of speare and jacke' were to be restored to the borderers. Calivers, powder, and shot were to be sent down from the Tower. The most peculiar order was Arundel's request for 2,000 brown bills, edged pole weapons that had become obsolescent during the late sixteenth century. One must sympathize with any English soldier who was expected to repel a Scottish attack with a spear, brown bill, caliver, or bow and arrows.[35] Arundel received information on the progress made in preparing his northern lieutenancy for war from Sir Francis Howard at Greystoke Castle.[36] The Lord Lieutenant could not be everywhere, and the captains did their best among strangers.

The garrisons at Carlisle and Berwick were the strategic points most likely to be attacked by the Scots. The Marquis of Hamilton, who observed the Covenanters, urged the strengthening of Carlisle and Berwick on 7 June 1638. Five hundred militiamen from Cumberland and Westmorland should be placed inside Carlisle, along with ammunition and more cannon.[37] Hamilton's advice was not always consistent. On 14 October 1638 he did 'humblie beg that Berwick and Cayrlyle be thoght on to be furnished uith good and strong garrissounes (and thatt with as greatt secresaie as may be)', but the next day he expressed doubt about a significant strengthening of the garrisons, fearing it might aggravate the Scots and provoke an attack.[38] By mid-November Hamilton judged that adequate forces and supplies could not be placed in Carlisle or Berwick until Christmas 1638.[39] The marquis, like his master, overestimated the capacity of English institutions, specifically the Ordnance Office, to sustain royal strategy at short notice. In spite of the mustering of the militia and rumours to the contrary, Berwick and Carlisle were not garrisoned at year-end.[40] On 25 February 1639, Charles told Wentworth that Carlisle (the logical staging-area for

---

[35] PRO, SP 16/397/6, Arundel's instructions to Bagg, 3 August 1638. For Bagg's response, SP 16/397/38, August 1638. For Arundel's role in the First Bishops' War, see Caroline Hibbard, *Charles I and the Popish Plot* (Chapel Hill, N.C., 1983), pp. 99–101, 117–120. Archaic weapons, though, did appeal to some of the prospective combatants. Huntly informed Hamilton that he had 'bene latelye muche solicited by dyvers Hyllanders for provyding a thousand hand-bowes with Arrowes', SRO, GD 406/1/412, 18 January 1638.

[36] Arundel Castle, Autograph Letters, no. 377, 31 January 1638/9.

[37] SRO, GD 406/1/10485, Hamilton Red Book; see also GD 406/1/10817, f. 3, 9 June 1638.

[38] SRO, GD 406/1/10509, Hamilton Red Book, 14 October; GD 406/1/10510, 15 October. At this stage Hamilton believed strong garrisons would make the Glasgow Assembly behave more reasonably, according to GD 406/1/570, Hamilton to Laud, 24 October 1638.

[39] SRO, GD 406/1/10521, Hamilton Red Book, Hamilton to Charles, 16 November 1638.

[40] SRO, GD 406/1/10794 Vane to Hamilton 18 November 1638.

Irish troops) or Berwick would not be secured until 8 April: 'You know that it is fit that Berwick and it [Carlisle] should be possessed at the same time. Now I thought I might have done it by the 1st of April; but I find it will be the 8th before this of Berwick can be performed.'[41] On 28 March 1639 Wentworth was to embark 500 Irish soldiers for Carlisle whether the garrison was in order or not. The mobilization could not tarry.[42]

Why did the Crown delay in strengthening the Carlisle and Berwick garrisons? First, Hamilton and the King simply could not judge the temper of the Covenanters while the Glasgow Assembly met, and they were uncertain of their opponents' response to any overt military act such as the build-up of the garrisons.[43] Second, the King had optimistic expectations regarding the projected invasion of the west of Scotland by the Earl of Antrim.[44] Third, the Scots were his subjects and had voiced their loyalty in spite of their protests over the introduction of the prayer book, which encouraged him to believe that major violence could be avoided by an appeal to negotiation or an offer of compromise. Fourth, the Council of War feared a Scottish counter-stroke. Should Charles mass troops and stockpile weapons at Carlisle and Berwick, he might precipitate an attack that England would be unable to withstand. Finally, assembling weapons and gathering reinforcements proved more difficult than anticipated, for it had been assumed that English institutions, lieutenancy, Ordnance, and Exchequer, could perform military tasks immediately and with limited resources.

When Charles's first grand strategy collapsed abruptly in late March 1639, the North of England lay defenceless as the Covenanters had extinguished royalist resistance in Scotland and could turn their energies to the borders. With the English still gathering at York, Charles sought an impromptu line of defence. Simultaneously he searched for an alternative landing site for Hamilton's forces (because the Covenanters held Aberdeen). Charles could not afford to lose Berwick, where his expeditionary force and Hamilton's troops might rendezvous and which constituted the

---

[41] Charles Petrie (ed.), *The Letters, Speeches and Proclamations of King Charles I* (New York, 1968), p. 102.

[42] By early March 1639 Wentworth was convinced that the Covenanters had gone beyond the point of reconciliation with their sovereign and would have to fight. Therefore, he recommended placing an army near Newcastle and garrisons in Carlisle and Berwick. Bodleian Library, Clarendon SP, XV, ff. 169v–170, to Secretary Windebank, 2 March.

[43] SRO, GD 406/1/10516, Hamilton Red Book, 5 November 1638. Hamilton wrote to Charles: 'be pleased to think of uhatt I formerlie uryt concerning Beruick and Cairlyle, for ther is nothing to be expected in this assemblie but madnes in the heyeghst degrie'. Later that month he urged Vane to hasten Charles's preparations, especially the installation of stronger garrisons at Berwick and Carlisle. See GD 406/1/713, 26 November 1638.

[44] See A. Clarke, 'The Earl of Antrim and the First Bishops' War', *Irish Sword*, 6, no. 23 (winter 1963), pp. 108–15; Hibbard, *Charles I and The Popish Plot*, pp. 97–8.

optimum 'jumping-off' site for an incursion into Scotland. The disintegration of the triple-pronged strategy might in fact have necessitated a royal border raid or invasion. Likewise, Carlisle needed to be secured so that Wentworth would have an avenue by which to send Irish troops from the west. Consequently, Charles's first tactical challenge was to hold the garrison towns.

The Berwick garrison remained England's northernmost outpost for military action against the Covenant, although on the eve of the Bishops' Wars it constituted little more than a shadow of its medieval strength. Construction of fortifications ceased after 1562.[45] Under Elizabeth only sporadic building programmes and garrison re-manning had been attempted. James I dissolved the garrison, leaving a scanty crew which numbered in 1639 eleven common soldiers, a handful of officers (including some pensioners), half-a-dozen or so gunners, eight horsemen and a preacher.[46] It would seem that Charles's decision to delay beefing up Carlisle and Berwick rested on the assumption that key points in Scotland would be secured. The loss of the Scottish strongholds undid the King's border strategy. Of the many disappointments suffered by Charles I in the First Bishops' War, the capitulation of Dumbarton, Edinburgh, and Aberdeen, without 'soe much as a bluddy nose' was the most humiliating.[47] Whether these citadels had been adequately manned and supplied to withstand siege is questionable.[48]

Berwick and Carlisle remained in English hands in 1639 through the foresight of Sir Jacob Astley and the decisive action of the Earl of Essex. Around 17 March Astley received word that the Scots were preparing to assault and occupy Berwick. He left York for the north, first ensuring Carlisle's safety by sending Sir Thomas Morton and Captains Waites and Gibson to the west to assist in the landing of troops from Ireland, and to escort them to Carlisle. On the afternoon of 22 March Astley met with the mayor of Berwick. Captains Fludd and Widdrington had surveyed the

---

[45] I. MacIvor, 'The Elizabethan Fortifications of Berwick-upon-Tweed', *Antiquaries Journal*, 45 (1965), p. 93.

[46] PRO, Declared Accounts of the Exchequer of Receipt 351/3518, account of Major Norton, 24 December 1638–24 December 1639. The annual cost of the garrison, pensioners and servitors came to £411 13s 7d.

[47] Frances Verney, *Letters and Papers of the Verney Family*, ed. J. Bruce, Camden Society, 56 (London, 1853), p. 212, Sir Edmund Verney to Ralph Verney, 4 April 1639. Vane describes Charles's rage in SRO, GD 406/1/1190, to Hamilton, 12 April 1639, comprising two letters. On the betrayal of Edinburgh Castle, see also GD 406/1/826, Sir William Stewart to Hamilton, 9 May 1639 and GD 406/1/864, Hamilton to Traquair, 10 July 1639. On Dumbarton Castle, GD 406/1/1081, Stewart to Hamilton, 13 April 1639.

[48] See Sir William Stewart's assertion that the Dumbarton garrison sympathized with the Covenant and was in no condition to hold out. SRO, GD 406/1/1081, to Hamilton, 13 April 1639.

town's fortifications and garrison.[49] The city fathers had mounted three old iron cannon at the bridge that spanned the Tweed.[50] On 30 March, the King reinforced Berwick with the Earl of Lindsey's Lincolnshire men. Charles did not know if Astley had occupied the town, or if the Scots had arrived beforehand.[51] Astley's forces had converged with the Earl of Essex's troops between Newcastle and the border. Essex was to secure the bridge across the Tweed, which the Scots wished to sever.[52] The Earl of Traquair, his loyalty already suspect, tried to convince Essex that the Earl of Montrose, with twice as many soldiers as the English, would fall upon Berwick before the relief forces could arrive. A Scottish army of 3000 with a train of artillery lay within three hours march of Berwick and had probably occupied the town. Traquair advised retreat.[53] Essex, not one to take fright at rumour, commanded Lord Clifford to muster the trained bands of Cumberland and Westmorland should the defenders of Carlisle require assistance or should the rumoured Scottish attack be in reality a feint. Essex then took nine companies mustered from Durham, four from Northumberland (which had joined him upon the march) and hurried north; again he succeeded in entering Berwick without sighting a single Scot. Lindsey arrived not long afterwards.[54] Astley took the bridge, marched across unchallenged and installed a 2,000 man garrison.[55]

These good tidings, coming in the midst of the news of the fall of Aberdeen, Dalkeith, Dumbarton and Edinburgh Castle to the Covenanters, temporarily buoyed the spirits of the King's men at York. Although the Carlisle garrison was intact, Arundel remained concerned. Two regiments of militiamen and eight brass cannon were hurried north. The strength of Berwick in the first week of April may be estimated at between 2,000 and 3,000 men.[56] Essex hurried back to the King's camp at York. There Charles

[49] PRO, SP 16/415/11, Astley to Windebank, 22 March 1639.
[50] HMC Cowper, Coke MSS., p. 217, Mayor William Nemo and the aldermen (?) to Essex, 28 March 1639.
[51] PRO, SP 16/415/73, the King to Lindsey, 30 March 1639.
[52] PRO, SP 16/415/78, Coke to Windebank, 31 March 1639.
[53] Clarendon, Edward Hyde, Earl of, *History of the Rebellion and Civil Wars in England* ed. W. D. Macray (Oxford, 1888), vol. I, pp. 151–2; PRO, SP 16/417/93, Essex to Windebank, 15 April 1639.
[54] PRO, SP 16/417/110, Rossingham newsletter, 16 April.
[55] PRO, SP 16/417/3, Rossingham newsletter to Conway, 1 April; PRO, SP 16/417/21, Coke to Windebank, 3 April 1639.
[56] Bristol Record Office, Smyth of Ashton Court MSS. AC/C61/3, 4, Poulett to Thomas Smith, 5 April, 11 April 1639; Verney, *Verney Papers*, p. 211, Edmund Verney to Ralph Verney, 1 April 1639; PRO, SP 16/417/30. Astley and Essex were accompanied by about 1,200 to 2,000 foot and several hundred cavalry with an 800 man garrison ensconced in Berwick. On 1 April, Charles ordered 'Sir William Pennyman to march with his [regiment] towards Berwick whethr [whither] on Saterday last were sent the forces of the Bishoppricke [of Durham] and Northumberland to keepe and fortefye itt'. BL, Add. MS. 18979, f. 44, Fairfax correspondence, Ferdinando Fairfax to his father, the first Lord

solicited volunteers to defend Berwick until the royal army arrived: 'the Earle of Essex was presentlye sent away agayne to Barwicke and the kinge declared that he would take it well if gentlemen of worth would put themselves into Barwyck'.[57] The King's request was mocked by one 'witty' but anonymous lord, who pointed out that there were no volunteers at York, since all came against their will.[58] The remark is lent some degree of credence by Poulett's observation that there were 'the fewest volontiers that I ever say in any army'. Nevertheless, Lindsey's succour of Berwick by sea with an additional 2,500 men promised to keep Berwick safe.

With the borders relatively secure, Charles could pursue one of two tactics: he might maintain a defensive posture indefinitely, or attack as soon as possible. The Lord Deputy of Ireland favoured postponement until adequate funds could be found. Meanwhile, Hamilton's fleet would blockade Scottish ports and intercept weapons and supplies. Wentworth's recommendations were well-conceived, but did little more than maintain the status quo, which the King found intolerable. The Covenanters had been in rebellion for nearly two years and Charles was impatient to bring them to heel.

Another tactical alternative at Charles's disposal was a variation on the strategy of 1638. Although the Scottish royalist faction had been fragmented and key harbours and forts lay in the Covenanters' control, the King might still concentrate his forces upon the eastern borders. While Carlisle and the threat of Irish intervention kept the Covenanters in check in the west, Charles's expeditionary force could advance to the Tweed and rendezvous with Hamilton's amphibious force, in a manner similar to the English strategies of 1544 and 1547. With Berwick under Lindsey's control, the King could strike at Edinburgh. Even if the blow could not be delivered, the threat might be enough to break the will of the rebels. Should he be unable to draw his sabre from its scabbard, Charles would rattle it loudly.

The King planned to leave York for Newcastle on 29 April, but a smallpox outbreak discouraged the court from moving there.[59] The royal army

---

Fairfax, 1 April 1639. On 12 April Vane informed Hamilton that 2,000 infantry had been installed in Berwick, along with fourteen artillery pieces. SRO, GD 406/1/1190, f. 4. On Essex's strength, see also BL, Add. MS. 18,979, f. 46, 5 April 1639.

[57] Peter Heylyn, *Cyprianus Anglicus or the History of the Life and Death of William, by Divine Providence Archbishop of Canterbury*, (London, 1668), book IV, p. 363; Bristol Record Office, Ashton Court MS. AC/C61/5, Poulett to Thomas Smith, 19 April 1639; *HMC Rutland*, p. 506.

[58] Bristol Record Office, Ashton Court MS. AC/C61/5, Poulett to Smith, 19 April 1639; Bodleian Library, Rawlinson MS. b. 210, ff. 3–6.

[59] PRO, SP 16/418/30, Thomas Windebank to Secretary Windebank, 21 April 1639; SP 16/418/52, Norgate to Reade, 25 April; SP 16/418/99, Rossingham newsletter, 30 April 1639.

had advanced north in piecemeal fashion, since victualling such a large body of men in one locale posed substantial logistical problems. Consequently, there were regiments spread out along the roads leading from York to Durham, to Newcastle, and to the borders. This was the first time an English army destined for Scotland had been organized upon a regimental basis.[60] The 1547 army had been divided into the traditional tripartite structure of vanguard, mainbattle, and rearward. The sheer bulk of the old style demanded a centralized commissariat which could supply and feed thousands within a single locale. The regimental configuration gave some tactical flexibility in battle, but upon the march stretched supply lines and communications and undermined deployment by separating the commanders.

April 1639: the situation at York

Charles hoped the slow but inexorable march to the borders would heighten the impact of the show of force. When the Covenanters did not come in to the King, however, and it appeared that a fight might erupt, the problems of distance and supply hindered the defence of northern England. The May 1639 march was comparatively chaotic after the army's sedentary stay at York. Officers competed for suitable lodgings and decent meals. Stormy weather dogged the march: 'there fell aboundance of raine, and made foule travelling'. Food was priced reasonably: 'good meate' for 6d, and provender beans and oats for the horses at 8d a peck. The most expensive commodity was beer, which cost 4d for a small flagon. The courtier John Aston ascribed the shortage of drink to the infantrymen who had passed through Northallerton the day before. He was disgruntled to find the price doubled when he arrived at Darlington.[61] On 29 April Aston came to Durham, where the King planned to remain before proceeding to Newcastle.[62] Once at Durham, Charles sent one of his Scottish cupbearers to the Covenanters with an offer of pardon for those who repented their resistance to the Crown. As he came nearer to Scotland, he reasoned, the more the Scots would seriously consider defecting. Their reply was polite and deferential, but firm. The Scots would not repudiate the Covenant until their grievances had been aired and their fears of innovations in religion

---

[60] Based upon conversations with Edward Furgol and Victor Stater.

[61] J. Aston, 'Iter Boreale, Anno Salutis 1639 et Dissidae inter Anglos et Scotos Inchoatus 1 Aprilis, finitum 29 Junii', *Six North Country Diaries*, ed. J. C. Hodgson, Surtees Society, 118 (Durham, 1910), p. 7, based upon the diary of John Aston, privy chamber man extraordinary, BL, Add. MS. 28,566.

[62] PRO, SP 16/420/7, Coke to Windebank, 1 May 1639.

allayed. It was said that this response further angered the King and increased his resolve to advance upon the rebels.[63]

Another logistical problem proved more formidable than Charles had reckoned: communication with London. With the King on the march, the Privy Council had been divided (physically and politically) for weeks. While Northumberland, Windebank, Cottington, and Sir John Heydon remained at Whitehall (in the Privy Council, Exchequer, and Ordnance Office respectively), their colleagues, Arundel, Coke, and Newport, kept pace with the King, which delayed communication between the capital and the army. The decision-making process had become more elaborate and less reliable due to the geographical split in the council. On 26 April, when Charles was still at York, the London councillors urged that communication be more rapid and discreet, complaining that 'things grow common and public here before we have knowledge of them.' Tardy correspondence, opened dispatches, harried post-riders, and shortages of post-horses (which were usually requisitioned from uncooperative civilians) fouled up communication and made tactical responses difficult to coordinate.[64]

The York rendezvous offered the first public opportunity to voice dissatisfaction with the mobilization. Of the many quarrels and confrontations that occurred in the King's camp, the most dramatic were the refusals of Lord Saye and Sele and Lord Brooke to take the military oath. Resistance to the Crown's policies during the Personal Rule had hitherto been localized and indirect. The sheriffs had deflected most of the criticism over ship money, while the justices of the peace, constables, and deputy lieutenants bore the brunt of complaints about military charges. But at York resistance was offered on the public stage: the two peers came face to face with the King in disagreement over the Scottish war. The older Lord Saye and Sele and younger Lord Brooke questioned the phraseology and legality of the royal military oath. In late February Lord Saye had objected that he was not obliged to supply horses, arms or men and had parleyed with Lord Brooke, possibly on the advice of Oliver St John. Later, they had returned more agreeable answers, assuring the council of their attendance at York.[65] Once there, however, they criticized the royal prerogative, the war against Scotland, and the legality of the form of summons. The grumblings of discontented nobles intensified when the King proposed an English equivalent to the Covenant. Such a pledge would unify the lords, he hoped, and silence discontent. The peers were asked to pledge

[63] Aston, 'Iter Boreale', p. 8

[64] HMC Cowper, Coke MSS., p. 223, 26 April 1639; PRO, SP 16/420/109, Rossingham newsletter concerning a duel fought over the use of a post-horse.

[65] M. L. Schwarz, 'Viscount Saye and Sele, Lord Brooke and Aristocratic Protest to the First Bishops' War', *Canadian Journal of History*, 7, no. 1 (April 1972), pp. 19–21.

'lyfe and fortune' in suppressing those who rebelled in the name of religion. It was one thing for a nobleman to venture his life, but quite another
to risk his wealth and family estate. That the King might lead them to
death on the battlefield was frightening enough; that their 'fortunes,' the
material security of their families and future generations, might be sacrificed to enforce the use of the prayer book in a foreign city was to ask too
much.

Lord Saye, like many others, sensed Charles's duplicity in the strategy
against Scotland. The letters summoning the lords to York spoke only of
defending the borders and repelling any Scottish incursion. No mention
was made of an invasion of Scotland. Charles's secretiveness (and,
perhaps, dishonesty) about the campaign did not conceal his predicament.
The King could not maintain an army on the borders indefinitely: the
Exchequer lacked the funds. Administratively the nation could not be
governed by a King residing at York or Newcastle. The crisis would not be
resolved until either the King gave way to the Covenanters' demands (an
unlikely development) or succeeded in overawing them with a sizeable
army (a substantial undertaking). The latter could include an invasion,
although the summoning of the nobility had mentioned only a defensive
war. The defence of the borders could quickly become an offensive foreign
expedition. Lords Saye and Brooke exploited these inconsistencies to great
effect, expressing their willingness to defend the realm, 'but to invade Scotland ther Lordships knew no law for to warrant the sam'.[66]

On 21 April Charles gathered his nobles in the council chamber at
York and announced that a new oath would be administered that very
afternoon. Called to subscribe, Lord Saye played for time, and requested
an opportunity to consider what was being asked of him. He offered to
take the traditional oath of allegiance, sanctioned by custom and Parliament, which was more specific in its demands. It pledged one to defend the
realm against the encroachment of foreign jurisdiction and invasion, but
excluded intervention in another kingdom. Lord Brooke also demurred. In
order to minimize this spectacle of public disobedience in the presence of
the King, Charles had the two peers taken into custody and interrogated

---

[66] HMC Rutland, p. 507; see the remarks of Sir Henry Vane who, along with the Lord
Chamberlain and Secretary Coke, examined Lords Saye and Brooke. SRO, GD 406/1/
1207, ff. 1, 3, to Hamilton, 23 April 1639; Schwarz, 'Viscount Saye and Sele', pp. 24–5.
The phraseology of the 'defence of the northern parts' proliferates in the official documents of the Bishops' Wars. Even in a mundane manuscript such as Sir William Uvedale's
declared account as army treasurer in the 1639, reference is made to money being disbursed (in this case, to Captain William Legge and Sir Robert Farrer) for assisting in the
defence of the northern parts. By stating that the measures were taken to protect a region
of the realm at large, rather than specific shires or for an incursion into Scotland, the King
and his councillors maintained the fiction that they were quite simply defending all of
England. See PRO, E 351/292, f. 16.

privately, probably more to isolate them from each other and their fellows than as a punishment or from fear of escape.

The 'Saye-Brooke' confrontation revealed an undercurrent of distrust of the Crown's real intentions and of the Personal Rule. Implicitly, the rejection of the military oath symbolized scepticism about Charles's sincerity and ability to govern, and underscored the necessity of calling a new Parliament. It also personified the erosion of political consensus. To some observers, the issue of a Parliament was 'the most critical aspect of this affair'.[67] Lord Saye portrayed Charles, in subtle tones of course, as another figure in the gallery of those sovereigns who had disregarded the privileges and advice of the nobility. The King had refused to call Parliament when that assembly could have assisted in the execution of royal policy. It is no coincidence that Lord Saye's assertion that his military obligation did not extend beyond the kingdom's borders resembled the statute 4 Henry IV c. 13, which declared 'that no Man be compelled to go out of his Shire, but where necessity requireth, and suddain coming of strange Enemies into the Realm; and then it shall be done as hath been used in Times past for the Defence of the Realm'.[68] Charles may have hoped to evade this statutory restriction by arguing that offensive operations within Scotland were under the command of the Marquis of Hamilton. Although his troops were recruited from East Anglia, the Marquis's invasion was (in the King's eyes) a Scottish invasion of Scotland. Continental armies were multinational; the make-up of the rank and file was less significant than the identity of the commander. Once Hamilton had precipitated a Scottish civil war, Charles might then seize upon any border incident to intervene with his English army as a defence of English territory which was necessarily threatened by violence in lowland Scotland.[69] Whether Hamilton would have been given joint command had the English force under Arundel linked up with this amphibious force is uncertain. Either way, invasion was most certainly planned. Very probably, Charles may have regarded statutory restrictions as null and void since Scotland was part of his dominion, hence English soldiers were not, technically, trespassing into a 'foreign' country.

Lord Brooke's contention that Parliament should be consulted was damaging to the King's position. If the Covenanters were as dangerous as Charles claimed and hostilities imminent, why had not the King summoned Parliament, the institution whose primary function, according to

[67] Schwarz, 'Viscount Saye and Sele', p. 27.

[68] J. H. Leslie (ed.), 'Statutes and Acts of Parliament – Army – From 1225 to 1761', *JSAHR*, 11, no. 44 (October 1932), p.219.

[69] A hint, but only a hint, can be found in PRO, E 351/293, f. 2, where the Commissary-General's account acknowledges what Charles's personal correspondence affirms, that Hamilton was to march into Scotland. That invasion failing to materialize, the victuals were sold.

old baronial theory, was to provide for war? Surely many of the lords and gentry who had assembled at York could have accomplished more at Westminster with their votes than with antiquated weapons on the borders? At the York rendezvous Sir Thomas Wilsford, a man of 'free speech and carelese,' who commanded a contingent of Kentish cavalry, told the King, 'I pray God send us well to doe in this busynes, but (said hee) I like not the beginning'. 'Why?' queried Charles. 'Because you go the wrong way to work,' came the answer. The King asked, 'What is the right way?' Wilsford replied, 'If you think to mak a warr with your owne purse you deceive your selfe, the only way to presper [prosper] is to go back and call a Parliament' which would grant 'monies enought, and do your busynes handsomely'. The King's sense of humor must have waned, for he snapped back, 'there were fooles in the Last Parliament'. 'True,' admitted Wilsford, 'but there were wise men too; And if you had let them alone the wise men would have bene too hard for the fooles.'[70]

The march to the borders

Through April and into May Charles consolidated and moved his forces across Yorkshire into Durham, arriving at Newcastle on 6 May 1639. His movements were synchronized to form one prong of the projected triple attack on Scotland. Wentworth, although sceptical about Charles's chances of success, was expected to send help from Ireland. Again, Hamilton, who likewise had doubts about the prospect for victory, flanked Scotland by sea from the east. Charles would surround and contain the Covenant with assaults from the east and west, a royal army on the borders, and the Highlands secured by clans hostile to the covenanting families. This tripartite attack had been suggested by a Scot.[71] Charles's strategy of western, eastern and southern 'fronts', abetted by strongholds of resistance within Scotland, failed. The eastern strategy (which comprised three metamorphoses, originally being a northern front joining Hamilton with Huntly's forces in the Highlands, then an Aberdeen landing, settling finally on penetration of the Firth of Forth with Leith as a major target) depended upon the Marquis of Hamilton's amphibious landing. Hamilton realized

---

[70] PRO, SP 16/422/65, extract from a letter by an anonymous eyewitness, written at Newcastle on 28 May 1639. See also Alan Everitt, *The Community of Kent and the Great Rebellion, 1640–60*, pp. 65–6; Henry Oxinden, *The Oxinden Letters*, ed. Dorothy Gardiner (London, 1933), p. 175; Peter Clark, *English Provincial Society from the Reformation to the Revolution: Religion, Politics, and Society in Kent, 1500–1640* (Hassocks, Sussex, 1977), p. 375; and Conrad Russell, *The Fall of the British Monarchies, 1637–1642*, p. 83.

[71] See Nithisdale's letter, NLS, MS. 9303, f. 17, and Donald, *An Uncounselled King*, p. 71. I am grateful to P. H. Donald for transcription and discussion of this manuscript.

that he could not assault the Firth of Forth and thus compel the Covenanters to retain a proportion of their forces in that area. The borders constituted the main theatre, and Hamilton was to be unleashed upon the
Covenanters once Charles's main army poised itself upon the frontier.
Should the Covenanters hold firm in the face of the royal army, Hamilton's
'marines' would strike near Edinburgh. But the unreadiness of the English
soldiers undermined this plan and Hamilton's activity degenerated into a
series of tactical diversions.[72] The King had assumed that all he need do
was pluck from the East Anglian militia an expert fighting force and hurl
them against eastern Scotland. Once again, he made a bad choice by divi-
ding his forces and expected too much from the men at his disposal.

The precariousness of Hamilton's position nullified his ability to take
the offensive. His soldiers' lack of training and the tenuousness of his
supply lines restricted his ability to attack. The tactical initiative lay with
the royal army on the Borders, which could not expect assistance from
within Scotland. They themselves would have to begin the war, and most
probably, win it on their own. Antrim's invasion of the west of Scotland
had come to nothing. Hamilton's impotence in the east was particularly
frustrating because he was now convinced that the Covenanters would
settle the issue on the field of battle. 'Resolved they ar to force your Majestie to a battle, being confident that they ar much stronger in infantry ... all
that is to be feared is that they pass by your army, and so gett betwixt
Newcastle and you, by which means they may cutt of [off] your victualls.'[73]
The Scots might avoid a headlong fight at the borders and instead penetrate deep into Northumberland, cutting off Charles's already strained
lines of supply, wheeling about and attacking the royal army from the
south. In fact, fighting the English army might not be necessary at that
point to force Charles to accept their demands.

Charles's army camped upon a hill called 'the Birks', 'Birkhill', or
'Brickhill', several miles west of Berwick on 30 May, 1639. A debate
erupted amongst the King's councillors, the two most vocal antagonists
being the Earl of Bristol and Sir Henry Vane.[74] The English lords' unea-
siness about the state of the army fuelled concern over the King's proximity
to the Borders. Since the Covenanters might strike at any time, and their
strength had been estimated as fairly substantial, the King was extremely
vulnerable. Bristol insisted that Charles should remain safely at Newcastle

---

[72] Hamilton's expedition will be dealt with in detail elsewhere. See also Mark C. Fissel,
'"*Bellum Episcopale*": The Bishops' Wars and the End of the "Personal Rule" in
England, 1638–1640', University of California, Berkeley, Ph.D. dissertation (1983),
pp. 72–3.

[73] SRO, GD 406/1/10554, Hamilton Red Book, 21 May 1639.

[74] PRO, SP 16/422/67, map of Birks and encampment; PRO, SP 16/421/169, Mildmay to
Windebank, 24 May 1639.

until the royal army entrenched properly and located the rebel army. He produced a Scot 'who offered to be hang'd if he did not see ten or 15,000 Scots upon theire march'. The King could not risk his person among 'an untaught inexperiencet army, untrencht, and perhaps as ill fed as taught'. Vane took offence, for he and Astley had surveyed the Borders and found the area safe; however, many experienced captains sided with Bristol. Nonetheless, Charles decided to remain.[75]

The situation of the English army, which numbered around 15,000 men, was a grim disappointment. The troops were mostly untrained, pay scarce, and morale low: 'Our Army is but weake; our Purce is weaker; and if wee fight with thes foarces ... we shall have our throats cutt; and to delaye fighting longe wee cannott for want of monny to keepe our Army togeather ... ther was never soe Raw, soe unskilfull and soe unwilling an Army brought to fight.'[76] Nine days later, Sir Edmund Verney, the standard-bearer, repeated his pessimism: 'Our men are verry rawe, our armes of all sorts nawght, our vittle scarce, and provition for horses woarce; and nowe you maye judg what case wee are in, and all for want of monny.'[77]

The situation was so bad that Thomas Windebank would not explain the situation in writing, preferring to relate it privately. Smallpox had broken out amongst the soldiers, one hundred stricken in Sir Thomas Morton's regiment alone.[78] Under these circumstances, talk of peace came as little surprise: 'The generall voice proclaimes peace and ... nowe there is strandge doctrine spread in the campe and swallowed by the officers and soldiers, soe that it is time to make an ende of this worke.'[79] The usually plucky younger Windebank confessed, 'we ourselves begin to be a little daunted when we looke uppon our enemies strength and cast our eyes back againe uppon our own confusion and wants'.[80] The standoff continued until about three weeks into May when skirmishing occurred which un-nerved both sides.

The first blood spilled in the *bellum episcopale* was that of an English cavalryman, although the Scot who wounded him paid for the honour with his life. Mr Garrald, a young colonel in Lieutenant-General Goring's horse, arrived at his quarters at Wark around 19 May, and immediately set off on

75 PRO, SP 16/422/78, Norgate to Windebank, 28 and 29 May 1639; PRO, SP 16/421/169, Mildmay to Windebank, 24 May 1639; Gardiner, *History*, vol. IX, p. 18.
76 Verney, *Verney Papers*, Sir Edmund Verney to Ralph Verney, 1 May 1639, p. 228.
77 Ibid. Sir Edmund Verney to Ralph Verney, 9 May 1639, p. 233; Gardiner, *History*, vol. IX, p. 15; C. H. Firth, *Cromwell's Army. A History of the English Soldier during the Civil Wars, the Commonwealth and the Protectorate*, 3rd edn (London, 1962), p. 13.
78 PRO, SP 16/423/13, Thomas Windebank to Secretary Windebank, 3 June 1639; SP 16/423/29, Edward Norgate to Robert Reade, 5 June 1639.
79 PRO, SP 16/423/110, Thomas Windebank to Robert Reade, 15 June 1639. PRO, SP 16/423/67, Sir Henry Mildmay to Secretary Windebank, 10 June 1639.
80 PRO, SP 16/423/14, Thomas Windebank to Robert Reade, 3 June 1639.

his own, fording the Tweed and entering Scotland, hoping to reconnoitre the area. Several townsmen of Wark observed Garrald's departure, and informed Captain Price of Goring's troop, who became alarmed. He dispatched two horsemen to find Garrald and bring him back. When the two riders did not return, he himself saddled up and led a contingent of eight to ten cavalry into Scotland. They located Garrald and the pair of messengers and made haste back to the Tweed. Before they entered the river, the English spied a group of horsemen, perhaps twenty or thirty, riding hard in their direction. Price and his dozen or so troopers held their ground. When the riders halted, the Captain called out, asking them if they were friends of the King. When the Scots answered affirmatively, Price suggested that they uncock their pistols, and his men would do likewise. The Scots refused. 'Why then,' replied Price, 'lett uss putt of [off] our hatts on boath sides and parte.' A shot rang out, striking Price's corporal, shattering his arm and wounding him in the torso.[81] An Englishman returned fire, and knocked the Scot from his mount. Both sides fled, the English cavalry plunging into the Tweed, and the Covenanters galloping northwards.

The skirmish is interesting in two respects. A mêlée was averted and the English commander of the horse, Lord Holland, and the Scottish noble in whose territory the skirmish occurred, the Earl of Home, were both conciliatory and apologetic in correspondence regarding the incident. The skirmishers showed no appetite for a pitched battle. Each side fired a solitary round, and the first shot seems to have been discharged spontaneously, without an order from an officer. The riposte which felled the Scot was triggered by the tension of the moment and the crack of gunfire. In the aftermath, Holland wrote to Home about the unfortunate incident, promising that the impulsive young colonel would be punished for violating Scottish territory, and acting without order. Home responded by reassuring Holland, telling him that he desired peace and would investigate the matter on his side of the border. Neither side, of course, had been instructed to engage the other. These were men who did not wish to fight, at least under these circumstances and at that particular moment.

On 22 May, a few days after the skirmish, much of Britain experienced an eclipse of the sun. This celestial event was interpreted by some as an evil

---

[81] The evidence regarding the skirmish is: SRO, GD 406/1/1188/1, 2, Vane to Hamilton, 23 May 1639, comprising two letters; PRO, SP 16/421/94, Earl of Holland to Earl of Home, 20 May 1639, Home to Holland, 20 May (reply), and note of Secretary Windebank (whose information regarding this incident is more extensive than the Holland–Home correspondence); HMC Rutland, p. 511, 21 May 1639; Verney, *Verney Papers*, pp. 240–1. It is mentioned in C. S. Terry, *The Life and Campaigns of Alexander Leslie*, p. 63. Charles Price served his monarch again, less than a year later, by championing the royal cause in the Short Parliament. See Mark C. Fissel, 'Scottish War and English Money: The Short Parliament of 1640', in *War and Government in Britain, 1598–1650*, ed. M. Fissel (Manchester, 1991), pp. 206–7, 222.

omen. Heaven itself had proclaimed against a war between English-speaking Protestants. On the eve of the eclipse the regiments quartered around Newcastle had been summoned in haste to Berwick, spinning rumours that battle was imminent. The eclipse overtook many *en route*, and the suddenness of the marching orders, coupled with the cosmological phenomenon, alarmed many a soldier. John Aston recorded that:

it was late in the afternoone before I set out, soe I began my journey just when the sunne suffered an ecclipse; ite was darke and misty before I came to Stannington . . . it was not superstition stayed mee, though rumours beeing then uncertaine, and our departure soddaine, there wanted not those who construed this ecclipse as an ominous presage of bad successe to the king's affaires.[82]

The retreat at Kelso

The omens were fulfilled when the English cavalry elected to retreat in the face of what was apparently a superior force at Kelso on 4 June. During the evening of 3 June 1639, intelligence reached the English camp at Birks that Leslie's army had entrenched near the border town of Kelso. With the Covenanters' location discovered to be within striking distance, Holland was to make a reconnaissance of their position and drive them out of Kelso if possible.[83] Holland departed from the royal camp with approximately 1,000 horse and 3,000 infantry, and marched off to find Leslie and the Covenanters.[84] The weather was exceedingly hot, and the infantrymen began to suffer fatigue. Some were so parched that they drank water from filthy pools, lapping it up like dogs, as an eyewitness described it.[85] As a

---

[82] Aston, 'Iter Boreale', p. 24. Aston's observation is confirmed by the diary of Robert Woodford, a steward in Northants, in HMC Woodford, p. 498, 'May 22nd. This day was an eclipse of the Sunne about 4 or 5 o'clock in the afternoon.'

[83] Arundel knew as early as 2 June that Covenanter forces were in the vicinity of Kelso. He may well have encouraged Holland's probe, for he told Hamilton 'it were a shame nowe wee are heere to lye idle with both our honor and army', SRO, GD 406/1/1066, 2 June 1639. There is some confusion regarding the verbal instructions Holland received from the King. Gardiner wrote that the Earl was 'entrusted with a reconnaissance in force' (*History*, vol. IX, p. 28), but contemporaries indicate that Holland was expected to drive the Covenanters out of Kelso if he could. See the letter of Sir John Suckling to the Earl of Middlesex, 'the horse had order to take in Kelsey, or dislodge the enemy, who was newly then intrenched', HMC de la Warr, p. 29; also, Reade (PRO, SP 16/423/16), that Holland was to force the rebels from Kelso if feasible. The anonymous account in the Bodleian Library, Rawlinson MS. b. 210, f. 15 (unfoliated) states that Holland's mission was to 'beate the Enemy out of their Trenches' at Kelso.

[84] The size of Holland's cavalry is difficult to determine, but seems to have numbered roughly 1,000. Secretary Coke estimated the horse at 1,000, as did George Weckherling and Sir Henry Vane (PRO, SP 16/423/11; SP 16/423/49; SRO, GD 406/1/1179). Sir Henry Mildmay calculated 1,200 (SP 16/423/22).

[85] PRO, SP 16/423/29, Norgate to Reade, 5 June 1639; SP 16/423/22, Mildmay to Windebank, 4 June 1639, who claimed the main cause of the retreat was the combination of the excessive heat and the march of eight to ten miles.

result, the foot began to lag behind the horse: 'the day was soe hotte and the way soe longe that a nomber of them fainted by the way and could not possibly marche any further.'[86] The cavalry soon outdistanced the weary foot soldiers. By the time the earl's thousand cavalry had arrived upon the outskirts of Kelso, the infantry plodded several miles behind.

The terrain around Kelso is for the most part a sloping basin, tucked into a ninety degree bend in the Tweed. The English approached the town from the southwest, along the northern bank of the river. They were flanked by the Tweed on their left and a marsh to the north, on their right. Adjacent to Kelso was a hill, from which the Covenanters observed the approaching English cavalry. Leslie had set a few pikemen, and perhaps some light horse, on the height, who scurried down the mount as the English drew near. Edward Norgate described what happened next in a letter to Robert Reade:

The horsetroupes approaching towards Kelsey saw on the topp of the hill a few Pikes, who seing we made towards them, hastened to their Trench downe the Hill, as if they fled. Our men ad-vancing, and yet perceaving a rising dust on each side of our troupes, and before us a river on the left hand, and a maras [morass] on the right, made a stand, when instantly appeared, a sudden and unexpected number of flying Coullors before us, yssuing out of the Trenches and from the towne behind. On each side appeared wings of foote and horse, in all above ten thousand. The danger was, that had wee advanced, wee had been entrapt and inclosed between the river and the marish [marsh], with the well fortified Trench and Town to frend before, and the wings falling on behind, had, in all probabilitie in respect of theire numbers so unequall, strength and advantages, slaine or taken off our people at their pleasure.[87]

Upon sighting the Scottish army, Holland's initial impulse had been to charge them immediately, without waiting for his infantry. He unsheathed his sword, hoping his cavalry would scatter the Covenanter infantry before they could settle into a defensive formation. 'When after a troublesome march, the weather being exceeding hote, our horse came in sight of the Scots, these came forth and put themselves in order, when presently the Earl of Holland drew his sword (as other commanders did) with intention and order to charge. But the nearer they went the more the Scottish troops encreased.'[88] The deeper the Scottish infantry formation, the less likely was Holland to breach it with a headlong charge. When more banners appeared on the field, and wings of Scottish foot began to outflank the royal cavalry, Holland faced the possibility that his horsemen would be pinned together and crushed. Without musketeers, whose fire could thin the Scottish ranks, and pikemen to protect from the shock of enemy pike,

---

[86] Bodleian Library, Rawlinson MS. b. 210, account of the campaign, f. 16 (unfoliated).
[87] PRO, SP 16/423/29, Edward Norgate to Robert Reade, 5 June 1639.
[88] PRO, SP 16/423/49, Weckherling to Conway, 6 June 1639.

the English cavalry might have been annihilated. Wisely, Holland cancelled the order to charge:

And on the Toppe of the Hill neere Kelsey about 200 Horse of the Scotch make a flourishe beinge little Bilders the Riders haveing Lances, and Speares and Carbens. My Lord Commaundes every man to Charge and bee ready and come upp to them, but not to give fire, the Scotch seeinge our Horse came on they all retreate with fast Trotte of purposeas itt was conceived to draw urs on, Then my Lord of Holland comes and standes in the same place where the Scotch Horse stood and had the viewe of some parte of the Enemy which they Conceived to bee about 4000 foote, then presently on the lefte hand comes a Companie with about 2000: and both Companies sett themselves in battaile Array.[89]

This description is supported by Sir John Suckling, who observed the Scots' attempt to draw on the English, and their use of lancers. 'The first that appeared (if our prospective glasses lied not) was Lord Car with a troop of Lancers, who hastily retired, our forlorn hopes pressing something too close upon him. (They got to the top of the hill much out of breath, suddenly a good number of the enemy were visible . . .)'[90]

Convinced that his troops were outnumbered by 6,000 to 10,000 foot, Holland dispatched a trumpeter, who approached the Covenanters' lines. The Englishman asked the Scots to explain their proximity, in violation of the agreement that the armies would not approach within ten miles of the Anglo-Scottish border. The Scots replied by asking the rather obvious question, why were English horsetroops trotting about the Scottish countryside? Leslie suggested to the messenger that the English should abandon the field immediately. Lieutenant-General Goring and Commissary-General Wilmot apparently found the Scots' recommendation persuasive, for they advised Holland to follow Leslie's advice and beat a retreat, which was done.[91]

How many Covenanters did the English encounter at Kelso that day? A French observer ventured the opinion that the Scottish forces hidden in the town, combined with the army in the field and trenches, amounted to at least 15,000.[92] Other estimates placed the number of Scots at 6,000, 8,000, or 10,000, but these approximations have met with scepticism from contemporaries and historians. The Covenanters' overwhelming numerical superiority at Kelso was more illusory than real. Leslie probably employed an old trick of the Thirty Years' War to hoodwink the English into believing that his ranks were much deeper than they really were. By arrang-

[89] Bodleian Library, Rawlinson MS. b. 210, ff. 17–18 (unfoliated).
[90] HMC de la Warr, p. 294, Sir John Suckling to the Earl of Middlesex, 6 June 1639.
[91] Aston, 'Iter Boreale', p. 24; Gardiner, *History*, vol. IX, p. 28, no. 2. The account in the Bodleian states that Sir Jacob Astley also counselled against battle, Rawlinson b. 210, f. 19 (marked with a '45' in the upper-right-hand corner).
[92] PRO, SP 16/423/29, Norgate to Reade, 5 June 1639.

ing the infantry in a compact but very narrow line, perhaps only a few men deep, he made it difficult for the English scouts to ascertain precisely how many soldiers faced them. 'Lesly had drawn his Army into a very large Front, his files exceeding thin and shallow: but intermingled with so many Ensigns, as if every twenty or thirty men had been a Regiment; and behind all, a great Herd of Cattel, which raised up so much dust with their feet, as did cloud the Strategem.' Such a ploy would explain Norgate's account of a 'rising dust' and 'a sudden and unexpected number of flying Coullors'. Clarendon provides an account similar to that of Heylyn: 'by the placing and drawing out their front in so conspicuous a place, by the appearance of other troops behind them, and by the shewing great herds of cattle at a distance upon the hills on either side, ... their army was very much superior in number.'[93] The deception seems likely, since the Scots did not dare assemble their entire army in one location for fear the English might strike elsewhere, for example at Tweedmouth. Also, the logistical problems of keeping so large an army in Kelso would have been formidable. Immediately after the English withdrawal, Leslie, Lyndsay, Balmerino, and the other Scottish commanders marched their forces north towards Duns, apparently in anticipation that the English might attempt another incursion. They slightly overestimated Holland's army at 4,000 foot and 1,500 horse.[94] Brinkmanship had failed Charles I. Yet the Scots still did not seek outright war but merely some security for their customs and kirk.

The ensuing retreat damaged Charles's army's morale and his political situation; the withdrawal of the English cavalry stunned the entire force. The psychological impact of this reverse seems disproportionate to its military significance. Holland lost not a single man or horse. Yet the Covenanters' seeming omniscience and their surprising appearance of strength and resolution worried English officers and soldiers. It was bruited that the

[93] Heylyn, *Cyprianus Anglicus*, Book IV, p. 363; PRO, SP 16/423/29, Norgate to Reade, 5 June 1639; Clarendon, *History of the Rebellion*, p. 157; Guizot remarked upon Leslie's 'skillfully disposed' troops in his *History of the English Revolution of 1640* (London, 1846), p. 75; strangely, Terry does not comment upon this matter in *The Life and Campaigns of Alexander Leslie, First Earl of Leven* (London, 1899), citing only Norgate's letter in the *CSPD*. Ironically, three weeks earlier Holland intimated to Hamilton that he suspected that the Covenanters had not raised as many men as their propaganda boasted. He suspected that they were only threatening and he now wished to see just what they could do. Such an attitude may account for his initial overconfidence. See SRO, GD 406/1/1086, ff. 1–2, 11 May 1639.

[94] National Library of Scotland, Crawford MS. 14/3/42, dispatch to the Committee at Edinburgh, 4 June 1639 (formerly in the John Rylands Library, now deposited in the NLS). Sir Henry Vane told Hamilton that although it was being said in the English camp that Holland had encountered between 8,000 and 10,000 Scottish infantry he reckoned that their true strength there was 5,000–6,000. The English force was about 1,000 horse and 3,000 foot. The King inspected the letter before it was sent off. SRO, GD 406/1/1179, f. 1, 4 June 1639. I am grateful to the Earl of Crawford and Balcarres for permission to examine the Crawford MSS.

Scots numbered 10,000. How many more troops the Covenanters had mustered at Edinburgh and beyond was a matter of disquieting conjecture. Few
Englishmen had been as enthusiastic about the war as the King, the Lord
General, and the bishops. The lukewarm support for this *bellum episco-
pale*, painfully obvious at York in April, evaporated. Leslie startled the
English by his stand at Kelso; his next tactic virtually broke the royal
army's will to fight. At six o'clock in the morning of 5 June a general alarm
sounded through the camp. On the heights of Duns Law, across the
Tweed, stood Leslie and a formidable Covenanter host, within sight of the
King's pavilion.[95] For three hours the English stood to arms, eyeing the
Scottish tents and fires. The more cynical in the King's camp suspected that
Charles had known beforehand of the Scottish advance, but declined to
inform his army: 'Some thought the king knew of their intentions to come
thither long before, but would suffer it [to] come as a soddaine alaram to
the campe to try their courage and affeccons, which, as the same polliti-
cians sayed, his majestie began now to distrust.'[96] Even in the face of an
ancient foe, Englishmen harboured suspicion and mistrust of their King.
Aston's remark reveals the degree of alienation between Charles and his
subjects and the essentially political dilemma which underlay the mobilization.

Alexander Leslie had not come seeking battle, however. He wished only
to overawe the English, and then arrange a treaty. Far from preparing to
storm the encampment, Leslie put on a brave show to intimidate the royal
army into coming to terms for 'the advance of their army to Duns Law had
been largely a bluff'.[97] When one of the King's Scottish pages arrived in the
rebel camp and suggested that both sides negotiate a settlement, the Scots
readily agreed. Still unsure of rebel strength, Charles had reservations
about the chances of achieving victory militarily. His poorly trained and
badly supplied army, which showed very little eagerness to fight, appeared
numerically inferior to the forces that impertinently entrenched themselves
within sight of their monarch. Even if he could win an engagement,
Charles would not necessarily win the war. He lacked at that moment the
financial and material resources necessary for the invasion of Scotland and
the occupation of Edinburgh because he had not drawn his English subjects
into his crusade. Hamilton and Antrim had failed; Wentworth advised
delay. The King must not risk his reputation and realm with an imperfect
army. Next summer he would have sufficient resources and a better army;
Charles must play for time through negotiation. Should he risk battle and

---

[95] For a detailed map of the royal encampment, see BL, Add. MS. 38,847, ff. 17v–18.
[96] Aston, 'Iter Boreale', p. 24.
[97] David Stevenson, *The Scottish Revolution 1637–44; The Triumph of the Covenanters*
(Newton Abbot, 1973), p. 145.

lose, northern England could be ravaged by a Scottish counter-attack. There would be no royal army to stand in the way of Leslie's victorious rebels. By negotiation he could gain time, and possibly divide his enemies and win with the pen what he might well lose with the sword. The tactic of delay strongly recommended itself. From the Covenanters' viewpoint, a peaceful settlement was imperative if the gains of the Covenant were to be preserved. They dared not attack the royal army or invade England: 'if the tramp of a Scottish army were heard on English soil, it might very well be that they would have to contend with an insulted nation. In Parliament, or out of Parliament, supplies would no longer be withheld, and the invaders would meet with a very different force from that which was now before them.'[98]

Many of the English lords and gentry distrusted the King's motives even more than they distrusted the Scots. The political context determined the tactical situation. However, the English were stronger than they themselves realized; the royal army was growing daily, while the army of the Covenant had begun to disintegrate. Additional regiments joined the royal camp: 'Our army encreaseth likewise, there being two regiments lately come to us, besides a troupe of horse and a regiment out of Northumberland, which Mr. Percy hath commaund of. Our comissary generall assured me this day that wee should have neere 4000 horse in our army.'[99]

Charles and his advisers knew little of the financial and logistical problems that beset the Covenanters. The number of soldiers raised by the Scots had not met expectations,[100] and the same problems of victualling, scarcity of coin, and weapons' shortages plagued the rebels.[101] But as they had done

[98] Gardiner, *History*, vol. IX, pp. 35–6.

[99] Verney, *Verney Papers*, p. 251, Temple to the Earl of Leicester.

[100] In neither war did the Covenanters raise as many men as their royal master. E. M. Furgol suggests that in the First Bishops' War Covenanter forces numbered at most 16,000 (E. M. Furgol, 'The Religious Aspects of the Scottish Covenanting Armies, 1639–1651', D.Phil. thesis, University of Oxford (1982), p. 3). The rebels contended with a 'shortage of manpower' (ibid, pp. 7). In 1640, they fielded a more substantial force, probably close to 18,000 (ibid, p. 15). Keeping these men around the standard was always a great concern. In the meantime, the English armies exceeded in size those raised in Scotland, pp. 32–3, 207–8, 262–3.

[101] The Crawford manuscripts reveal the rag-tag nature of the army of the Covenanters. Communities scoured their inhabitants for arms and money. Interestingly, the coastal parishes often found that seafaring men were among the most able and best equipped, but could not be easily recruited as they were often at sea (14/3/14, 14/3/28, parish of 'Gilcongh'). The motley assortment of weapons, including a plethora of 'hag butts', is also illustrative of the irregularity of the Covenanter arsenal (ibid, and 14/3/15; also 14/3/17, general memorandum regarding arms, and the returns for Kilconquhar, 14/3/18). With regard to money, the stringent pledges of security and occasional seizure of rental monies from the unwilling testify to the need for cash. See especially 14/3/36. On these procedures see 14/3/22, especially articles three to six. Also, 14/3/24, regarding rentals and debts. For a protest, 14/3/30. The system, which was fraught with 'shortages of ready money', is also discussed by David Stevenson, 'The Financing of the Cause of the

at Kelso, the Scots masked their weaknesses successfully. Their bluff at Kelso having worked they tried a similar ploy at the Tweed; nonetheless it was only a matter of time before the English discovered the deception. Once the main Scottish force had moved within view of the English camp, and potentially of the King himself, maintaining the bluff became increasingly difficult.

Sir Edmund Verney, shocked by the apparent strength of the Scots' force at Kelso, which he estimated at between 6,000 and 8,000, assumed that the forces under Holland had been fortunate to escape destruction. Leslie, Verney wrote, 'is within fiveteene mile of us with a verry strong army'.[102] The situation seemed worse the following day: 'The Scotts are verry strong; they have 15,000 men within 12 miles of uss on the one hand ... Lasly himself will bee as neare uss, eyther this night or to morrow, on another side, with 30,000 men more.'[103] Verney, a perceptive and honest observer, fully believed that aggregate Scottish forces numbered around 45,000. Charles had endeavoured to raise 30,000 and had got half that number. The Council of War had abandoned the plan of creating such a gigantic army, settling for a nucleus of 6,000 soldiers to be supplemented by the retainers of the nobility.[104] In early June, however, it appeared that the Covenanters had succeeded where the King had fallen short. Charles's commanders were stunned that the comparatively poorer nation had fielded such a colossal array. Holland wrote in the wake of his retreat that the surprisingly large number of Scots he encountered stemmed from the Covenanters' excellent intelligence regarding the movements of the royal army. Knowing where and in what strength the English would attack, they could deploy sufficient troops. He added, 'intelligence is the soule of armyes'. So persuasive was Scottish propaganda, and so lamentable English intelligence-gathering, that Verney and the English lords were convinced that these warriors truly existed and were marching to the borders.[105] He summed up the tactical situation:

The covenanters sayes they will in all humility petition the king for redress of theyr greevances. If that maye bee heard remidyed, they will laye downe theyr armes; if not, yett they will not assault any army wher the king is in person, but they profess they will instantly breake into Ingland with all the power they can make, and make the seate of the warr heere, for if the suffer the king to block them upp, they shall starve at home. All this they maye easily doe in spight of uss, for our army is very weake, and our supplyes comes slowly to uss, neyther are thos men we have well

Covenants, 1638–51', *The Scottish Historical Review*, 51:2, no. 152 (October 1972), pp. 89–94. The mobilization instructions, especially for impressment, can be found in 14/3/32, wherein anyone evading service could be 'hanged to death publickly'.

102 Verney, *Verney Papers*, pp. 243–4, Edward Verney to Ralph Verney, 4 June 1639.
103 Ibid., p. 246, Edmund Verney to Ralph Verney, 5 June 1639.
104 HMC Devonshire, p. 40, Northumberland to Clifford, 5 February 1639.
105 Verney, *Verney Papers*, p. 247; PRO, SP 16/423/27, Holland to Windebank, 5 June 1639.

orderd. The small pox is much in our army; ther is a hundred sick of it in one regiment. If the Scotts petition as they ought to doe, I beleeve they will easily bee heard, but I doubt the roages will be insolent, and knowing our weakness will demand more then in reason or honner the king can graunt, and then wee shall have a fillthy business of it. The poorest scabb in Scottland will tell uss to our faces that two parts of Ingland are on theyr sides, and trewly they behave themselves as if all Ingland were soe.[106]

A man of Verney's intelligence would no doubt perceive something incongruous in all this. Would an army of 45,000, whose leaders had been proclaimed traitors, simply lay down their arms if only the King would consider their grievances and make some concessions? Was their trust in Charles so unqualified that they would disarm themselves when their angry sovereign and a foreign army were poised upon the borders? On the day negotiations opened between King and Covenanters, Verney's tone changed dramatically:

The Scotts have a good army, but farr short of what they have bragd on; trewly I thinck wee shall have the better army, for now our supplys are come to uss, wee shall bee able to make really 13,000 foote and 2,200 horse. They will have more foote, but are weake in horse, nor are they so well armed as wee, soe that I thinck they will hardly bee drawne to meete uss in open feeld, and wee have 2,000 foote more readdy att a dayes warning.[107]

Some assessments were accurate as early as 1 June, when Lord Feilding estimated the Covenanters' strength at no more than 13,000. Archibald Campbell walked among the Covenanter troops and numbered them at 15,000 infantry and 1,500 cavalry, though a last-minute levy may have swollen the camp at Duns to closer to 20,000. Either way, the royal and Covenanter armies were of roughly equal size around 1 June.[108]

June 1639: the pacification of Berwick

On 6 June the Scots implored Charles to select some English nobles 'who are well affected to the true religion' as intermediaries in negotiations for peace. The Covenanters professed a desire only for 'the preservation of our religion and lawes'. It was in the interest of the nobility of both kingdoms to settle the issue of innovations in religion, they argued, since England and Scotland were equally afflicted. In reply, Charles sent one of his Scottish pages to Duns, who urged his countrymen to petition for a settlement. The page appeared to act upon his own initiative, despite suggestions from contemporaries and modern historians alike that he was secretly instructed

---

[106] Verney, *Verney Papers*, p. 246, Edmund Verney to Ralph Verney, 5 June 1639.
[107] Ibid., p. 252, Edmund Verney to Ralph Verney, 11 June 1639.
[108] SRO, GD 406/1/844 f. 4, report to Hamilton; GD 112/40/2/2/84, Breadalbane muniments, 2 June 1639.

to make the overture on the King's verbal order.[109] On the next day the Earl of Dunfermline arrived in the English camp as the Covenanters' emissary and asked Charles to choose English 'commissioners' to meet with representatives of the Covenant. Charles responded by sending to the Scottish camp Sir Edmund Verney, whom he entrusted with the task of arranging a conference. Verney later wrote to his son: 'I was sent by his majesty with a message to them, wherein thoughe I had a hard parte to playe, yett I dare bouldly saye I handled the business soe that I begatt this treaty, otherwise wee had, I doubt, beene at blowes by this time.'[110]

The retreat from violence owed much to the English nobility's willingness to intercede between the Scots and the King, as the Covenanters had reckoned. The disaffection of his nobles led the King to the conference table. The Earl of Holland, who had received the initial olive branch, and the King's standard-bearer, Verney, who seems to have misled Charles into thinking a declaration against the Covenant had been read to the Scots army (as a precondition of the pacification), showed through their actions that this was the King's war, not England's. The nature of the conflict being what it was, the lords of both kingdoms sought a compromise. Moreover, the affinities between them were such that it was not surprising to find collusion between English and Scots nobles during the First Bishops' War, the subsequent Short Parliament, the 'Peers' Petition' in September 1640 and ultimately in the summoning of the Long Parliament in November 1640.[111]

Much of the conduct of the First Bishops' War was theatrical. The progress of Charles's army was compared to the procession of an Eastern prince, in contrast to the resolute march of an English fighting force. The review at York was likened to equestrian frolics in Hyde Park.[112] And, of course, there were the performances of the King himself. Charles gazed nonchalantly at the Scots' encampment across the river, remarked that there were not so many as to cause alarm, and retired to dinner. It was appropriate, then, that the peace negotiations should convene with a touch of theatre. Perhaps Charles wished to utilize the Thespian skills he had acquired while taking part in the many masques staged at Whitehall. The Scots were given the impression that they would parley with the English commissioners. But the architect of the Personal Rule could not resist indulging in a little melodrama. Once the Covenanters had seated them-

---

[109] Gardiner, *History*, vol. IX, p. 36; C. V. Wedgwood, *The King's Peace 1637–1641* (New York, 1969), pp. 274–5; Stevenson, *The Scottish Revolution*, p. 151.

[110] Verney, *Verney Papers*, p. 249, Edmund to Ralph Verney, 9 June 1639.

[111] P. Donald, 'New Light on the Anglo-Scottish contacts of 1640', *Historical Research*, 62, no. 148 (1989), p. 223. See also Holland's association with the Covenanters, and his conciliatory correspondence with the Earl of Home, above p. 25, note 81.

[112] Aston, 'Iter Boreale', p. 5.

selves, Charles made a sudden entrance: 'My Lords, you cannot but wonder at my unexpected coming hither; which I myself would have spared, were it not to clear myself of that notorious slander laid upon me, That I shut my ears from the just complaints of my people of Scotland.'[113] Thus did the King justify his presence.

Charles aimed at preventing the English and Scottish representatives from collaborating or expressing opinions critical of royal policy. He undermined any common ground between the Covenanters and those 'sympathetic to the reformed religion' who had been selected as English commissioners because they were responsive to both sides. The King instead orchestrated the negotiations so as to justify his actions and intimidate the Covenanters. He was both magistrate and prosecutor. When Rothes tried to vindicate the Covenant, the King swiftly brought him to heel:

My Lord, you go the wrong way in seeking to justify yourselves and actions; for though I am not come hither with any purpose to aggravate your offences, but to make the fairest construction of them that they may bear, and lay aside all differences; yet, if you stand upon your justification, I shall not command but where I am sure to be obeyed.[114]

Finding themselves face to face with their prince and subjected to probing questions and sharp rebuttals from the King's own mouth, cracks developed in the Covenanters' facade of unity. The comparatively moderate Scots, like Henderson and Baillie, responded more cautiously than zealots like Johnston of Wariston, who accused Charles of playing for time.[115] The King told Wariston that even the devil could not have delivered such a slur. 'The King's indignation was genuine because in his anger at such insolence he had probably forgotten that this devilish interpretation of his actions was unquestionably correct.'[116]

As both sides wanted a speedy peace, the terms could be left vague in the interest of averting war. Neither side considered pacification a permanent solution. In this sense the ambiguity of the conditions was not only tolerable, but desirable. The Covenanters demanded that the legislation of the Glasgow Assembly 'shalbe Ratified by the ensueing Parliament to be holden at Edenborough July 23'.[117] They argued that such recognition was

---

[113] Hardwicke, Philip Earl of (ed.), *Hardwicke State Papers. Miscellaneous State Papers from 1501–1726*, vol. II (London, 1778) p. 132; PRO, SP 16/423/92, Borough to Windebank, 12 June 1639. Borough's powers of observation were acute. It was he who took copious notes of the Treaty of Ripon negotiations the following year.

[114] Hardwicke (ed.), *Hardwicke State Papers*, vol. II, p. 132.

[115] Wedgwood, *The King's Peace*, p. 276.

[116] Ibid. See also PRO, SP 16/423/97; Hardwicke (ed.), *Hardwicke State Papers*, vol. II, pp. 139–40.

[117] Alnwick Castle, Northumberland MSS., Letters and Papers, XV, f.204.

essential because kirk and state were one body. The civil power must contribute its 'sanction and authority to the constitution of the kirk'.[118] The
second demand dovetailed with the first. All matters ecclesiastical were to
be determined by the General Assembly and matters civil by the Scottish
Parliament.[119] 'The demand is so vague that it is impossible to know how
wide the powers were that the covenanters intended at this time to give
parliaments and general assemblies, and what authority they would leave
to the king.'[120] Finally, the English fleet was to be recalled from Scottish
waters, the royal army withdrawn from the borders, and 'Excommunicate
Persons, Incendiaries, and Informers' returned from Charles's court.[121]

When the parties met on the 13 June Charles suggested the preservation
of the laws and religion of Scotland as the basis of a settlement. On 15 June
he reiterated his opposition to the legislation of the Glasgow Assembly and
to the proposition that assemblies might alter or 'protect' the religion and
laws of Scotland. Although aware of their own military weaknesses and the
fragility of their power, the Scots risked carrying their bluff one step
further. Should the commissioners fail to reach a settlement at the conference scheduled for the 18 June, they would stop talking and start fighting.
If the impasse could not be solved by political means a military solution
was the only alternative. 'If there was to be a battle, the Covenanters would
prefer it to be as soon as possible, before the strength of their army was
eroded by delay.'[122] Charles, conscious that his restless nobles and ill-
trained army were impatient for peace, realized that some bargain would
have to be struck. Both sides agreed to withdraw and disband their armies
(hardly much of a concession from either side, since the Covenanters' host
was melting away daily while many royal soldiers wished nothing more
than to return home). For the most part, the agreement aimed at restoring
the status quo ante. Royal castles were given up to the King, and all
prisoners freed. A parliament was to be held at Edinburgh during the late
summer to deal with particulars. Most Scots and English were relieved that
war had been averted. The prospective combatants, waiting anxiously in
tents and trenches, understood little as to why the extravagant military
preparations had come to nothing more than a truce. If the King and
Covenanters had been capable of reaching a peaceful settlement, why had

---

118 PRO, SP 16/423/97; PRO, SP 16/423/104, journal prepared by Arundel for Laud; Hard-
       wicke (ed.), *Hardwicke State Papers*, vol. II, p. 139.
119 Alnwick Castle, Northumberland MSS., Letters and Papers, XV, f. 204.
120 Stevenson, *The Scottish Revolution*, pp. 153–4.
121 Alnwick Castle, Northumberland MSS., Letters and Papers, XV, f. 204.
122 Stevenson, *The Scottish Revolution*, p. 154; for the negotiations see also PRO, SP
       16/423/97, a list of Scottish proposals presented on 13 June. For an 'official account', see
       Charles I, King of England, *His Majesties Declaration Concerning his Proceedings with
       his Subjects of Scotland* (London, 1640).

they gone to the trouble and expense of assembling their armies? Neither side seriously desired war under these circumstances. The Scots honestly craved peace, provided they retained their laws and their presbyterian religion.

There were those who suspected the King was playing a bluff. The Venetian ambassador Giustinian theorized that the King and council were 'trying, by the mere noise of military preparations to bring that people [the Scots] to its original loyalty and to re-establish the royal authority in that kingdom'.[123] Nor did Charles's scheme fool Clarendon, who recalled that the King 'more intended the pomp of his preparations than the strength of them, and did still believe, that the one would save the labour of the other'.[124] More revealing is the memorandum of Secretary Windebank regarding Wentworth's Irish troops. The deployment of the Lord Deputy's forces against Scotland was a stratagem of questionable wisdom, since their removal would leave the Anglo-Irish population in the Pale vulnerable to an Irish Catholic rebellion. Windebank asserted that the danger would be minimal because Wentworth's army would be needed for a short while only:

for I think ther [the Irish soldiers] stay neids not be long In Scotland for the work will be done very shortly; for I think ther will be noe man soe made [mad] when the Kinges Army is in the feildes to hazard both ther lyff and estat, Albeit ther is many will say weill to the [thee] now bot, when they see a Armie in the fields the [they] will towrne ther Coat and will be glad to com In to the Kinge.[125]

A show of force would be sufficient to scatter the rebels. Moreover, Charles felt confident that only a disaffected minority lay behind the prayer book rebellion. Drawing near the borders with an English army, he would intimidate the malcontents and bring them to their knees. The Covenant did not enjoy universal support, and few, if any, Scots contemplated the overthrow of monarchical government. But such was the momentum of the National Covenant that the majority of Scots placed more faith in the phrase 'Christ's Crown and Covenant' than they did in the threats and vague assurances of a sovereign who dwelled in a distant, foreign city. That Charles expected the Covenant to collapse is indicative of how unaware he was of the growing delegitimation of his regime. How could the Scots trust what they regarded as an innovative, inconsistent, and unfaithful sovereign who seemed oblivious, and sometimes hostile, to the survival of the kirk?

The most telling metaphor was that which compared Charles to the sun, and the Covenanters to a murky Scottish mist: 'the beliefe of the bishops

---

[123] *CSP Venetian* (1636–9), XXIV, p. 484, to the Doge and Senate, 7 January 1639.
[124] Clarendon, *History of the Rebellion*, vol. I, p. 153.
[125] PRO, SP 16/400/65, Windebank's memo, 20 October 1638. See also below, pp. 166–7.

was that the King once heere [on the borders], the faction in Scotland, like a mist by the breaking forth of the Sunne, would dissipate and vanish'.[126] Sir Francis Seymour, in the heady first days of the Short Parliament, likened Charles to Sol: 'His Majesty is the Sunne, which though it ever shines alike in it selfe gloriously; yet by reason of Clouds, many times it doth not so appeare, and if his Majesty, by reason of bad members may not appeare in such splendor, Let us labour to cleere those Clouds.'[127] Edward Norgate employed this metaphor when he wrote in early June, 'Wee are as ignorant as before, and know as little as wee did, for this foggie Scotch mist is not yet cleared.'[128] Earlier he had written rather apprehensively that the tale that the Covenanters would break and run as the English army approached was being disproved daily. He estimated Scottish strength at 40,000 soldiers.[129] Lord Poulett wrote: 'those that were of opinion that the kinges drawinge neere Scotland with an Army would disunite those people and drawe a party to the kinge find themselves deceaved'. The Lord General was genuinely surprised when no Scots defected to the royal standard.[130]

Ironically, Charles had been much closer to victory than he ever imagined. Had he postponed negotiations for another week or two, the Scottish army would probably have disintegrated, as its money and food were exhausted. In reality, the pacification was a draw. The Covenanters had successfully induced the King to discuss the issues that had sparked the rebellion. They did not succeed in securing recognition of the Glasgow Assembly, but Charles had given his word to honour the laws and religion of Scotland (though the King was free to interpret this as he pleased). On his side, Charles, as we have noted, remained adamant that the Glasgow Assembly acted without royal authorization and that its legislation was illegal. By negotiating with the rebels he had therefore lost nothing. His failure to destroy them could be ascribed to his forgiving nature. Instead of appearing weak, he was seen to be magnanimous. Lord Poulett deserves to place the epitaph upon the First Bishops' War:

If you saw our men with their feathers and buff cotes and bigg lookes you would say the Scotts are like to have but a bad bargeyn in meddling with us. For my part that am not yet come to my buff cote and feather I pray for peace and that the shocke of our arms may not be tried.[131]

126 Aston, 'Iter Boreale', p. 5.
127 Cope and Coates (eds.), *Proceedings of the Short Parliament* , p. 214, citing Worcester College MS. 5.20.
128 PRO, SP 16/423/15, Norgate to Reade, 3 June 1639.
129 PRO, SP 16/421/34, Norgate to Reade, 16 May 1639.
130 Bristol Record Office, Ashton Court MS. AC/C61/5, Poulett to Smith, 19 April 1639; SRO, GD 406/1/1066, Arundel's letter of 2 June 1639.
131 Bristol Record Office, Ashton Court MS. AC/C61/5, Poulett to Smith, 19 April 1639. I am certainly not the first to suggest that Charles and the Covenanters were bluffing in

Politics had started the war and could have ended it, but no political remedy could be found in the pacification. Late 1639 saw the King change his advisors rather than abandon his purpose or his methods. He dismissed Arundel, Holland, and those who had failed to bring off a victory. Laud and Strafford (for Wentworth had been elevated to an earldom) took their places at Charles's side.[132] Laud, who was widely condemned for the shunning of parliaments, would assist Strafford in overseeing a War Parliament which would sustain the campaign.[133] It was a policy which Strafford felt confident of realizing.[134] The consequent collapse of the Short Parliament demonstrated that the King's chief lieutenants had no more sense of the political and religious concerns of the realm than did their royal master. Strafford had been ensconced in Ireland for six years and Laud, who had never served as a parish priest, still failed to comprehend the sensibilities of the laity. The Short Parliament made Charles's predicament in 1640 much worse than in 1639 in three ways. First, the elections raised political consciousness throughout the kingdom. Second, the enunciation of grievances at Westminster brought political issues into sharper focus. Inchoate local grievances became defined national issues. Third, the breakdown of the Parliament mirrored the rift between governors and governed. It made for a most inauspicious start to the Second Bishops' War.

THE SECOND BISHOPS' WAR, JUNE–AUGUST 1640

Whereas the campaign of 1639 was badly conceived, the mobilization of 1640 was foolhardy. Explaining why the King went to war in 1639 is comparatively easy: he genuinely believed that a show of force and an uncompromising rebuff of the Covenant would stifle unrest in Scotland. Why Charles and Strafford persisted in pursuing war in 1640 is not so easily fathomed. The coercion of the Scottish assemblies and the Edinburgh Parliament had failed in the face of profound political and religious differences between the Scots and the King. The protests of the Edinburgh Parliament in particular had clarified the problem. Scotland would have no bishops; the King insisted (at least in the long run) that episcopacy be preserved. Charles could not force the acceptance of bishops except by the

<hr/>

1639. In 1955 David Mathew wrote that the First Bishops' War was 'a game of double bluff', *Scotland under Charles I* (London, 1955), p. 293.

[132] See pp. 66–72, 86–7 on the Council of War and the command structure.

[133] See for example the seditious conversation that alleged that as long as Laud lived there would be no Parliaments: Bodleian Library, Bankes MS. 18/2. The reasoning was explained quite clearly to Ambassador Hopton by Windebank in a letter, Bodleian Library, Clarendon SP, XVII, ff. 215–215v, 13 December 1639.

[134] Strafford's confidence in early 1640 brought out the worst in Charles I, encouraging the King to believe matters were not as desperate as they really were. See Hugh Kearney, *Strafford in Ireland, 1633–41. A Study in Absolutism* (Cambridge, 1989), p. 189.

sword, which he had failed to do in 1639. Charles's foreign policy had
come to naught. He further aroused the suspicion of his subjects when he
appeared to be aiding the Spaniards by allowing them to shelter their fleet
in an English harbour in October 1639 while a Dutch squadron lay in wait
in the Channel. The royal position had further deteriorated because the
King's actions bred mistrust of his political agenda. The Short Parliament
had taken its cue from the Edinburgh Parliament, being forced to challenge
royal policy in what both assemblies perceived as a matter of survival of
their religious liberties and rights as subjects. Regardless, Strafford pushed
on with the King's war in a celebrated tirade delivered at the momentous
council meeting of 5 May 1640, hours after the dissolution of the Short
Parliament. In spite of the King's failure to play off the French, Spaniards
and Dutch against each other, he attempted once again to secure foreign
money and mercenaries.[135] In the face of doubts about his solvency and
motives, loans were solicited in a shameless and swaggering fashion. Ship
money and coat-and-conduct money were collected with renewed diligence
and county communities were bidden to another mobilization; raw
soldiers were to be collected and armed amid rumours of continental
invasions and foreign conspiracies that would break out as soon as the
armed might of the nation marched north.

In 1639, as a consequence of the Crown's failure to occupy Berwick early
with a sufficient garrison, the Earl of Essex had marched hurriedly to the
town, fearing that a Scottish army might already have taken it and established a 'beach-head' in English territory. The King learned from this
mistake: in the Second Bishops' War he made certain that royal garrisons
and forts remained securely in the hands of loyalists before any military
action commenced. Since Edinburgh controlled lowland Scotland, the
security of Edinburgh Castle was paramount. The castle's commander,
General Ruthven, was convinced that the Covenanters would first make an
attempt on the citadel before sending their main force to the borders in
1640. A hostile garrison in the capital would place an enemy at their backs.
Ruthven and the Council of War agreed that the castle should be prepared
for a siege of six months to a year. The garrison was reinforced secretly,
and soldiers dressed as mariners slipped in in twos and threes. Powder and
arms were smuggled in packed in beer casks. The castle's well and water
supplies were inspected and the fortifications improved. The preparations
attracted attention. The garrison consisted mostly of lowland Scots, and
their food was purchased directly from Edinburgh tradesmen, who
delivered the provisions. Communication existed between the garrison and
the townspeople. Ruthven admitted his distrust of the Scots under his

135 Discussed below, pp. 119–20, 162–6, 172–3.

command, and asked for English soldiers. The influx of foreigners, even if disguised as innocuous seafaring men, bred suspicion amongst the populace. To make matters worse, sections of the walls and bulwark crumbled during the winter of 1639–40, and Ruthven searched for sufficient stone and timber to repair the damage by spring. The Scots, understandably, were not keen on assisting. The garrison fortress stood as a symbol of the Crown's intransigent opposition to the Covenant and Charles's threat to use foreign troops in the coming summer. The King's soldiers were abused when venturing out of the castle's confines. Workmen refused to repair the fortifications, and contractors declined to supply materials. In March, soldiers from the garrison scaled the walls and deserted. Ruthven pleaded for English reinforcements and more weapons. Tension became violence in May 1640, when Ruthven fired upon the town, allegedly killing thirty Scots civilians.[136]

The vulnerability of Edinburgh Castle was matched by that of the Berwick garrison. Combined operations by the Covenanters against Berwick from land and sea would have disrupted the English mobilization by removing Charles's forward outpost. The Scottish East Marches and Edinburgh would then be out of harm's way. Victuals, ovens and mills in Berwick would fall into Covenanter hands. Holy Island's strategic value to the English would be considerably diminished while the Scots controlled the harbour, and the supplies stored on that island could be taken. Replenished, the rebels might then have pushed further into England. Such logistical successes would have placed Charles at a distinct disadvantage had he chosen to give battle in summer 1639.[137] In order to prevent this he had calculated that his 'beach-heads' in Scotland, the royal fortresses, would keep the Covenanters from concentrating all their forces along the frontier. As it happened, in 1639 the King's Scottish strongholds fell, but the Covenanters did not press this advantage by moving against Berwick or Carlisle. Instead, they held their ground, hoping for a peaceful settlement. In 1640 the Covenanters were not so sanguine. The royal strategy of 1640 dictated again that Berwick and its garrison serve (as had been the case in the mid-Tudor mobilizations) as a staging area for an invasion of the Scottish East Marches and Edinburgh, or as a vantage point from which to launch a counter-stroke against an invading Scottish force.[138] One would

---

[136] Patrick Ruthven, *Ruthven Correspondence. Letters and Papers of Patrick Ruthven, Earl of Forth and Brentford, and of his family: A.D. 1615 – A.D. 1662*, ed. W. D. Macroy (London, 1868), pp. xvii-xix, 13–69; Gardiner, *History*, vol. IX, p. 148, citing SP 16/454/51, 75, and 98; see also the account in SRO, RH 13/18, anonymous diary, unfoliated, ff. 16–17 (In cases where a longer manuscript is unfoliated, I have counted the leaves and provided an *ad hoc* folio reference.)

[137] PRO, SP 16/457/4, 17 June 1640. See also PRO, Signet Office 3/12 f. 95.

[138] Colvin, *King's Works*, p. 614.

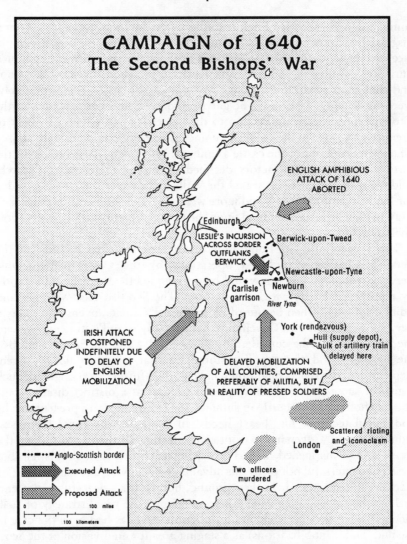

CAMPAIGN of 1640
The Second Bishops' War

ENGLISH AMPHIBIOUS
ATTACK OF 1640
ABORTED

Edinburgh

LESLIE'S INCURSION
ACROSS BORDER
OUTFLANKS
BERWICK

Berwick-upon-Tweed

Newcastle-upon-Tyne

Carlisle   Newburn
garrison
River Tyne

York (rendezvous)
Hull (supply depot),
bulk of artillery train
delayed here

IRISH ATTACK
POSTPONED
INDEFINITELY DUE
TO DELAY OF
ENGLISH
MOBILIZATION

DELAYED MOBILIZATION
OF ALL COUNTIES, COMPRISED
PREFERABLY OF MILITIA, BUT
IN REALITY OF PRESSED SOLDIERS

Scattered rioting
and iconoclasm

London

- ·—·—■—·— Anglo-Scottish border

Executed Attack

Proposed Attack

Two officers
murdered

0   100   miles

0   100 kilometers

2   Campaign of 1640: the Second Bishops' War

have expected the Covenanters to follow the eastern coastline south, their
modest artillery train in tow, and then to lay siege to Berwick. Instead, the
Covenanters employed the strategy which Hamilton and Charles had
feared in 1638, and which they had chosen, wisely, not to pursue in
1639.[139] They bypassed Berwick and struck into the heart of England.

[139] See NLS, Wodrow MSS., Church and State Papers 1618–85, XXXI, no. 4, ff. 27–28v.

The Covenanters anticipated successfully the royal strategies of 1639 and 1640 and made the correct counter-manoeuvres. Conversely, Charles and his councillors, in spite of the benefit of having expert Scottish advisors such as Hamilton and Traquair, were uncertain about the intentions and movements of the Covenanters. Strategically, the Covenanters won the war to the same extent that Charles effectively lost it by making the wrong decisions.

Nevertheless, the cautious but effective shielding of Berwick remained a strategic imperative through both Bishops' Wars, although greater efforts to protect it were made in 1640. The more likely the combat, the better prepared the garrison needed to be. The 'dissolved,' or skeleton, garrison was increased in strength throughout the Second Bishops' War.[140] Reinforcements from London were sent up.[141] In addition to the periodic tactical presence of various companies from the expeditionary forces, 300 infantrymen under Captains Foulthorpe, Wren, and Gifford augmented the garrison for at least a fortnight; and 600 dragoons of the regiment of Sir Francis Howard occupied the fort for eight months.[142] The Earl of Lindsey's 2,000 Lincolnshire men gave way to a more varied and stronger garrison presence, which boosted the town's strength at a minimum cost of £45,000 per annum. The nature of the new forces revealed a more aggressive royal strategy for 1640. Four troops of carabines under Lord Wentworth, Sir John Byron, Sir William Bronker, and Governor Sir John Conyers were available for rapid deployment. They were supported by fifteen companies of infantry (and horse, it would seem), though the tours of duty varied and it is doubtful if all fifteen companies quartered there simultaneously.[143] The town's security rested also upon assistance from adjoining shires. The Northumbrian lieutenants and the Bishop of Durham were ready to furnish 500 militiamen if need be (much as in 1639).[144] Six

---

[140] PRO, E 351/3519, Norton's account for 25 December 1639 to 16 December 1640, wherein the skeleton garrison cost £386 10s 11d; for the ideal garrison, see the pay table in Alnwick Castle, Letters and Papers, XV, ff. 5–6, 22 January 1640.

[141] Corporation of London Records Office, *Journals of the Court of Common Council of the City of London, 1558–1640*, vol. XXXIX, f. 61v, 200 pressed men from London; PRO, Signet Office 1/3, f. 157, 10 January 1640, 100 pressed men from Middlesex.

[142] PRO, E 351/3520, Sir Alexander Davidson's account, 20 March 1639 to 16 February 1640.

[143] PRO, E 351/3521, account of George Payler, June 1639 to November 1640. The settlement of pay for some units at the close of the First Bishops' War are included, though the terms suggest the majority of companies listed occupied the garrison in preparation for the summer 1640 campaign.

[144] Captains were to raise four companies for Berwick, see *CSPD* (1639–40), XV, p. 50, 23 October 1639; PRO, SP 16/431/66, Ernley informs the council that reinforcements are needed, 28 October 1639; SP 16/432/93, more gunners needed to supplement the fourteen already in the garrison, 20 November 1639; SP 16/436/29, Bishop of Durham to use militiamen to reinforce the garrison, under Captain Gifford, 25 December 1639; SP 16/436/34, 35, Council informs Ernley that the trained bands will be used to assist the

companies of Northumberland and Durham militia actually served at Berwick even though they were very much needed with the royal army.[145] The Crown envisioned a restored garrison of 1,400 men, equipped with an artillery train, costing £22,268 per annum.[146] Because Berwick had reached its nadir as a fortress in 1638, during the winter of 1639–40 its fortifications were repaired and improved. Construction proceeded in spite of inclement weather and a shortage of carpenters.[147] Precautions were taken to prevent a surprise attack;[148] Covenanter spies were to be ferreted out, though apparently this operation met with little success.[149] All of this points to greater resolution on the part of Charles I to fight.

The borders in 1640 were mobilized more effectively than in the previous year. Sufficient pay was to be supplied to the King's soldiers for the campaign's duration. Six hundred Cumberland dragoons, 200 of whom were tenants of the Earl of Northumberland, were equipped by the King and placed under Colonel Trafford. Another 400 dragoons were to be raised so that an entire regiment was available from Cumberland. The Council of War drafted an army list of 20,000 foot and 3,000 horse, including twenty regiments of ten companies of one hundred men each, plus officers, and throughout January 1640 set about appropriating sufficient firearms, swords, powder, and match. Money would be obtained when Parliament met in the spring.

The politics of the Second Bishops' War

If the Scots were sure of the King's intentions in 1640, others were not. In England, with the first parliamentary election in more than a decade under way, the stockpiling of arms and the presence of English mercenary cap-

---

garrison, 26 December 1639; SP 16/436/42, 43, where Charles urges Windebank and Ernley to remind the Bishop of Durham that he must aid Berwick, 28 December 1639.

[145] Ibid, f. 8. It is unclear whether the sixty Northumberland men pressed on 16 April 1640 were in fact militia, a grievance just then coming before the Short Parliament. See PRO, SP 16/450/100 and 100 I.

[146] Alnwick Castle, Northumberland MSS., Letters and Papers, XV, ff.5–6, 22 January 1640.

[147] For the repair of Berwick fortifications, see the business of re-supply (PRO, SP 16/438/9); the impressment of workmen (SP 16/441/115, council to Lloyd, 13 January 1640); account of ordnance in Berwick (SP 16/453/94, 16 May 1640); survey of buildings (SP 16/444/20, 3 February 1640 and SP 16/446/91, *c.* February 1640). See also *CSPD* (1640), XVI, under 17 June 1640 for several entries. See also SP 16/432/94 I, works to be undertaken at Berwick, 20 November 1639; SP 16/436/30, 31, 32, reports on progress at Berwick, 25 December 1639; SP 16/441/67, on the shortage of carpenters, 8 January 1640.

[148] PRO, SP 16/431/53, Windebank to Ernley, 24 October 1639; SP 16/436/35, Windebank to Ernley, 26 December 1639; SP 16/436/43, Windebank to Ernley, 28 December 1639.

[149] PRO, SP 16/435/59, Ernley to Windebank, 10 December 1639; SP16/436/34, Windebank to Ernley, 26 December 1639; 16/436/35, Windebank to Ernley, 26 December 1639; SP 16/436/41, the King to Traquair, 28 December 1639; SP 16/436/54, Ernley to Windebank, 31 December 1639.

tains in the capital was viewed with foreboding. Were Charles's soldiers intended to suppress the Covenanters or intimidate the new Parliament? Richard Cave confided to Sir Thomas Roe, 'The raising of troops before a Parliament begets discourse and censures.'[150] On 30 December 1639 he noted:

The public pretext for these extraordinary preparations is given as the need for checking the ardour of the Scots, but I find that his Majesty and his more confidential ministers have other and more secret intentions. The chief one is to keep within bounds, by the fear of these forces, the Parliament which they have decided to open on the 13th April.[151]

Giustinian later reported, 'His Majesty has ordered that they [the royal troops] shall be quartered in the most remote parts, in order to disarm the mischievious suspicion of the people that the assembling of such great forces is intended rather to kill the demands of the English Parliament than to beat down the violence of the rebels.'[152] In New England John Winthrop heard, 'Wee are now neere our parliament ... Our King vppon his own charge prouides for warr Thirty Thousand foote and 7 or 8 thousand horse. *We say against the Scotts; but we know not.*'[153]

While parliamentary candidates and those 'preciser sort' opposed to Arminianism felt uneasy about the gathering of an army and a Parliament simultaneously, continental powers entertained similar uncertainties. More than any other European power, the French had confounded Caroline foreign policy. Louis XIII had imprisoned Charles's nephew, the Elector Palatine. Cardinal Richelieu was encouraging (perhaps inciting) the Covenanters' revolt and forging a new 'auld alliance'. Fears of English reprisals were confirmed by the presence of the Queen Mother, Marie de' Medici, at Whitehall since the autumn of 1638. The Duchess of Chevreuse, supposedly Marie's confederate in opposition to the regime of Richelieu, worked to animate the English court against Louis XIII. During late 1639 and the first few months of 1640 events in England convinced some French observers that an Anglo-Spanish alliance had been struck in order to assail France and her possessions.

Strafford's influence grew dramatically after the failure of the First Bishops' War, and his disdain for Richelieu's France was common knowledge. It was deduced that he plotted a grand alliance against France, which could ill-afford a major conflict with England in 1640.[154] The nation

---

[150] *CSPD* (1639–40), XV, p. 321, 10 January 1640.
[151] *CSP Venetian* (1636–9), XXIV, p. 605, n.750.
[152] Ibid., XXV, p. 4, n. 6, 13 January 1640.
[153] Wright to Winthrop, 26 March 1640, printed in *The Winthrop Papers* Massachusetts Historical Society (1929), vol. II, p. 220 (my italics).
[154] Indeed he was. See J. H. Elliot, 'The Year of Three Ambassadors', in H. Lloyd-Jones, V. Pearl, and B. Worden (eds.), *History and Imagination, Essays in Honour of H. R. Trevor-Roper* (London, 1981), pp. 165–181.

was war-weary and Louis XIII's finances as badly strained as those of Charles I.[155] It was in the interest of France to keep England embroiled with Scotland, and Charles with domestic discontents. Should Charles quell his problems at home, he might intervene on the continent to liberate the Protestant Elector Palatine. On 30 December, 1639, Giustinian noted:

If the parliament here produces the results desired, the King does not mean to leave this army idle, but will use it to encourage revolts in Normandy, in order to express his resentment with France for the arrest of the Palatine and the secret pecuniary assistance afforded to the Scots ... These are vigorously supported by the suggestions of the Queen Mother and by the malcontents of France who sojourn at this Court.'[156]

The army of 15,000 infantry and 2,000 horsemen could fulfil 'some hidden intention against France in case the disturbances in Scotland are settled'.[157] When the French ambassador Bellièvre departed from London in mid-January, a serious breach between France and England was predicted. Once in Paris, he provided Louis and Richelieu with a very accurate assessment of Charles's predicament. Although the Spanish, especially the ambassador, the Marquis de Vellada, were promoting an Anglo-Spanish alliance, Charles could not provide much assistance while Scotland was in revolt: 'the King of Great Britain is in no condition to undertake anything against France this year. His wrath at the detention of his nephew is much less than the necessity of employing his forces against the Scots.'[158] Bellièvre's evaluation (if we can believe Correr's account of it) was very near the mark. The subjugation of Scotland took precedence over all continental projects, including aid to the Elector Palatine. 'The King is not yet come to any resolution concerning our treaties with France and Holland', Northumberland wrote. 'The truth is, we think so much upon reducing Scotland to obedience, that other matters of no less importance are wholly neglected.'[159] While the Covenanters' revolt continued, English prestige abroad suffered. The Dutch, too, took comfort from the prayer book rebellion. It was said that the Dutch 'derive great hopes from the movements of the Scots, and they believe here that more serious disturbances will occur'.[160] The courtship of Spain by Cottington and other Caroline courtiers convinced the Dutch that Charles I was not to be trusted. Better that the Scots should keep him out of European affairs, for he might (and could) be bought by Spanish gold.

155 Geoffrey Parker, *Europe in Crisis 1598–1648* (New York, 1979), p. 246.
156 *CSP Venetian* (1636–9), XXIV, pp. 605–6, no. 750.
157 Ibid., XXV, p. 13, no. 20, 28 January 1640.
158 Ibid., pp. 16–17, no. 27, Ambassador Correr's summary of Bellièvre's report to the French King, 14 February 1640.
159 HMC Northumberland, p. 79, to the Earl of Leicester, 26 December 1639.
160 *CSP Venetian* (1640–2), XXV, p. 9, no. 21, Correr to Doge and Senate, January 1640.

Even more than the Dutch, however, many Englishmen 'took comfort' from the Scottish unrest which had compelled the issuing of writs for a parliament. After more than a decade without parliaments, the calling of that body to Westminster was hailed as the proper remedy for all England's ills, from ship money to Archbishop Laud. Eleven years' absence had endowed Parliament, in the popular imagination at least, with miraculous healing powers.[161] Those too young or inexperienced in national politics to recall the tumultuous sessions of the 1620s believed that the summoning of Parliament *was* the solution, not merely the means to arrive at a solution. That Charles changed his mind in 1640, agreeing to call Parliament when the year before he had refused to do so even in the face of war, showed the centrality of the Scottish problem in the governance of this British King. He even listened to counsel upon this occasion, though only because it seemed the best way to obtain his desired goal: the conquest of Scotland.

The King's revenew upon examination appeered to be so anticipated, as litle could be hoped for from thence; laying excises, inioyneing eache countie to mentaine a certaine number of men, whilst the warre lasted, and such like wayes, were by some farre prest but mett with so many weightie obiections, that those Lords that were all this while most averse to parlaments, did now begin to advise the Kings makeing triall of his people in parlament, before he used any way of power. This being advised by their Lordships (who to say truth found themselves so pusseld that they know not where to begin) the King was soon gained, and resolved the next Councell day to propose it to the rest of the Lords, which accordingly was donne, and though it came very unexpectedly to them, yet it passed without opposition.[162]

But those who saw the occasion of a parliament as an opportunity for domestic reform, or as a chance to make a lasting peace, were to be disappointed. War hastened the calling of Parliament, and the Crown's insistence that its military policies remain uncompromised precipitated its dissolution.[163]

The dissolution of the Short Parliament on 5 May 1640 set in motion the most important council meeting of the reign of Charles I. On that afternoon the King, Laud, Cottington, Northumberland, and Vane decided the fate of Scotland and the Personal Rule. Parliament's refusal to grant supply without discussion of grievances deprived the Crown of revenue needed to fund a royal army. What policy could the Crown now pursue in response to the Covenanters' rebellion? Could Charles afford to fight the Scots?

[161] Esther Cope, 'Public Images of Parliament During its Absence', *Legislative Studies Quarterly*, 7, no. 2 (May 1982), pp. 221–34.
[162] Centre for Kentish Studies, De L'Isle and Dudley MSS., Sydney Papers, U 1475 C 85/4, f. 1v, Northumberland to Leicester, 12 December 1639.
[163] Fissel, 'Scottish War and English Money', pp. 206–11.

Opinions were divided, but once again Strafford's dynamism prodded the Council into action, and sustained the King's resolve to subjugate the Scots.

Incomplete and hasty as they are, Secretary Vane's notes convey the tension that permeated the council chamber. Strafford declared there was 'Noe danger in undertakeinge this warr.'[164] Were the Covenanters to be crushed or left alone? The King should 'reduce them by force; as the state of this kingdome standes'. Now second-guessing the Crown's strategy in dealing with Parliament, Strafford reflected that if Charles had not 'declared himselfe soe soone, hee would have declared himselfe for noe warr with Scotland', and consequently, Parliament would probably have voted subsidies. Strafford's argument seems to have been that had the King refrained from making known his strategy he would not have encountered unified resistance to his policies. Strafford's reasoning is confusing. It was the war's imminence which justified the granting of supply before the broaching of grievances. An unhurried Parliament would have taken time to review the Personal Rule in excruciating detail, and awakened the issue of the hasty dissolution of 1629. On the other hand, if Charles had remained relatively noncommittal about the future actions of his government, such a course would not have coalesced opposition as rapidly, since doubt remained as to his intentions. But it did not matter: the City of London's merchants and guilds could assist by loaning £100,000.[165] Ship money would 'bee putt vigorously uppon collection. These two waies will furnish his Majestie plentifully to goe on with armes and warr for Scotland.'

Strafford proposed a blow against the enemy's capital. An 'Offensive warr' into the heart of lowland Scotland would bring victory in a matter of months. Northumberland, cognizant of the Crown's financial weakness, inquired as to where the money could be found. Strafford had erred in his assessment of Parliament. Could he be certain that the City would loan £100,000? What guarantee existed that local administrators, already hard-pressed after eleven years of Personal Rule and a pointless war against Scotland in 1639, would succeed in collecting ship money speedily and completely? 'If noe more mony then what proposed, howe then to make an offensive warr?' Strafford's retort, even if fragmentary, deserves quotation at length:

Goe vigorously on or lett them alone, noe defensive warr, losse of honour and reputacion. The quiett of England will hold out longe. You will languish as betwixt

---

[164] This discussion is based upon the manuscript preserved in the House of Lords Record Office, Main Papers (April–September 1640), ff. 99–100. T. G. Barnes kindly provided a transcript of that document.

[165] See pp. 118–24 below.

Saul and David. Goe on with a vigorous warr, as you first designed, loose and absolved from all rules of government beinge reduced to extreame necessitie, everthinge is to bee done that power might admitt, and that you are to doe. They [the Parliament] refuseinge you are acquitted towardes God and man, you have an army in Ireland you may imploy here to reduce this kingdome. Confident as anythinge under heaven Scotland shall not hold out five months. One summer well imployed will doe it. Venter [venture] all I had, I would carry it or loose it.[166]

Laud seconded Strafford. Charles had 'Tried all waies' and been 'refused alwayss'. The King was entitled by 'the lawe of God' to have 'subsistance', and being denied the funds to maintain his government, he had lawful and moral grounds for taking what he needed. Cottington, the Chancellor of the Exchequer, who should have heeded Northumberland's warning, stressed the seditiousness of the Scots. Because the Covenanters had invited foreign intervention, as Finch and Charles had attempted to prove at the outset of the Short Parliament, the suppression of the Scots was indeed a defence of the realm. The Commons worked towards the destruction of 'King and Church'. Given this predicament, Charles was obliged to defend the realm as he saw fit.

Northumberland's worst fears regarding the royal army's fortunes had been realized by the Short Parliament's obstinacy. His misgivings about prosecuting the war with insufficient money in the Exchequer had not blunted Strafford's impassioned call for a crusade. Although the council debated whether the war should be offensive, defensive measures were essential in order to prepare the way for Charles's grand army. The reinforcing of the Edinburgh and border garrisons and improvements in fortifications had been undertaken precisely in anticipation of a Second Bishops' War. On the very day of the council meeting, Northumberland informed Lord Conway that Alnwick, Morpeth, and Hexham should be fortified and garrisoned. The 1640 strategy aimed at nothing short of a massive attack upon Edinburgh: 'we are going upon a conquest with such a power that nothing in that kingdom will be able to resist us'.[167]

We know how Charles planned to approach Scotland and understand the strategy that he laid out. It is unclear, however, just what he would do once across the border. No plans for the occupation of Edinburgh

---

[166] In addition to the document in the House of Lords Record Office, another copy is preserved as PRO SP 16/452/31. It was published verbatim in the third report (appendix) of the Historical Manuscripts Commission (1872), p. 3. Another specimen is included amongst the Earl of Northumberland's papers in Alnwick Castle, Northumberland MSS., Letters and Papers, XV. See HMC Northumberland, p. 81. A discussion of the versions can be found in Gardiner, *History*, IX, pp.120–1.

[167] *CSPD* (1640), XVI, p. 114; Sir John Borough, *Notes of the treaty carried on at Ripon between King Charles I and the Covenanters of Scotland. A. D. 1640*, ed. J. Bruce, Camden Society, first series C (1869), p. viii.

apparently exist.[168] Charles had insisted, even to Hamilton, that his border preparations were defensive.[169] How such a strategy could have coerced the Scots remains something of a mystery, and one cannot help but wonder if Charles had thought through the ramifications of his actions. The almost casual strategy of 1639, which discounted the resolve of the Covenanters, had aimed at bluffing them into submission. Some fighting there might be, but the three-pronged assault would, in Charles's opinion, allow him to march into Edinburgh and extinguish the opposition. He was, however, out-bluffed by the Scots. In 1640 the King resolved upon force. So fixed was he upon this goal that he had relented and called an English Parliament. So obsessed was he with the challenge to his authority that he prosecuted the war in spite of the dissolution. The lack of parliamentary support, financially and politically, placed Charles at a strategic and, ultimately, a tactical disadvantage. Conversely, the Scots won the battle of Newburn in September 1640 because of a tactical superiority seized by a bolder strategy than that of their sovereign. They had to be bold, for politically the King would not compromise with them. Their political situation forced them into action.

Charles's strategy for 1640

The English tactical blunders of the Bishops' Wars proceeded from the ill-conceived strategies of 1639 and 1640. Different as they were, both strategies aimed at solving a political problem, the unrest in Scotland. It was a political dilemma, not a military challenge, that Charles faced. Neither strategy gave English military institutions the resources or time to make a military solution feasible. Incomplete military preparations and poor strategic thinking placed English forces at a disadvantage, which led to tactical setbacks. Those setbacks compounded the political problem by demonstrating the King's military impotence, which in turn further bedevilled the political problem. Charles should not have launched either campaign until he had sufficient forces and resources to sustain his strategy.

The success of the bluff and the reverse at Kelso in 1639 had repercussions upon tactical responses in the Second Bishops' War. In 1640 the King expected to fight, as did the Covenanters. The likelihood of a Scottish blow inculcated within Charles a certain apprehension about being surprised by the Covenanters, as had occurred in 1639. Consequently, even though his design was offensive, Charles's tactical response, undercut by Sir Jacob

---

[168] Though Strafford makes reference to the relief of the castle in August 1640. SRO, GD 406/1/1232.
[169] SRO, GD 406/1/422.

Astley's unwillingness to commit unpaid and unreliable soldiers, spread the English forces too thinly. The delayed mobilization meant that too few soldiers were reaching the borders and that those stationed there simply had too much ground to cover. In the late summer of 1640, Berwick and Carlisle were virtually conceded to the Scots in hopes of drawing a defensive line at Newcastle.

Expected to prosecute the war to its fullest extent, the English commanders in the Second Bishops' War had fewer resources at their disposal than were available in 1639. The political stalemate made pay and discipline greater problems in 1640, making deployment that much more difficult. Particularly galling to Lord Conway, in the field in place of the stricken Strafford and Northumberland, was the accusation that he had failed to take sufficient precautions for protecting Newcastle.[170] As a matter of fact, Charles's personal instructions to Conway regarding the defence of Newcastle smacked of defeatism. Conway was to torch outlying settlements and the suburbs should the Covenanters overwhelm his forces; ships were to be burned or sunk to prevent their falling into Scottish hands; he was to keep his forces intact and prevent arms from being captured. The defensiveness of these tactics makes one wonder if Charles should have marched in 1640.[171] Sir Henry Gibb, who had visited the borders and spoken with the Covenanter Thomas Hamilton, second Earl of Haddington, believed that the Scots would strike in August with an army of 30,000. Conway relayed this information to Northumberland and Strafford, who were sceptical. Strafford responded:

It is true, it is observed to be contrary to all your Lordship hath formerly wrote, wherein you judge England to be secure of the Scots this year; and to believe so mightily an increase of number above what you formerly mentioned, in truth, cannot probably be really so, upon no more ground than the bare relation of Gibbs, a known Covenanter in heart, and too in his own view [upon hearsay, in other words], but only in the credit and report of the Lord Haddington, is not a little wondered at ... But also those, who wish you not well, severely interpret to your prejudice, that, upon so slight an advertisement, and from a person you had so little cause absolutely to trust in that business, you should so suddenly pronounce the town of Newcastle lost ... for the love of Christ, think not so early of quitting the town, burning the suburbs, or sinking of ships.[172]

Defeatism irritated Strafford. Conway was a friend and ally, and he regretted that Conway contemplated such desperate measures. Northumberland, too, liked Conway, and did not wish his detractors to find cause for

---

[170] Northumberland was immobilized by illness in summer 1640. The reins of command then fell to Conway and Strafford. The latter, too, was plagued by bad health. See Gardiner, *History*, vol. X, pp. 139–40,185,188.

[171] Bodleian Library, Clarendon SP, XIX, ff. 167, 171v, Conway's relation.

[172] Ibid, ff. 168–168v.

censure. Haddington, however, was correct. The Covenanters were indeed preparing to strike a blow. Between the Scots and Conway stood only Sir John Conyers and the Berwick garrison, and that border town could be bypassed easily. Northumberland agreed that Conway would be hard pressed to halt the Scots with his modest contingent of cavalry. Obviously, a large number of infantry was needed, but the troops at Selby were 'so unskillful in the use of their armes, so disaffected, and so illpayed that I can hope for little helpe from them for the present'.[173] Shortages of weapons, too, discouraged deployment.[174] Conway could not rely upon Yorkshire, then. Any Scottish advance would have to be met with his cavalry and whatever support he might raise from the trained bands of Northumberland and Durham.

On 20 August 1640, the Scots forded the Tweed, committing the act they had so studiously avoided in 1639. Violation of English territory altered significantly the King's legal, constitutional, and political position with regard to the military obligations of his English subjects. In 1639 many Englishmen insisted that the *bellum episcopale* was a war of conquest, a foreign expedition undertaken to bolster the authority of the bishops. The King characterized the Scottish war as a rebellion that by its very nature threatened the peace and security of England. Religion cloaked a wicked design that included invasion. In 1639 the Covenanters undermined Charles's argument by refraining from trespassing on English soil, but in 1640 they had no choice. A preemptive campaign could disable the English war effort and prevent an attack on Scotland. Such a move required the violation of English territory. Now the Scots could no longer maintain that they had no intention of intervening militarily in England. By entering Northumberland, Montrose and Leslie committed an act of war. There could be no quibbling over whether the King might demand military service from the English nobility and gentry. The arguments of Lords Saye and Sele and Brooke in spring 1639 had little relevance to the Anglo-Scottish situation after 20 August 1640. Strafford saw this clearly, and exhorted the Yorkshire gentry: 'It is now no time of Disputation, but of Preparation and Action ... we are bound unto it by the Common Law of England, by the Law of Nature, and by the Law of Reason, and you are no better than Beasts, if you refuse in this Case to attend the King, his Majesty offering in Person to lead you on.'[175] The realm had been invaded by predatory Scotsmen, and the King was marching to the borders to meet the challenge directly, risking his person. The Covenanters no longer restricted

173 PRO, SP 16/463/71, Northumberland to Conway, 10 August 1640.
174 Discussed below pp. 59–60, 106–10, 288, 293; see also C. Russell, *The Causes of the English Civil War* (Oxford, 1990), p. 13.
175 John Rushworth, *Historical Collections* (London, 1722), vol. III, p. 1235.

themselves to an indirect role in English domestic politics; military intervention and alliance with the opponents of the Personal Rule in the south, with the accompanying political complications, had become unavoidable. For the Scots, the Tweed was their Rubicon.[176]

Newburn: the Covenanter counter-stratagem

By crossing the Tweed, the Covenanters ended speculation on the likelihood of invasion. The question was, *where* would Leslie strike? The choice of Coldstream as the point of entry into England kept the English unsure as to the Scots' destination. Could the southerly march be a feint intended to lull the garrison of Berwick into a false sense of security, followed by an assault from the rear? Would Newcastle be attacked from the north or west? Could a lightning stroke overwhelm the Carlisle garrison so that the Covenanters could penetrate the borders at their southernmost point, making their presence felt in the heart of England? Some English commanders suggested that the Covenanters meant to overrun Hexham. By keeping the English commanders, especially Conyers, Conway, and Astley, uncertain as to whether or not they would invade in summer 1640, the Scots discouraged the King from massing his entire army on the borders. The Crown could not maintain a large army for months at a time. Nor could the Covenanters. Shortages of money had strategic repercussions. The Covenanters would have to strike quickly. Now that war had begun, Charles could mobilize all England. Moving rapidly, the Scots might entrench themselves in a position of strength with the minimum of bloodshed. Their goal was the occupation of Newcastle. The English commanders guessed as much. But which route would Leslie take? Since Newcastle was fortified on its northern side, and virtually defenceless on the south, a siege of the southern approach to the town seemed almost certain.[177] To execute this flanking manoeuvre, the Scots would have to ford the Tyne, a tidal river. Conway suspected that Leslie would traverse the bridge at Hexham, about twenty miles to the west of Newcastle. Logically, English troops would have been disposed in two main segments, at Newcastle and Hexham. The intervening ground would be patrolled, and a sizeable force held in readiness in case the Scots crossed anywhere between the two towns. The largest contingent should remain at Newcastle, to reinforce Berwick if necessary and to await the main body of the English army when

---

[176] The comparison is contemporary. See Bodleian Library, Carte MSS., LXXVII, f. 452 and PRO, SP 16/464/52, an undoubtedly apocryphal speech by Leslie composed by a source hostile to him. It is printed in Terry, *The Life and Campaigns of Alexander Leslie*, pp. 108–9.

[177] Illustration of Newcastle defences, PRO, MPF 287. Of course, the Scots would have to take the Tyne bridge intact.

it moved up from Yorkshire. All English units would converge upon the Scottish invaders, once located.

Leslie bisected the English strategy by wading across the Tyne near Newburn, six miles from Newcastle. The English strategy was flawed by an irreconcilable contradiction: Conway's forces were too slender to garrison Newcastle and field an army against Leslie. Conway and Strafford gambled that the Scots would make their passage at Hexham, so that a skeleton force might guard Newcastle while Conway's cavalry and the local militia intercepted the crossing at Hexham. Instead, Leslie encamped at Heddon-Law, on the northern bank of the Tyne, on the hills above the town of Newburn, on 27 August.[178] Learning of the Scots' whereabouts, Conway gathered his men at Stella Haugh, a village southeast of the Newburn ford, at a bend in the Tyne, on the Blaydon road. The Durham men hastily erected two earthworks on the southern bank of the Tyne.[179] The Scots did nothing to conceal their campfires on the heights above Newburn, perhaps to draw the attention of the English while they quietly arranged their ordnance in the forested areas of the hill and buildings of the town, within cannon shot of the English breastworks at the ford.

On the morning of 28 August, the tide ran too deep to accommodate a crossing, so that the opposing sides eyed each other but exchanged no gunfire. In fact, Scots and English cavalrymen watered their horses on their respective sides of the river, 'without affronting one another or giving any reproachful language'. In the early afternoon an incident triggered the battle. John Rushworth, who had arrived at Stella Haugh only an hour or two before, recorded the event:

A Scottish Officer well mounted, having a black Feather in his Hat, came out of one of the thatcht houses in Newburne and watered his Horse in the River Tyne, as they had done all that day. An English Soldier, perceiving he fixed his Eye towards the English Trenches on the South-side of the River, fired at him (whether in earnest or to fright him is not known), but wounded the Scotish man with the shot, who fell off his Horse, whereupon the Scotish Musqueteers immediately fired upon the English, and so the fight begun with Small-shot, but was continued with great Shot as well as small.[180]

The Covenanters replied with a fusillade, and the battle commenced with a

---

[178] For a Scottish eyewitness account, see BL, Add. MS. 57,929, 'A full relation of the skirmische at Newburne betweixt the Inglishe and the Scottis, Agust 27, 1640.' Andrew Thrush supplied a transcript of this letter: see also NLS, Advocates' MS. 33.4.6, Register of the Committee of Estates, ff. 7–9 and SRO, RH 13/18, ff. 23–7 (unfoliated).

[179] The positioning and the number of sconces is discussed in Terry, in *The Life and Campaigns of Alexander Leslie*, p. 114, n. 1.

[180] Rushworth, *Historical Collections*, vol. III, p. 1237.

general exchange of musketry.[181] In terms of terrain and numbers, the Scots enjoyed the advantage in skirmishing with Conway's 3,000 infantry and 1,500 horsemen. Most of these were held in reserve on Stella Haugh, within view of the ford but out of harm's way from Covenanter cannon. Leslie had easily triple the number of soldiers that the English had ranged against him.[182] Numbers alone did not assure Scottish victory, however. Ordnance did. The Covenanters deployed at least forty, perhaps as many as eighty, cannon, most of which seem to have been demiculverins (which fired a ten-and-three-quarter-pound ball). Conway, whose hurried departure for Newburn prevented him from assembling a sufficient artillery train, had only eight cannon, the largest being sakers which propelled six pound shot.[183] Equally telling was the disposition of the Scots' cannon. Camouflaged in the wooded heights and hidden amongst the structures and hedges of Newburn, their ordnance was well concealed from English musketeers and artillerymen. Scottish snipers crouched behind the cover afforded by the 'Church, Houses, Lanes, and Hedges'. The musketeers and artillery were able to fire upon the vulnerable English breastwork, which provided minimal protection, being little more than 'a trench halfe a yard high'.[184]

Leslie next probed the English defences and prepared to ambush the enemy cavalry. By afternoon the Tyne had receded enough to become fordable. Three hundred Covenanter cavalry attempted a crossing, triggering a volley from the English behind the earthworks. The advance of the cavalry might force a retreat from the sconces, the 800 musketeers being isolated and not too well disciplined, which Leslie probably suspected. Or, a withdrawal of the 300 horsemen back across the river might lure the English cavalry to pursue the Covenanters, bringing Conway's horsemen within range of Leslie's concealed cannon. The English soldiers sheltering behind the insubstantial bulwark held fast and unleashed a barrage of gunfire, which repelled the attackers. The Covenanter horse 'wer so galled by the English musketeers from behynde the breest worke, that they wer forced to

---

[181] Gardiner, drawing upon Balfour's account, claims that the English fired upon the Scottish position for three hours, without answer. The diary, SRO RH 13/18, ff. 23–4, states that the English drew up eleven troops of horse around noon on a height a little to the east of the ford, where they remained until after 2.00 p. m. when nine English artillery pieces zeroed in on the Scots who approached the waterside. The Covenanters did not, says the diarist, return fire until after 5.00 p. m.

[182] The diarist in SRO, RH 13/18 reckoned English strength at 5,000 foot and 2,500 horse, f. 24 (unfoliated). The size of the armies is discussed by Terry in *The Life and Campaigns of Alexander Leslie*, pp. 120–1, no. 7.

[183] The artillery train was still at Hull! Stafford RO, Dartmouth MS. D (W) 1778/I/i/8, Newport to Legge, 30 August 1640.

[184] Rushworth, *Historical Collections*, vol. III, p. 1237. Account of James Gordon, parson of Rothiemay, printed in Terry, *The Life and Campaigns of Alexander Leslie*, p. 137. See also SRO, RH 13/18, f. 23, (unfoliated) and BL, Harleian MS. 6801, f. 15v.

reteer'.[185] Having failed to dislodge the entrenched troops or snare the English horse, Leslie commenced to harry the sconces with intense cannon-fire. The ferocity of the cannonade ultimately compelled the foot soldiers to evacuate the trenches:

About 4 a'clocke in the afternoone, after some fewe muskettes shotte, the Scottes mownted some ordinance on the steeple of the church of that vyllage, which com-maunded our workes and battered them so muche that they that weare in one of them fled And for-sooke the work: the other stayed makynge a lyttle resistance, but not long After lykewyse fled.[186]

Balfour described the bombardment:

some of our grate ordinance and some of our feilding peices which we planted in conuenient places aboute, did discharge vpone the foottemen that wer in the workes, and having killed about 20 of them, did so affright them, that all the foottmen fled confusedly.[187]

The soldiers in the beleaguered sconce were commanded by thirty-year-old Lieutenant Colonel Thomas Lunsford, 'a young outlaw' and 'swagger-ing ruffian' who had been pardoned for an alleged murder attempt the year before. Lunsford's march to the borders had been marred by brawls with his own soldiers arising over issues of religion, pay, and discipline. By his own admission, he and his fellow officers had slain some of their own enlisted men, in self-defence, of course.[188] Unfortunately, the plight of the roughly 800 Somerset infantry under bombardment could not be remedied solely by the bellicosity of their leader. The troops in both sconces under-stood the alternatives they faced. Either they would be battered to the point of surrender and then mowed down by the Covenanter cavalry as the river became fordable, or they might fall back to Stella Haugh, safe from the withering fire. As successive barrages exploded about them, the latter choice looked more attractive. When the breastwork nearest the Tyne took a direct hit, killing several officers as well as infantrymen, a spontaneous retreat was averted only by Lunsford's exhortation. Whether or not Luns-ford's reputation as a man who had no compunction about slaying disobedient soldiers inhibited desertion is a matter of conjecture.[189] The fact that reinforcements had not come to their aid, and that the main body of the army was being held in reserve until the Scots began to cross

[185] Account of James Gordon, in Terry, *The Life and Campaigns of Alexander Leslie*, p. 137.
[186] HMC Middleton, p. 193.
[187] Sir James Balfour, *The Historical Works* (Edinburgh, 1825), vol. II, pp. 385–6. See also SRO, RH 13/18, f. 23 (unfoliated).
[188] The descriptions of Lunsford's character are those of Lord Dorset, quoted in P. R. Newman, *Royalist Officers in England and Wales, 1642–1660* (New York, 1981), p. 242. 195. PRO, SP 16/457/91, 22 June 1640, Lunsford to Northumberland.
[189] See p. 270.

the river, gave the distinct impression that they were being sacrificed. With each passing minute, more projectiles ripped through the flimsy earthworks. As the Tyne ebbed a Scottish charge appeared imminent. The tension became very difficult for these 'raw' men. When another shot crashed amongst the soldiers, Lunsford was unable to stop the men from abandoning the sconce and fleeing back towards the horse. As they withdrew many cast away their arms, and the stores of gunpowder were exploded, either by accident or design. A Scot observed that the Covenanter guns had 'a perfyt view of the English trenches' and 'did play so hard vpone them, that they were forced to throw away there armes, disband in confusion, and blow up there owne pulder [powder]'.[190]

The evacuation of the 'Greater Sconce' allowed Leslie to concentrate his ordnance upon the secondary earthwork. The musketeers and artillerymen there soon followed the example of the occupants of the other fortification and fled their position. Seizing the opportunity, with disorder on the southern bank and the Tyne fordable, a contingent of Scottish cavalry splashed across the river. The horsemen were to establish a bridgehead so that the army might follow without fear of being driven back into the Tyne by the English. Several English commanders perceived that should the Scots capture and hold the southern bank, the day would be lost. The resulting counter-charge of the English cavalry produced the most notable acts of bravery of the Bishops' Wars. Leslie had placed a battery near enough to the Tyne to be within range of the King's horse gathered in a meadow behind and to the east of the sconces. With the musketeers and artillery in the breastworks now out of action, these nine cannon could fire across the river with impunity. They began to harry the royal cavalry, hoping to put them to flight along with the infantry from the riverside sconces. In fact, just the opposite happened. Impetuously, several officers charged the Scots, who were now coming ashore, with a general advance close behind. Specifically, Commissary-General Wilmot, Sir George Vane, Sir John Digby, Captain Daniel O'Neill, and (perhaps) Sir John Suckling, threw themselves into the fray. Their courage inspired others, but not all. Wilmot galloped directly into the Scottish forces, and killed two or three men 'with his owne handes after he had receved a pistoll shott in his face; he chardged them alone where his troops was left ingage'.[191] Captain George Vane led the first charge and managed to blunt the Scottish advance, forcing many Covenanters to fall back. Vane's horse was wounded under him, and his

---

[190] 'Sure Newis from Newcastell and from the Scottish Army', printed in Terry, *The Life and Campaigns of Alexander Leslie*, p. 136. Note also the crucial role of artillery at Pinkie in 1547.
[191] HMC Middleton, p. 193. Wilmot's wound was apparently not too serious.

company suffered numerous casualties, which ultimately caused him to withdraw.[192]

In the meanwhile, Commissary-General Wilmot found himself overwhelmed by the counter-attack. Both he and Vane had given their utmost in stemming the tide, but neither the royal infantry nor the cavalry pressed hard behind the officers. The foot-soldiers were especially reluctant to hurl themselves into the breach. An English account related, 'Our commaunder of horse chardged them bravely, but there troopes for the most parte ran awaye .... Had our men followed there leaders and not fled, the[y h]ad gotten the honour of the victorye.'[193] In spite of the check to their cavalry, 10,000 Scottish infantry surged across the Tyne. With their feet planted firmly on shore, Leslie's musketeers peppered the remaining Englishmen, and the Scottish cavalry pursued those who fled. Sir Jacob Astley tried to rally the foot in a nearby forest, and brought them up in support of the cavalry. But by then the Scottish numbers were too great. Wilmot, Digby, and O'Neill, the most gallant of the defenders, were captured.[194]

The Scots had won the battle by means of superior artillery and a well-orchestrated cavalry charge; Leslie did not need his infantry, who did not even advance far enough to see the battle let alone fire in support of the horse.[195] The arrival of the Covenanter army on the southern bank precipitated a general retreat of Conway's forces. The infantry straggled off in the direction of Newcastle, and the cavalry rode towards Durham. English casualties numbered perhaps several hundred, although exact figures are lacking.[196] It would seem that the Scots lost a similar number. At Newburn, as at Kelso the previous year, a solitary setback lost the campaign. The ensuing confusion compounded the psychological impact of the loss. The Covenanter advance had occurred more quickly and with greater numbers than the English army had anticipated. Royal commanders were scattered about the north. The Master of the Ordnance, searching for the King first at York and then at Northallerton, got word of the retreat, and relayed the news to Captain Legge at Hull, where the train of artillery sat.[197] With

[192] BL, Harleian MS. 6801, ff. 15v–16; PRO, SP 16/465/38, Secretary Vane to Windebank, 29 August 1640.

[193] HMC Middleton, p. 193; see also PRO, SP 16/465/38, Vane to Windebank, 29 August 1640.

[194] CSPD (1640–1), p. 38, cited in Terry, *The Life and Campaigns of Alexander Leslie*, p. 132. Balfour, *The Historical Works*, vol. II, p. 187; Rushworth, *Historical Collections*, vol. III, p. 1238.

[195] SRO, GD 406/1/1219, Loudoun to Hamilton, 2 September 1640.

[196] PRO, SP 16/465/38, Secretary Vane to Windebank, 29 August 1640; Gardiner, *History*, vol. IX, p. 194; Terry, *The Life and Campaigns of Alexander Leslie*, p. 120. According to Bodleian Library, Clarendon SP, XIX, f. 11v, Windebank to Hopton, 5 September 1640, 100 common soldiers were lost on the English side.

[197] Stafford RO, Dartmouth MS. D (W) 1778/I/i/8, Newport to Legge, 30 August 1640.

communications erratic, his cannon far to the rear, key units held back in Yorkshire for want of pay, and his front-line forces in retreat, Charles had lost his war in a single day.

The summer campaign of 1640 dwarfed the military debacles of the 1620s. On the march north troops rioted, murdered, and became 'the greatest law enforcement problem in living memory'.[198] It finally came as no surprise when the English army was routed by the Covenanters on the banks of the Tyne. When accused of bungling the campaign, Lord Conway defended himself by questioning the wisdom of starting the war.[199] Charles I had insisted upon war, and now he had got it – an army of Scots occupied the north of England, and in effect blackmailed the King into summoning an English parliament in November 1640.[200] Why did England suffer a military disaster in the late summer of 1640? For that matter, who was defeated – England or its King? And to what degree was Newburn a disaster? Humiliating, yes, but English casualties were counted in scores, not thousands. Newcastle and the north were occupied, not burned. How did this reverse occur, and why was England left relatively unscathed?

Defeat often demands a scapegoat, and in the case of the Second Bishops' War that man was Edward, Viscount Conway and Kullultagh, General of the Horse and Deputy General of the Army. Those around the King, and the courtiers safe in London, found it incomprehensible that the Scots should defy an English army and cross into England. The aristocracy's anachronistic concept of war and the natural inclination of its members to snipe at one another led them to blame the debacle upon the carelessness and timidity of one of the royal commanders. Victory stemmed from will and leadership, hence an honourable lord would have halted the Scots in spite of his army's weaknesses. In response to these criticisms, specifically the charge that he had not taken sufficient precautions for the defence of Newcastle, Conway enumerated the causes of military failure in August 1640. For the historian, it is a very useful document; instead of blaming subordinates, or casting doubt on the integrity of other commanders, Conway set forth the reasons – financial, organizational, and ultimately, political – that prevented him from repelling the Covenanters.

The Crown's defence of the north was too little and too late to stem the tide of Scots sweeping across Tweed and Tyne. The infantry had mustered at the York rendezvous too slowly and in insufficient numbers. The quality and quantity of weapons for the royal army proved a disappointment. Charles had not issued the proclamation to muster the militia for active

---

[198] See below pp. 264–86 and Barnes, *Somerset 1625–1640*, p. 277.
[199] See pp. 60, 294–5.
[200] C. Russell, 'Why did Charles I Summon the Long Parliament?', *History*, 69, no. 227 (October 1984), pp. 375–83.

service until the day before the Covenanters forded the Tweed. As it was, the Durham trained bands committed themselves to the defence of the Tyne only when the King arrived at York, four days after the Scots entered England, and a mere four days before they advanced across the Tyne. Meanwhile, the artillery train sat useless at Hull.

Tactical miscalculations stemmed from ill-conceived royal strategies which extended from the political policies fashioned by Charles I.

Now, upon the whole matter, it may easily be judged, whether these two single actions, of the retreat of Newburne, and quitting Newcastle, were the causes of our losses, or the defect of ill-grounded designs, to make a war without monies to go on with it, and to begin it at sea; thereby giving the Scots a pretence to attempt us by land, before we were able to resist them.[201]

Conway realized that the tactical errors in themselves had not brought defeat. The repulse at Newburn and the abandonment of Newcastle did not lose the war. Rather, politics had doomed the campaign. The Crown's policies had brought about a major war without parliamentary financial assistance and with a depleted Exchequer. Making war without money had led to these straits.[202] The designs for an amphibious assault on Scotland had forced the Scots' hand and led to a land war for which the English were not prepared. They were unprepared because the King had not harnessed the might of England by establishing first a political consensus through Parliament. The Covenanters' objective in 1640 was a military victory which would, after their consolidation of the north of England during August and September, force the King to a negotiated settlement through the agency of an English Parliament. Thus their ultimate goal was political.

The remainder of this book attempts to explain how that 'most shameful and confounding flight that was ever heard of' at Newburn came about.[203] It will be seen that Charles expected too much from royal institutions, namely his councils, officers, Ordnance Office, Exchequer, and paymasters. Unrealistic expectations characterized the King's management of people and institutions. Still, both muddled through.[204] The army came into being, twice. But the mobilization brought together men who were not armed or trained well enough for the task at hand, nor deployed properly.

---

[201] Bodleian Library, Clarendon SP, XIX, f. 175v.
[202] In assessing the failure of the Second Bishops' War, Conrad Russell has written that 'money, rather than politics, is likely to have been paramount', *CECW*, p. 13. The two, of course, are inseparable. This book argues that the dearth of money was a direct result of misguided political decisions by the King.
[203] Clarendon, *History of the Rebellion*, vol. I, p. 190.
[204] L. J. Reeve, *Charles I and the Road to Personal Rule* (Cambridge, 1989), pp. 194–200, 261, 295–6 and Russell, *CECW*, p. 200.

For that matter, the mobilization compounded Charles's political problems and once assembled the English army became as much a threat to England as to Scotland. The King managed armies about as well as he managed Parliaments.

2

Institutions

Interpretation of the failure of Caroline government has passed from emphasis on the structural weakness of institutions to laying blame on Charles himself. The Bishops' Wars provide evidence of the King's handling of the instruments of government, in particular how he expected executive authority to manage the war (the Council of War), how royal leadership would be translated through the ranks (the army's chain of command), and how the materials of war were collected, distributed and maintained (the Ordnance Office). Conversely, the Covenanters organized their mobilization upon Scottish forms of counsel, command, and armament procurement. In the Bishops' Wars, as in the Civil War, Charles mismanaged his resources whereas collectively his enemies found means to achieve victory.[1]

THE COUNCIL OF WAR

The Caroline Council of War should be considered in the plural, for a series of Crown-appointed subcommittees administered the war effort under the King and Privy Council. The Council of War was a committee of the Privy Council. As such it was further subdivided into committees of the Council of War which dealt with specific duties in the war effort. Military matters fell within the parameters of the Council of War, but internal Scottish affairs could not, for the *English* Council of War had no such jurisdiction. Better equipped was the Scottish Committee, which occupied itself with negotiations with the Scots, often through Scottish intermediaries. Subcommittees therefore addressed specific problems facing the Council of War as a whole. Thus circumstances created the subcommittees, which reacted more than they initiated. Their task was to meet the contingent

[1] Russell, *FBM*, pp. 71–146 and *CECW*, pp. 11–13, 186–7, 200, 211; E. M. Furgol, 'Scotland Turned Sweden: The Scottish Covenanters and the Military Revolution, 1638–1651', *The Scottish National Covenant in its British Context, 1638–51*, ed. J. Morrill (Edinburgh, 1990), pp. 134–48.

demands of war rather than to engage in long term or strategic planning. Again, changes in personnel prompted by political and administrative manoeuvres periodically altered the style, and occasionally the jurisdiction and focus, of the Council of War and its subcommittees. As a result, the Council of War was political in composition though military in activities and responsibilities.

Politics and the predicament of the Council of War

Crown policy placed the Council of War in a quandary at the outset of the mobilization. Since the King eschewed Parliament in 1639, the Council of War carried the political burden of engaging in military activities that were neither endorsed by statute nor subsidized by Parliament. The Personal Rule spared councillors from parliamentary interference like that from 1624 to 1626.[2] However, by autumn 1640 the ambiguity and fragmentation of the Council of War's authority, combined with the Crown's lack of money, particularly after the dissolution of the Short Parliament, inhibited the councillors from assisting Charles in achieving victory over the Covenanters. Like the Privy Council and lieutenancy, the Council of War relied on cooperation from the county communities. The power to ensure stringent compliance was lacking. Moreover, the Crown's insolvency meant that administrative duties, such as the purchase of weapons and transport of stores, were compromised.[3] Orders and elaborate plans in 1640 were undercut by an empty Exchequer over which the Council of War had no control. Hemmed in by the limitations of administration and finance, its task was made more difficult by a King who demanded action not excuses; for Charles made exact demands of the Council of War, unheedful of its handicaps in enforcing and financing the mobilization. Its administrative structure and its very procedures were conditioned by the King's own political and military agenda.

A functional dichotomy between advisory and administrative duties raised questions about the Stuart Council of War's jurisdiction and purpose. In 1621 the Jacobean Council of War functioned as an advisory board, with minimal administrative duties. It existed only when the King felt the need to address military matters. The councillors, predominantly old soldiers rather than politicians, answered directly to James I. Their opinions affected policy, as for example when their cautionary assessment of a projected campaign to restore the Elector Palatine dissuaded the King

---

[2] M. B. Young, 'Revisionism and the Council of War', *Parliamentary History*, 8, pt. 1 (1989), pp. 1–27.
[3] See pp. 93–4, 96–9, 102–3, 110, 115–16, 123–4, 137–51 below.

from engaging in such a war.[4] In 1624, the increasingly volatile situation in Germany demanded a more powerful and adaptable instrument for managing military affairs. The hand of young Charles Stuart, guided most certainly by Buckingham, can be seen in the refashioning of the Council of War. The Prince presided over the Committee on Munitions, recently created by the House of Lords, which promoted the commissioning of a new Council of War.[5] The council's genesis owed as much to the sitting of the 1624 Parliament as to the bellicosity of Buckingham and Prince Charles. In order to secure money for a continental war, James allowed the Commons to encroach upon one of the 'peculiar Prerogatives of Kings', the sphere of war.[6] Medieval precedents established that the Commons might monitor their subsidies. So the Commons, wary of James's fiscal manipulations, voted supply provided that the moneys remained within the grasp of special treasurers rather than deposited in the Receipt of the Exchequer.[7] This manoeuvre may well have had ramifications in 1638, for Charles saw that Parliament might meddle with the Crown's prerogative regarding defence of the realm. In his eyes, Parliament's unseemly interference, proven time and again in the 1620s, made that body an unsuitable partner in time of war. In 1624–5 the Commons tried to browbeat the Council of War, creating precedents for conflict between Parliament and royal servants engaged in military affairs.

On 21 April 1624 the Council of War, on the authority of a royal signet letter, received advisory and bureaucratic responsibilities that would synthesize during the actual management of war. On the one hand James I still perceived the Council of War as largely advisory, almost exclusively part of the royal household. The Council of War, on the other hand assumed a critical administrative role in the war effort. It allocated funds, drafted warrants, decided the fate of the Commons' subsidies. Parliament, which allocated the funds, regarded mere consultation as insufficient to influence the management of a war. The Council of War supervised military expenditure and therefore answered for the manner in which the subsidies were spent. The House controlled only the disbursing agents.[8] Of course the exhaustion of parliamentary subsidies freed the council from budgetary duties, but questions lingered about the authority and jurisdiction of the institution, and who should serve upon it.

When the Council of War was resuscitated in April 1625, it again found its function shaped by the Crown and Parliament. The first act of the 1625

---

[4] S. J. Stearns, 'Caroline Military Organization: The Expeditions to Cadiz and Rhé 1625–7', Ph.D. dissertation, University of California, Berkeley, 1967, pp. 129–30.
[5] Stearns, 'Caroline Military Organization', p. 131, note 40.
[6] Young, 'Revisionism and the Council of War', p. 3.
[7] Stearns, 'Caroline Military Organization', p. 132.
[8] Young, 'Revisionism and the Council of War', pp. 2–5.

Parliament inquired into the Council of War's military expeditures. In 1626 the Commons again poked into the council's business.[9] Badgered to give an answer to the House, the council relented, creating something of a precedent and again confirming in Charles's mind Parliament's capacity for meddling.[10] Most disturbing was the Commons' insistence on calling the council members to the bar. The experience of being summoned, accompanied by fears of impeachment or prosecution, made councillors wary of parliamentary authority. However, they successfully drew the line against disclosure of their deliberations so that Buckingham and Charles felt secure enough to broaden the scope of the body's authority.[11] Now the council emerged as an organ which might inquire into any business which affected the military preparedness of the nation, from trained band administration to disbanded officers from abroad.

Throughout the 1620s and 1630s and during the Bishops' Wars the enforcement arm of the Council of War was the Privy Council. Not surprisingly, as the scope of the institution broadened, courtiers, politicians and Privy Councillors increasingly sat upon the Council of War. These men, more than the old soldiers, regarded Parliament as a threat or at least an obstruction. The longer the Council of War existed, the more confident and sturdy it became. The institution attained a degree of maturity when a permanent commission under the Great Seal came in February 1629, and the Council of War received jurisdiction over all matters 'tending to the advancement' of the King's 'Martiall Affayres'.[12] But, ironically, with the advent of peace and Personal Rule the Council of War went the way of Parliament, into dormancy.

The council's entry book bears witness to the hiatus of the 1630s as the entries become more sporadic, written in a variety of hands, punctuated by blank folios, with no entries at all between 11 June 1632 and 21 February 1638. On 10 March 1638 the council demanded an account from the Ordnance Office, at which point the book ends.[13] In late July 1638, the Council of War regained life and again raised the question of its jurisdiction. What proportion of the council's duties would be advisory and to what extent would it administer? What power would the King and Privy Council delegate to the Council of War? Was the 'Committee for the North' to advise on the wisdom of going to war, or strictly to implement the mobilization? The answers to these questions are coloured by the nature of the extant

---

[9] Ibid, pp. 10–18.
[10] Stearns, 'Caroline Military Organization', p. 140, note 6.
[11] Ibid, pp. 141–2, quoting the commission.
[12] PRO, SP 16/28, f. 85v, Council of War entry book, commission dated 23 February 1629.
[13] Only seven attended the meeting, the Lord Treasurer, Lord Wimbledon, the Comptroller (Vane), Secretary Windebank, the Lieutenant of the Tower, and (from the Ordnance Office) Newport and Heydon; PRO, SP 16/28, ff. 158v–163.

records. Whereas the entry book for 1626–38 reveals debate, deliberation, and discussion, that for 1638–9 contains warrants to pay out sums, letters to the country, and orders to permanent establishments such as the Ordnance Office, approximating to the Privy Council's registers. Perhaps the King, who sat at the table periodically, insisted they restrict themselves to the tasks at hand, for he saw no point in debate or deliberation. Privy Council meetings were, according to the procedure dictated by the Personal Rule, to avoid wholesale debate. Councillors declined to keep accounts of discussion, for they might be copied or fall into the hands of a hostile Parliament or, in the King's absence, annoy their royal master. Minutes were regarded as secret, and clerks were in fact banned when Charles discussed policy.[14]

While the Council of War proper concentrated most closely upon straightening up the garrisons and fortresses of the south during 1638, the more imposing task of creating a northern army fell to the 'Scottish Committee' created in July 1638, whose initial members included Arundel, Coke, Cottington, Hamilton, Juxon, Morton, Lennox, and Vane.[15] Circumstances brought visitors to the table, as on 3 December 1638 when the Earls of Essex and Newport, accompanied by Sir Jacob Astley, hammered out details for the Yorkshire rendezvous.[16] Although ostensibly acting in an advisory capacity, in practice the Scottish Committee occupied itself with the mustering, arming, and paying of Englishmen. A subcommittee, *sans* the Scots (Hamilton and Lennox), attended to the 'providing of arms for the North'.[17] The latter was, in effect, the Council of War.

The Council of War and related subcommittees financed their initial activities with £200,000, allocated by Juxon on 26 July 1638. The council devoted most of its time to disbursing these funds and sending off letters to the county authorities, orchestrating the mobilization. Advisory functions

---

[14] On Charles and counsel, see Reeve, *Charles I and the Road to Personal Rule*, pp. 195, 199. No council entry book should be considered comprehensive especially during the Personal Rule, when secrecy encouraged omissions. According to Bodleian Library, Clarendon SP, XV, f. 36, much of what was discussed at the meeting of 11 November 1638 was not disclosed by the brief entry in PRO, SP 16/396, ff. 49–50. On that meeting, see pp. 68–70. Matters referred to informal subcommittees may have been documented in supplementary notes, the details of which were not registered in the formal council entry book. On a secretary to the Council of War, see PRO, E 351/293 where Robert Scawen [?], received 10s a day for 163 days from 1 June to 10 November as well as a tent and a wagon. He got an allowance of 20s a month for writing commissions, warrants, and acts of the Council of War. Apparently these have not survived.

[15] PRO, SP 16/396, f. 4 and M. J. Havran, *Caroline Courtier: The Life of Lord Cottington*, (London, 1973) p. 140, where Havran mentions Irish, Admiralty, and Ordnance committees on which Cottington sat.

[16] Bodleian Library, Clarendon SP, XV, f. 48; on 17 January Essex and Newport were sworn in as members of the committee. See PRO, SP 16/396, f. 60 and SP 16/409/106.

[17] PRO, SP 16/396, f. 4.

seem to have been minimal and the Council of War and its tangential committees executed the King's wishes rather than assisting in the formulation of war policy. Charles desired obedience and diligence, not advice.

As the enforcement power of the Council of War emanated from the Privy Council, one would suspect that the more exalted body fulfilled the advisory role. But in fact, Privy Councillors complained that the King excluded them from Scottish affairs.[18] The Privy Council was not taken into Charles's confidence as to the likelihood of war with Scotland until a council meeting of 1 July 1638.[19] The matter had been broached in late June 1638 at the 'Foreign Committee', though in general terms and on the assumption that the ensuing military preparations were defensive.[20] Charles was more eclectic than systematic in the matter of counsel. Confident that his royal perception was flawless (the same discerning eye that could appreciate fine painting and noble architecture), he remained sceptical of the views of lesser men. If his counsellors and subjects did not see things his way, it was not so surprising; they were not Kings. Charles was blinded by his lofty monarchical perspective. Although awkward in his younger years, he had compensated by at least trying to give the impression of confidence. Now he had arrived at a time in his life when he thought that a brave show would steady those around him and that events would necessarily change their course and flow in the direction of the royal will. So when it came to the matter of the Scottish War his certitude was such that to pose the question of the purpose of the campaign to the Council of War was ridiculous. His counsellors knew better than to dissuade him from a policy which in the royal view of things could not and should not be questioned. Naturally, he listened to those who had some glimmering as to what was at stake. When it seemed someone understood and could be counted upon to do the job, for example the Earl of Arundel, Charles took him into his confidence. When the Earl failed to deliver the goods in 1639, the King looked elsewhere. It was comforting to the King that some did agree with him – Vane, Nithisdale, Arundel, Windebank. Those that did not entirely agree with the course the King had charted apparently minimized their objections, for they knew they could not dissuade their royal master, as seems to have been the case with Northumberland and Conway. Even if he suspected that certain servants were lukewarm, Charles had no

---

[18] See above, pp. 3–4, 115, 292.
[19] Gardiner, *History*, vol. VIII, p. 349. The Privy Council had not been consulted when Charles opened the Spanish peace negotiations at the beginning of the decade. Why consult them now that he was charting a new course in 1638? See Reeve, *Charles I and the Road to Personal Rule*, pp. 198–9.
[20] SRO, GD 406/1/423, f. 1, Vane to Hamilton, 25 June 1638.

doubts about their loyalty. He knew they would carry out their duties, and in this assumption he was right.[21]

Whereas James I had preferred the Council of War to perform a truly advisory function, his son felt quite the opposite. Charles reached his own decisions and expected the Council of War and its subcommittees to implement those policies. Institutional functions reflected the style of royal government. For all James's absolutist pretensions, the royal administration of Charles I was far more closely tied to the person of the monarch. Policies radiated from the King, and the councils merely implemented those policies; they rarely altered them.

The Council of War in 1639 and 1640

In one hitherto unnoticed episode the Council of War did presume to advise His Majesty. At the Council of War meeting of 11 November 1638, Charles being absent, the members proposed the elimination of 'projects as yeelded his Majesty noe considerable proffit and were greevous to his Majesty's Subjects'. They specified fines on the erection and occupation of cottages in contravention of the statute of 1589, abuses of shrievalty (particularly selling the office of under-sheriff), regulation of the export of butter, licensing and marking of iron, 'taking of Bonds in the Countrey concerning venison and partridges', the commission on butter cask, the licensing of coaches, bricks, and hats, sale of linen and bone lace, and Nova Scotia baronetcies.[22] Here the Council of War assumed its advisory duties with some courage, for, regardless of the disclaimer that they were cultivating the hearts and affections of the King's subjects, they raised sensitive domestic issue that fell beyond the scope of their jurisdiction; patents, monopolies, and commissions remained bitterly controversial in spite of the statute of monopolies of 1624.[23] The recommendation implies some unanimity amongst councillors often divided by faction and temperament. The Council of War, acting in harmony, attempted to shape domestic policy, if very politely, and the King proved receptive. On the day

---

21 See Donald, *An Uncounselled King*, especially pp. 88–9 and 320–7, and Reeve, *Charles I and the Road to Personal Rule*, pp. 1–7, 195–207, 247–8, 293–6 for the origin of Charles's independent style of rule. One must emphasize how ardently the King listened to those whose views matched his own, especially the Earl of Nithisdale. The latter told Charles what he wanted to hear, that the Covenanters aimed to 'extirpat monarkie' and that they boasted of an English faction that would prevent the King from harming the Covenant. He also relayed news of Covenanter military preparations. See SRO, GD 406/1/883, ff. 1–2, 13 December 1638.

22 PRO, SP 16/396, ff. 49–50.

23 E. R. Foster, 'The Procedure of the House of Commons against Patents and Monopolies, 1621–1624', *Conflict in Stuart England. Essays in Honor of Wallace Notestein*, ed. W. Aiken and B. Henning (New York, 1960), pp. 59–85; Russell, *FBM*, pp. 80-1.

before the rendezvous at York, 31 March 1639, Charles revoked numerous obnoxious patents and monopolies. The revocation was immensely significant, for it implied that the King was willing to redress grievances. It is no wonder that in the following spring many members of the Short Parliament believed that reform was possible if the King were properly counselled.

Historians have ascribed this act of royal grace to the Privy Council's fear of a future parliament or alternatively to a triumph of 'thorough', Laud and Wentworth's governmental philosophy of uniformity and rigour.[24] The genesis of the revocation occurred in the Council of War, however, not at the Privy Council; nor did Laud and Wentworth, who did not sit on the Northern Committee, propose the reforms.[25] At the meeting

[24] W. H. Price, *The English Patents of Monopoly* (Cambridge, Mass. 1906, reprinted, New York, 1978), p. 45 and G. Aylmer, 'Attempts at Administrative Reform, 1625–40', *EHR*, 72, no. 283 (April 1957), pp. 232–3.

[25] The evidence regarding the 11 November 1638 Council of War meeting is PRO, SP 16/401/59, SP 16/396, ff. 49–50; Bodleian Library, Clarendon SP, XV, f. 36 (notes of Windebank and Cottington) and f. 82 (Cottington's notes). The stray undated sheet calendared amongst the Clarendon State Papers as 'Minutes concerning provisions and other necessaries. In Lord Cottington's hand. No date' is in fact a list of fifteen grievances virtually identical to those raised at the Council of War on 11 November, drawn up by the Chancellor of the Exchequer. After each 'project' Cottington penned in the name of the owner(s) of the respective patents and commissions. Predictably, names of courtiers especially close to the King dominate the list. For example, the commissions for marking iron and licensing coaches were held by the Marquis of Hamilton: Lord Stirling possessed the licences on brick and hats as well as on baronetcies of Nova Scotia; Henry Rich, Earl of Holland, held the commission regarding fines for the dressing of venison and partridges in inns and taverns; Endymion Porter, another of Charles's intimates, enjoyed the commission on abuses of the shrievalty. Other holders included Lord Morton (soon to join the Council of War, for cottages), Lord Goring and one Hungate (exportation of butter), Captain Read (the sealing of butter cask), Cunningham (sealing of buttons), Bray (linen), and Webb (bone lace). Finally, at the bottom is scrawled, 'cum multis aliis, quae nunc etc.', translated roughly as 'with many other [things], which now . . .' These 'other things' could refer to patents and commissions abolished in spring. More likely, it referred to other measures with which Cottington and the Council busied themselves. At the top of the paper, in the hand of Secretary Windebank, are sentence fragments, 'Musters in Yorkshire presently. Arms to be sent thether', which date and identify the manuscript. Yorkshire musters were needed in early winter 1638–9 because local authorities had failed to review the militia in spite of orders from the central government. These notes dovetail perfectly with minutes of the Council of War meeting for 11 November which are part of the same collection. Those notes reveal that in addition to contemplating the withdrawal of patents and commissions, the council dealt with the more routine business of ordering the lieutenancy to ready their forces, selection of officers, preparation of coastal defences, raising money, and calling upon the nobility. According to the *Dictionary of National Biography*, Goring was the leader of the monopolists. See also M. F. Keeler, *Members of the Long Parliament* (Philadelphia, 1954), p. 193. One wonders if ties of patronage which existed among the monopolists led to a kind of fraternity among the commanders. See the Earl of Holland's note to the Attorney General announcing the commission of his co-monopolist, Lord Goring, in Bodleian Library, Bankes MS. 65/45, 19 April 1639. Hungate could be Sir Henry Hungate, who was either commissary or muster-master in Pembroke's regiment of horse appointed to the guard the King, recorded in PRO, E 351/292, f. 12. He

of 11 November 1638 the Council of War discharged both duties, advisory and administrative, and achieved success in both areas. The six men at the council table – Arundel, Juxon, Cottington, Vane, Windebank, and Coke – realized that the King should render justice as well as demand obedience. By demonstrating his willingness to reform abuses, his subjects might be rendered more malleable to the demands of a Scottish war. Cottington might well be the author of this proposal, for he drew up the list of patent and commission holders and as Chancellor of the Exchequer recognized more than most the fiscal challenge of fighting this war without parliamentary subsidies. Finally, it is significant that Charles's inner ring of councillors recognized dissatisfaction with the Personal Rule, for 1638 was also the year of Hampden's trial, and urged some token relinquishment of financial exactions in order to lessen resistance to mobilization; the entry book makes clear that the concession could win public support. The political chasm between the regime and the country was to be bridged, if modestly. In late March 1639 the councillors 'mett all againe' to consider the future of about thirty-two patents, putting aside several which Charles regarded as untouchable. The transportation of butter precipitated some controversy due to alleged grave abuses, followed by a 'warm debat' over the cards-and-dice patent, which the King had left open for revocation. However, the latter patent generated £6,000, and Secretary Windebank suggested that it be left intact. The King responded, instructing the council that the butter patentees should be consulted and another meeting arranged. Lord Goring would speak for the butter patentees on the following Wednesday as would the corporation of brickmakers regarding brick.[26] The episode illustrates that the councillors recognized that a serious gulf existed between their royal master and the country at large, and that some political action would be needed to bridge that gulf should the King ask for military support from the realm.

In evaluating the performance of the Council of War in 1639, one must acknowledge that the army did arrive at York and that the shires did in fact cooperate with the central government. In the absence of Parliament and in

was certainly a courtier, receiving an appointment as a royal gamekeeper. On 17 January 1639 a warrant was issued to Hungate for preservation of game at Half Moon Park, Wimbledon, and to take care that no person hunt within four miles of the park, according to *CSPD* (1638–9), XIII, p. 323. The supply of butter may be a connection between the monopolists and the army. See SP 16/425/80, Coke to Windebank, 16 July 1639, from Berwick, where he informs him that the King has received Sir Henry Hungate's petition, and the Privy Council may give the order to take off the proclamation regarding Welsh butter, which was interdicted to supply the army now dissolved. Martin Havran and Conrad Russell kindly provided advice regarding the identification of the Bodleian manuscript.

26 Bodleian Library, Clarendon SP, XVI, ff. 42–42v and 72v, Windebank letters of 31 March and 13 April 1639, both apostiled by the King.

the face of protests over ship money and religion, this was no mean accomplishment. What is particularly remarkable is that the tenuous connection from Council of War to Privy Council to lieutenancy to shire functioned well, comparatively speaking, in 1639. During the following year, the Council of War would be less successful because the political situation worsened and ruptured the linkages.

On the eve of the First Bishops' War the 'Committee for the North', or Council of War, had consisted of fifteen members: the Duke of Lennox, the Marquis of Hamilton, the Lord Chamberlain, the Earls of Holland, Dorset, Salisbury, and Morton, the Vice-Chamberlain, Juxon, Arundel, Northumberland, Cottington, Vane, and Secretaries Coke and Windebank.[27] Although other committees, such as the Scottish Committee and the Privy Council, touched upon martial affairs in their daily business, the onus of the mobilization fell squarely on the Northern Committee. The apparent preference for the title of 'Committee for Providing Arms for the North' stemmed from euphemistic considerations, namely that Charles claimed to be defending the borders, not launching an assault on Edinburgh.[28] The Council of War which met on 30 December 1639 to lay the plans for the Second Bishops' War had its responsibilities quite clearly defined by the previous year's council. The twelve royal servants seated at the council table were entrusted with mobilizing a nation that had been further shaken by the Short Parliament's dissolution, as well as the 1639 exercise. The men selected not only possessed different opinions about the King's Scottish policy, but shared some distrust and personal animosity as well. The councillors included the Bishop of London, Lord Treasurer Juxon; the Earl of Northumberland, Lord High Admiral; the Marquis of Hamilton; Sir Thomas Wentworth, currently the Lord Deputy of Ireland, soon to become Lord Lieutenant of Ireland and Earl of Strafford; Sir Henry Vane, the Treasurer of the Household, soon to be elevated to Secretary of State, and arch-rival of Wentworth; Secretary Windebank; Lord Conway (who would ultimately come eye-to-eye with the Scottish army); Lord Cottington, the Chancellor of the Exchequer; Sir Jacob Astley; Sir John Conyers, who would govern Berwick; the Earl of Newport, Master of the Ordnance; the Earl of Arundel, Lord General of the preceding year's army and soon to be sacked; Sir William Uvedale, the harried Treasurer at Wars; Sir Nicholas Byron; and Lord Goring.[29] Also in attendance was Secretary Nicholas (whose notes are preserved), and often the King

---

[27] PRO, SP 16/396, f. 59; SP 16/409/100.
[28] HMC Cowper, Coke MSS., p. 210, for Council of War minutes for 22 January–7 February 1639. The Coke manuscripts are now deposited in the British Library.
[29] PRO, PC 2/51, f. 1, Privy Council register, a list of the Council of War, entered around the beginning of October 1639.

himself.[30] The membership of the Council of War, as established on 30 December 1639, was flexible, including the Privy Councillors present, as well as Uvedale and Goring, who were absent.[31] A quorum of five members permitted business to be transacted formally, and meetings were scheduled for eight o'clock in the morning on Thursdays and Saturdays, at Whitehall.[32]

The Second Bishops' War saw the council complete the transformation from advisory to bureaucratic responsibility. Ironically, the 1640 council demonstrated the institutional resiliency of Caroline government in a losing cause. As Conway suggested, the war very well may have been lost from the start.[33] But in spite of an appalling shortage of cash and a hostile political climate, the Council of War assumed the business of managing a war and organized the mobilization fairly well, if much too slowly and with chaos in some shires. The myriad of details involved in assembling twenty regiments of foot, six regiments of horse, and auxiliary support were dealt with thoroughly by a council that often involved itself in matters directly under the jurisdiction of other governmental institutions.[34] For example, the council complemented the services of the Exchequer in that once the Receipt had disbursed funds to the Treasurer at War, Sir William Uvedale, it set pay levels and coordinated Uvedale's agenda. Since he, as well as the Lord Treasurer and the Chancellor of the Exchequer, sat regularly at the council table, the business of army pay was closely monitored. The council engaged in 'long debate' over the rate of pay for infantry file leaders, and there is every indication that they laid plans to ensure that the troops received steady payment[35]. That the soldiers did not always receive their wages was the result of fighting the war with insufficient resources, not the incompetency of the paymasters. Charles did not appreciate debate on that strategic concern. Rather, the councillors were simply to work out a pay scale. Likewise, matters regarding the Ordnance Office, which were of paramount concern in late 1639, also overlapped with the careful management of the Council of War.[36] Although the council positioned itself well to coordinate the activities of Caroline institutions (Ordnance Office, Exchequer, and lieutenancy), it could neither

[30] PRO, SP 16/436/38, Secretary Nicholas's notes, 30 December 1639. At this meeting Charles announced his decision to appoint a Council of War by a commission under the Great Seal.

[31] PRO, SP 16/441/119, Robert Reade to Thomas Windebank, 13 January 1640.

[32] PRO, SP 16/436/47, Nicholas writes, 'anie fyve to sit'.

[33] Bodleian Library, Clarendon SP, XIX, f. 175v and above, pp. 59–60.

[34] These regiments totalled 20,000 infantry and 3,000 cavalry, according to PRO, SP 16/441/83, f. 2, council minutes of 10 January 1640.

[35] Nicholas originally wrote 'much debate', then changed the entry to 'long debate', apparently as 'much' implied disagreement. PRO, SP 16/441/14, f. 3, minutes of 2 January 1640.

[36] See below, pp. 95–6, regarding Newport's complaint about the Ordnance Officers.

increase the resources the King had made available to these institutions nor alter appreciably the time constraints which had been imposed upon them by the King and ultimately the Covenanter invasion. The English Council of War could urge Sir Job Harby to bring over weapons from Flanders more rapidly but could not cast record numbers of cannon. It could tell captains how to disburse wages but could not send extraordinary agents into the shires to raise funds to pay the soldiers. It could issue orders for musters and pressing, but could not compel men to attend the standard except through the accepted channels of law and tradition. What the council did succeed in doing was to enable old institutions to fight a war with no parliamentary revenues.[37]

The Scottish committees of war

While Charles resuscitated traditional institutions, the Covenanters imposed a new administrative framework upon their nation. As would be the case during the Civil War, the opponents of the Crown developed reliable committee systems which harnessed the energies of the countryside in spite of the questionable legitimacy of the rebel government in the capital city. In January 1639 a score of Covenanter lords fashioned a bureaucracy of subordinate committees linking Edinburgh to the parishes via shire and presbytery. By rotating elected positions, prescribing regular meetings and designating specific dwellings for the transmission of news and transaction of business, they established sturdy conduits of authority which gave the impression that the impulse of the war effort derived from the locality, with Edinburgh serving as a nerve centre. The parishes and presbyteries took responsibility for defending themselves and, if necessary, the kingdom and kirk at large. They fashioned a community of political consensus stronger than that which existed in Caroline England.

The various Scottish committees of war lay within the network monitored by the commissioners at Edinburgh, who represented their respective shires for a term of three months. Below them each shire designated an individual who served as a link between Edinburgh and the shire. Thus, at the apex of the pyramid, the localities participated in the formulation and communication of governmental policy. For the larger shires a pair of respected, ostensibly godly, men directed the course of the rebellion (smaller counties had a single representative, or combined to elect a commissioner). Their policies came to the locality borne by one of their own

---

[37] An analysis of the 1640 Council of War may be found in an examination of a cross-section of Secretary Nicholas's notes and supplementary materials. PRO, SP 16/435/28; 436/48; 441/14; 441/83; 442/14; 442/130; 443/25; 444/1; 444/3; 445/33; 446/6; 447/7; 447/9; 447/74; 448/11; 448/30; 448/71; 449/42; 450/49; 450/111; 451/75; 457/20.

residents, a man selected for that task, who convened weekly meetings with the commissioners representing their presbyteries.[38]

The experiences of decades of religious self-government facilitated mobilization, for the presbyteries served as useful administrative units for managing the war effort. No equivalent existed in England. In mobilizing, the burgh community of Scotland organized more effectively than the shires of England or Wales, though the evidence suggests that the respective inhabitants' commitment to the war determined the success of the call-up as much as administrative efficiency. The presbytery official, with the assistance of the clergy, saw to it that the parishes cooperated with instructions from above. Again, a specific individual stood accountable; in this case a commissioner elected from within the parish, who answered to the presbytery commissioner directly. The kirk, too, enforced authority, for the parish minister assisted the parish commissioner in his duties, lending ecclesiastical authority to the activities of local government.

Each administrative unit, shire, town, presbytery, and even parish, seems to have had a corresponding committee of war. Shire committees of war came into being in January and February 1639, made up of shire representatives and three or four men from each presbytery, so that military preparations were conducted from the perspective both of shire and presbytery. They supervised the enrolling of able men, drilling, amassing of stockpiles of victuals and material, and the sensitive matter of raising money from the parishes. A parish commissioner answered to the committee, so that their instructions could be translated down to the basic unit of Scottish rural life.[39]

Although the English Council of War was highly centralized and carried the authority of the King, it lacked the integration with the localities that characterized the Covenanter system, for its membership derived from the court, not from the realm at large. The committee at Edinburgh compelled the localities to join in the preparations, engendering a sense of collective responsibility (and vulnerability) directed by an elected member of the community who answered personally for his neighbours as well as for himself. Nor did the exactions of the Personal Rule hang over him in the same way as they weighed upon the activities of justices of the peace and

---

38 SRO, GD 16/52/19, Airlie Muniments, ff. 1–2, an original copy of circular instructions regarding the meetings of the commissioners and the maintenance of the army. An English copy, apparently intercepted and sent up to London, is catalogued in PRO, SP 16/410/167 II. See also Stevenson, *The Scottish Revolution*, p. 129.

39 SRO, GD 16/52/19, Airlie Muniments, ff. 2–3. On the functioning of Scottish committees of war see the Burntisland committee of war notes *circa* 15 May 1639, NLS, Crawford MSS. 14/3/32, 33, and J. Nicolson (ed.), *Minute Book kept by the War Committee of the Covenanters in the stewartry of Kirkcudbright in 1640 and 1641* (Kirkcudbright, 1855), pp. 1–4, 6, 9–28, and 30–2. For a 'grassroots' meeting at which the formation of a Council of War was moved and then implemented, see GD 406/1/769, 28 January 1639.

deputy lieutenants in England. The commissioners responded to an extra-ordinary situation, whereas the justices and lieutenants could be regarded as tools of a policy of arbitrary government forced upon an unwilling community. Resentment lay deeper in the English parishes.[40]

The authority of the Covenanter Council of War lay in self-preservation and the protection of the kirk. The council's actions served not the mysterious designs of a prince intent on buttressing his stature, but the subject's right to preserve his life and the compelling mission to stand firm for Christ's church. The councillors declared how they had appealed 'many tymes' to their sovereign but received 'no other answer' than the positioning of hostile armies on their various borders, with certain intelligence that 'our adversaries' intended to keep up this military posture.[41] A national threat prompted a national response. The cooperation of the national committee of war with the local committees was apparent in the requisitioning of horses and horsemen.

The committee determined the number of cavalry to go to the Borders who were able to afford such service, and then exercised power to 'taxe'. Those unable to 'ryd [ride] themselves they shalbe oblished [obliged] to sell the horse' to those who had the means to buy and the authorization of the committee. Those possessing 'landrent able to susteine the rank [?] of horsemen' should buy horses and send them. The local committees requisitioned horses from those most capable of supplying them. The inhabitants were gathered and instructed 'to cast lots which of the two thirds goeth'. One-third would then be excused. Whoever refused the service was 'incarcerat and fyned in his goods and the horsemen that comes shalbe interterned [entertained] horse and men'. Wages would be paid only for riding to the border or for returning home. The Covenanters saw service as essentially defensive, as did Charles I, but did not have to spend large amounts of money in keeping their cavalry on guard. While horsemen patrolled the Borders, the shire committee remained ready to receive instructions from the national committee at Edinburgh. If the committee consisted of lairds owning horses, they were obliged to send them to the border with able men fit for service. In other words, serving on the shire committee did not exempt one from contributing steeds, men, and money. Horses belonging to 'anti-covenanters' were 'seased' by the committees of shires or presbyteries and 'put out for the publick service'. The horses which remained at

---

[40] The phraseology of orders for mobilization issued from Edinburgh made explicit the collective nature of their security. See for example the preamble to the commission issued for raising troops, which invoked the authority of the nobility, the commissioners of 'Shires and burrowes', and the Scottish Parliament. SRO, GD 112/43/6/35, Breadalbane Muniments, 9 May 1639 (?).

[41] NLS, Crawford MS. 14/3/33, articles from the committee of war, 18 May 1639.

home were listed with colonels so that they might in turn relieve those at the Borders.

All men between sixteen and sixty were to be ready with arms at twenty-four hours' notice with '*a moneths provisione* and if come upon anie part of the country of the sea coast order shalbe given' to leave as many in each area as need be to resist the enemy. The shire committee enforced the universal military obligation and readied an expeditionary force. The 'fourth man' marched from each parish with *ten days provisions*.[42] Vict-ualling problems were the business of the soldiers themselves, for the Scots had no commissariat on the scale of that of the English. 'And if they refuse ther persones to be incarcerat and ther goods seased upon.' If someone were appointed to be a horseman 'and comes not foorth', he 'shalbe put in closse prisone' and fined 1,000 'merks' if a baron, or 500 'merks' if a gentleman of inferior quality, or 40 'merks' if a yeoman. The colonels and committees stockpiled in each parish 'jacks and lances pickes swyn feathers' and other weapons, made and priced 'at one easier rate at the sight of the Committee'. Weapons were confiscated from anti-covenanters.

The Covenanter war committees kept a tight rein over money and officers. Foot captains of gentle status who possessed good horses were either to sell them or sponsor a rider. Burgh and country committees brought before them those reputed to have money and upon a 'great oath' required them to lend upon sufficient security (based upon future rents). If they refused, lied, or otherwise doubted, the committee empowered a search, so that what was concealed was taken. The goods and rents of anti-covenanters were 'seased upon' except for entertainment of wives and babies, with chamberlains appointed to this end. All money in readiness at the term for paying of debts was taken from the creditor 'upon good securi-tie for the publick service'. If not enough was secured by this means, then all 'silver work and plat' in burgh or land was to be given up upon oath 'and brought to the mint house and struken in money upon securitie'.[43]

The power and authority of the committees of war (national, shire, and presbytery) far exceeded the English Council of War and its subcommit-tees. When Charles tried to lay hold of men's wealth, the cry of the liberty of the subject was raised up. Englishmen accused the King of breaking the contract between subject and ruler. But in Scotland, a new contract, the Covenant, legitimized the committees of war which represented the will of the nation.

The English Council of War, however, reflected the political tempera-ment of the Privy Council. When the proponents of 'thorough' gained

---

[42] Ibid. My italics.
[43] Ibid. For similar orders, see SRO, GD 112/43/1/6/30, Breadalbane Muniments, 3 May 1639.

ascendancy around the time of the Short Parliament, those more rigid policies were implemented. Muster defaulters would be persecuted vigorously
along with coat-and-conduct-money refusers. Militia units would be
fielded regardless of their objections.[44] Strafford's off-hand remark about
hanging those who would not defend the realm is emblematic of the more
forceful posturing of the Council of War in 1640. Yet any factional domi-
nation of the Council of War (or command of the army for that matter)
was rendered impossible by the periodic illnesses of Northumberland (the
Lord General) and Strafford (the Lieutenant General). The former understood the limitations placed upon the Council of War, just as he grasped
the present weakness of the Exchequer of Receipt and the unpreparedness
of the Ordnance Office. Northumberland's selection as Lord General was
propitious in that he understood how politics affected Stuart institutions,
as a result of his involvement with Charles's navy.[45] Strafford, like his
royal master, preferred to bully institutions, for example the Irish Parliament and his small army. His fallibility in judging the predicament of
English institutions was illustrated in his miscalculation of the Short
Parliament.[46] Strafford's techniques had sometimes succeeded in Ireland
but in England only prompted legalistic reaction from a system of government based upon cooperation rather than intimidation.[47]

Political considerations shaped the success of the councils. In England
the political situation bound the council. In Scotland a more vigorous and
aggressive political posture, based upon religious conviction, enabled the
Covenanters to build an effective committee system. The highly structured
pyramid of committees rested upon the presbytery and parish, giving cohe-
sion and responsiveness to the system administered from the committee at
Edinburgh. The Scots mobilized fairly quickly due to their efficient administration, but their limited resources made retention of those forces difficult. Conversely, the personalized system supervised by the English
Council of War made the assembly of the royal army in 1639 more sluggish, with unfortunate consequences. The test came in 1640. The English
Council of War laid its plans and the task of winning the war became the
responsibility of the army then assembling. The councillors assumed their
places: Northumberland, Newport, Conway, Goring, Conyers, and Astley
with their regiments, Juxon and Cottington at the Exchequer. Whitehall's
council chambers became quieter as the enterprise fell upon the shoulders
of the commanders.

[44] See below, pp. 207–14.
[45] He had served as Lord Admiral from 23 March 1636.
[46] Fissel, 'Scottish War and English Money', pp. 197–212, 217–18.
[47] P. H. Hardacre, 'Patronage and Purchase in the Irish Standing Army under Thomas
Wentworth, Earl of Strafford, 1632–1640', *JSAHR* 67, no. 269 (spring 1989), pp. 40–5. See
especially the comment on 'Wentworth's straining of military law', p. 45.

THE CHAIN OF COMMAND

The Bishops' Wars began with a chivalric rendezvous at York on 1 April 1639, an instance of the 'theatre of reality' Thespianism Charles later demonstrated at the attempted seizure of the five members and ultimately, with great effect, upon the scaffold. Although he stopped short of commissioning Inigo Jones to build a review stand at Selby, or Davenant to compose a military masque, the theatrics of this rally round the royal banner were apparent to all. By the time of the Second Bishops' War the poet Sir John Suckling would be commanding a troop and Davenant would be serving as 'commissary of the draught of artillery'.[48] Fighting Scots was traditional stuff for northerners, and Charles struck a pose reminiscent of grand predecessors such as Edward I. The Recorder of York further extended the historical context and likened Charles to a new Constantine, asserting that this mounted Christian warrior promised to restore order and religion to the British Isles.[49]

Charles chose his commanders predictably. John Hale's remarks are relevant here – 'as far as leadership was concerned, armies were still seen as the claws expanding naturally from the tensed body politic as a whole. Command structure was the least modernizable of the elements of armed force.'[50] The great border magnates therefore constituted the logical choices for generalship. In 1639 Thomas Howard, Earl of Arundel, served as Lord General, not the least because of his influence amongst his northern tenants.[51] In 1640 Algernon Percy, Earl of Northumberland, took command.[52] His hereditary seat at Alnwick Castle and his northern lieutenancy should have worked to the royal advantage. Finally, Lord Clifford assisted actively in both wars. Thus the three most prominent border families, the Howards, the Percys, and the Cliffords, played leading roles in the mobilization.[53] But border society had changed under the early Stuarts so that, although pacification enhanced the authority of great landlords by reinforcing law and order, improved relations between English and Scot-

---

[48] PRO, E 351/293, Sir William Uvedale's declared account as Treasurer at Wars for the Second Bishops' War, f. 15 (Suckling) and f. 227 (Davenant). See also Roy Strong, *Van Dyck: Charles I on Horseback*, pp. 45–63, and Graham Parry, *The Golden Age Restor'd. The Culture of the Stuart Court, 1603–42* (Manchester, 1985), pp. 184–5, 190, 203, 221–2.

[49] *CSPD* (1638–9), XIII, p. 626, speech of Thomas Widdrington, 30 March 1639.

[50] J. R. Hale, *War and Society in Renaissance Europe 1450–1620* (London, 1988), p. 132.

[51] PRO, SP 16/396, f. 150; SP 16/412/74, 9 February 1639. See for example Arundel Castle, autograph letter, no. 377, ff. 387–387v.

[52] Northumberland's commission is printed in Rymer, *Feodera*, vol. IX, p. 237 and in Rushworth, *Historical Collections*, vol. III, pp. 988–90; his regiment, however, consisted of 1,200 Hampshire men.

[53] See Clifford's correspondence with Wentworth in Sheffield City Library, Strafford MS. Xb, ff. 158–61.

tish lords made them less inclined to quarrel, as had been the case in the Middle Ages.[54] But the inherent conservatism of military command meant that the campaign would be officered and planned in traditional English fashion.

A 'quasi-medieval' command structure led to the use of archaic strategies and weapons; for example, in 1639 Arundel urged the sending of bills and bows to the border militia.[55] Reliable English veterans of the continental wars needed to be placed directly below the aristocratic generals so that the command structure would not be entirely out of date in its grasp of the art of war. Charles I seems partly to have appreciated this when he selected Sir Jacob Astley as Sergeant Major General of the infantry. Astley later distinguished himself under the royalist banner, notably at Edgehill. Schooled in the Low Countries' wars since the age of nineteen, he was arguably the finest soldier at Charles's disposal and certainly the best command appointment.[56] Astley appears to have fought under Protestant military commanders including Counts Maurice and Henry, the Elector Palatine, and Gustavus Adolphus.[57] Sir Jacob's stiffening of the trained bands in the north and assiduous care in provisioning and in the repair of fortifications facilitated the campaign immeasurably. He guided the supply of arms through John Quarles, Captain Legge and the agents of the Ordnance Office, while he browbeat local authorities into heeding the council's orders. But Astley represented the exception rather than the rule, for the majority of Charles's commanders were lords, knights, and gentlemen who had never experienced battle. With a year's training and with seasoned troops at their disposal, the inexperienced might have become suitable officers. But Charles wanted speedy mobilization and would not allow time for preparation. The rank and file were as new to war as their officers and difficult to drill, for a dearth of experienced non-commissioned officers made training at best fitful. Nor did foreign commanders serve Charles. Few mercenaries found rank in the royal army, except for a pair of French cornets.[58] A rivulet of British officers trickled across the Channel amid rumours of an Anglo-Scottish war. Whether they returned to serve the

---

[54] R. T. Spence, 'The Pacification of the Cumberland Borders, 1593–1628', *Northern History*, 13 (1977), pp. 59–160. See for example the remarkably conciliatory correspondence between the Earl of Home and the commander of the English cavalry, the Earl of Holland, p. 25 above.

[55] PRO, SP 16/397/6, to Sir James Bagg; Bagg's reply, SP 16/397/38. See above, p. 13.

[56] PRO, SP 16/396, ff. 54–7; Rymer's *Feodera*, vol. IX, p. 190. See above, p. 288.

[57] Wentworth's discerning eye spotted Astley as well, and Sir Jacob was offered the rank of Sergeant-Major General in the Irish standing army. He refused it, however: Hardacre, 'Patronage and Purchase in the Irish Standing Army', p. 44.

[58] On mercenaries, see pp. 162–73. On the French, see PRO, SP 16/473/52 I, one of whom may have been the culprit from Captain Cowper's troop in the 1639 shooting incident. See Fissel, '*Bellum Episcopale*', p. 318 and SP 16/459/90.

Covenant or their Stuart master was not always entirely clear, judging from a number of petitions from Scottish soldiers of fortune who had been imprisoned upon returning from the continental wars. Understandably, they protested their loyalty to the Crown.[59] It may well have been the paucity of field-grade officers that prompted Windebank to exclaim to the King that he prayed for commanders as well as money on the eve of the Battle of Newburn.[60]

The First Bishops' War made clear the need for experienced commissioned and non-commissioned officers. In seeking officers for the Second Bishops' War the Council of War solicited the aid of the English ambassador at Hamburg, Sir Thomas Roe, who was no stranger to the profession of arms.[61] By late February, the Venetian ambassador remarked that English captains had forsaken their Dutch commissions and now swaggered about London.[62] Roe composed successful letters of recommendation in March for several officers.[63] Others advertised their expertise to the secretary of the Privy Council, Francis Windebank, as did Thomas Dymock, who secured a captaincy in Colonel Sir Thomas Glenham's regiment of 1,200 west-country men.[64]

It is possible that at the captaincy level and above there were sufficient takers (though not as qualified as the King might have wished) to fill posts adequately. One of the more celebrated captains and military theorists, Henry Hexham, received a pass to go to Holland on 27 July 1640, at the height of the mobilization for the Second Bishops' War. Surely during a state of emergency this veteran should have been dispatched north rather than allowed to go abroad.[65] Hexham could have trained officers between the wars, for example, if the government had taken the initiative. The greatest shortage existed at the non-commissioned officer level, especially sergeants. On 6 February 1640 the Council of War ordered Sir Nicholas Byron, who had endured Hamilton's amphibious exercise in 1639, to seek out a hundred expert sergeants and corporals for immediate service in England.[66]

---

59 PRO, SP 16/439/54 (Barclay); 55 (Forbes); 58 (Furbish and Browne); 63 (Hunter).
60 Bodleian Library, Clarendon SP, XVIII, f. 273, 1 September 1640.
61 *CSPD* (1639–40), XV, p. 371, Windebank to Roe, 24 January 1640.
62 *CSP Venetian*, XXV, p. 20, note 30, Giustinian to Doge and Senate, 24 February 1640.
63 PRO, SP 16/447/108 (Sergeant-Major Thelwell, probably Sergeant-Major Anthony Thelwell of Colonel Fielding's regiment of 1,400 soldiers from Essex, Huntingdonshire, and Bedfordshire); 109 (Captain Thurland, possibly Captain Richard Thurland in Colonel Culpepper's regiment of 1,200 Dorsetshire and Devonshire men).
64 PRO, SP 16/399/15 and 15 I and Rushworth, *Historical Collections*, vol. III, p. 1247; see also Willoughby in SP 16/452/82, 8 May 1640.
65 PRO, SP 16/461/23; Hexham had published *The Principles of the Art Militarie Practised in the Warres of the United Netherlands* in 1637.
66 PRO, SP 16/444/43, Nicholas notes.

The chain of command was complicated by another reality of military life in the era of the Thirty Years' War: religious division. As John Morrill reminds us, the Civil War of 1642–5 can be described as the last of the wars of religion.[67] And certainly a campaign fought for religious uniformity (and autocracy) falls squarely under such a rubric. As the existence of a Catholic conspiracy was bruited in these years, naturally a fifth column was detected within the officer corps. Rumours abounded that the entire officer corps was Romanist, which explained the war against Presbyterian Scotland. Since some Irishmen, such as the Earl of Barrymore, served their King as officers, the belief that Catholic sentiments permeated the chain of command gained currency. In 1640 some common soldiers alleged loudly that their officers practised the Roman religion. Anti-catholicism manifested itself in the murder of two officers during the Second Bishops' War.[68] The Long Parliament later attempted to identify officers who preferred the Old Religion. Lord Conway's tally numbered one colonel, two lieutenant-colonels, two sergeant majors, ten captains, thirteen lieutenants, thirteen ensigns, one quartermaster, twelve sergeants, a total of fifty-four popish officers; these included Captain James Maxwell, a Scot serving in Colonel William Vavasor's regiment, and his lieutenant Hugh Maxwell, Ensign James Maxwell and Sergeant James Maxwell, all apparently kinsmen and co-religionists. Barrimore's Welsh regiment was officered by ten Roman Catholics.[69]

The Covenanters, however, used religion to unite their army while simultaneously balancing experience with social status. Again, the political context of the war favoured Scottish arrangements. The Covenanters concocted a formula which integrated aristocratic and gentlemanly leadership with military expertise. In so doing they succeeded in placing regimental command within the power structure of the locality while improving military preparedness by inserting proven veterans into the chain of command directly below the man of local influence. When shires were divided into regiments and companies under the supervision of local commissioners and the shire committees of war, the colonels appointed were noblemen or gentlemen of quality. However, the lieutenant colonels 'Quho ar pryme

[67] 'The Religious Context of the English Civil War', *TRHS*, fifth series, 24 (1984), pp. 155–78.
[68] See below, pp. 277–84.
[69] PRO, SP 16/473/52; 52 I; 53. See below, pp. 225, 285. Arguably, Romanists could not be tainted with sympathy for the Covenant, which justified the royal trust reposed in them. See Hamilton's recommendation to Windebank (himself a 'crypto-catholic') of a servant, who could be trusted because he was a 'Romane Catholique'. See SRO, GD 406/1/940, f. 2, 15 April 1639.

officers' were to be veterans of the German or Dutch service, and paid by the shire.[70] This system extended into the company, where the captain and ensign came from noble or gentle stock, and the lieutenants and sergeants were overseas veterans. Even if this ideal balance was not entirely achieved, a clear policy on social rank and military experience existed to keep order, acknowledging that victory required both attributes. A similar compromise was hammered out between national military command and allowance for local autonomy in naming officers. Presbytery committees, sometimes towns and parishes themselves, made the choice of captains, who then chose their subordinates. The Covenanters could go so far as to say that the Earl of Montrose had been 'ellectit' colonel by the common consent of the whole shire and that the parishes possessed the powers to 'ellect and ordaine' under-officers.[71] The Covenanter system, more than the English, involved the locality more intimately in the leadership of the war effort and circumvented the political problems which beset Charles's selection of officers.

Military success in England depended on the country's pliability and willingness to contribute to the war effort. Terms of service, such as who was mobilized, how they were paid, and the appointment of officers, constituted issues which central and local government had to resolve. The naming of officers was especially delicate during the Bishops' Wars for mistrust dogged the Crown's dealings with the country. If militia or conscripts were to cross the shire boundaries, the locals preferred that men of standing from their own community carried the conduct money and gave the orders. However, the Crown had learned that royally appointed officers, strangers to a community, could 'use rougher hands', in other words enforce discipline.[72] This led to negotiations over the appointment of officers and the receipt of their pay. Durham in 1639 'was in very good forwardness, for providing Armes, and trayning our forces', the alacrity of the captains and soldiers commendable. But trouble had arisen over local officers and their pay. The bishop had received a royal letter appointing Sir Thomas Morton colonel of the regiment and empowering him to select officers who should be paid by the bishop as long as the forces remained in

[70] SRO, GD 16/52/19, Airlie Muniments, f. 3, document detailing arrangements for the meeting of commissioners from the shires and the maintenance of the army, *circa* 1639 and SRO, RH 13/18, p. 23 (unfoliated) where the diarist records that every regimental colonel of noble birth 'had old Souldiers to be theire Leiutenant Colonells and Maiors'.

[71] SRO, GD 16/50/6, Airlie Muniments, f. 1; SRO, GD 112/43/1/6/30, Breadalbane Muniments, f. 1, article one, instructions from Perth dated 3 May 1639. See also Stevenson, *The Scottish Revolution*, p. 129. There were, however, protestations when these arrangements ran roughshod over clan honour, as expressed in regard to the Campbells in GD 112/43/1/6/31.

[72] Avon Reference Library, Bristol, MS. B 28176, Buckingham (?) to Lord Poulett, 7 March 1639.

the bishopric. However, 'when they shall march out of the Countie, then his Majestie would pay them'. When the 'Captaines and Countrie' learned of this it bred distraction because it was contrary to the King's former arrangement, published by Sir Thomas Morton upon his arrival, that the Crown would not 'put any gentlemen of the Countrie from their places that were willing to continue those which gave them good satisfaction'. Now they all expected to be 'displaced', and wondered even more if they were the only men in the kingdom considered unworthy (or not trusted) to be in Charles's employment: 'and lastly, to have soe great a Charge, as the payment of soe many officers, and the like in noe other countie, makes all feare his Majestie may have had some sinister information'.[73] The Durham authorities protested against disruption by outsiders and registered their dislike of centralization and interference in the organization of local defence. The politics of the court had upset the politics of the locality. Moreover, these 'outsider' officers were to be paid from local money, reminiscent of the despised muster masters of the 1630s. Local officers represented a defensive posture and would be less rash in marching the forces out of the county. Crown-appointed officers might take the offensive using the expeditionary force in 'illegal' fashion.

Another 'outsider' was the Marquis of Hamilton, whose dealings illustrate the links between commander, royal officers, and lower field grade officers. Hamilton did not inform his officers that their destination was Scotland, telling them instead that they were headed for Holy Island. He complained of the insufficient preparations made by the local officers for the provision of victuals for their troops. Hamilton was appalled that the local officers had not made 'any provision of victualls. So as from the Colonel to the Corporal, they live upon the King's store laid in for the common soldiers which doth not only waste it but causeth a general desire to be on land.'[74] When admonished for failing to bring sufficient victuals, the officers said they had not been advanced money to get victuals. Further misfortune followed from the choice of officers for the English army. Sir Thomas Morton reported from Gravesend that one of his Captains had 'gone madd'; he lacked one captain and four or five lieutenants. The officers of Colonels Byron and Harcourt were inexpert, some missing. Harcourt himself was seasick, unable to survive a week at sea, which was confirmed by a physician's certificate.

The greatest cause of the officers' misfortunes was the clause in the council's letters to the lords lieutenant sparing trained soldiers and allowing able bodied but unskilled men to serve instead. Hamilton intended to select

[73] SRO, GD 406/1/690, f. 1, Sir William Belasys to Hamilton, 22 February 1639.
[74] SRO, GD 406/1/1209, Hamilton to Vane from Yarmouth Roads, 23 April 1639.

militiamen as non-commissioned officers.[75] The scarcity of soldiers of the
trained bands reduced the number of sergeants and corporals for the regiments. Militiamen were to be spread amongst the companies to manage the
inexperienced recruits. A greater percentage of local officers and militia
might in fact have made the expeditionary force a considerable weapon.
The perfect militia spawned leaders. Hamilton described the local officers
as generally obedient, respectful, and careful of their charges.[76]

In addition to consulting with the local authorities, Hamilton, like other
commanders, had to contend with the recommendation of officers by his
colleagues. Arundel recommended to Hamilton Lieutenant Colonel
Waytes and Sir Charles Vavasor, 'a very gallant gentleman and worthy of
a Regimente', probably to replace the seasick Harcourt. The Marquis did
not know Waytes or Vavasor, but had to consider them, although only
one lieutenant colonel's place was available.[77] Hamilton's was a British
command designed for a war fought for British ecclesiastical uniformity.
Mixed regiments existed, such as English commanders and Welsh or Irish
soldiers. But often politics and bureaucracy led to division, as for example
over different pay arrangements for English and Scottish officers.[78] It was
imperative that Scotland should be invaded by an army under the
command of a Scottish noble, for in Charles's view this was a matter of the
suppression of internal conspiracy, not a war fought between two ancient
foes.

From the outset of the First Bishops' War, the appointment of officers
sparked disagreement and ill-feeling. Clarendon observed years later that
the Lord General, the Earl of Arundel, 'who had nothing martial about
him but his presence and looks', had been chosen 'for his negative quali-
ties: he did not love the Scots; he did not love the Puritans; which good

---

[75] Hamilton's need for officers prompted Secretary Vane to dispatch Captain Thelwall, who
had done well in preparing the trained bands of the north, to the amphibious force. In the
message borne by Thelwall, Vane specifically blamed the 'substitution clause' (see
pp. 241–63) for the lack of officers. SRO, GD 406/1/1207, f. 3, letter of 23 April 1639. See
also GD 406/1/820, Windebank's comments of 12 April and GD 406/1/938, 938 I, 938 II,
Hamilton's of the same date.

[76] SRO, GD 406/1/847, Hamilton to Arundel, 26 May 1639.

[77] SRO, GD 406/1/831, Arundel to Hamilton, 10 May 1639 and the latter's response, GD
406/1/835, ff. 2–3, 14 May 1639.

[78] PRO, E 351/296, declared account of Sir J. Lockhart, paymaster of Scottish officers, for
the period 21 March 1640 to 6 November 1640; also E 351/297, additional account of Sir
J. Lockhart; E 351/298 and 299, accounts of Francis Vernon, paymaster of Hamilton's
forces. There were of course English officers under Scottish commanders, receiving pay
under these accounts. On Vernon's activities as a paymaster, see SRO, GD 406/1/1176, 22
June 1639, where he made up his reckonings with Sir William Uvedale; GD 406/1/1177,
where he arrived in the nick of time to pay the soldiers. Although Vernon had English
soldiers in his pay lists (GD 406/1/1182, 26 May 1639 and GD 406/1/1121, 11 June 1639),
Sir James Lockhart's funds were for Scottish troops only (GD 406/1/1197, f. 1, 14 May
1639).

qualifications were allayed by another negative, he did love nobody else'.[79] The Earl of Holland received command of the royal cavalry through the intercession of the Queen and thus shared command with the more mature Arundel. Overlooked was the 'darling of the swordmen', the Earl of Essex, son of the Elizabethan traitor, whose staunch Protestantism and serious bearing recommended him as a commander. When Holland was chosen over Essex, Arundel was outraged. Only the personal urging of the King dissuaded the earl from declining his post. Essex was forced to accept the place of Lieutenant General, second in command to Arundel. 'The seeds of jealousy were thus sown before a single regiment was formed.'[80] In mid-April Arundel clashed with the Master of the Ordnance, the Earl of Newport, when they 'had a difference about the marchinge away' of Newport's cavalry, 'which grew to high speaches betwixt them'.[81] A command structure drawn from the Court brought with it the fractures that occurred between courtiers, as when an intriguing and violent argument erupted between two officers responsible for the supply of the army: Captain Hunnywood, a quartermaster for the infantry, and Wilmot, Commissary-General for the horse, later to be a hero at Newburn. Rossingham's newsletter states that Wilmot had drawn his sword upon one of Arundel's captains for allegedly encroaching upon his office, and was jailed by Colonel Goring.[82] It appears that the dispute arose over the functioning of the commissariat and the duties and privileges of the officers. The Earl of Rutland entered in his diary under 8 April what 'happened betwixt Hunnywood, Quarter-Master Officer to the General, and Sir Wilmot, Commissary of the horse'. Goring, Lieutenant General of the cavalry, investigated the matter and, after examination, Hunnywood was committed 'by the Kinge and Councell of War'.[83] The quarrel is interesting for two reasons. First, it reveals conflict within the commissariat, an institution vital to the maintenance of an army. Second, it is noteworthy that the dispute occurred between a captain of Arundel's infantry and an officer of Holland's cavalry, for there was a degree of animosity between the respective generals as well as between cavalry and infantry.

John Aston, one of the King's privy chamber men, recorded in his diary that some infantrymen

[79] Clarendon, *History of the Rebellion*, vol. I, p. 150; Charles's commision to Arundel: PRO, SP 16/396, f. 150 (Council of War entry book) and PRO, SP 16/412/74, 9 February 1639.
[80] Gardiner, *History*, vol. VIII, pp. 385–6; Wedgwood, *The King's Peace*, pp. 251–2.
[81] *HMC Rutland*, p. 307, 8 April 1639.
[82] PRO, SP 16/417/110, Rossingham to Conway, 16 April 1639.
[83] *HMC Rutland*, p. 505, 8 April 1639.

intermixt with the horse, which bred some disorders and quarrells (yet without bloud-shed), there beeing ever an aemulation betweene the horse and foote for presendecy, and therefore not to bee quartered together, the auncient dispute reviving, especially in their distemper with wine, the foote then not contented that common opinion should bee theire umpire.[84]

It has been suggested that this rivalry was exacerbated by the ill-will between Essex, the Lieutenant General of the infantry, and the Earl of Holland, Commander of the Horse.[85] The deleterious effect of court politics upon the chain of command would not have been as drastic except that the shortage of non-commissioned officers allowed the reverberations of faction to permeate the lower ranks. The billeting arrangements at York aimed at keeping civilians, horse, and foot separate in order to avoid the 'disorder which common souldiours are apt to occasion in great townes'. Only the King's servants and courtiers lodged within the walls of York, while the cavalry camped at Selby-upon-Ouse, ten miles from the city. The infantry were scattered among the villages.

Contemptuous though Sir Thomas Wentworth was of the effete court factions, he too attempted to secure military positions for his friends. In 1639 he promoted Viscount Conway. Little did they know that in the following year they would together shoulder the generalship of the Second Bishops' War. Wentworth told Conway on the last of August 1638, 'I have layd the Plott to make you a Captaine of Horse' and that secrecy was necessary for he intended to approach the King directly. Two courtiers could impede their design: Sir Jacob Astley and Lord Cromwell, who had ambitions of their own. Wentworth manoeuvred around Astley 'by moveing in his behalfe for a Troope of Horse, and the Sergeant Majors place'. Conway would have to deal with Cromwell on his own: 'But as I take Sir Jacob off your shoulders, so must you take his lordship [Cromwell] off mine.'[86] Sir Thomas argued that court-appointed commanders often undermined the quality of the officer corps, as when the late Lord Kirkcudbright's horse troop was bestowed upon the Earl of Desmond. Poor choices for military leadership meant the 'very soule of all Actions [was] cast into a Dead Sleepe'. In Ireland Wentworth had been forced to elevate a 'youth' to a captaincy at the King's command with the result that he had 'had more Trouble, the Kings Payments more Scandall, then from the whole Army besides'.[87] Patronage and faction shaped the chain of command more than purely military consideration, for the appointment of

---

[84] Aston, 'Iter Boreale', p. 6.
[85] Wedgwood, *The King's Peace*, pp. 264–5.
[86] Sheffield City Library, Strafford MSS., Xb, ff. 173, 177–8.
[87] Bodleian Library, Clarendon SP, XV, ff. 163–163v, 165, to Secretary Windebank, 2 March 1639.

officers was determined too often by local and personal politics, and conditioned by the inherent rivalries.[88]

Court rivalries could strain the chain of command. When Wentworth, newly elevated to the nobility as Earl of Strafford, assumed the lieutenant generalship, he found his authority circumvented. The personal animosity between Strafford and Secretary Vane spilled over on the eve of hostilities with Scotland. Strafford in fact may have been asking Hamilton, a friend of Vane's, to intercede in the quarrel. But the bitterness between the King's servants was quite apparent. Wentworth complained that the officers of the army addressed Vane 'rather than me, for since I was declared Lieutenant General I have not had one word from any of them, not so much as from my Lord Conway ... I take my self to be a far better Captain than himself [Vane], and ... I know myself to be infinitely the better secretary'.[89]

The English were commanded by faction and patronage while the Scots were commanded by committee, formula, and consent. Oftentimes the high command had to weigh the influence of a friend or client desirous of a command against the autonomy of a locally fielded force that wished to have a familiar face as an officer.[90] In short, the English commanders achieved appointment through consideration of personal connection, regional loyalties, and court politics for the most part. Turning to Scotland, one finds a chain of command reflective of Scottish society as a whole, not an extension of a royal court. The Covenanters integrated social rank and military training to forge a chain of command largely unblemished by court politics. Survival demanded it. Religious allegiance and a national covenant kept patronage in check, so that appointments could be balanced between social leadership and military expertise. In the latter category, the Covenanters were amply blessed for 10 per cent of the male population had seen service in the Danish or Swedish armed forces.[91] Hence the Scots were quite well led on the non-commissioned officer level at a time when the English had tremendous difficulty finding such men. Likewise, the preponderance of court politics in English command appointments undermined officer-corps continuity between the Bishops' Wars.[92] The consequences affected the level of expertise available to Civil War armies.

[88] Ibid. See correspondence between Strafford and his nephew, Sir William Saville, ff. 102–105, 208–210, letters of 13 and 19 September 1638.

[89] SRO, GD 406/1/1230, 25 August 1640.

[90] One of the many examples that could be cited is 'Mr. Alesburies desires', expressed to the Earl of Northumberland, for the command of a company. Centre for Kentish Studies, De L'Isle and Dudley MSS., Sydney Papers, U 1475 C85/8, f. 1v, Northumberland to the Earl of Leicester, 12 March 1640.

[91] G. Parker, *The Military Revolution*, pp. 49, 174 note 18; Furgol, 'Scotland Turned Sweden', p. 136.

[92] The turnover of the officer corps is apparent when contrasting the list of officers in PRO, E 351/292 with E 351/293.

Did the creation of an English officer corps in 1639–40 provide nuclei for the parliamentarian and royalist armies? Did participation in the Bishops' Wars predispose officers to choose one side over the other? Of 747 officers of the royal army serving at the time of Newburn, only 178 (23 8/10 per cent) appear to have fought in the English Civil War.[93] In general, the higher the rank, the greater the inclination towards royalism. Such a trend of course reflects court influence in appointment to the chain of command. Numerically, many regimental officer corps split between parliamentary and royalist commissions. In some, a marked preference was evident, as for example in Sir Thomas Glenham's regiment, where 75 per cent followed the King. Of the thirty-eight officers of the Earl of Northumberland's regiment in 1640, fourteen went on to fight in the Civil War, ten as royalists and only three as parliamentarians. Ensign Robert Brandling switched sides and cannot be easily categorized.[94] Some commanders who enlisted with Parliament would not have pleased their former colonels, the Marquis of Hamilton and Sir Jacob Astley. Of the seven Civil War officers from the former's regiment, all aligned with Parliament. Astley's parliamentarians amounted to 80 per cent, four out of five.

Certainly familial ties and patronage created 'clusters' of loyalties. Both Ballards in Lord Grandison's regiment, Lieutenant Colonel Thomas and Lieutenant Philip, served the roundhead cause. Ensigns in particular tended to accompany senior officers into new regiments, as in the case of Lieutenant Colonel Robert Hammond who was joined by half a dozen lower company grade officers (two lieutenants and four ensigns) when he declared for Parliament. One, Ensign Edward Gray, accompanied Hammond to Ireland in 1646.[95] Birth, patronage, and the camaraderie shared with subalterns accounted for the allegiances. That captains usually joined the royalist side is of note since generally they were of higher social status than the lower grade company officers such as ensigns and lieutenants. During the early modern period, elevation from the ranks or noncommissioned officer level to a captaincy was rather rare, for captains were

---

[93] The following statistics, which presume to be no more than conjecture in this matter, were constructed from a compilation consisting of officer lists, the declared accounts of Sir William Uvedale (E 351/292 and 293), John Rushworth's list of the Earl of Northumberland's officers at the end of the Second Bishops' War, and the popish officer lists of SP 16/473/52 and 53. These were checked against E. Peacock's *The Army Lists of the Roundheads and Cavaliers* (London, 1983) and Newman's *Royalist Officers in England and Wales*. Phillip Norris analysed the lists and greatly assisted in sorting out the trends.

[94] One must keep in mind the various routes by which officers gathered under the standard of a given commander. Some came by virtue of an allegiance based upon professional and personal association. For others, the 'old boy network' secured a commission through patronage. Still others were inherited from the locality. For example, local contingents' officers were attached to the regiment.

[95] However, one should note that just because they declared for Parliament didn't mean they were 'following'.

still regarded as a more refined social breed.[96] The subsequent perambulations of the captains reveals a professional and social tendency to royalism. Lord Fielding's regiment spawned seven Civil War officers; all three captains became royalists, along with a lieutenant. Three ensigns aligned with Parliament. Colonel Brett's regiment followed a similar pattern. Of the dozen officers who were on active service after 1642, all five captains remained faithful to Charles I. In general, the officers tended to split evenly between King and Parliament. However, the higher company and field grade officers leaned strongly to the royalist side. Colonel Byron's regiment illustrated this quite clearly; the eighteen officers divided evenly in Civil War allegiance, but all five captains adhered to the Crown. What command experience the parliamentary armies gleaned from the officer corps of the Bishops' Wars came out of the ranks and non-commissioned level, whereas the royalists enjoyed a greater percentage of the captains and colonels.[97]

Three hundred and seventy-two individuals are listed in the declared accounts of Sir William Uvedale, virtually all of whom are officers, comprising 200 for the First Bishops' War and 172 for the Second Bishops' War.[98] Only sixty-nine are repeated, which indicates a surprising turnover of military leadership. That only a third, or possibly less, went on to fight the Civil Wars implies that military professionalism was not readily transmitted between 1639 and 1645. This may well be a result of a court-faction-tainted command structure that allowed politics, and amateurism, to flourish. The Covenanters, like the Dutch rebels against Philip II, devised a chain of command which recognized social status but did not allow pettiness and political patronage to impair military leadership. Their political predicament and religious convictions made this possible.[99] Superior leadership brought victory to the Scots at Newburn. Leslie and his commanders knew well the value of cannon and made sure they were in place.[100]

---

[96] See Hale, *War and Society in Renaissance Europe*, p. 133.

[97] As colonels came from rather exalted backgrounds, generally being denizens of the court, their allegiances are not quite as intriguing as those of the officers below them. On the Covenanters' officers, see E. M. Furgol, *A Regimental History of the Covenanting Armies* (Edinburgh, 1990), pp. 16–79.

[98] PRO, E 351/292, 293. These are not comprehensive records, of course, as the secretary sometimes omitted lesser officers in one regiment and included them for others. Discussions with Phillip Norris proved very useful in reviewing this material. Some later celebrated commanders, such as George Monk of Restoration fame, got their start in the Bishops' Wars. Monk, a captain at the outbreak of hostilities, succeeded his commanding officer, Sir William Legge, as Sergeant Major of the Earl of Newport's infantry regiment in 1639 (see E 351/292, f. 5v).

[99] See M. D. Feld, 'Middle-Class Society and the Rise of Military Professionalism, the Dutch Army 1589–1609', *Armed Forces and Society*, I, no. 4 (August 1975), pp. 419–42.

[100] See above pp. 54–9 and Russell, *CECW*, p. 13, n. 37 and *FBM*, pp. 142–5.

THE ORDNANCE OFFICE

The Bishops' Wars comprised the enforcement of Caroline military policy through largely Tudor institutions, particularly the lieutenancy and the Ordnance Office. The Ordnance Office, given its proximity to court, was more susceptible to management, coercion, and reform than the lieutenancy, for its key officers could not exploit distance to insulate themselves from the Crown's wrath should they fail in their instructions. Also in contrast to the lieutenancy, the officers of the Ordnance were neither amateurs nor part-timers. Laxity might characterize the officers' work in time of peace, but the fact that a staff existed when a state of war did not imbued the Ordnance with extraordinary, perhaps unique, longevity.[101] Under the steady hand of Sir John Heydon they had received the opportunity to refine their procedures, while the maintenance of the ship money fleets raised the level of their activities. In the era of 'thorough', when Charles I possessed councillors with reforming zeal – Strafford, Laud, and Northumberland – it is remarkable that the Ordnance Office escaped drastic overhaul. Gerald Aylmer's assessment of Caroline administrative reform concluded that the 1639 mobilization 'once more found the Ordnance office wanting'.[102] That Ordnance Office administration needed to be reformed was painfully obvious. At the very least, its financing demanded an increase. But did institutional flaws doom Charles's Scottish campaign? Was the institution to blame, or the royal policies that asked so much from an admittedly understaffed and underfinanced institution?

It is ironic that an institution so close to Whitehall and so centralized under the rather broad authority of the Lieutenant of the Ordnance could be so fragmented and divided against itself. Sir John Heydon shouldered most of the office's responsibilities, and it was his misfortune that the unexpected conflict with the Scots occurred while he laboured to fit out the ship money fleet and restore decaying fortresses on the southern coast. Like the predicament of royal servants in the counties, too many duties too often fell to a single man. Heydon coordinated the office, monitoring daily

---

101 This section is very much influenced by the work of Richard Stewart, particularly his 'The "Irish Road": Military Supply and Arms for Elizabeth's Army during the O'Neill Rebellion, 1598–1601' and 'Arms and Expeditions: The Ordnance Office and the Assaults on Cadiz (1625) and the Isle of Rhé (1627)', in *War and Government in Britain, 1598-1650*, ed. Fissel (Manchester, 1991), pp. 3, 7–8, 16–32, 112–29.

102 'Administrative Reform', p. 245. He notes that greater care was taken in 1640 and that neither can be judged as 'disgraceful' as the Cadiz voyage preparations. For a persuasive corrective to Aylmer's view, see Andrew Thrush, 'The Ordnance Office and the Navy, 1625–40', *The Mariner's Mirror*, 77, no. 4 (November 1991), pp. 339–54. See also Stewart, 'Arms and Expeditions', pp. 112–32. On attempts to reform the Ordnance Office, see M. B. Young, 'Illusions of Grandeur and Reform at the Jacobean Court: Cranfield and the Ordnance', *Historical Journal*, 22, no. 1 (1979), pp. 53–73.

operations while answering for its expenditures to the Exchequer.[103] The Lieutenant found himself caught between the Privy Council and his underlings. Heydon's 'external responsibility for finance conflicted with his subordinates' internal control of expenditure'. The scope of the office's activities increased the pressure. Heydon accounted for all equipment, continued his investigation of royal garrisons, and provided for the ship money fleet. The acrimonious relationship between the Lieutenant and the staff necessarily coloured documents drawn up during investigation of the office. Apart from hyperbolic complaints, however, these inquiries, such as the one undertaken in late 1639, expose the inner workings, strengths, and limitations of the office. Unfortunately, criticism of the Crown's use of the office lay beyond their purview.[104]

The Ordnance Office prepares for war

The royal army envisioned by the King began to coalesce in June 1638. 'My traine of Artillerie consisting of 40: Peece of Ordinance (with the apurtinances,) all Drakes halfe and more of which, ar to be drawen with one or two Horse a peece) is in good forwardness, and I hope will bee reddie within Six Weekes; for I am sure, ther wants nether Monie, nor materials to doe it with'.[105] Vane told Hamilton five days later that the Ordnance officers had received their monies and would be prepared to march in twenty to thirty days.[106] Charles's Privy Council did not hear of the matter, at least formally, until 1 July 1638. A privy seal enabling Heydon to assemble the artillery train did not come until 14 July 1638.[107] If the King expected a complete train in August, he was disappointed, for a train consisted of much more than cannon, carts, horses, powder, shot, and gunners. The office moved swiftly to collect the requisite equipment, once the privy seal had been issued, gathering in stores of spades, pulleys, ladles,

---

[103] Heydon is ubiquitous in Exchequer documents, for example in the Pells issues books kept during the Bishops' Wars (PRO, E 403/1752, 1753, 1754), order books (E 403/2813), naval ordnance declared account (E 351/2663), and privy seals authorizing payments (E 403/2568), listed by date. Also on naval ordnance, see for example PRO, WO 49/69, ff. 112v–113 regarding £14,617 allocated on 12 February 1639 and WO 49/73, ff. 1–47, from August 1639 into autumn 1640.

[104] Aylmer, 'Administrative Reform', p. 243; Thrush, 'The Ordnance Office and the Navy, 1625–40', pp. 348–50.

[105] SRO, GD 406/1/10490, Hamilton Red Book, to Hamilton, 20 June 1638. The forty pieces probably included three demi-cannon, eight culverin, twelve demi-culverins, and twenty-two sakers. See PRO, WO 49/68, f. 8.

[106] SRO, GD 406/1/422, f. 1, 25 June 1638.

[107] Fissel, 'Bellum Episcopale', p. 8; PRO, SP 16/396, f. 3 for the sum of £7,247 by way of imprest. See also E 403/2568, f.72v for £9,756 ordered 5 August 1638, confirmed by SP 16/396, f. 3 and SP 16/395/85 II.

wheels, nails, etc.[108] A myriad of items made up the equipment of the artillery train: spare wheels, ladles, pickaxes, wheel-barrows, linch-pins, 'Palisadoes', 'Handspikes', ropes, shovels, spades, 'Leaver Crowes', 'Formers', 'Spare Ladlestaves', 'Hedging bills', lanterns, sheepskins (for cleaning ordnance), 'Budge Barrells', 'Brasse morters and pestles', nails, leather powder bags, hoops, pitch, tar, scaling ladders, tackle, baskets, horseshoes, and many other items. At least fifty sturdy horses and several types of carriage were required as well.[109] However, the demands upon the office came at a particularly bad time.

The needs of the navy, coupled with renovation of southern defence points, had depleted stores to an unusually low level. In December 1637 garrisons and forts located on England's southern coast and the Channel Islands reported deficiencies in their ability to repel an invasion force. The success of French arms on the continent had convinced them to look to their weapons. Sir John Manwood, Lieutenant of Dover Castle, reported that the castle's defences had lapsed into an advanced state of decay. The garrison possessed 'not one Muskett or Bandelere for a Musket serviceable'. As for pikes, a survey of 1632 had revealed that 300 were either broken or in some way unfit for use. Since the defective pikes had not been replaced there 'remayneth but a small number fitt for service'. The castle bulwark required extensive repair, as did the garrison's church, whose steeple had partly collapsed. On the ramparts facing the sea only a single demi-culverin lay in place, the other cannon being strewn about on the ground for lack of proper carriages and mountings. Nor could the night watch keep guard effectively, as only one workable lantern was available.[110]

Conditions were little better on the Isles of Scilly. The Governor, Sir Francis Godolphin, noted that supplies had arrived, but until the fortress was enlarged and repaired storage of those supplies was impossible. In manpower, the garrison was so deficient that a defence of the island was impossible even with the active assistance of local civilians. Godolphin

108 PRO, WO 49/68, esp. ff. 5–15, and WO 49/71, ff. 12v–16, 22v–23v and WO 49/72, ff. 10–25 for contracts and expenditures.

109 For structure, see PRO, SP 16/397/55; for equipment, see PRO, WO 49/68, ff. 5v, 10v–15; for the pay in 1639, see SP 16/415/27; SP 16/415/35; SP 16/415/89; SP 16/415/91; SP 16/438/24; for the Second Bishops' War, SP 16/442/15; SP 16/444/59; SP 16/447/95 and SP 16/457/29.

110 PRO, SP 16/385/4, 4 I, and 4 II, Manwood and Increased Collins on conditions at Dover, *circa* March 1638. SP 16/387/38 provides an inventory of ordnance and ammunition at Dover when Manwood took over on 26 April 1637. HMC Cowper, Coke MSS., p. 187, letter of 3 July 1638 regarding Manwood's dispute with the Dover magistrates; also, for example, Heydon's £4,495 for garrisons of Guernsey and Alderney 19 August 1638, in PRO, PC 2/49, f. 394; also PC 2/50, f. 134, ordnance and arms for Plymouth garrison, 3 March 1639; SP 16/382/59; 60; 61; 62. On expenditures for the southern forts, see PRO, E 403/2568, ff. 50–1.

closed on a sour note by reminding the council that 'wee are at this present much necessitated by reson of our want of paye there being near two yeeres and a halfe ... owing to the soldiers'.[111] The lack of money and arms was symptomatic of the general decrepitude of royal fortresses. The problems of the southern forts were formidable. The restocking of stores and weapons was complicated since no big arms supplier existed in London. The office purchased armaments from numerous small producers who could not supply arms on the continental scale.[112]

The King's unreasonable expectations were reinforced by reliance upon a single man to brief him about the Ordnance Office's situation. Charles's information came from the Earl of Newport who, as Master of the Ordnance, did not involve himself in the daily operations of the office; Sir John Heydon served as the chief executive officer. In fact Newport complained that in 1639 the staff routinely transacted important business without his knowledge and sometimes refused to obey his warrants.[113] The tenuous linkage between the Master (who was quite literally at the King's side) and his primary administrator, Heydon, required memoranda. The earl knew only as much as Heydon's reports told him, yet the King expected answers momentarily. Newport only discovered the plight of the office when he inquired as to its readiness.[114] Captain Coningsby, who inspected the quality of the contractors' weapons, lay ill; Edward Sherburne, who kept the accounts that Heydon maintained for inspection by the Exchequer of Receipt, languished in gaol. The clerk of deliveries, who kept track of the issuing and recovery of the Crown's weapons, was not in London. Several clerks to these officers remained absent. The master gunner had died, with no replacement yet selected, and the yeomen of the ordnance and the gunners were apparently stationed elsewhere. The office was as understaffed as it was exhausted of supplies. Charles chose to be oblivious to this situation as preparations proceeded.[115]

The challenges faced by the Ordnance Office entailed contracting and importing sufficient arms and equipment from a variety of suppliers, then inspecting, packing, and dispatching them north. At Kingston-upon-Hull the office maintained a key supply depot, though frequently caches of arms piled up at locations further north, such as Newcastle and Holy Island.[116]

---

[111] For Godolphin and his garrisons in 1640 see PRO, E 403/2568, ff.121–3.
[112] The contractual arrangements for such purchases are well documented in the various order books preserved at the Kew PRO. See for example WO 49/68, purchases for the artillery train, and WO 55/455 and 456, warrants relating to stores, 1638–41.
[113] Aylmer, 'Administrative Reform', p. 243; PRO, SP 16/436/48, 30 December 1639.
[114] PRO, SP 16/397/37, 'An answere to his Lordshipp's propositions', dated 9 August 1638. See Aylmer's comments on Oppenheim's taking Heydon's remarks out of context, 'Administrative Reform', p. 245, n. 5.
[115] See Andrew Thrush's verdict in 'The Ordnance Office and the Navy', p. 346.
[116] Bodleian Library, Clarendon SP, XV, f. 38, for Legge's reports on the buildup.

Scores of vessels found employment ferrying the tools of war along the eastern coast, while keel boats later carried shipments to Selby and York from the Hull magazine.[117] The volume of war material compounded the problem of distance. The First Bishops' War drew more heavily upon the Ordnance Office stores than the 1625 and 1627 campaigns combined, with regard to great ordnance, powder and musket shot. In 1639, the office issued 62 pieces of great ordnance, 166 lasts of powder, and 80 tons of musket shot. The aggregate for Cadiz and Rhé equalled 32 pieces of ordnance, 152 lasts of powder, and 57 tons of musket shot.[118] Hamilton's expedition posed the greatest challenge, for his lines of supply would be stretched to the utmost.[119]

In spite of shortages and delays, arms arrived and were distributed at Hull.[120] The Ordnance Office achieved no small measure of success in simply delivering the arms, although in 1640 the failure to get the large ordnance to the front rendered the office's efforts useless. But the task asked of the Ordnance Office was too onerous for the time and resources Charles had allocated. Heydon's prediction that the office's means and manpower were spread much too thin came true. The departure for the north had fragmented the Ordnance much as it had the Council of War and, to a lesser extent, the machinery for paying troops from the Receipt. The Lieutenant had informed the King personally, three weeks prior to the journey to York, that the understaffing of the office would hinder the mobilization of an artillery train. Newport had not made adequate arrangements prior to his own departure, and his disclosure that the King wished to make a second artillery train available (though surely not as substantial as the one destined for the north) 'in these southerne parts' increased the burden beyond the institution's capabilities. Newport's laxity was a failure of leadership, not of the institution, and the second artillery train was a bad idea on the part of the King.

In the midst of the spring 1639 mobilization the few Ordnance personnel available scattered throughout the realm. Four engineers attended Newport at York. The battery master went south to assist with the second

---

[117] Stafford RO, Dartmouth MS. D(w) 1778/I/i/5 details the cargoes dispatched to the Yorkshire rendezvous points. For further lighterage charges see PRO, WO 49/71, ff. 24v–25, 26v–27; WO 49/72, f. 36.

[118] PRO, SP 16/433/37.

[119] For a personal view of the problem, see the efforts to fit the colliers serving as troop transports with sufficient ground tackle in SRO, GD 406/1/814, 12 April 1639. Spring was a difficult time for the provision of large proportions of victual since the supply was seasonal, as was pointed out in GD 406/1/815, 17 May 1639, to Hamilton. See also GD 406/1/935, Hamilton's instructions on 6 May 1639. The Marquis did complain of the Ordnance Office's backwardness in delivering ammunition, further evidence that the distribution of arms was slow. See GD 406/1/940, to Windebank, 15 April 1639.

[120] PRO, SP 16/438/10.

artillery train. The Clerk of the Ordnance worked at Portsmouth delivering provisions to the royal navy, while Mr Sherburne attended at Yarmouth by order of the Privy Council (helping out with Hamilton's expedition).[121] Two of the ablest and most experienced clerks accompanied Newport as keepers of the magazines of the train and army, so that only a solitary man remained to discharge the duties of Clerk of the Ordnance at the Tower. Other officers were dispersed, one at Dover (though recently summoned to Newcastle), one had disappeared and another was insubordinate. Brooks the cannoneer lay sick in Kent, whilst officers tried to press ten more cannoneers.

Probably Heydon drew upon the talents of master gunners in the royal navy who held gunners' places in the Tower. Enrolled on a list of the skeleton staff available were 'Filcott' and 'Dalbye', two of four Gentlemen of the Ordnance. The former may have been Peter Filcott of the *Prince Royall* and the latter Gerald Dalby of the *Due Repulse*.[122] The gist of Heydon's assessment was that 'so many ymployments as well for sea as land service at once are on foote, and so litle tyme and so few hands to afford assistance'. Had orders been 'seasonably' given and the 'accustomed course of the office observed', the King would have been better served. The demands placed on the Ordnance Office asked too much of too few. Extraordinary monies (above and beyond the 'Grand Proportion' designated) had not yet been received.[123] The hastiness of the expedition, of which Heydon complained, was the fault of the King.

On 30 December 1639, when planning for the Second Bishops' War was under way, the Ordnance Office became the target of reforming councillors. Newport himself raised the issue of inefficiency before the Council of War. An investigative committee was appointed to oversee and review operations; it consisted of councillors who were familiar with the technical and logistical problems of war, but not associated formally with the office. Newport, not surprisingly, wanted it made clear who was in charge. Nicholas noted that:

there are some differences betweene his Lordshipp and the Officers of the Ordinance who act diverse services themselves without his Lordshipps notice, and refuse to obey his Lordshipps warrants in some businesses and alleage that they do so by vertue of certeyn Instructions which are given to that office for ordering of the affaires and service belonging to the same.

---

[121] For example, SRO, GD 406/1/941, Hamilton to Sherburne, 17 April 1639.
[122] Birmingham Reference Library, Coventry papers, DV 896/200, for Filcott's grant of a gunner's place on 5 June 1632; for Dalby see PRO, SO 3/12, March 1639. Andrew Thrush provided these references.
[123] BL, Coke MSS. C60/22a and 22b, 18 April 1639. Andrew Thrush transcribed this letter and enclosure.

The King instructed Newport to record the specific disputes and 'particular exceptions'.[124] The bureaucratic sprawl and over-extension of personnel had made the Ordnance Office more quarrelsome then ever.

The investigative committee, appointed in October 1639, consisted of Juxon, Arundel, Dorset, Cottington, Coke, and Windebank. Neither Newport nor Heydon sat. The committee queried the officers on matters ranging from the supply of carbines, match, and timber, to the presentation of a 'Modell' musket stock to the King for his personal inspection.[125] In addition to this extraordinary committee, Lord Conway, Sir Jacob Astley, and Sir Nicholas Byron, all officers in the royal army, were instructed to 'advise' on equipping the King's forces. Newport's complaint of 30 December no doubt stemmed from the fact that he was under scrutiny by the Privy Council and court, and that his underlings now looked to the committee as the ultimate authority, which effectively divided authority and confused an already tangled bureaucracy. The newly appointed committee held greater sway than the Master of the Ordnance. Hence the establishment of the committee exacerbated the already disrupted lines of authority inherent in the office's procedures.

The arms market, 1638–1640

In addition to putting in order Newport's relationship with the under-officers, the committee also inquired into the solicitation of fees which could be considered bribes or forms of extortion. These bribes were believed partly responsible for the high prices the Crown paid. Firearms sold on the open market for less than the Crown had paid to the Gun-makers' Company. An inquiry was to be made to ascertain the lowest prices at which muskets, carbines, and pistols could be obtained from domestic gunsmiths. Complaints of this nature were nothing new. The office's purchasing procedures were not always observed. If sums imprested were insufficient, the officers sometimes ordered more weapons and then set about trying to raise the balance from the Crown after the fact.[126] Officers sometimes conspired with manufacturers so that the Crown paid exorbitantly. Like the divisive quarrelling within the office, these complaints were characteristic of the early Stuart Ordnance Office in general, not just the particular performance in 1639. Another reason why the prices the government paid were higher than current market levels was

---

124 PRO, SP 16/436/38, Nicholas's notes, 30 December 1639.
125 On Charles's interest in military gadgetry, see M. Fissel, 'The Identity of John Bishop, Gunner, 1625', *JSAHR*, 68, no. 274 (summer 1990), pp. 138–9 and 'Tradition and Invention in the Early Stuart Art of War', *JSAHR*, 65, no. 263 (autumn 1987), pp. 133–47.
126 PRO, SP 16/457/108.

the office's tardiness in paying its bills. The financial weakness of the office (the annual budget being a paltry £6,000) drove up prices, since arms merchants were unsure as to when payment would be forthcoming. 'Poor royal credit meant paying excessive prices.'[127] When asked about extraordinary fees Heydon claimed that:

hee never demanded or received any more or other fee, allowance or acknowledgement, but barely and only the same sixpence on the pound that from the first institution was allowed ... and hitherto hath forborne to receive any Poundage of the wages yearely payable to the Officers, Clerks, and all other the Members of that office, so to this day hee hath forborne to take the Poundage of the Powder Monies, the charges in receiving and discompting whereof have bene the same with other the monies by him received and disbursed, and his paines therein much greater.[128]

The officers of the Ordnance enjoyed an arrangement similar to the army officers' 'dead pays'. The Lieutenant of the Ordnance, officers, and clerks retained a percentage of the business transacted. The more arms and powder were bought, the greater their salaries. In theory, this policy paid officers according to their labour, but was conducive to corruption, that is, price gouging so that the Crown paid more, resulting in bonuses for the officers and excessive profits for the arms merchants. Two types of allegations were made, that officers received 'kick-backs' from arms merchants and that they conspired with the merchants to inflate prices. Francis Coningsby, the Surveyor of the Ordnance testified:

hee never demanded any Fee from any Artificer or others bringing in Provisions into his Majesties Stoares; though it is true that some of them after they received their Monies, have voluntarily and freely (according to the quality and disposicion of the party and the some of Money by them receaved) sometymes presented him with some small gratuity, yet hee hath not either directly or indirectly at any time or upon any Consideracion advanced the King's price to the value of one Farthing for any perticuler ends or advantage to himselfe.[129]

Coningsby drew an annual salary of £36 10s, while his allowance upon the ordinary amounted to £56, being two years in arrears. The Crown owed him £92 10s. The Clerk of the Ordnance and the Keeper of the Stores told the council that inflation rendered insufficient the customary fees granted to the officers. The allowance for the officers had been established during the reign of Henry VIII, when twelve pence went further than ten shillings in 1640.[130] According to Heydon, Coningsby, Sherburne, and

---

[127] Aylmer, 'Administrative Reform', p. 244. See Andrew Thrush's incisive comments in 'The Ordnance Office and the Navy', pp. 348–51.
[128] PRO, SP 16/441/11.
[129] PRO, SP 16/441/11, 2 January 1640.
[130] PRO, SP 16/441/12, 13, 2 January 1640. Conrad Russell, 'Parliament and the King's Finances' in his *The Origins of the English Civil War*, p. 95.

March, Ordnance Office salaries had not kept pace with the inflationary trend which simultaneously made the cheap purchase of good arms increasingly difficult. Not only did market conditions make guns more expensive due to continental wars, but the transition from the relatively simple matchlocks to the more intricate and expensive wheel-locks and snaphaunces made firearms exceedingly highly priced. Regardless of whether the Ordnance Officers conspired with the Gunmakers and the arms manufacturers to boost prices, the cost of arms was most certainly on the rise during the era of the Thirty Years' War, as were the costs of food and transport for armies.[131]

The relative immaturity of the English domestic arms market induced the Crown to purchase foreign-made weapons, a reality which Charles I grasped immediately. The first Englishman to seek out arms abroad for the impending mobilization was John Quarles, a merchant whose ancestors had served Elizabeth in a similar capacity. When the King told Hamilton that he had already 'sent for armes to Holland for tenn Thousand Foote and two Thousand horse', he referred to Quarles's mission, which began in spring 1638. As Charles intended originally to field 35,000 foot, Quarles aimed to arm about a third of the proposed army.[132] To plunge into the frenetic weapons market during the Thirty Years' War entailed certain risks, especially when a private merchant carried the responsibility of contracting for massive quantities of weapons, destination unknown. Sir Jacob Astley assisted Quarles in the Low Countries, as he was a veteran of the Thirty Years' War and had recently inspected the trained bands. He realized that the firearms should be of uniform bore, for variations in calibre would wreak havoc in supplying ammunition to the English militia.[133]

Perhaps Charles hesitated to place his initial orders in the more visible London arms market for fear of alerting the Covenanters; it was more discreet to buy muskets and pikes across the Channel, but also more expensive in carriage and customs duties. However, security dictated the safer, more anonymous route of using a private citizen well-versed in the ways of Dutch commerce to obtain the arms. Quarles spent over £38,000 overseas, though this figure includes freight and £2,391 in Dutch customs duties. He shipped the weapons across the Channel, and William Legge inspected and catalogued them into the royal stores.[134] Their quality left

131 Fissel, 'Scottish War and English Money', pp. 193–7.
132 SRO, GD 406/1/10490, Hamilton Red Book, the King to Hamilton, 20 June 1638. See PRO, E 351/2711, Quarles's declared account. See this work, pp. 112–14.
133 BL, Coke MS. C 59/11a, Astley to Coke, 6 October 1638. Andrew Thrush transcribed this letter.
134 PRO, E 351/2711; PRO, SP 16/404/52 I and SP 16/421/76. Charles should have started the English arms manufacturers as soon as possible. However, since they could only produce

something to be desired. Some pikes had rotted, the firearms were badly assembled and of different bores, and some bandoleers were lined with brown paper and flimsy, poorly tanned leather.[135] These disappointments may have spurred on Charles's negotiations with domestic suppliers, particularly for swords and guns.[136]

The officers of the Ordnance often expressed scepticism about the quality of foreign weapons. Since their salaries drew heavily upon fees and arrangements with domestic arms contractors, the purchase of weapons from abroad robbed them of perquisites. Here lay a problem of some magnitude, for a major expedition such as that envisioned by the King required more arms and equipment than could be supplied by domestic manufacturers in less than a year. A more plentifully supplied Ordnance Office would have rectified the problem. When foreign weapons were imported they had to be judged by the officers and the English arms-makers, the two parties most hostile to their intrusion into the market. Quarles encountered this problem, as did Sir Thomas Roe.

On 11 March 1639, little more than a fortnight before the rendezvous at York, Juxon and Coke instructed Ambassador Sir Thomas Roe to purchase immediately arms for infantry and cavalry at Hamburg.[137] He contracted with Albert Bearnes, the Danish King's arms merchant, for 3,000 muskets (standard and shortened), 1,500 pikes, armour for horse and foot, firelock pistols and other accoutrements, costing over 20,000 rix dollars (a northern European monetary unit used in international commerce, valued between 2s 3d and 4s 6d). As Roe reached into his own pocket, assured that the Exchequer would reimburse him through a bill of exchange, his venture was as costly as it was inconvenient. Still attending to ambassadorial duties, he had no time to inspect thousands of weapons individually, but he did arrange for their examination by several veteran commanders, who adjudged the arms as comparable in quality with those in use in the Thirty Years' War. Loaded on the English ship *William and Daniel*, they were conveyed to the Tower by the end of April 1639. There they encountered their greatest hurdle, for in spite of Roe's efforts these weapons apparently never saw service in 1639 or 1640. The officers of the Ordnance who had already shaken their heads over the quality of Quarles's consignment now balked at receiving Roe's shipment. In fact, they simply refused to take the weapons into the royal stores, so that the new weapons were badly stored and became damaged and rusted. No officer

so many, and since they were at least in proximity to the Tower, obtaining the foreign weapons might well have been Charles's top priority.
[135] PRO, SP 16/404/110 III and 110 III 1, 7 December 1638; SP 16/427/98, 28 August 1639.
[136] PRO, WO 49/71, ff. 56–74.
[137] PRO, SP 16/458/98.

would lift a finger to keep the Hamburg arms cleaned and oiled; they lay derelict.[138] Such actions can only be explained as the officers' attempt to protect their purchasing system and salaries from the incursion of foreign imports. The King's war became a secondary consideration, through self-ishness masked as quality control.[139] Examination of 3,191 firearms pur-chased through Roe revealed that one-third of the muskets were 'under bore' (smaller calibre), while 1,513 of the 2,356 bastard muskets were alle-gedly unserviceable due to short barrels, defective works, stocks, locks, or undersized bores.[140] The judges had a vested interest in the verdict, however, for they were Henry Rowland, Warner Pynn, and Robert Compton, substantial London gunmakers, in effect evaluating foreign competitors' workmanship. Imported arms may have been disgraced, but nonetheless the utility of foreign arms purchases remained a viable alter-native to sole reliance upon native arms-makers. The shabby treatment of Roe's arms, more than bureaucratic disharmony, and faulty book-keeping, exposes the Ordnance Office's worst characteristics. No excuse justifies the wanton refusal to maintain the Hamburg weapons during a time of war. Regardless of the suspicious scepticism of the London gunmakers, the majority, if not all, of the imported arms could have been salvaged. All of this reflects on the ill-judged decision to go to war before everything was ready.

In December 1639 the government contemplated a grand scheme to obtain weapons for an army of 60,000 foot and 3,000 horse, amounting to a cost of £65,564. This included £3,850 for weapons apparently already contracted for through Sir Thomas Roe. The new consignment consisted of £5,223 worth of cavalry arms and there was a hefty £56,491 to equip an infantry of 16,256 pikemen and 16,257 musketeers.[141] Even if the order were placed immediately, at the New Year, the armourers could not fashion the whole quantity of pikeman's arms until late 1643! Perhaps the King or his servants hoped to solve their weapons problems once and for all. If the domestic manufacturers were going to be relied upon to this extent, then the order should have been placed in the spring of 1638, when Charles had sent Quarles abroad. Again, poor judgement by the Crown hamstrung the Ordnance Office.

Rather than plunge back into the Hamburg market, the Crown in 1640 sent Sir Job Harby into Flanders with £17,000 (in three installments by way of imprest).[142] Meanwhile the Council of War and the Ordnance Office

---

[138] PRO, SP 16/458/98, 100, 101, depositions of Sir Thomas Roe.
[139] PRO, SP 16/427/98. See also the council summons to Mr Ashwell in SP 16/433/37, f. 2.
[140] PRO, SP 16/427/98.
[141] PRO, SP 16/435/87.
[142] See Harby's account, PRO, E 351/2712.

resolved that in 1640 a greater effort would be made to secure the relatively scarce handguns and carbines from domestic weapons manufacturers, which would make quality supervision easier and eliminate the shipping expense. Likewise, the purchases would invigorate the English arms industry, and less currency would be spent abroad. It was decided that the Crown should contract with the London Gunmakers' Company for the complicated but reliable wheel-lock and snaphaunce carbines and pistols. Prior to 1637 English guns were fashioned by blacksmiths (who cast the barrels) and locksmiths (who produced and attached the gunlocks). Such an arrangement was not conducive to professionalization, high quality manufacture, or technological innovation, since production was divided between two companies. Charles I had incorporated the Company in 1638 and its formation simplified the purchase of firearms (since the Crown could deal with the manufacturers as a whole), but the arrangement was not entirely satisfactory.[143] The price of guns remained high, since materials and highly skilled labour were still at a premium. Independent, particularly foreign, gunsmiths were discouraged from working in the metropolis, which stifled competition and kept costs high. In addition, the newer, complicated gunlocks required the services of an experienced gunsmith while the old matchlocks could be repaired by a good blacksmith. The London Blacksmiths, supported by the Armourers' Company, had opposed the enrolment of the Gunmakers' Company.[144] Repairs on an expedition would be increasingly difficult and costly to effect. The more sophisticated the firearms of Charles's expeditionary force, the more gunsmiths would be needed to accompany the army north.

In spite of the creation of the Gunmakers' Company, firearms' purchases had to be arranged through a variety of manufacturers. Gunsmiths could now bargain collectively, as they did in a sense by enumerating the hindrances, delays, and costs they tolerated when attempting to secure payment from the Ordnance Office.[145] The structure of arms manufacture in England, then, compelled the Crown to place orders early and pay its bills punctually. The craftsmen had, on an individual basis, limited production capacity. A large number of weapons demanded the planning and negotiation of quite a few contracts, and the specialities and idiosyncracies of each arms maker had to be dealt with. Since the members of the Gunmakers' Company worked with comparatively modest capital, they needed

---

[143] Guildhall Library MS. 5228, roll of vellum with seal, charter of incorporation granted under the Privy Seal, dated 14 March 1638. Corporation of London Records Office, *Journals of the Court of Common Council*, XXXVIII, ff. 60–67v.

[144] See the *Repertories* of the Court of Aldermen of the City of London (1558–1650), in the Corporation of London Records Office, *Rep.* 52, f. 221v (12 July 1638) and *Rep.* 53, f. 289 (26 Sept. 1639).

[145] PRO, SP 16/435/85.

to be paid on time to maintain solvency and keep the weapons production system in operation. The Crown therefore had to pay a lot (for no significant wholesale discounts or intensive competition amongst producers existed under this system) and plan ahead. Finally, the Gunmakers needed time and practice if they were to perfect the art of fashioning the new gunlocks, and make them more reliable and cheaper. They explained to the council, 'The afore mentioned carbines and pistolls have not beene here many yeares in use, nor long beene made, and we doubt not but here after upon Encouragement we shalbe more ready in the makinge of them and soe shall afford them at cheaper rates.'[146]

The Gunmakers, however, wished to resolve some unfinished business before undertaking to supply Charles's new expeditionary force. More than a third of the 10,000 muskets they had supplied in the First Bishops' War had still not been paid for. If the King wished the Gunmakers to set about making 2,000 muskets per month, immediate payment was necessary. Without 'ready money att the rate agreed upon', they could not complete the work already undertaken for the Second Bishops' War, as their stores were depleted. The Gunmakers enumerated the obstacles and individuals they had to circumnavigate before obtaining payment: a warrant signed by Newport had to be issued, attesting to the manufacture and testing of the weapons prior to acceptance into the royal stores. The officers who inspected firearms demanded a fee, and, upon approval, rendered a charge. The time which elapsed between the arrival of the arms at the Tower and their certification made for a significant and costly delay in recovering the manufacturer's investment. A bill of impress, which would get money from the clerk of the Lieutenant of the Ordnance, also required a warrant. The speed with which that clerk, Mr Strechy, processed the Gunmakers' bill depended on the size of the gratuity. A small fee provoked a delay of several days. Similar fees had to be paid to the keeper servant of the small gun office, the surveyor, and those officers who handled their debentures. The heaviest fee was the fifty shillings deducted by Mr Strechy for every £100 they received.[147] From the Gunmakers' point of view, selling firearms to the Crown entailed three drawbacks: complex bureaucratic procedures, excessive fees and late payment.

The relationship between the Crown and the manufacturers was not entirely collective. Individual gunmakers contracted to produce specific numbers of certain types of firearms, especially wheel-locks and snap-haunces.[148] For example, on 20 December 1639, each of twenty-seven

---

[146] PRO, SP 16/441/75, 9 January 1640.
[147] PRO, SP 16/438/33, petition conjecturally dated late 1639. See also Thrush, 'The Ordnance Office and the Navy', p. 350.
[148] PRO, WO 49/76, f. 10 for snaphaunces.

London gunmakers listed the number of muskets he would manufacture monthly for the Crown at a price of sixteen shillings and sixpence. Individual gunmakers would receive 'redy monyes' before beginning to make the firearms, and 'bee freed from paying any manner of Charges out of it and the charge of the proofe for powder and shott bee allowed to us as is usuall'.[149] The same principle was applied to the making of wheel-locks and snaphaunces for the officers and dragoons. Ten gunmakers agreed to manufacture 80 pairs of wheel-lock pistols, 120 wheel-lock carbines, 200 'Spanish' carbines, 300 'halfe-bent' snaphaunce carbines, and 200 pairs of 'halfe bent' snaphaunce pistols. Each gunmaker specified a quota. For example Thomas Barnes promised to deliver monthly 5 pairs of wheel-lock pistols, 5 wheel-lock carbines, 13 'Spanish' carbines, and 20 'halfe-bent' snaphaunce pistols. Each gunmaker manufactured a percentage of each type of firearm ordered.[150] There was no specialization of the kind where certain manufacturers monopolized the production of particular types of gunlock.

During the First Bishops' War, the King's commanders (Astley, for instance) requested more wheel-locks and snaphaunces. The nobles summoned in spring 1639 found the new-style pistols hard to come by.[151] There are several reasons why guns fitted with the wheel-lock and snaphaunce were slow in displacing the matchlock. First of all, the newer, more complicated mechanisms were more expensive to make as opposed to the straightforward design of the matchlock. Secondly, England was insulated from direct and sustained involvement in the Thirty Years' War. Consequently, domestic arms makers in England did not keep abreast of the technological improvements in firearms manufacture as closely as did their continental counterparts. Any quality arms that were made were snapped up, like English gunpowder and iron ordnance, by the continental buyers.

The King's purveyors fared better with edge weapons. With a Scottish war imminent in 1638, the Crown was fortunate in that Benjamin Stone, a maverick sword-merchant, was engaged in an effort to break the London Cutlers' Company's virtual monopoly on supplying the Ordnance Office with blades. Stone succeeded, to the degree that he was appointed 'Cutler for the Office of the Ordnance' during the Scots' rebellion.[152] Stone's challenge to the Cutlers comprised an important chapter in early Stuart weapons manufacture. In 1629 Sir William Heydon and King Charles invited German swordsmiths from Solingen to settle in England and

---

[149] PRO, SP 16/436/18.

[150] PRO, WO 49/71, ff. 52v–53, 55–8, 66–74.

[151] HMC Buccleuch, Montagu MSS., p. 282, letter of William Montagu to his father, 14 March 1639.

[152] PRO, SP 16/407/60, SP 16/407/61, undated petitions whose contents date them as *circa* 1638–9.

manufacture their wares in the continental fashion. It is quite possible that Charles was dissatisfied with the quality and cost of blades provided out of the stores of the Ordnance Office during the war years of the 1620s. The Solingen swordsmiths resided around Hounslow, west of London, although some lived at Greenwich, where the royal armouries had employed foreign (especially German) craftsmen during the Tudor period.[153] The Solingen craftsmen forged an alliance with Stone, a Sussex man once apprenticed to the London Cutlers' Company.

Hounslow's suitability as a site for a swordmill was enhanced by its distance from the City and the Cutlers' jurisdiction. Windsor Castle, with its capacity as a royal arsenal, lay only a few miles distant, and blades could be transported to the Tower via the Thames. Stone assisted the Solingen swordsmiths in managing the mills and marketing the blades. Englishmen were employed in the Hounslow factory, while German craftsmen acted as supervisors and shared their expertise. Stone was the key figure in retailing the Hounslow blades. He had fallen foul of the Cutlers and was only too happy to undermine their business. In 1630 the Company had judged him in contempt of an order forbidding him to stamp the mark of a bunch of grapes upon his blades.[154] The episode was the first blow in a long war. By his own admission, Stone had also got into trouble with several London lenders, going so far as to request from the King a letter of protection, 'being indebted to persons in the city of London, he dares not walk about in respect they threaten to arrest him'. Stone received support from Attorney-General Bankes and Solicitor-General Littleton, who annexed to the petition a statement confirming Stone's claim to have expended a great deal of money in manufacturing blades for the King's stores, and that he had 2,000 swords available for immediate delivery. Without 'present money', Bankes and Littleton continued, Stone was 'like to be undone.'[155]

Stone exploited the complaints of royal servants, including Sir Thomas Wentworth, in his attack upon the quality of the swords of the Cutlers' Company. In his petitions he often equated the prosperity of his swordmill with the good and safety of the realm. On the eve of the Bishops' Wars, Stone petitioned the Council of War, extolling the excellence of his blades for use in the royal army. He said that his swords were the finest ever supplied to the Tower, implying that the Cutlers' blades were of inferior

153 J. F. Hayward, 'English Swords 1600–1650', *Arms and Armor Annual*, ed. R. Held (Northfield, Ill., 1973), vol. I, pp. 158–60; M. B. Colket, 'The Jenks Family of England', *The New England Historical and Genealogical Register*, 110 (January 1956), p. 206. See the map between pp. 205 and 206.
154 Colket, 'The Jenks Family', pp. 14–19; Charles Welch, *History of the Cutlers' Company* (London, 1922), vol. II, p. 346.
155 CSPD (1636–7), X, p. 45.

quality. He pledged security for producing a thousand swords per month, and requested the Council of War to order the Cutlers to stop harassing his business.[156] Stone also took steps to prevent domestic swordsmiths from striking foreign marks upon their blades, particularly those of Spanish producers. In so petitioning Stone suggested that the Cutlers and other domestic swordmakers were passing off their own work as high quality foreign blades. Although Stone had been affiliated with the Ordnance Office as a 'blade-maker' and 'Cutler', his association ceased sometime in 1639, for reasons unknown. In a petition addressed to the Master of the Ordnance, Stone described himself as 'Blademaker on Hounsloe Heath' and requested a warrant to bring swords into the royal stores. Stone produced many blades for Charles's expeditionary force, but the size of the army led the King to secure edge weapons from a variety of sources, including London cutlers Robert South and Nicholas Brether and foreign importers.[157] The Cutlers' Company retrieved the gauntlet that Stone had tossed before them, and tried to discredit him. Stone had no patent, nor any right to one, since he was not among the original importers of this particular type of manufacture. Stone had brought before Captain Legge 600 blades of questionable origin, even though he had promised 3,000. Although the Cutlers had accepted the condition that they must sell to the Crown on credit, Stone had refused to deliver any more swords without ready cash, hardly patriotic conduct. Worse, he had incited some soldiers to damage their weapons so as to make the Cutlers' blades look inferior.

The Cutlers further alleged that the officers of the Ordnance and many of the common soldiers were in league with Stone. To eliminate Stone's influence at the Tower the Cutlers advocated that the Ordnance Office be relieved of the duty of proving swords, or inspecting the wares brought into the Tower, and rejecting them if they did not meet royal standards. The Cutlers suggested that the inspection procedure had been so corrupted that Stone and his cronies could easily secure approval of their poor quality swords and then discourage purchases from the Cutlers' Company. 'There is a difference betweene the offices of th'ordnance and armoury which hath bin the cause of this Resurvey and proofe againe' and the Officers 'may defect as manie of ours on purpose to make roome for Stone who is theire Engin to restore theire lost profitt; whereas the swords now in question for a Resurvey are as good as those receaved into the office of ordnance and much better then Stones and cheaper to the King by 500£'. The Cutlers closed by asking that, if a resurvey should be undertaken, the Council

---

[156] PRO, SP 16/407/61.
[157] Hayward, 'English Swords', p. 156. For debentures between Stone and the Ordnance, see PRO, WO 49/71, ff. 9, 53v, 62v, 64v–65. For Robert South, see ff. 9v, 10, and for Nicholas Brether, see f. 10.

would delay until the return of the Master of the Ordnance or the Master of the Armoury[158]. The Council of War did purchase 3,000 blades from Stone's Hounslow factory for use in the Second Bishops' War. But its biggest order, for 22,503 swords, was divided between Stone and his competitors because a single manufacturer could not produce such a large number of weapons.[159]

Arms procurement and logistics

The quarrels of the gunmakers and the feuding of the swordmakers underscore the fact that many of the problems of supplying a royal army stemmed from the immaturity and fragmentation of the English arms industry. For all its woes, the Ordnance Office contended with the capricious demands of the central government and the inelasticity of domestic weapons manufacture. One must keep in mind that the English arms makers, from common founders to handgun-makers, were more involved in continental war profiteering (as was the Crown, for that matter, from 1629 to 1638) than in building up an arsenal in the Tower.[160] Short-term revenues took precedence over long-term military preparedness. The King in 1638 had only himself to blame. He had shown little inclination to streamline the Ordnance Office for any future war, or the Exchequer for that matter. One would think that Charles's interest in military matters, as witnessed in the 1620s, would have encouraged him to evaluate the capability of his government if threatened by war. The central government seemed impervious to change when compared to the reforming pressures placed upon the counties – the Book of Orders, the perfect militia, and ship money. Perhaps Charles knew what historians have sometimes forgotten: central institutions, whatever their flaws, had proved efficacious; innovation might bring breakdown. As Richard Stewart has demonstrated, new life could be breathed into old bodies. Those bodies, though, had limited endurance.

Contemporaries, such as Sir Francis Windebank, were inclined to point to the slackness of individuals, rather than to any belief in institutional weakness: 'there is no little neglect in the officers of the Ordnance; and if

---

[158] PRO, SP 16/377/47, 'Reasons humbly offered by the London Cutlers as to why the Office of Ordnance should not prove swords'.

[159] PRO, SP 16/441/83, Council of War notes, 10 January 1640; SP 16/442/32, 18 January 1640.

[160] See Reeve, *Charles I and the Road to Personal Rule*, p. 207. It was at this time, too, that Swedish iron cannon competed with English ordnance in the continental marketplace. After 1638, in fact, Swedish ordnance was being imported into England. See C. M. Cipolla, *Guns, Sails, and Empires: Technological Innovation and the Early Phases of European Expansion 1400–1700* (New York, 1965), pp. 54–64.

the Master of that office be not quicker with them, your Majestys service will dangerously suffer'.[161] Criticism of the institutional nature of the Ordnance Office has been perpetuated by historians. Corruption, inefficiency, understaffing, and nepotism most certainly plagued the institution. But with the scholarship of Andrew Thrush and Richard Stewart a healthy revision of the history of the Ordnance Office is now under way. The fact is that in 1639 and 1640, as in 1598 to 1601, 1625, and 1627, the Ordnance delivered the goods. Besides delivering the equipment, the Ordnance Office succeeded in mustering a small array of support personnel, all of whom were paid, in 1639, the sum of £5,800,[162] and, in 1640, £6,326 8s 8d.[163] The material may not have been the best, but the cause of that problem lay with the under-financing of the office and the Crown's unwillingness to provide adequate time, facilities, and staff for the purchase and preservation of war goods. In both Bishops' Wars the train of artillery got under way. Its tardiness in reaching the front had much to do with the manner in which the King and his councillors orchestrated the mobilization. The Ordnance, like the perfect militia, never received an adequate test in 1639–40. In 1639 a settlement was reached before the combatants came to blows. In 1640, rapid deployment of Scottish men and cannon proved decisive at Newburn ford. The English ordnance was for the most part still at Hull. Most of the English forces were deployed in the wrong areas. Deployment was affected by slowly arriving pay as well as by logistical hurdles. The lack of English cannon at Newburn was not so much the fault of the office but of the spasmodic fashion in which Charles I carried out the mobilization. The King simply expected too much from institutions (and from men, for that matter). The Ordnance Office was squeezed between the manufacturing limitations of the modest English arms industry and the unrealistic military demands of the Crown, while trying to maintain an unreasonable mobilization schedule on a miniscule budget. In 1639 the dilatory gathering of forces provoked so much comment that Charles and his council should have been aware of the problem in 1640. But as was the case with the militia 'substitution clause', discussed below, the Crown failed to learn from recent experience. And it was not only the Ordnance Office that

---

[161] Bodleian Library, Clarendon SP, XVI, f. 72, Windebank to the King, 13 April 1639.
[162] PRO, E 351/292, f. 16, declared account, to Captain William Legge, Lieutenant to the Train of Artillery, for imprests of 30 May 1639, £1,800; warrant of 18 May; £1,000; warrant of 12 June, £1,500; and warrant dated 23 June 1639, £1,000 for a grand total of £5,300; also moneys to Sir Robert Farrer for Legge's use as keeper of the magazine in Hull, to convey overland cannon, muskets and other munition totalling £5,800.
[163] PRO, E 351/293, declared account for the standing train of artillery, including the wages of Captain William Legge, at £17 5s 10d a day for a grand total of £6,326 8s 8d.

mobilized slowly; the 6,000 pressed soldiers and the army's pay came up slowly as well.[164]

Institutionally, what happened to the Ordnance Office was more or less what happened to the Exchequer. In both cases Charles expected his bureaucracy to mobilize more speedily than an administratively astute sovereign would have expected. Of course, few if any early modern monarchs had such insight. Paying the army entailed more than loading chests of coins onto wagons; arming the forces involved more than handing out muskets at the Tower and harnessing horses to caissons. The King and his councillors may be excused, in 1639 if not 1640, for finding the logistics of a Scottish war beyond their imaginations. Such an expedition had not been attempted in living memory. Fitting out seaborne assaults was a different matter. The arms, ordnance, and pay for the most part were packed aboard a single fleet. In supplying the armies in Ireland after 1598, regular caravans moved through England to specific ports where the carts were transferred to ships without unloading, and then transported to Ireland.[165] The Bishops' Wars involved the equipping of as many as three geographically removed expeditionary forces and cooperation with shire authorities who were accustomed to be rid of their military obligation once they had collected coat-and-conduct money, pressed some riff-raff, and trundled them across the county border. In terms of complexity, the Bishops' Wars harked back to the 1569 rebellion of the Northern Earls and the Edwardian and Elizabethan campaigns in Scotland.

Deploying artillery and arms against Scotland was a task of great difficulty, for the heart of the English weapons industry and the Tower lay at the opposite end of the island. To assemble a train *en masse* at the Tower and, like a grand procession, move through the shires on seventeenth-century roads would have been virtually impossible. The artillery train was brought together piecemeal, the heavy ordnance loaded on ships (as were most of the weapons and munitions) and sent off to ports such as Grimsby, Hull, Newcastle, and Holy Island. If the measure of the Ordnance Office's

---

[164] Around 12 April 1639 the King instructed Vane to solicit advice from Hamilton, a familiar triangle of counsel. The first matter raised by Charles was 'the slowe comminge upp of the 6000 pressed men, and the slowe motion of the officers of the ordinance in the sendinge downe of Armes', which would keep his already lean force of 10,000 foot and 1,200 horse from the 'frontiers' until the first of May. This delay in the mobilization would, of course, affect Hamilton's plan of attack. Worse, however, was the unarmed condition of the main expeditionary force. Charles could not fully equip even the existing 10,000 infantry! Vane and the Master of the Ordnance were to go to Hull the very next day to sort out the weapons problem. See SRO, GD 406/1/1190, ff. 2–3. The English forces experienced the same problems the next year. While an insufficient number of troops occupied Yorkshire, leaving the borders vulnerable, essential weaponry bottle-necked at the Hull depot.

[165] R. Stewart, 'The "Irish Road"', pp. 23–6.

performance was its ability to convey equipment to its depots, then it achieved success in 1639 and 1640, in spite of the King's limited resources and erratic timetable. What happened afterward was the responsibility of the leaders of the royal army. Had central government taken up the proposal made in 1639, that regional supply depots based upon strategic locations be established, then the royal army might have been better supplied with arms in 1640. But the Crown chose not to act.[166]

The 1639 campaign took sixty-two pieces of great ordnance out of the Ordnance Office stores, some of which, especially brass cannon, were destined for installation in fortifications, and forty or fifty cannon to comprise the artillery train which would support the royal expeditionary force. This amounted to almost double the ordnance issued for the 1625 and 1627 campaigns combined. Cadiz and Rhé had taken 152 lasts of powder; the First Bishops' War at least 166, not counting the contributions from county stores. Over 57 tons of musket shot were provided for the 1620s voyages; the initial Scottish campaign took 80 tons.[167] Issues from the Tower cannot fully gauge the efforts of the Ordnance Office during the Bishops' Wars. In addition to drawing upon the shire stores, the Ordnance officers made certain that supplies would be available in the localities for reasons of preparedness and to reduce freight costs. Apparently they kept up their magazines at Hull and elsewhere between the wars. The shortages of arms available in the localities which had plagued the 1639 campaign were to be avoided. This activity accounts for the reduced supply of powder, match, and shot sent from London in 1640. For example, 80 tons of shot had been issued in 1638–9; only 24 additional tons were sent from the Tower in 1640.[168]

When mobilization resumed in 1640, the Ordnance Office succeeded in re-assembling a train of fifty brass cannon, including six culverins, four demi-culverins, ten six-pounders and thirty three-pounders. Remaining in the north were two of the culverins, a pair of demi-culverin, four six-pounders, and twenty three-pounders. Thus seventeen cannon of the artillery train, and a dozen or so smaller drakes, were conveyed north by sea, to be fitted into an artillery train by William Legge at Hull. Half a dozen of the largest ordnance were consigned aboard the *Mary* on 10 July 1640, along with their carriages, iron shot, wagons, carts and other

[166] Thrush, 'The Ordnance Office and the Navy, 1625–40', pp. 342, 352, citing Alnwick Castle, Northumberland MS. X, f. 201.

[167] PRO, SP 16/433/37, folio marked '143', computations at bottom of page, figured *circa* December 1639. For brass ordnance ordered in July 1638 see PRO, WO 49/72, ff. 9–9v, which includes brass ordnance provided as early as 1634.

[168] Stafford RO, Dartmouth MS. D(w) 1778/I/i/5; account of ordnance and carriages belonging to the train issued out of the Office of Ordnance, drawn up by Legge on 19 August and filed with the Ordnance Office on 12 September 1640.

accoutrements of the train. Additional brass cannon, grenades, carpenters' tools, etc., followed on 18 August 1640 on the *White Lyon*, also destined for Grimsby. Vessels plied the east coast dispatching weapons, equipment, and carts northwards, some, like the *Mary*, making multiple trips. Fifteen documented voyages involved in relaying the artillery train set sail between 20 May and 10 August 1640, remarkably late in the campaign season but understandable in the light of Charles's postponement of the rendezvous.[169]

The problem of arms was much like the problem of money. The Ordnance Office scraped the bottom of the barrel to find weapons just as the tellers reached into the recesses of their coffers to find sufficient coins. Shortages there were, given the way the King set about going to war. But just as serious as lack of availability was distribution. Strafford saw this clearly in August 1640 when he learned that a quarter of the royal army lagged behind because they were waiting for weapons. He instructed the Earl of Newport to issue arms from Hull and to speed up deliveries to Sunderland, so that the full number of regiments could get to the front and Newcastle be safeguarded.[170] Timing and fiscal weakness, both dictated by Charles I's political agenda, hampered royal institutions.[171] Like the Council of War, like the King's commanders, and like the Ordnance Office, the Exchequer found that impossible demands were made by the Crown. This was Charles's fatal error, for money, not royal will or righteousness, made full mobilization possible.

---

[169] Stafford RO, Dartmouth MS. D(W) 1778/I/i/5; for ordnance ordered from John Browne between the wars, see PRO WO 49/71, f.33.

[170] SRO, GD 406/1/1229, to Hamilton, 20 August 1640.

[171] The Covenanters, on the other hand, began preparing for a Second Bishops' War as early as July 1639. They set about inventorying weapons 'within the Shyres' and placing orders for Dutch arms. See SRO, GD 406/1/967, Traquair to Hamilton, 17 July [1639].

3

Military finance

THE FINANCIAL CONDITION OF THE CROWN

'Brittle' best describes the state of royal finances at the end of the Personal Rule. Income flowed steadily but modestly: annual revenue ranged from £377,243 in cash receipts for 1634 (though partial figures for 1632 suggest a worse year) to peaks of £527,322 in 1631 and over £498,000 for 1630 and 1636. Predictably, Charles spent what he got. In this he was no better and no worse than most monarchs, for the 'ordinary' was not designed to generate surpluses, since custom dictated that Parliament would grant extraordinary funds. No war chest was filled at Westminster. Rather, yearly expenditures approximated revenues, even exceeding them slightly in some years.[1] Coupled with the royal fondness (or compulsion) for the assignment of tallies, Charles's 'ordinary' was just that – sufficient to get by, but inadequate for an emergency. Tallies and anticipations discouraged the accumulation of surpluses. He had succeeded in living 'of his own', but found his policies constrained by financial limitations.

In 1638 the Crown took in £489,358, while the original proposal for the royal army envisioned 40,000 men costing in excess of £900,000 per annum.[2] Even if the army were halved and deployed only for a campaigning season of six months, the estimated £225,000 cost overwhelmed the current budget. Charles's experiences in the 1620s had exposed him to the expense of wars, but those had been overseas expeditions.[3] The Personal Rule had demonstrated that resources could be extracted from the localities if done so within what was regarded as the customary obligation of the subject. The King had already fashioned his perfect militia in this way. In the case of a Scottish war the King could demand that Englishmen

---

[1] F. C. Dietz, 'The Receipts and Issues of the Exchequer during the Reigns of James I and Charles I', *Smith College Studies in History*, 13, no. 4 (July 1928), pp. 148–9; 164–5.
[2] PRO, SP 16/415/119 and Gardiner, *History*, vol. VIII, p. 384, n. 2; see also SP 16/396, ff. 66–7, 72–3; SP 16/409/115; SP 16/409/118.
[3] The cost of the 1625 and 1627 campaigns is dealt with by Tom Cogswell in a forthcoming book on Parliament and war in the 1620s.

mobilize in order to defend the realm, exploiting border service and the duty to defend the locality against foreign incursion. On English soil he could create an army from trained-band contingents, fortified by noble horsemen and gentry armed at their own cost, with gaps in the ranks filled with pressed men. Therefore he relied heavily on the vitality of institutions such as the Exchequer and the Ordnance Office, as well as the goodwill and cooperation of the countryside. By the summer of 1640 it was plain that he had misjudged the preparedness of the institutions as well as the temper of the realm.

Charles did not see into his Exchequer further than the figures of Juxon and Cottington nor could he discern the workings of the Ordnance Office beyond Newport's hand. In summer 1638 he asked the chief executive officers if certain tasks could be performed – in Juxon's case, obtaining £200,000 to commence a Scottish war, in Newport's assembling an artillery train within eight weeks. Like Juxon, Newport later qualified his estimate upon consultation with his officers. Their immediate subordinates, Cottington as Chancellor of the Exchequer and Heydon as Lieutenant of the Ordnance, possessed a clearer notion of the immediate state of their respective institutions. Juxon and Newport served on the council and answered for their bureaucracies; Cottington sat beside Juxon, a marked advantage for the Exchequer since Heydon had not the privilege to sit at the Board. Cottington, too, enjoyed the advantage of the King's ear. Charles expressed his need for £200,000 and Juxon assured him that the funds would be found. The King told Hamilton that he had 'consulted' with Juxon and Cottington regarding the availability of £200,000, 'which they doubt not but to furnishe mee with all'. The letter clearly implies that Charles himself had estimated the initial cost of the expedition (to him at least) at £200,000. Juxon and Cottington apparently chose not to question the figure. The smallness of the figure might have been a product of optimistic thinking that the war would be short or that the mere sound of mobilization would destroy the Covenanters' resolve to resist.[4]

By mid-July 1638 it became apparent that Juxon had spoken too soon. The Lord Admiral, Northumberland, had recently been admitted to the council's deliberations. He confided to Wentworth (in Dublin) that the

---

[4] SRO, GD 406/1/10490, 20 June 1638. See also Bodleian Library, Bankes MS. 5/45 for Juxon's belief that voluntary contributions would be significant. On Juxon's relationship with the King, see T. A. Mason, *Serving God and Mammon: William Juxon, 1582–1663* (Newark, Delaware, 1985), pp. 12, 16, 34, 95–8, 107, 136–40, 145–6, 159; on Cottington, see Havran, *Cottington*, pp. 65–7, 70–8, 80–1, 124–53. P. H. Donald suggests that Laud may have advised on some money matters (*An Uncounselled King*, p. 8), yet even so Laud's input was minimal, especially as Charles moved towards war (ibid, p. 131, note 53). The point is that Laud (and Wentworth for that matter) had little to do with the 1639 mobilization; it was different in 1640. In retrospect, the best advice came from of the Earl of Northumberland.

state of the Exchequer of Receipt had been 'examined upon this occasion' and a paltry 'two hundreth pounds' found. Allowing for hyperbole, since accurate estimates of the cash holdings of the four Tellers of the Receipt changed hourly, clearly Crown financial resources were limited. Even by pledging their personal security, Juxon and Cottington could raise only £110,000 in Crown loans at this time.[5] But Charles proceeded with his war nonetheless. At the meeting of 26 July, Juxon allocated £200,000 for military expenditure, to be issued under the Privy Seal by Sir Robert Pye.[6] The arms merchant John Quarles received £15,230.[7] The Lieutenant of the Ordnance, Sir John Heydon, collected £300; Leonard Pinkney, Commissary General, received £500.[8] Sir Thomas Morton, soon to be entrusted with organizing the defences of the northern counties with Sir Jacob Astley, got £295, while Hamilton accepted £5,000.[9] Juxon could initiate the war on anticipations, as the largest sums would go to the Treasurer at War, Sir William Uvedale, but not until March 1639, giving the Exchequer time to generate revenue, especially by loan and tally.[10]

Receipts during the autumn and winter lagged behind expectations.[11] By January 1639 the financial prospects for the war seemed as bleak as the winter landscape. The King, observed Northumberland, 'declares not where he expects to have the money that must defray the expense of his army'.[12] It would be a familiar refrain over the next two years as the Exchequer struggled to find ready cash for the King. The political reality of the Personal Rule meant that the King's finances were the subject of conjecture. When the royal army assembled at York on 1 April 1639, the troops were to receive wages from the Crown. The Treasurer at War, Sir William Uvedale, did not appear that day and his tardiness sparked rumours about the availability of cash.[13] Where others, including army officers, expressed uncertainty, the King remained confident. Charles informed Hamilton on 13 May 1639 'the truth is that I fynde my state of Monies to bee suche, that

[5] Sheffield City Library, Strafford MS. Xb, ff. 1–2, miscellaneous correspondence, 23 January 1638. The document is damaged by damp but the word 'two' can be discerned and the word 'hundreth' is clear.
[6] PRO, SP 16/395/85, Charles to Juxon and Cottington; SP 16/396, f. 1; F.C. Dietz, *English Public Finance 1558–1641* (New York, 1932), p. 284.
[7] PRO, SP 16/395/85 I, Juxon to Pye; SP 16/396, f. 2.
[8] Pinkney's commissary accounts, 1 October 1638–1 May 1639, are preserved in PRO, Exchequer of Receipt, Declared Accounts, E 351/579.
[9] PRO, SP 16/395/85 II, notes on expenditures; SP 16/396, f. 3, Council of War entry book.
[10] Mason, *Serving God and Mammon*, pp. 126, 131 and below, pp. 141–8. T. A. Mason has been generous in sharing his knowledge of Juxon and the Exchequer, for which the author is grateful.
[11] PRO, E 401/2460–1.
[12] See Mason, *Serving God and Mammon*, p. 127.
[13] See below, pp. 144–5.

I shall be able (by the grace of God) to maintain all the Men I have a foote for this Somer; but for doing anie more, I dare not promise'. But actions spoke louder than words. The King forbade him to engage in further expenditure, save to pay some few officers.[14]

The financial condition of the Crown during the First Bishops' War is summed up neatly by Secretary Windebank's report to the King on 24 May 1639. With the royal army occupying the north, there was no money to maintain it through the summer. Charles had reckoned that with an army in the field his English subjects would be compelled to lend. He had not counted on 'this coldnesse of the Citizens' which left him precariously exposed. He had misjudged the temper of England and had taken for granted the unqualified consent of his subjects. On this tenuous assumption he waged a war that involved all Britain. 'With your Majesties owne Revenue, the Lord Treasurer and the Lord Cottington assured it is impossible', Windebank wrote. Even if moneys could be borrowed, they would not salvage the royal finances. Supposing that the merchants were better able or inclined to do so, 'the moneyes now borrowed must be paid againe and the interest in the meane time answered. So that this is still an Anticipation of your revenue.'[15] It is not surprising that the King made peace within a fortnight. The next time he intended that his servants should find better ways to pay for an army.

In October 1639, the committee for Scottish affairs, a subcommittee of the Privy Council, further subdivided to plan the Second Bishops' War. One group conjured ways to finance the war (Juxon, Laud, Strafford, Cottington, and Windebank) and another dealt with strategy (Laud, Strafford, Northumberland, and Hamilton). The architects of 'thorough' sat on both committees, a deliberate change in leadership.[16] Arundel, Holland, and Coke had fallen from grace in a general purge precipitated by the King's displeasure with the 1639 campaign. In their place came Strafford and Laud with the tenacity which characterized their institutional management. Strafford's aggressiveness at the table is well documented. Laud single-handedly organized a boycott of the Lord Mayor of London's procession, telling Charles that the City had dishonoured him in failing to provide adequate support for the First Bishops' War. The Lord Keeper reversed the Privy Council's resolution to participate and Laud obtained the desired end. Eight months later the King was asking the Lord Mayor for help once again, making Laud's tactlessness quite expensive.[17] New ministers did not guarantee new circumstances.

[14] SRO, GD 406/1/10558, Hamilton Red Book.
[15] Bodleian Library, Clarendon SP, XVI, f. 124v.
[16] Henry E. Huntington Library, Ellesmere Collection, Bridgewater Papers, John Castle newsletters, EL 7810, Castle to Bridgewater, 30 October 1639.
[17] Ibid.

In the Second Bishops' War fiscal problems continued to bedevil the war effort. Northumberland wrote, 'Many consultations are held for our military preparations against the next summer; a mighty army is intended for the north, but no man knows how it will be paid.'[18] His opinion was seconded by the Chancellor of the Exchequer, who threw up his hands and exclaimed, 'How we shall defend ourselves without money is not under my cap.'[19] The foolhardiness of ignoring Parliament in 1639 was now compounded by clumsiness in failing to manage and enlist Parliament in spring 1640. But coercing a Caroline Parliament was no easy matter.[20] Nor could it be assumed that given inflation, undervaluation of assessments, and the tight-fistedness born of a recessionary economy, enough money would be forthcoming from the Houses. The Privy Council estimated the cost of the 1640 mobilization at a million pounds per annum. 'To perswade a parlament to furnish the King presentlye with so much, was conceaved a very unlikely thing.'[21] The Earl of Northumberland had calculated the cost of the 1640 royal army by comparing the projected expenses of the forces intended for the relief of the Palatinate in the 1630s. The current army was to have forty pieces of ordnance, double that of the Palatine army, and 35,000 infantry, 10,000 more than the 1630s relief force. That smaller army cost £8,000 per month,

but if the designes that are now proposed goe on, the Kings expence will farr exceed that estimate; the train of artillerie for this intended army will be more then double the proportion of the other .... lesse then a million a yeare will not defray this expence. If the Parlament supplie not the King, God only knowes how this money will be gotten.'[22]

Furthermore, Ireland, from which Charles expected help not hindrance, dealt a serious blow to Crown finances at the height of mobilization in 1640. Prior to departing Dublin to join the King, Strafford had manipulated the Irish Parliament to grant four subsidies to the Crown. Once the Lord Deputy was gone from that kingdom, however, the assembly fell back on the old book of rates, which Strafford had not foreseen. Consequently £120,000 rather than £200,000 would be making its way across the Irish Sea, infuriating Charles, who desperately needed cash.[23] Chronic shortages

---

[18] HMC Northumberland, p. 79, 26 December 1639.
[19] Quoted in Havran, *Cottington*, p. 142.
[20] See Fissel, 'Scottish War and English Money', pp. 193–218, for the Parliament most germane to the subject of this book.
[21] Centre for Kentish Studies, De L'Isle and Dudley MSS., Sydney Papers, U 1475 C85/4, Northumberland to Leicester, 12 December 1639.
[22] Centre for Kentish Studies, De L'Isle and Dudley MSS., Sydney Papers, C85/5; HMC De L'Isle and Dudley, pp. 219–20.
[23] HEH, EL 7840, Castle newsletter of 26 June 1640. The extent to which the Irish Parliament outwitted Strafford is apparent in the letter's boasting of the alacrity with which supply was voted. See SRO, GD 406/1/803, to Hamilton, 24 March 1640.

of money crippled the Crown's ability to deploy its army, which contributed to the debacle at Newburn.[24] Perhaps as much as one quarter of the English army lacked weapons.[25]

The Crown's inability to raise as many regiments as anticipated left the Lord General short-handed. The tardiness in fielding regiments, complicated if not caused by lack of money and defaults in coat-and-conduct money, meant that many of the companies arrived in the north without proper training. Units lingered far from the front, in most cases for lack of pay and officers. The artillery train rested at Kingston-upon-Hull.[26] Soldiers awaited arms expected from Flanders, prompting Sergeant-Major General Sir Jacob Astley to comment that a good occasion was to be lost due to lack of money.[27] Shortages of money therefore plagued the arming as well as the financing of the army.

Military failure demanded a scapegoat, and the blame fell upon Edward, Viscount Conway. General of the cavalry, Conway failed to stem the Scottish advance at Newburn and was compelled to explain the defeat.[28] In his justification Conway's most consistent theme was the Crown's lack of funds. Neither the withdrawal at Newburn nor the abandonment of Newcastle caused the disaster, rather, 'ill-grounded designs, to make a war without monies to go on with it'.[29] The consequences of the shortage of money were disorderly, and thus undependable, troops and insufficient equipment and arms.[30]

When Conway wrote to Astley at York for reinforcements, he found that the old soldier had troubles of his own. Northumberland had ordered him to march between 4,000 and 5,000 infantry north to assist Conway, but Astley lacked sufficient men to send a force of that size.[31] Now the army's pay had arrived, and it too did not meet expectations. Officers dispatched north would encounter disorderly troops and have no money to pay them. Commanders pestered Astley for wages for their companies, and the enlisted men were more badly behaved than ever.[32] With the 'arch knaves' of

---

[24] See for example Bodleian Library, Clarendon SP, XIX, f. 171, where the Vice President of the Council of the North suggested that it would be better to let the Scots advance rather than deploy unpaid English troops. See below, pp. 149–51, 272, 292.

[25] SRO, GD 406/1/1229 and Russell, *FBM*, pp. 142–3 and *CECW*, p. 163. See also pp. 59–60, 96–103, 110, 293–4.

[26] Stafford RO, Dartmouth MS. D(W) 1778/I/i/8, Newport to Legge, 30 August 1640.

[27] PRO, SP 16/463/41.

[28] See above, pp. 59–60.

[29] Bodleian Library, Clarendon SP, XIX, f. 175v.

[30] Nearly a quarter of the army lacked arms as late as 20 August, as documented by SRO, GD 406/1/1229, Strafford to Hamilton. Conrad Russell kindly supplied this reference.

[31] In addition to the tactical ramifications of the shortage of cash, which kept sufficient soldiers from the front, one must also acknowledge the strategic limitations imposed by the smallness of the English force, dictated by the King's meagre resources.

[32] See below, pp. 151, 271–3.

the kingdom rioting on his doorstep and clamouring for pay, Astley was in no position to aid Conway. As an alternative he proposed sending troops north at Conway's summons upon news of the Scottish advance. This would enable Astley to restore order at Selby, gather a sufficient contingent, and the troops would remain at York (where their pay was to be delivered) as long as possible.[33] The depletion of ready money at the front prompted some spontaneous solutions. Conway latched onto some ship money intended to pay the Berwick garrison, which he distributed amongst the cavalry at Newcastle. Northumberland acknowledged Conway's appropriation of the ship money and commented, 'make yourselves merrie this month for after those moneys are spent we shal see how farr your credites will reache, unless the Scotts come into England'. Northumberland ordered that no more than a week's pay be issued.[34] Arrears of pay proved disastrous, for lack of funds prompted Astley to refrain from arming his restive infantrymen at precisely the moment when they should have been deployed near the Tyne to repulse the Covenanter advance.[35] In this case, the weapons were available, but the officers dared not distribute them.

The economic condition of England and Wales was as inflexible as the King's finances. Part of the difficulty in gathering taxes lay in the sluggishness of the economy, exacerbated by the scarcity of small coin, the stagnant cloth-trade, and the aftermath of decades of inflation. Contemporaries lamented the 'dead marketts' and dearth of trade, which sometimes figured as a justification for slowness in paying taxes such as coat-and-conduct money.[36] Robert Woodford, a steward, entered into his diary, 'Our markets here [in Northamptonshire] are very dead, people want moneyes, and those that have it are loath to part with it.'[37] The recessionary phase through which the English economy trudged meant that loans, large or small, were difficult to raise. 'Mony is very scarce and hard to be gotten.'[38] Depressed domestic markets are mirrored in James Hunt's assertion that

[33] PRO, SP 16/459/64, Astley to Conway, 9 July 1640; Bodleian Library, Clarendon SP, XIX, ff. 163–166v. See also below, pp. 144–51, 293–4.
[34] PRO, SP 16/460/55, Northumberland to Conway, 21 July 1640; PRO, SP 16/460/13, Northumberland to Conway, 15 July 1640.
[35] HEH, EL 7855, f. 2, Castle newsletter, 26 August 1640.
[36] *Winthrop Papers*, vol. IV, p. 224, John Tinker to John Winthrop, 13 April 1640. See also PRO, SP 16/454/86, certificate of George Glamfield, a Suffolk constable, who on 23 May 1640 cited scarcity of money and a slow commodities market in his explanation about the difficulty in collecting coat-and-conduct money. The failure of the Short Parliament had not engendered optimism about the English economy, while simultaneously providing political reasons for non-payment.
[37] HMC Woodford, p. 498.
[38] PRO, SP 16/463/98, George Beare, 13 August 1640.

deadness of trading and commerce caused a paucity of capital so that when bailiffs seized a distress they were unable to auction the goods.[39]

The outbreak of war with Scotland simply aggravated the bleak economic conditions, as Sir Robert Bell noted at the same time as Hunt was writing: 'If this Scotch rebellion (which tyes up all menns purses) be turned (as there is great hope) into conformetie there will be open and free mart again and every man will trade.'[40] Some predicted a slump, for example William Moorhead of London, who reported 'A great complaint here that trade doth muche decay: and if it continew in this posture long men far so bakward from adventuring that his Majesty's customes may muche diminish'.[41] The economic slowdown not only diminished chances for loans, but also deprived the customs farmers of their revenue, further damaging the monarchy's economic base. The London aldermen, pressed for loans during the First Bishops' War, pointed out that the Merchant Strangers had called in their monies and shut their banks due to the scarcity of cash and general dampening of trade. The political situation made markets that much more uncertain.[42] Thus the King's financial resources were remarkably limited from 1638 to 1640 and the realm's stagnant economy made loans, anticipations and above all taxation unusually difficult to raise.[43]

The reputation of royal credit, and by implication confidence in the feasibility of Caroline policies, had been eroded at home and abroad. Lack of confidence implied that something was amiss with the government. The King's inability to work with Parliament grew out of mutual distrust. Like the gentry, merchants showed some scepticism and apprehension about the trustworthiness of Charles and his ministers. From major lenders to minor victuallers the notion that the King might not deal evenly with his creditors undermined their willingness to lend.[44] Likewise, failure to reach an agreement with Parliament implied that the monarchy might have difficulty putting its finances in order and might renege on loans. If Charles's non-parliamentary sources of revenue had been substantial enough to fund massive mobilizations in consecutive years, royal credit would have been a consideration of secondary importance.

The Exchequer could only issue as much as it received from fairly fixed

[39] PRO, SP 16/427/47, 13 August 1639 and C.A. Clifford, 'Ship Money in Hampshire: Collection and Collapse', *Southern History*, 4 (1982), p. 97.

[40] HMC Lothian, p. 85.

[41] SRO, GD 406/1/848, 29 May 1639.

[42] Bodleian Library, Clarendon SP, XVI, f. 124, Windebank to Charles. Some merchants were 'refractory' about royal loans, according to SRO, GD 406/1/848.

[43] B. E. Supple, *Commercial Crisis and Change in England 1600–1642*, pp. 125–9, 192, 225–53 and C. G. A. Clay, *Economic Expansion and Social Change: England 1500–1700, II, Industry, Trade and Government* (Cambridge, 1984), pp. 251–81.

[44] See below, pp. 120–9. See also HEH, EL 7837, where it was reported that the victuallers refused to supply the fleet unless paid in cash. Castle newsletter of 9 June 1640.

sources of income; unanticipated and abnormally large military costs could swamp the Tellers.[45] The Lord Treasurer could not mint his own money. But the King could, within certain limitations. English rulers had long tinkered with the intrinsic metal content of the coinage, but in 1640 Charles's attempted seizure of bullion and the 'brass-money project' triggered a storm of protest from mercantile interests on both sides of the Channel. Threatened debasement and schemes at the Mint in summer 1640 proved fatal when the Crown searched for creditors in time of military crisis.

Foreign wealth did reside within the King's domain; however, the Merchant Strangers had tightened their lending in those times of uncertainty. More accessible was Spanish precious metal destined for the paymasters of the Army of Flanders. The Spanish King had entrusted his British cousin with bullion, housed in the Tower, awaiting minting and shipment across the Channel. The Spanish had secured a conduit through which they funnelled pay to the Low Countries with relative security and the English King collected a percentage for storage, minting, and safe conveyance to Dunkirk.[46] If the Spanish would not lend voluntarily, then the state of emergency justified a forced loan. The chaos of June 1640 had the earmarks of a national catastrophe, with a delayed mobilization and rioting in the capital and elsewhere. 'Borrowing' £300,000 of bullion or more from Charles's 'cousin', the King of Spain, would assist in quelling the domestic problems of summer 1640; however, such a breach of trust threatened a trade embargo. More cognizant of the ramifications of the royal action than Charles himself, some officers of the Mint begged the King to think again, in the same way as the Councillors of War had asked him in November 1638, over monopolies and patents. Speaking on behalf of his colleagues Sir Ralph Freeman explained that the £300,000 in bullion demanded by royal warrant had been partly coined, but that the Mint men dreaded the results of such an action. To requisition the King of Spain's treasure would 'trench upon his Majesties Honour both at home and abroade', triggering retaliation. Economically and politically, such an act spelt 'the ruyne and destruction of all Confidence and commerce'.[47] On 6 July the Merchant Adventurers took the bit between their teeth and confronted Strafford with a deputation. Fear of reprisals such as seizure of cargoes and forfeitures in Spain, the Habsburg dominions, and elsewhere had forced their hand. Black Tom (Strafford) then fashioned some blackmail. In return for a £40,000 loan (secured on the customs farmers, not the government, the

---

[45] See below, pp. 141–9.
[46] The Battle of the Downs in August 1639 cast serious doubt on Charles's ability to protect Spanish vessels.
[47] HEH, EL 7842, f. 2, Castle newsletter of 6 July 1640.

deputation countered), the seizure would be cancelled. For £40,000 the Crown had suffered an indelible tarnish upon its already stained reputation in money matters.[48] Mistrust further deepened when the King contemplated debasing the coinage rather than seizing Spanish bullion from the Tower.

As the King's numerous requests for loans had been rebuffed at home and abroad, he had no other way of meeting his needs and so touted the brass money project.[49] Sir William Parkhurst and Mr Palmer, who had collaborated with the remonstrance against the bullion seizure presented by Freeman, were ordered, around 11 July 1640, to hammer out with a committee of Privy Councillors a scheme to produce debased shillings (intrinsically worth threepence) from an alloy of silver and copper. The milling of small coin from copper or brass was in fact practised earlier during the reign of Charles I. Similar proposals circulated among the royal ministers.[50] A clamour about brass money sounded in London, primarily amongst the City merchants.[51] The county communities shared their apprehension, generating petitions in some areas and reporting 'heere is much feare of Brass mony'.[52] Again, Charles turned a deaf ear to servants who expressed reservations about his policies. He would not take advice. Of the drastic measures contemplated to fund the mobilization of 1640, the brass money project loomed most ominously for it threatened the very lifeblood of the English economy, its currency. Political and religious unrest had already shaken mercantile confidence, so the advocacy of this fiscal expedient was extraordinarily ill-timed, especially considering Charles's desperate need for credit from the London merchant community. In retrospect, the project may have been a crude attempt at extortion, for by threatening debasement, the King pressured merchants to relent and lend to him.[53]

According to Charles's scheme the new currency would finance the war effort and then be withdrawn when the Scots rebels were crushed and peace restored. It would be used temporarily and selectively. Soldiers were to be paid in 'good coyne' for armed conscripts posed a threat to public order should they be angered by debased wages, while the obstinate

48 The decline of Charles's credit is set forth in Robert Ashton, *The Crown and the Money Market* (Oxford, 1963), chapter 7; Gardiner, *History*, vol. IX, pp. 169–70.
49 Huntingdonshire Record Office, Manchester MS. 32/5/17. I owe this reference to Conrad Russell.
50 Copper farthings were in circulation in Caroline England. G. Brooke, *English Coins* (London, 1932), pp. 217–18; see also PRO, SP 16/461/74; 75; 76; 77.
51 Bodleian Library, Clarendon SP, XVIII, f. 239v, Windebank to Hopton, 24 July 1640.
52 Huntingdonshire RO, Manchester MS. 32/5/17; PRO, SP 16/463/98, 13 August 1640.
53 See Rossingham on brass money in PRO, SP 16/460/56, f. 2; and the Venetian verdict, Giustinian to the Doge in *CSP Venetian* (1640–2), XXV, pp. 58–60, 27 July 1640.

London victuallers and tradesmen were to receive brass money.[54] This policy could be rationalized on the basis of the numerous complaints about scarcity of coin in the localities, thereby denying the locals one of their excuses for non-payment of ship money and coat-and-conduct money.[55] More seriously, Sir Robert Heath and others pointed to an imbalance between the value of coins domestically and their intrinsic worth abroad to explain why bullion flowed out of the kingdom. The King must 'reduce his coins to such a value as ... the ordinary current coins of Christendom' by minting pennies from base metal. Smaller moneys only would be alloyed, the greater simply placed on parity. Thus debasement could be dressed up as an attempt to make available small change to the general public and simply to adjust larger-sized coins to their true market value, all for the benefit of the kingdom. Of course, the brass money project, with its threepenny shillings, would not suit Heath's recommendations.[56] The English system of coinage did suffer from problems such as the hoarding by speculators of 'heavy' coins, whose intrinsic worth was greater than their face value.[57] But overweighted shillings would not be eliminated by way of debasement. In fact, the King's proposals promised further to degrade the minting and circulation procedure, to the detriment of the economy.

The most forceful condemnation of the brass money project came from Sir Thomas Roe. An ambassador who had spent the First Bishops' War abroad, mainly in Hamburg, he had only recently become a member of the Council, and was well versed in international trade and diplomacy. Roe's assessment of the Crown's fiscal situation lacked the more 'economic' tone of Heath's analysis. But its allusions were powerful enough to arouse Strafford's ire.[58] History proved that kingdoms fell as the value of their coinage plummeted. As long as emperors retained the 'Standard of their Coin' Rome stood, but when the coinage was altered, glory and solvency were shaken, and 'that Empire fell by degrees'. Tracing briefly the monetary policies of Edward I, Roe argued persuasively that a stable currency brought national prosperity. What short-term gain might be obtained would be small compared to long-term losses in royal customs revenues. Debasement would trigger hoarding and the export of precious metals.[59] Most grievously, though, Charles's profile would be stamped on a shilling

[54] PRO, SP 16/459/77.
[55] Fissel, *'Bellum Episcopale'*, pp. 180, 406 and this book, pp. 117–18, on scarcity of coin.
[56] PRO, SP 16/460/60; *CSPD* (1640), XVI, pp. 498–500; Gardiner, *History*, vol. IX, p. 171.
[57] J. Craig, *The Mint* (Cambridge, 1953), pp. 145–6.
[58] Gardiner, *History*, vol. IX, p. 171.
[59] A change in the gold/silver ratio was sometimes 'sufficiently wide to make the export of the undervalued metal worthwhile', according to J. D. Gould, 'The Royal Mint in the Early Seventeenth Century', *EconHR*, second series, 5, no. 1 (1952), p. 241.

coin whose true value was threepence. 'Princes must not suffer their Faces to warrant Falshood' was Roe's candid judgement on the business.[60]

The officers of the Mint received an order to prepare dies. Councillors examined the phraseology of the proclamation of debasement. And the Lord General, Northumberland, wrote with sage detachment that the milling of copper coins signified that money was not as plentiful as it should be at the outset of a campaign.[61] The extortionate inspiration behind the project came to light on 22 July 1640, when the King wrote to Sir Henry Garway, who was sympathetic to his plight, that brass money was a last resort, the only lawful alternative to raise money for the defence of the realm. If the London merchants could see their way to loaning his Majesty £200,000 upon reasonable security the scheme would be cancelled.[62] Charles's proposition betrays a certain deviousness. A Great Council held at Hampton Court debated brass money and recommended the the City be approached for a loan of £200,000, rendering the project unnecessary. Secretary Vane, Dorset, and Cottington then delivered a letter to the Lord Mayor and Common Council and made persuasive, eloquent speeches. The Common Council deliberated (while the courtiers waited in another room). When the Lord Mayor emerged he spoke the mind of that assembly, that they were not of themselves furnished with money to lend, and they knew not where or from whom to borrow, considering that the solicitation of loans from the nobility and others had so exhausted the banks of the City. When Charles learned of the rebuff, the Lord Mayor was summoned and chided again. The officers of the Mint then gathered with some coined specimens of the brass money. When they were gone there was a new round of consultation amongst the King's councillors about a way to call into the Mint the silver and gold of the kingdom. Agreement was hard to come by but slowly the consensus emerged that the project should be abandoned.[63] It would be the Chancellor of the Exchequer, Lord Cottington, who offered the next alternative.

Cottington's ingenious pepper ploy nearly salvaged the campaign's finances, but too late. He learned of the arrival of an East Indies ship laden with a cargo of pepper valued at around £70,000. With the cash available to the Crown at around £19,000 and little more in sight, the seizure and sale of the cargo promised some fiscal relief.[64] Regulation of commerce fell

[60] Rushworth, *Historical Collections*, vol. III, pp. 1217–20.
[61] PRO, SP 16/460/3, Northumberland to Astley, 14 July 1640.
[62] PRO, SP 16/460/62, 22 July 1640.
[63] HEH, EL 7844, Castle newsletter of 25 July 1640.
[64] Strafford indicated that around the time of the collapse of negotiations for a loan from the Merchant Strangers and the genesis of the pepper deal, the Exchequer was down to about £19,000. Without more money, regiments (the Middlesex ones in particular) were going to be disbanded. SRO, GD 406/1/1234, Strafford to Hamilton, undated, but internal evi-

within the King's prerogative, and the Chancellor exploited that right. Cottington went into the City on 22 August and subscribed for the entire cargo, pledging as sureties himself, Sir George Ratcliff, and another. The merchants, having wrestled bitterly with the Crown over a loan throughout the summer, their confidence eroded by schemes such as the bullion seizure and brass money project, balked at this. Cottington made a counter-offer involving the Farmers of the Great Customs, but it was pointed out that the Farmers 'had as much upon their backs alreadie as they could beare'. Regardless of this, a precedent existed which prevented subscription for such a valuable cargo.[65] Undeterred, Cottington pressured the merchants, offered sufficient private securities, and requisitioned the cargo for his royal master.

In the long run, the pepper deal saw the cargo sold below value (by probably 30 per cent) and 16 per cent interest, twice the market rate, paid.[66] But for the Tellers of the Receipt it was a godsend, though it took much of September to find buyers and lay hold of the money.[67] This drastic solution illustrates the quandary in which the Chancellor and the tellers found themselves. Although the Crown succeeded in raising a great deal of money in 1640, close to £900,000, the army took two-thirds of that amount, and still more was needed. Amid all the rumours surrounding the war, the dismal state of royal credit was apparent to all.

Credit rested to a degree upon reputation, so that Charles repeatedly countered rumours of his government's tottering finances.[68] But Strafford's uncompromising attitude had as always soured relations. Without the pepper money all was lost: 'unlesse wee get the pepper money the whole Armye will disband most shamfully, and all will be lost, and therfore his Majesty must resolve by one meanes or other to have it'.[69] The tone echoed the 'army in Ireland' speech of 5 May. The oblique references to gaoling the East India merchants if they resisted also sounded familiar.[70] The tangible limitations of Stuart absolutism prevented the rescue of Crown finances. Having lost the goodwill of Parliament to grant extraordinary revenue, and the goodwill of the country to shoulder the war effort,

---

dence suggests a date of 20–21 August. See also GD 406/1/1232, Strafford to the King, also written about this time.

[65] HEH, EL 7855, f. 2, Castle newsletter.

[66] PRO, E 403/2568, f. 138v for 2,500 bags of pepper bought from East India Company at £56,000.

[67] Description in HEH, EL 7856, f. 3; Dietz's figures show a receipt of £41,581 ('Receipts and Issues', p. 152); Gardiner, *History*, IX, p. 190.

[68] HEH, EL 7836, Castle newsletter.

[69] SRO, GD 406/1/1234.

[70] SRO, GD 406/1/1231. One recalls Strafford's remark to Charles that lynching a few aldermen might be the best course in coercing Londoners to cooperate with the Crown. See Gardiner, *History*, vol. IX, p. 130, citing Rushworth's transcript of Strafford's trial.

Charles had also lost the trust of his merchants to lend money for the waging of his Bishops' War.

The cost of fighting a Scottish War had by 1639 increased significantly over Tudor campaigns of a similar size. The Crown's ability to draw upon loans, benevolences, and contributions had not kept pace with inflation. However, Charles's alternatives remained those of his predecessors: free gifts and contributions from individuals, loans from domestic corporate bodies and foreign sources. Unfortunately, although he depended upon loans and contributions, Charles had little sensitivity to the feelings of his prospective creditors.

Charles's approach to finance closely resembled that of medieval rulers. For the Bishops' Wars he presented a time-honoured formula – a foreign threat endangered the whole realm and the monarch planned to meet that threat in person, and invoked the feudal obligation of the subjects to support their liege in these straits. As the situation in 1638–9 was an emergency, time prevented Parliament from assembling. In spring 1640, the Parliament was made to understand that immediate supply must precede discussion of grievances.[71] As Parliament extended support in good faith, Charles would reciprocate with a quid pro quo at a later date. Thus the door was opened for those who preferred to contribute, through gift or loan, rather than to serve in person. Couched in these terms, Charles's campaign was identical to earlier Scottish campaigns. Some disagreeable memories, however, chafed against the traditional form. The forced loans of 1626–8 cast a dark shadow over Charles's methods of raising loans from the county communities. Reinforcing the armies of Christian of Denmark might have been a matter of personal honour for the King, but his attempts to raise money through the prerogative in this business were politically controversial.[72] Then, as in 1639, the assertion that there had not been time to summon Parliament was less than honest. The trust and goodwill which facilitated the individual's willingness to lend to his sovereign had been eroded during the 1620s.[73] Given the poor credit which dogged Charles's regime at this time, the King could not easily turn to professional financiers; rather, he needed the assistance of his loyal private subjects.[74] Natur-

---

[71] Fissel, 'Scottish War and English Money', pp. 200, 211–12.
[72] Richard Cust, *The Forced Loan and English Politics* (Oxford, 1987), pp. 39–40.
[73] Young, 'Charles I and the Erosion of Trust', pp. 217–35.
[74] See *CSP Venetian* XXV, pp. 61–2, where Giustinian informed the Doge that Charles had 'no money ready in the Treasury' and that his government could not succeed in all its plans due to 'lack of credit, a result which generally dogs the proposals of this court', pp. 61–2.

ally, Charles looked to the men sitting at the council table. The mobilization required immediate cash, regardless of how successful would be the Parliament in spring:

Before the King can have any supplie from the parlament it is conceaved that he will have greate occation for the imploying a good summe of mony for the strengthning his Northerne garisons and secureing thos parts with some troupes, both of horse and foote; His owne credite not serveing for the takeing up of these moneys his Majesty is forced to ingage his Councell. Some of them undertake the furnishing 10, some 20 thousand pounds.[75]

The author of this observation, the Earl of Northumberland, put up £5,000 against the impositions on lawns and cambrics. Tallies were struck and he was to receive the 'first moneys' collected and reap a profit of 8 per cent.[76] The King then turned to the nobility in general.

Loans, contributions, and gifts from the nobility must be evaluated against the background of their summons to serve in a feudal host in defence of the realm.[77] The interchangeability of military service and hard cash made possible negotiations between Crown and lord. Although nobles often loaned money to the King in time of peace, war-time contributions were customary rather than unusual. The question was, how able were the lords to raise significant cash sums quickly? And, if able, how willing would they be to aid a sovereign who had imposed on many of them antiquated forest laws and the burdens of lieutenancy?[78]

Those nobles closest at hand were courtiers, most of whom owed their positions to the King's goodwill. Their names head the lists of creditors. For the Second Bishops' War Lord Newburgh loaned £3,000, repayable out of the firstfruits and arrearages of tenths in the years 1640 and 1641.[79] The Lord Privy Seal loaned £4,000, assigned out of the duty of £8 per ton of soap in the years of 1640 and 1641. The Lord Privy Seal told John Castle 'from his owne mouth' that he would give the King £500 and asked Castle and 'some other Clarkes of the P. Seale' if it was a fitting gift. They agreed. The Lord Privy Seal said if they knew what he received and what he expended they would regard it as a 'faire' gift.[80] Charles's courtiers had to sort out amongst themselves how much to give the King. The Earl of Newcastle tendered £10,000, assigned out of the new impositions upon strangers'

[75] Centre for Kentish Studies, De L'Isle and Dudley MSS., Sydney Papers, U 1475 C 85/4, f. 2, to the Earl of Leicester, 12 December 1639.
[76] PRO, SO 3/12, f. 67v; CSPD (1639–40), XV, p. 191, docquet of 31 December 1639; also Ashton, *The Crown and the Money Market*, p. 53.
[77] See pp. 152–62.
[78] Schwarz, 'Viscount Saye and Sele', pp. 17–36.
[79] HEH, Bridgewater MS. EL 6979, 'Assignments upon Loane /1639/'.
[80] HEH, EL 7807, 13 February 1639, Castle to Bridgewater.

goods in the Port of London for the years 1640 and 1641.[81] The Lord Chamberlain loaned £7,000, assigned out of the Receipt of the Court of Wards and Liveries in the years 1641 and 1642 and another £13,000, to be covered by the new Imposts for Merchandizes Outwards: £5,000 in 1640 and £8,000 for 1641. Lord Coventry loaned perhaps as much as £9,000.[82] On 6 March 1640 the Earl of Holland paid £10,000 as a loan to the Exchequer. Tallies were struck for the Earl's repayment upon collection of the 'westerne Imposicons', £5,000 for the year to end at Michaelmas 1640, and the remaining £5,000 for the year ending at Michaelmas 1641.[83] In February 1640 John Castle reported that the assignment for the Lord Privy Seal's money on the soap monopoly was brought to pass the Signet, 'which *mutatis mutandis* runs much after the same manner with this'. Castle informed Bridgewater that he was not wise enough to advise on the security of Bridgewater's money but suggested that he should go the way of the Lord Privy Seal, who 'is very wary and has searched this business to the bottom'.[84]

The King borrowed money from his nobles, who in return were given specific assignments of the royal revenue (anticipations) as security. The Lord Privy Seal chose the soap monopoly, and Castle suggested that Bridgewater 'invest' in the same manner. The solicitation of loans in early 1640 was facilitated by the knowledge that Parliament would be meeting, ostensibly to rescue the royal finances. Castle heard from Lord Keeper Finch that writs for a new Parliament would be sent out. Castle further counselled Bridgewater to follow Captain Davies's suggestion that he distribute his loan to the King as the merchants do in their lading, not trusting in a solitary ship. Therefore Bridgewater should place his great loan upon several branches of royal revenue. In spite of some anxiety over this situation, Charles received £5,000 from Bridgewater on 21 February 1640, secured on the Clerks of the Hanaper, ending at Christmas 1640 and 1641.[85]

Sir Robert Pye loaned £2,000, of which £600 was assigned out of the Customs for 1640 and another £500 out of the new Impositions; £500 would come out of the collections made from Merchant Strangers plus

[81] *CSPD* (1639–40), XV, p. 493. Also, Margaret Cavendish, Duchess of Newcastle, *The Life of ... William Cavendish, duke of ... Newcastle*, ed. C. H. Firth (London, 1886), p. 6. It is likely that the King's reluctance to eliminate impositions stemmed from their potential use in securing credit.

[82] *CSPD* (1639–40), XV, 14 March 1640.

[83] PRO, E 404/234, unfoliated, warrant from Juxon to Pye.

[84] HEH, EL 7821, 5 February 1640, Castle to Bridgewater.

[85] HEH, EL 7822, 12 February 1640, Castle to Bridgewater; EL 6613, warrant from Juxon to Pye, diplomatic similar to those in E 404/234. Bridgewater paid £452 on 26 April 1639 to teller Saville, according to E 401/2461.

£400 out of recusant fines and rents.[86] The Lord Chief Justice of Common Pleas loaned £1,000.[87] Sir Charles Caesar received as collateral £2,000, assigned out of the fines for compositions for the alienations in the year 1642. Sir Edward Littleton's £1,000 was assigned out of the annual revenues of the clergy in the diocese of London with £500 for the year ending at Christmas 1639, and £500 for the year ending at Christmas 1640. James Morely loaned £2,000 against the new impositions collected by Henry Garway for the year 1642. Sir Henry Martin's [Marten?] £3,000 was assigned out of the collection of the duty upon wines for the year 1642.[88] Sir John Lambe, Sir Sydney Montagu, Sir Edward Powell, Sir Thomas Merry, and Mr John Parker (all creatures of the King's court) were solicited directly by summons of the Privy Council. They demanded of Lambe £6,000, Montagu £4,000, and the rest £3,000 apiece. Sir Sidney got himself down to £2,000 and Parker to £1,000, but the others were ordered to pay the sums designated.[89]

According to Gerald Aylmer these were 'genuine loans', secured at the maximum rate, 8 per cent, as dictated by statute. Only the loans of Laud and Attorney General Bankes were given interest free. There was, however, no 'general levy on all office-holders', though certain parts of the royal bureaucracy, such as the Exchequer, were squeezed collectively.[90] A loan or contribution sometimes lessened an official's obligation to provide forces from his shire:

Mr Pitt, one of the Tellers of the Exchequer having already contributed in a good proporcion towards the present imployment into the North: It is not conceaved reasonable (although according to his Majesties pleasure signified by the Lord Trearer, he hath provided an Horse and Armes for the defence of the County where hee lives) that hee should upon this occasion send the said Horse or Armes from thence

The deputy lieutenants were to see that Mr Pitt's horse and arms were

---

[86] PRO, E 401/2461. £100 received by teller Saville from Pye on 29 April 1639.

[87] £500 at Christmas last, £500 at Christmas next, Juxon to Pye, PRO, E 404/234, unfoliated. See G.L. Harriss, 'Aids, Loans and Benevolences', *Historical Journal*, 6 (1963), pp. 16–17

[88] HEH, EL 6979.

[89] HEH, EL 7825, Castle to Bridgewater, 27 February 1640. See also Sir Sydney Montagu's giving up of the office of Master of Requests over the £2,000 loan and Mr Parker's jeopardy in coming up with the £2,000. HEH, EL 7839, Castle to Bridgewater, 24 June 1640.

[90] *The King's Servants: The Civil Service of Charles I 1625–1642* (New York, 1961), p. 201. Aylmer cites PRO, SP 16/408/53 (the plan to raise £1,150,000), SP 16/423/67 (Mildmay's letter), SP 16/539/6 (loans anticipated from Exchequer officers), CSPD (1639–40), XV, pp. 337,567, Rushworth, *Historical Collections*, vol. II, ii, p. 912, and PRO, T 56/5, ff. 65–103.

spared and remained in the county.[91] Sir Peter Osborne, the Lord Treasurer's Remembrancer of the Exchequer paid into the Receipt £1,000 by way of loan; the tallies were cut against revenues for respite of homage for 1640 and 1641.[92]

Solicitation of loans was accompanied by the collection of old debts. The Earl of Huntingdon learned that he had to pay a debt of £4,055 10s 8d to the Crown.[93] Yet Charles characteristically did not live by the rules he imposed upon his subjects. He began to demur to his own creditors. Although among the first to be solicited, the King's servants found themselves the first to be denied repayment:

> those Lords, and others, your Majesty's servants, that have lent you monies, and who are shortly to receive them again upon assignments, may be dealt with by you Majesty to forbear them for a year longer, your Majesty causing the interest due to be paid in the mean time. Those that are best affected to your Majesty are first to be treated with.[94]

The devices for raising extraordinary revenue outside of parliamentary channels always carried a political price. By borrowing from the Anglican clergy, Roman Catholics, and even the Queen, Charles brought attention to those whose political and religious agendas were suspect.[95] By drawing upon the resources of Arminian bishops and papists, Charles gave credence to the allegations that an unholy alliance had been forged which would eradicate mainstream Protestantism and Parliament. The financial benefit was modest and the political cost incalculable. The final incrimination came when Charles stooped to borrow money from his own wife, an alleged ringleader of the popish plot. 'It is of ironic interest that the queen advanced a loan to the king of £8,000 "out of my treasure" on 26 May 1640, that was to be repaid out of the clergy benevolence.

---

91 PRO, PC 2/50, ff. 401–2, 31 May 1639. Also received by John Savile according to PRO, E 401/2461, receipt book, Easter 1639; Savile paid £50 on 2 May for the defence of the realm. Also, entry below Savile, one John Elston, receiver in the Exchequer, paid in 100 shillings on 2 May 1639. This arrangement was not unlike the one offered to Lord Montagu regarding substituting cash in lieu of raising horsemen. See discussion of the summoning of the nobility on pp. 154–6.

92 PRO, E 404/234, Juxon to Pye,

93 HEH, Hastings Collection (box 16), HA 7997, Juxon to Huntingdon, 28 April 1640, regarding a declaration of the Receiver of Accounts for Warwickshire and Leicestershire concerning rents enrolled in the Pipe Office.

94 Bodleian Library, Clarendon SP, XIX, f. 35v, Windebank to the King, *circa* 23 August 1640.

95 C. M. Hibbard, 'The Contribution of 1639: Court and Country Catholicism', *Recusant History*, 16 (1982), pp. 42–60, *Charles I and the Popish Plot*, pp. 90–167 and 'Episcopal Warriors in the British Wars of Religion', in M. Fissel (ed.), *War and Government in Britain, 1598–1650*, pp. 164–92.

After the Long Parliament declared the benevolence void, she had to write off the debt.'[96]

Summer brought a rash of borrowing as the mobilization demanded a steady cash flow. Archbishop Laud loaned £4,000 on the security of the Customs.[97] Strafford appears somehow to have raised £20,000, lent against future recusancy fines. Sir Richard Wynne presented £7,000 and the Lord Maynard a comparatively modest £500.[98]

Charles's frantic attempts to raise money elicited some uncharacteristically panicky responses from the King. By August he was asking for money to be raised in any way possible. If none were sent, the war would be lost. In such straits, he was dependent upon the cooperation of the counties. Yet those who dwelt in the towns and countryside had contributed as little as possible in most cases and very often refused outright. This recalcitrance was most apparent in the lack of enthusiasm, and sometimes defiance, in the matter of the collection of coat-and-conduct money.

COAT-AND-CONDUCT MONEY

Coat-and-conduct money was 'a general rate levied throughout the county ... to buy each soldier a good coat and maintain him on the march' until he came under the King's pay, either at an embarkation point, when the shire boundary was crossed, or arrived at the royal standard.[99] A raw soldier received 8d a day, and his coat and shoes could cost about fifteen shillings. Many regarded coat-and-conduct money, like other Caroline exactions, as of dubious legality, for the assessment lacked statutory authority. The subject's obligation to defend the realm was originally customary and then defined by medieval statute. Coat-and-conduct money was regarded as one component of that obligation. Opposition to the rate, however, did not focus on the solitary issue of what constituted defence of the realm, for coat-and-conduct money had been collected most commonly for foreign expeditions, which added to its ambiguity in the case of the Bishops' Wars. In sixteenth-century campaigns against Scotland, which could fall under the rubric of defensive wars, the Tudors had used the rate

[96] C. M. Hibbard, 'Episcopal Warriors in the British Wars of Religion', p. 190, note 91, citing PRO, LR 5/57, f. 50, the Queen to Sir Richard Wynne, 20 December 1641. The date would indicate that Charles was scrambling for cash in the wake of the dissolution of the Short Parliament.

[97] On the Laud loan see PRO, E 403/2568, ff. 112v–113.

[98] See PRO, E 403/2568, ff. 127v–129v, privy seals from May to June 1640.

[99] Barnes, *Somerset 1625–1640*, p. 254, note 6. The estimate on clothing is my own. For a rough Scottish equivalent to coat-and-conduct money, see the receipt for £10 in SRO, Breadalbane muniments, GD 112/43/1/7/51.

to get soldiers north. But in these cases the Tudors had summoned Parliament and consequently reimbursed the county communities at least partially from the coffers of the proceeds of parliamentary subsidy. Because the First Bishops' War was waged without benefit of parliamentary assistance, the Crown relied particularly heavily on the coat-and-conduct money assessment to get levies to the York rendezvous. The non-parliamentary nature of the mobilization constituted something of an innovation, as did the footing of the bill. Charles I expected the localities to provide for their pressed men until they formally entered royal pay, without reimbursement or compensation.

In the guise of coat-and-conduct money the Crown greatly increased the military obligation upon its authority alone. The coincidence of its vigorous collection immediately after Hampden's case conflated coat-and-conduct money, ship money, and other financial exactions of the Personal Rule with the constitutional battles between Crown and Parliament in the 1620s. Just as the forced loan of 1626–8 placed a cloud over Crown borrowing in 1639–40, so too the military charges and parliamentary rhetoric of the 1620s seen through the prism of the 'eleven years' tyranny' gave coat-and-conduct money an ideological character identical to ship money.[100] Inchoate resistance in the counties coalesced with the calling of Parliament in April 1640.

John Pym recited coat-and-conduct money and other military charges in his litany of grievances before the House of Commons on 17 April 1640.[101] In doing so, he defined coat-and-conduct money as a constitutional issue and linked military charges and ship money, making military grievances stemming from the First Bishops' War consistent with the parliamentary attack on the exactions of the Personal Rule. As a result the military charges of the Bishops' Wars became inseparable from ship money and led to the 'taxpayers' strike of 1640'.[102] Sir Francis Fane told the Earl of Rutland, 'I have beene in the west with my brother, and find a strange concurrence in men's minds concerning the Scottish business and shipping

100 See pp. 40, 48, 121, 131, 192, 194, 208–9, 215–16, 294–5.
101 Aylmer, 'Administrative Reform', p. 240; see also proclamation of 20 August 1640 in J. F. Larkin (ed.), *Stuart Royal Proclamations* (Oxford, 1983), vol. II, pp. 728–30; and Rushworth, *Historical Collections*, vol. III, pp. 1228–9. This theme is developed in M. Fissel, 'Scottish War and English Money', pp. 202–6, 212.
102 Maltby (ed.), *Aston's Diary*, p. 22 and note 49 on p. 30: 'The melitary chardges by letters from the Lords [of the Privy Council], or king, pressing of men, munition, horses and such like by Lord Lieutenants of theyr owne heads.'; also Cope and Coates (eds.), *Proceedings of the Short Parliament*, p. 154: 'The Millitary charges or Imposicons on the people, raysed by Princes lrs or by Lords of the Councell, as Armour money, conduct money, and the like; these are imposicions agt all Lawe, which as they are very burthensome soe is the consequence very dangerous.'

mony', an observation which linked the suppression of the Covenant with the tyranny of the Personal Rule.[103]

Coat-and-conduct money, unlike ship money which fell upon the shrievalty, was collected by the lieutenancy, with assistance from the constabulary. As with the Exchequer, the efficiency of the apparatus through which revenue flowed was as important as the amount collected.[104] Whereas ship money tested the sheriff, coat-and-conduct money tested the constables.[105] At the pyramid's apex, the Privy Council oversaw the Lords Lieutenant setting in motion the process of collecting conduct money. The tireless deputy lieutenants, who shouldered many military responsibilities, also had the thankless task of collecting cash from each shire's residents. In this they were aided by the chief and petty constables who listed and rated inhabitants according to their wealth, and then collected the prescribed sums. In effect, the King had chosen to place a tremendous burden on local officials rather than endure the objections of MPs at Westminster. He showed little understanding of the dilemma in which he placed his loyal but amateur and unpaid servants as they struggled to collect the non-statutory tax from their neighbours.

On Sunday 31 May 1640 the announcement of the impending tax rang from each parish pulpit, fitting for a war fought for religious uniformity. The Short Parliament had been precipitously dissolved that very month, and recountings of speeches such as Pym's now circulated into the country. Coat-and-conduct money which, even before the Bishops' Wars 'had all the signs of another military tax' like ship money, now mushroomed as a full constitutional issue at a crucial time in the mobilization process.[106] The Short Parliament had brought the issue to the fore, as was dramatized at a Common Council meeting in the City. The Lord Mayor's pressing of 4,000 men had been stymied by the Common Council's refusal to levy coat-and-conduct money. After the Lord Mayor and Recorder's exhortation of obedience to the Crown, a citizen stood and offered to donate half his estate to the royal cause if three questions were answered satisfactorily. First, had the recently dissolved Parliament embraced the Scottish war or not? If not, could the Common Council in conscience pursue a policy that had been spurned by Parliament? Secondly, were the Scots at that specific time truly in rebellion? If a state of rebellion did *not* exist, would it be wise to provoke the Scots? Thirdly, could an Englishman in all conscience enable soldiers to kill the Scots (as they were 'cousin' Protestants) whilst he

---

[103] HMC Rutland, p. 522, cited in Hibbard, 'Episcopal Warriors', p. 190, note 92.
[104] See Fissel, *'Bellum Episcopale'*, pp. 396–403.
[105] Ibid, p. 397, citing Barnes, *Somerset 1625–1640*, p. 121.
[106] Anthony Fletcher, *A County Community in Peace and War: Sussex 1600–1660* (London, 1975), p. 195. According to Fletcher (p. 194), 'Delays in the repayment of coat and conduct money were normal.'

remained ignorant of the motives and grounds of the war? These considerations were joined to the constitutional objection that no statutory basis
existed for military charges, as subsequent speakers pointed out, citing the
Petition of Right.[107] Clearly, the dissolution of the Short Parliament
without clarification of the legality of military charges provided a useful
excuse for non-payment. In late May the Buckinghamshire deputy lieutenants were so exasperated that of the £2,600 to be raised for coat-and-
conduct money, they had secured only £8 10s.[108]

In August 1640 the Berkshire Grand Jury petitioned against 'the newe
tax of coat-and-conduct mony, with the undue means used to inforce the
payment of it by messingers from the Counsell ... the compelling of some
freemen by imprisonment or threatenings to take presse money coat-and-
conduct money refusers punished by being conscripted'.[109] By enforcing
the assessment in this manner, the refusers received punishment that circumvented due process of law. The penalty was worse than the offence. In
Hertfordshire the constitutional objections helped local authorities explain
why the rate met with unusually consistent opposition. The deputy lieutenants and constables summarized the sentiment of their locality that coat-
and-conduct money must be implemented through the ancient course of
Parliament. That body's expressed doubts provided sufficient justification
for non-payment, or at least further consideration. The constables of
Aldenham reported that they had caused a warrant for the raising of
£10 10s to be read from the pulpit and announced a community gathering
to discuss how the collection and rating could be made equitably. This
occasion for the articulation of opposition rallied the parish around the
argument that coat-and-conduct money was not to be due by the 'Lawes
established in the Realme'.[110]

Returns from adjacent parishes in Hertfordshire bore remarkable,
indeed suspicious, resemblance, suggesting some collaborating in the compilation. Abbots Langley, Watford, Windridge, and Parkward (in the
parish of Stevens) convened meetings like that of Aldenham whose returns
approximated each other not only in language but also in handwriting,
suggesting that the extant returns are not the originals, though they bear

---

107 HEH, EL 7838, Castle to Bridgewater, 25 June 1640.
108 Bodleian Library, Tanner MS. LV, f. 78, Robert Crane to Sir Robert Crane, 29 May
     1640. The correspondent claimed to have learned this personally from a Bucking-
     hamshire deputy lieutenant.
109 PRO, SP 16/463/33, newsletter of Edmund Rossingham, 4 August 1640. The phraseology
     of Rossingham's letter approximates closely John Rous's diary: 'The newe taxe of Coate
     and Conduct Mony, with undue meanes used to inforce payment of it, by messengers
     from the Counsell table.' John Rous, Diary of John Rous incumbent of Santon
     Downham, Suffolk, from 1625 to 1642, ed. M. A. E. Green, Camden Society, first series
     (London, 1856), p. 92.
110 PRO, SP 16/456/71 I, Herts constables' returns June 1640.

the constables' signatures. Five other Hertfordshire returns, Brandfield (Bramfield?), Codicte, Norton, Newen (Newnham?), and Shephold specify the need for parliamentary authorization, what one constable termed 'the usuall and Ancient waye'.[111] In these five returns there is a similarity in the clerks' hands; the size and texture of the paper is almost identical, as is the composition of the certificates. Chronology accounts for the consensus amongst the Hertfordshire parishes. Given the proximity of the parishes, it is likely that the local authorities, lieutenants and constables, met to discuss the resistance they were encountering, hoping to make some sense of it to the Lord Lieutenant.[112] On 11 June they declared:

Yesterday we attended againe at Hertford, to take the rates made by the high and petty Constables of this County, for the Coate and Conduct moneys and other Services ... we doe finde much disobedience in this service, few of the petty Constables haveing made any rates, and little or noe moneys collected, but denialls or delayes generally returned by them in writing under their hands.[113]

The constables were caught between the inhabitants and the government, and thus enunciated the problem as local governors saw it, very much in the language of the dissolved Parliament. The raising of coat-and-conduct money as an issue before the Short Parliament, coupled with the parliamentary dissolution in May, made assessment and collection very difficult. In describing the dilemma, the returns reflect the collective opinion of local governors and not necessarily those of the refusers themselves.

If coat-and-conduct money had a potential Hampden, it was William Pargiter. Imprisoned for refusal to pay, this Northamptonshire gentleman seized upon the Petition of Right and applied for a writ of habeas corpus, which obliged the King's Bench to demand of the Crown the cause of Pargiter's committal.[114] It could not have happened at a worse time for the mobilization of the King's army. The impending prosecution justified wholesale refusal of coat-and-conduct assessments, crippling the fielding of the pressed infantry.

Resourceful Crown lawyers found a solution, the Commission of Array. Unlike the 1620s, it could be argued that in 1640 England faced imminent invasion. According to Gardiner,

In the reign of Henry IV, it had been decided in Parliament that, when an invasion was impending, the King might issue Commissions of Array. All that were capable of bearing arms in each county would be bound to march in person to the defence

---

[111] PRO, SP 16/456/71 I, certificate marked '146'.

[112] The papers of the Lord Lieutenant, the Earl of Salisbury, are printed in HMC Salisbury, Cecil MSS., XXII, especially pp. 296–322.

[113] PRO, SP 16/456/71, 11 June 1640. See V. Stater, 'War and the Structure of Politics', in *War and Government in Britain, 1598–1650*, ed. M. Fissel, pp. 87–109, for a recent interpretation of how local governors mediated between central and local government.

[114] Gardiner, *History*, vol. IX, p. 161.

of the realm. Those who were incapacitated by age or infirmity would be bound to contribute both to the equipment of the force raised, and to its support till it passed the borders of the county in which it had been levied. After that it would be taken into the King's pay.[115]

Commissions of Array, an unprinted statute, resolved the question of payment in favour of the central authority and established a legal basis for the military preparations of 1640. The council could with some smugness disregard the argument that the Crown should repay coat-and-conduct money after the cessation of hostilities, for with Commissions of Array the initial outlay and obligation to contribute clearly came from the pockets of the countrymen, not the Receipt.

As was the case with Hampden, Charles had satisfied the law but not his subjects, who regarded this as another trick from Westminster.[116] Sir Gilbert Gerrard expressed Middlesex's resistance to military charges. During the pivotal and disastrous parliamentary session of 4 May 1640 he described the burden of military charges and specified the similarities which ship money shared with coat-and-conduct money, as had Hampden, Hotham, and St John.[117] Although his remarks in the House sounded sufficiently confrontational to spark a reply from Sir Henry Vane, Gerrard did not seek conflict when the constables came round to collect coat-and-conduct money later that month. No fewer than four Middlesex constables sought to collect from the baronet. Rated in four parishes (Harrow-on-the-Hill 18s, Sudbury 20s, Roxeth 4s, and Northall 13s 4d), constables called at his residence repeatedly from 24 May to 15 June and were informed of his absence or inability to see visitors because of indisposition. He did, however, pay his 18s coat-and-conduct money assessment in Harrow-on-the-Hill while privately encouraging non-payment among his neighbours.[118]

Middlesex provides the richest documentation of coat-and-conduct money collection. The Privy Council monitored the returns and compelled refusers to appear before the board.[119] The parishes of Middlesex being

---

[115] Ibid, p. 162.

[116] On the Commissions see A. H. Noyes, *The Military Obligation in Mediaeval England, with Especial Reference to Commissions of Array* (Columbus, Ohio, 1930), pp. 55–65; 104–63; for an apparent case of repayment of coat-and-conduct money in the 1620s, see PRO, E 404/234.

[117] Cope and Coates (eds.), *Proceedings of the Short Parliament*, pp. 192,194; Fissel, 'Scottish War and English Money', pp. 204, 209. On Gerrard see Keeler, *The Long Parliament*, pp. 185–6 and Russell, *FBM*, p.134; for Hampden's connection of ship money with military impositions, see Maltby (ed.), *Aston's Diary*, p. 43.

[118] PRO, SP 16/457, f. 76, abstract of constables' activities; Russell, *FBM*, p. 134.

[119] See Fissel, '*Bellum Episcopale*', p. 385, n. 29; Danvers was committed to the Fleet; PRO, PC 2/51 ff. 573–5; Maltby (ed.), *Aston's Diary*, pp. 26, 31, 104, 198; on Gerrard, see also Fissel, 'Scottish War and English Money', p. 209; also Keeler, *The Long Parliament*,

close at hand and comparatively wealthy allowed the council to pursue delinquents stringently. The deputy lieutenants, justices of the peace, and constables not only drew up accounts of the moneys collected but also individualized lists of refusers enumerating their excuses. Some, like one Shambrooke of Hornsey, characterized themselves as a 'poore' men, while others did not elaborate on their poverty, simply (and vaguely) stating that they 'cannot pay'. Or the rating might be disputed: Philip Briscoe responded that he was 'willing to pay parte but conceaveth himselfe over rated', as did William Gibbs. In fact, the coat-and-conduct money rate was often modelled upon the poor rate, but that did not prevent disputes. There were about a dozen pleas through which one might delay payment or conjure up an excuse for non-payment. Besides poverty and the equity of the rate, one could offer a percentage, disappear, claim non-residence, question the legality of the charges (especially in 1640), take refuge behind a general refusal of the parish or hundred, request time to consider the demand, argue that the absence (or opposition) of one's spouse prevented compliance, or most interesting of all, tell the authorities that one 'did not understand what was meante by Coatte and conductt money'.[120]

Special-interest groups posed a problem. For example, the Middlesex justices of the peace found defaulting endemic in the parishes and hamlets of Stepney, St Katherine's, Whitechapel, and Smithfield. The main source of resistance came from the 600 militiamen assigned to guard the Tower of London which, they asserted exempted them from paying coat-and-conduct money. Likewise, certain London seafaring men and ships' carpenters claimed immunity under the charters of the Trinity House and Shipwrights' Company.[121] In a similar vein, William Geene requested dismissal of his 6s 8d assessment on the grounds that he served as a captain in the trained bands.[122]

The nature of the Scottish war made coat-and-conduct money a more truly national issue than billeting, for it affected each county. But billeting charges (a more onerous expense) still stirred controversy among those who remembered the 1620s, and sometimes compounded the resentment associated with coat-and-conduct money. The council's shortage of funds in spring 1640 postponed the admission of levies into the ranks of the royal army. The central government's political incompetence as much as the revived legal objections to coat-and-conduct money had made refusal fairly

pp. 185–6; Maltby (ed.), *Aston's Diary*, pp. 14, 115, 181; Cope and Coates (eds.), *Proceedings of the Short Parliament*, p. 194.

[120] PRO, SP 16/460/80.

[121] PRO, SP 16/460/80; 80 I, certificates of the Middlesex justices of the peace, 22 July 1640.

[122] PRO, SP 16/461/103 I, f. 240, Middlesex returns of Sir John Francklyn *circa* July 1640. Geene is listed under defaulters from Highgate Side in the parish of Hornsey; Rushworth, *Historical Collections*, vol. III, pp. 1203–4, 12 July 1640.

common. In addition to the doubts sown by the protestations of the Short Parliament, a more eminently practical justification for delay of payment or refusal existed. Anthony Fletcher has pointed out that the feverish changes of plan in the mobilization penalized those counties which were obedient to the council's orders. Their reward was billeting. The Crown's failure to obtain money from Parliament, coupled with the bottleneck at the Receipt, delayed mobilization.[123] The colonels could not take command of raw soldiers without ready money, for they were in the King's pay upon delivery to the captains. The colonels therefore had to see that the captains possessed money to keep the troops together. Mobilization ground to a halt until the field officers possessed sufficient money. The Sussex deputies assembled their force of 600 men by the end of April and began drilling in anticipation of the 20 May county rendezvous. On 1 June, the men were to be transferred to their royal commanders and placed on the King's pay. But the delay ordered on 6 May meant that the locality shouldered the maintenance of these six companies until embarkation. Ensuing billeting charges compounded the cost of coat-and-conduct money so that by 22 May Sussex faced a debt of nearly £4,000! And the amount grew as June proceeded. Those counties which had failed to raise their men due to widespread resistance to coat-and-conduct money benefited, for without the rate they could not field a force and thus did not sustain billeting charges when the council delayed mobilization.[124]

The anticlimax of the Pacification of Berwick and the failure of the Short Parliament provided ample reason to evade payment of coat-and-conduct money. Again, one might say that the obedient had the greatest grievance. Those counties which had successfully raised coat-and-conduct money in 1639 saw an inconclusive campaign waste their funds. The Short Parliament only increased doubts about the wisdom of the war. Therefore, why squander further coat-and-conduct money if the King and the Scots simply sat down again at the conference table? The 1639 'masque' cost the county communities a great deal of money and they did not look forward to a second performance, particularly after the bad reviews at Westminster in April and May 1640.[125]

The collection of coat-and-conduct money in 1639 and 1640 further underscored the political insensitivity and ineptitude of the King. Those who paid obediently in 1639 and 1640 were taken for granted. Again, Charles's inability to work with Parliament in spring 1640 made the func-

---

[123] See pp. 140–50.
[124] Fletcher, *Sussex*, p. 194; but see also C. Russell, *Parliaments and English Politics 1621–1629* (Oxford, 1979), p. 346, where he comments on the relation between coat-and-conduct money and billeting in Sussex in 1628.
[125] Fletcher, *Sussex*, p. 194; see also his citations of *CSPD* (1640), pp. 202, 539–40; HMC Rutland, p. 520.

tioning of government that much more difficult during the Second Bishops' War. However, hard as the local governors struggled to make ends meet, their predicament was not nearly as desperate as that of the Tellers of the Receipt at the Exchequer.

THE MACHINERY OF THE EXCHEQUER

Charles pursued a variety of courses to finance his armies in 1639 and 1640, many of which drew upon traditional fiscal expedients (excluding Parliament). The inherent financial weakness of the Crown made it imperative that the royal army be properly paid, for the King had no reserves of cash from which to fund unanticipated military costs. There was little margin for error. Fiscal weakness had inclined the Crown to borrow more than it should have done, with the result that royal credit in 1638 stood rather low. For essentially commercial reasons loans were difficult to obtain from big lenders, while the 'forced loan' episode of 1626–8 had poisoned the minds of lesser lenders and quite a few citizens. This procedure had managed to get a modest army to the borders in 1639, but was insufficient to meet the needs of the 1640 campaign. Ideological (as opposed to purely economic) resistance to Charles's attempts to fund the Second Bishops' War grew largely out of the issue of coat-and-conduct money, since its collection could be tied to loftier constitutional issues. Issues of principle combined with fiscal weakness. In 1640, politics weakened the system of military finance by encouraging non-payment of taxes and loans, but the overheating and final malfunctioning came within the Receipt itself, when the demands placed upon the machinery of the Exchequer jammed that institution, severing the connection between the central administration and the paymasters.

Historically, war stimulated the development of the Exchequer, yet its resultant complexity impeded the flow of funds into the captains' pockets. The bureaucratic thicket of the Exchequer, made even more dense by the motley collection of fiscal expedients and a tangled web of deficit financing, complicated the exchange of funds from the administration to the paymasters. Given the ponderous mechanism of the Exchequer, it is not enough to ask whether Charles could have afforded to fight in 1639 and 1640. The fiscal problem was twofold: how much money could the King get, and, just as important, how efficiently could it be collected and disbursed? The second problem, even more than the first, hampered the war efforts of 1639–40. Unwarranted optimism regarding the availability of money and inflexible scheduling led the government into the fiscal crisis of August–September 1640. The shortage of ready money experienced during the First Bishops' War should have alerted the King to the perils of deficit finance. The diversion of pay and supplies from theatres regarded as marginal to the royal strategy opened up holes in the defence perimeter of the borders. The demoralized condition of the units guarding areas near Carlisle indicate that an incursion through that sector might have undone the English army entirely through encirclement or bypass. The men lacked 'Amunition and paye havinge neither pouthr nor match nor monye from the Treasurer'.[126] If the King planned to fight in 1640, he should have had sufficient money. Lacking a war chest, Charles pinned his hopes on Parliament and loans, and hemmed himself in by allowing little time between the convening of that assembly and the consequent gathering of the anticipated subsidies in time to fight a war that summer. He may have been thinking of the political benefits of a successful Parliament at the expense of considering the obstacles involved in securing its economic rewards.

Parliament opened on 13 April 1640. By that time the lieutenancy, especially in the north, was expected to have begun mustering and drilling county forces. All counties were to hold a general muster and review on 20 May, a bare five weeks after Parliament's opening. No wonder Charles warned that delay in granting subsidies for the war was worse than outright refusal. The money was needed straightaway, and the Parliament men were to vote the subsidies, then hurry back to their counties for mustering, administering, and collecting. Mismanagement and then dissolution of the Short Parliament jeopardized the timetable for the mobilization.[127]

In spite of the utter failure of the Parliament and a hard-pressed Exchequer, Charles insisted on prosecution of the war. The Earl of Northumberland's correspondence confirms to the historian what all Privy Councillors knew; the King would have his way regardless of the results: 'Notwithstanding this dissolution, the King intends vigorously to pursue his former designes.' The 30,000 man army would assemble, with 3,000 cavalry, even though it was not clear to the councillors how it could be sustained for even a month. The earl could not fathom 'by what meanes we are certaine to gett one shilling, towards the defraying this great expence'.[128] Strafford assured Charles – telling the King precisely what Charles wanted to hear – that there was 'Noe danger in undertakinge this warr':[129] £100,000 could be pried loose from the merchants of London, and expedients such as ship money could raise more. Remedies required

---

126 British Library, Add. MS. 18,979, ff. 56–59v, Sir Ferdinando Fairfax to Lord Fairfax, 11 and 18 June 1639.
127 Cope and Coates, *Proceedings of the Short Parliament*, p. 198. For an account of how the Short Parliament was bungled, see Russell, *FBM*, pp. 92–123.
128 Centre for Kentish Studies, De L'Isle and Dudley MSS, Sydney Papers, U 1500 C 2/42, f. 1v, to the Earl of Leicester, 7 May 1640; Russell, *FBM*, p. 123.
129 House of Lords Record Office, Main Papers (April–September 1640), ff. 99–100; Fissel, *'Bellum Episcopale'*, p. 173, note 2.

time, so the council amended the schedule for raising pressed soldiers and postponed the general musters. Levies remained in the pay of the counties until 10 June 1640, or later.[130] That delay in the mobilization was the first of two delays which ultimately rendered the English army unprepared to flex its full strength when the Scots crossed the Tweed and the Tyne in August.

In 1640, Charles raised £857,712 in cash receipts and assigned in tallies an additional £102,381.[131] The government's estimate that the 1640 campaign would cost a million pounds or so was fairly accurate.[132] Where they erred was in assuming that the money could be collected, and collected quickly. However, it was a remarkable achievement, considering that the annual cash revenues of the Crown during the Personal Rule rarely reached £500,000.[133] But most of it came too late. Uvedale's £300,000 should have been infused into the army in July, not in late August and early September. Certainly money trickled in through mid-August 1640. Each teller would collect comparatively small amounts. From the Great Customs, Teller Brooke received £2,500 on 13 August, Squibb £2,500, Pitt £5,000 (followed by £1,000 six days later), and Savile £5,000.[134] But the volume was insufficient and tardy. The Farm of the Great Custom garnered £87,566 in 1639, increased to £177,883 in 1640, and the new impositions brought in £76,169, followed the next year by £141,285.[135] During the crucial late summer, Brooke received only £2,000 from the new imposition on wine and nothing from exports. Squibb gathered a total of £5,785 from those sources in August. Pitt received £4,855 from the exports under the new imposition in July and August and £4,200 from the wines. Savile got £7,255 from the exports and £700 from the wines during July and August.[136] But these sums, the major receipts for the totality of Crown finance, did not sustain the immense needs of a 20,000-man army as its mobilization reached high gear. While the troops lacked weapons, arms lay waiting to be purchased from the makers.[137] Income failed to keep pace with expenditure by imprest.[138] The royal political agenda had failed to account for the limited resources available.

---

[130] PRO, PC 2/52, ff. 472–3, Privy Council to Lords Lieutenant; PRO SP 16/452/57; Rushworth, *Historical Collections*, vol. III, p. 1171.
[131] Dietz, 'Receipts and Issues', p. 152.
[132] Russell, *FBM*, p. 92.
[133] Dietz, 'Receipts and Issues', pp. 148–9.
[134] PRO, E 401/2463, unfoliated, by teller, with Savile's water damaged.
[135] These figures do not include the 'new increase of new impositions', £6,850 (1639) and £2,800 (1640), according to Dietz, 'Receipts and Issues', p. 150.
[136] For July and August, see PRO, E 401/2463, unfoliated, entries listed by teller, fund, and date.
[137] HEH, EL 7844, f. 3.
[138] See PRO, E 403/2813, ff. 64v–80v.

In the August heat, tempers frayed. Rumour circulated that when the Privy Council informed Charles of the City's recalcitrance in refusing yet another loan, he denounced his councillors, asking them what had become of their promises of money, made when they advised dissolution of the Short Parliament in May 1640.[139] It was in this context that Strafford, fighting illness as well as impatience, uttered his recommendation that hanging a few aldermen might get better results.[140] Drastic action alone could salvage the situation, and Charles's insistence spurred his councillors into action.[141]

The King's belated conjunction with his army in the north in August 1640 gave him first-hand knowledge of the financial anaemia that beset his army. The desperation and irritation in Charles's dispatches betray his frustration over lack of funds. The tellers had run short of ready cash. Secretary Windebank informed his royal master on 2 September 1640 from Drury Lane, 'Sir William Uvedale partes from hence tomorrow with: 15000 £: and if he colde have staid: 3: or 4: dayes longer he might have had: 30 m £: more, which shalbe sent with all the speed that may be'. By 4 September the cash available to the tellers had dwindled to slightly more than £1,000.[142] The Receipt strained to make available as much cash as possible, but the resources were too scant and the process too slow.[143] The Second Bishops' War was lost because money, men, and arms came too slowly to the Borders. These defects brought about the tactical blunders that led to the loss at Newburn.

The Crown generated substantial sums during the Bishops' Wars. How much cash filtered into the King's hands?[144] Initially, £200,000 was allocated for the 1639 war and £300,000 for 1640.[145] The latter figure was higher due to the experience of 1639, the prospect of Parliament's coming together to vote supplementary funds, and the greater certainty of war in 1640. In spring 1640 the Lord Keeper estimated that the royal army cost £100,000 per month. In a speech before the Short Parliament (which must be taken with some scepticism), Finch referred to £300,000 allocated for the 'preservation' of Berwick and Carlisle, so phrased as to imply that Charles's preparations were entirely defensive, which was a lie.[146] He went

139 HEH, EL 7849, f. 2, Castle to Bridgewater, 15 August 1640.
140 R. Ashton, *The City and the Court 1603–1643* (Cambridge, 1979), p. 199; on loan solicitation, see pp. 124–9.
141 Bodleian Library, Clarendon SP, XVIII, ff. 263–273v.
142 Bodleian Library, Radcliffe Trust MS. c. 36, f. 4; Russell, *CECW*, p. 164.
143 PRO, E 403/2813 chronicles this process.
144 The auditors' receipt books are E 401/2462, 2463, 2464, which compare with the abbreviates of the Pells, E 401/2342, 2343, 2344, 2345. Dietz gives aggregate revenue totals in 'Receipts and Issues'.
145 See PRO, E 403/2568, f. 72 for the First Bishops' War.
146 See above, pp. 4–6.

on to say, with truth, that the initial £300,000 would be 'of noe use' without further supply. If the £300,000 is added to the twelve subsidies asked of Parliament, historians can ascertain the amount Charles needed to get the war under way (making the £200,000 outlay for the commencement of the 1639 campaign look quite paltry in contrast). Gardiner and Russell estimated a single subsidy from a Caroline Parliament at about £70,000.[147] Thus twelve subsidies equalled about £840,000 with some flexibility for varying rates of assessment. In 1639, £600,198 in cash was disbursed, along with tally assignments of £124,408. For 1640, the tellers disbursed £851,603 in cash, with tallies amounting to £102,381.[148] Yet at the climax of the Second Bishops' War Charles dispatched urgent appeals for cash to Westminster: for 'God's sake haste Monies all you can by all wais'.[149]

The apparent contradiction of an Exchequer issuing comparatively substantial sums of money and a King and his officers desperate for ready cash came about because the initial outlays for the campaigns were insufficient to fight a Scottish war on the scale envisioned by Charles.[150] Although the size of the 1639 army was later trimmed, from 30,000 to 20,000, the demand on the Ordnance Office (whose annual budget was merely £6,000) was unreasonable in the light not only of available money but also of available personnel and stores. Considering that the bulk of infantry weapons were to be purchased abroad, the allocation of £200,000 to begin the mobilization of the First Bishops' War was a gross under-assessment of the costs of war. This error was not so much institutional but administrative. Charles and Newport should have paid greater heed to the Lieutenant of the Ordnance. In 1640 some improvement was made by setting aside a larger initial sum, £300,000. Yet the fact that a quarter to a third of the English foot were unarmed on the eve of battle indicates that weapons' procurement remained a problem. Purchase of armaments, which depended on the disbursement of substantial sums of money promptly, still did not operate as smoothly as it should have done, especially in the light of the experience of 1639. One cannot blame the institutions, the Exchequer and the Ordnance, but rather the unrealistic timetable set by

---

147 Conrad Russell gives the figure of £55,000 for 1628 in *The Origins of the English Civil War*, p. 96; Esther Cope, 'Compromise in Early Stuart Parliaments: The Case of the Short Parliament of 1640', *Albion*, 9 (1977), p. 139, n. 14 and Gardiner, *History*, vol. IX, p. 148. Dietz, *English Public Finance*, p. 285.
148 Dietz, *English Public Finance*, p. 285.
149 Bodleian Library, Clarendon SP, IX, f. 262, annotation on Windebank's letter of 24 August 1640.
150 Tudor and Stuart monarchs (aside from Henry VII) knew or cared little about the practice of the Exchequer. See J. D. Alsop, 'Government, Finance and the Community of the Exchequer' in *The Reign of Elizabeth*, ed. C. Haigh (Athens, Ga., 1985), pp. 101–23. Gloriana may have had a dim notion of her Exchequer's procedure but knew enough to economize whenever possible.

Charles I for the conquest of Covenanter Scotland. Furthermore, the inherent sluggishness of the Exchequer apparatus meant that the receiving and issuing of funds was slower than the King wished. The money moved through the 'ancient course' but did not arrive at its destination speedily enough. This was particularly true in 1640 when the twelve subsidies solicited from the Short Parliament failed to materialize, so that ready money had to be raised from other sources. Charles bears some of the responsibility for this situation, as his unfamiliarity with royal financial institutions tempted him to plan strategies which stretched his resources to the fullest extent.[151] Juxon and Cottington, too, were initially more sanguine than circumstances justified; in 1638 their naivete regarding war and in 1640 their optimism over Parliament led them astray. They did not understand the 'ancient course'.

Money passed linearly through bureaucratic channels which might at any point be delayed. It began with the Receivers General, appointed by the Lord Treasurer, or in some cases the treasury commissioners, by letters patent under the Great Seal with tenure for life. Bi-annually, around Lady Day and Michaelmas, they proceeded through their circuits, collecting funds at predesignated meeting places, where farmers, tenants, collectors, and bailiffs of the Crown proffered hard currency derived largely from Crown lands. Most often a Receiver General bore responsibility for two, three, or sometimes four counties. The Receivers General deposited the money with a specific Teller of the Receipt, who recorded the transaction.[152] The auditors of the Crown lands, also known as the 'auditors of the land revenues' examined the accounts of the Receivers General, placing the collections from the seven land-revenue districts under the eye of the Augmentations Office. The number of receivers, usually fewer than thirty, remained small, since each position was only as lucrative as the size and wealth of the collection area.[153] The fees kept by the receivers, which could be as high as 10 per cent of the total received, denied some of the money to the Crown. The Receivers General were a hybrid of 'salaried' Exchequer officers and local governors. Some military revenues did not originate with the receivers, but rather with local administrators. For example, coat-and-conduct money was collected under the authority of the deputy lieutenants, along with the constables. They, too, accounted for these funds to the Exchequer of the Receipt.[154] Under certain circumstances, justices and

---

[151] See below, pp. 290–5 and Russell, *FBM*, pp. 142–3.
[152] See PRO, E 401/2461–64, unfoliated, entries by teller under the heading 'De Exit Receptor genal dui Regis'.
[153] L. Squibb, *A Book of all the Several Officers of the Court of Exchequer .... *. ed. W. Bryson, *The Camden Miscellany v. 26*, Camden Society, fourth series, vol. XIV (London, 1975), pp. 118–24.
[154] See p. 131.

lieutenants were later reimbursed from the Receipt, for example when money was given to captains along with a contingent of pressed men.[155] *En route* to the rendezvous, the county paid the soldiers' wages, but the troops then entered the pay establishment of the Crown once they had been delivered to their royal commander.

The drawbacks of this system of collection for the Bishops' Wars were distance and transportation. For example, when John Braddill gathered up the royal revenues in Cumberland and Westmorland, those coins were apparently sent up to London for proper accounting unless authorization was given by the Lord Treasurer to re-route them to a temporary receiver or a commander who was in desperate need of hard currency. Thorough accounting demanded that the money should go through London, even if anomalies such as requisition of ready money in an emergency were occasionally permitted. Royal revenue would have been better employed in the north, as hard currency which could have been disbursed for the planned landing from Ireland, or to pay the Carlisle garrison,[156] or simply stored in a northern Treasury (at Durham or York) for the payment of the expeditionary force. The problem of a 'regional' Exchequer for military operations seems not to have been dealt with.

The Receivers General of Yorkshire often functioned as a conduit between Westminster and Major Robert Norton's garrison at Berwick. Thomas Talbot in 1639 and Thomas and John Bland in 1640 funnelled cash to Norton and were then reimbursed.[157] The Mayor of Newcastle, Sir Alexander Davison, also dispensed money to Berwick, supplying £16,000 he had obtained from Sir William Uvedale, the army's treasurer, to George Payler, the paymaster, in 1639.[158] In Davison's case, the money was prepaid by Uvedale, whereas the Yorkshire receivers appear to have imprested the money from their coffers, and then got reimbursement from the tellers themselves. Other examples of payments directly from temporary receivers exist. The Lord Treasurer authorized payment by the temporary receivers, which solved problems in the short run, but circumvented the central officers of the Exchequer, lessening the flow of currency into their coffers and thus making the tellers short of cash to issue by way of imprest or to honour the tallies that were coming in for repayment.[159]

[155] PRO, E 404/234, unfoliated, 18 December 1627, Lord Treasurer Marlborough to Sir Robert Pye, and others in this series.
[156] See PRO, SP 41/1, folio marked '19' – £13,776 per annum.
[157] PRO, E 404/234, unfoliated, Juxon and Cottington to the Receiver-General for Yorkshire, 21 March 1637. E 351/3518, f. 1v for Talbot and also issue book of the Auditor of Receipt, E 403/2813, f. 38 for two issues regarding Norton; E 351/3519, f. 1v for the Blands.
[158] PRO, E 351/3520.
[159] Havran, *Cottington*, p. 142.

During the mutinies of summer 1640, the Privy Council went so far as to allocate recently collected ship money for the payment of discontented soldiers.[160]

Sir William Uvedale linked the central government and the captains in the field. Appointed 'Treasurer at Wars' by commission under the Great Seal for both Bishops' Wars, he also functioned as Treasurer of the Chamber.[161] The success of the mobilization rested as heavily upon Uvedale as on the Lord General or the King, for he relayed the periodic payments from the Tellers of the Exchequer of Receipt to the regimental commanders. Time and distance were his enemies and he had to rely upon the efficiency of others to keep the common soldiers in pay. He was authorized to pay out sums by order of the King, Juxon, Arundel, Essex, Newport or some combination of three privy councillors. By necessity, then, he answered to many and disbursed money for virtually every need of the royal army. For his pains he received forty shillings a day and the 'hundredth penny'; in other words he deducted as a commission 1 per cent from the revenues he handled. The Auditor of the Imprests periodically examined Uvedale's accounts, usually in the form of a ledger book drawn up for that purpose by one Matthew Bradley. Payments by the temporary receivers confounded his book-keeping (and undermined his and the tellers' income). Those records were kept in a two chamber office at Westminster, where coins were padlocked in chests and guarded by a watchman at all times. When sufficient funds were amassed, they were packed in chests and loaded upon wagons bought expressly for that service. The caravans were coordinated by Uvedale's deputy paymasters and driven north with Ushers of the Guard providing security.[162] More portable sums could then be relayed in leather valises placed on horseback, as when £4,000 was sent from York to Newcastle during the First Bishops' War.[163]

Uvedale's first commission began on 20 March 1639, a week before the rendezvous at York, and he was hard pressed for funds at the very outset.[164] The Lord General complained, 'We are heere, in private be it spoken,

---

160 J. T. Cliffe, *The Yorkshire Gentry from the Reformation to the Civil War* (London, 1969), p. 318. Similar arrangements had been forged before, as in May 1627 when £500 in recusant fines destined for the Receipt and, ultimately, to finance fortifications at Landguard, were diverted to pay coat-and-conduct money to recruits for the Isle de Rhé. See PRO, E 404/234, unfoliated, 3 May 1627.

161 PRO, E 351/292 and 293; E 403/2568, ff. 90v, 91v, 132v (privy seals), and PRO, SP 16/442/80, 23 January 1640.

162 PRO, E 351/292, ff. 15–15v; PRO, PC 2/50, f. 192, 24 March 1639, warrant for guards for safeguarding of the treasurer through Yorkshire; PC 2/50, f. 411, 4 June 1639 warrant for the safeguarding of treasure for the army (or for safeguarding Uvedale?).

163 PRO, E 351/292, f. 15. Wages were paid in gold as well as silver, of course. SRO, GD 406/1/11148A, Vernon on transporting pay, 21 June 1639.

164 PRO, E 351/292, ff. 1–1v.

without Sir William Uvedale, or soe much as one penny of mony till he come: how much then, God knowes.'[165] Uvedale did not arrive until several days after the rendezvous date of 1 April 1639. Luckily, the Treasurer at Wars did not have to provide for 'distant' expeditions which lay outside his responsibility. Since Hamilton's amphibious forces in 1639 (the 1640 voyage was cancelled for lack of funds) operated in another theatre, so to speak, Captain Francis Vernon acted as paymaster for that army.[166] Likewise, Sir James Lockhart served as paymaster for Scottish officers serving the King.[167]

Uvedale received his moneys from the hands of four men, John Savile, Arthur Squibb, Edward Pitt, and John Brooke, the Tellers of the Exchequer. Revenues at the disposal of the Receipt were divided and assigned to each teller, usually on the basis of its county of origin and its source.[168] They accounted for the currency immediately upon its arrival, making out a parchment bill listing the source, county, sum, and cause of payment.[169] These bills were sent down to the Tally Court, where the payer received his tally. Money would be issued upon warrant under a privy seal from Sir Robert Pye, the Auditor of the Receipt. Uvedale received a series of at least five privy seals as Treasurer of War.[170] Possession of the warrant under the privy seal did not guarantee payment in full, as large sums were usually paid by the tellers in instalments.

Because the bureaucracy of the tellers was in almost constant operation, halting only on Sundays and major holidays, it was exceedingly difficult to ascertain exactly how much money was in the Receipt at any given time. The fluidity of the system allowed for disbursement of money, constrained by availability, at the cost of precise accounting. Since the military expenditures of 1639 and 1640 came by way of imprest, in currency, the speedy supply of coin from the tellers was the lifeblood of army finance. But the

---

165 PRO, SP 16/415/79, 31 March 1639.
166 PRO, E 351/298, 299; PRO, PC 2/50, f. 228, 3 April 1639, warrant to Vernon to pay the three regiments of English trained bands serving in Hamilton's force; SRO, GD 406/1/1176, Vane to Hamilton, 22 June 1639, and GD 406/1/1177, same correspondents, 21 June 1639. Vernon received £30,000 to be disbursed according to private instructions on 31 March 1639, the same day as Lockhart received his allocation. See E 403/2568, f. 94.
167 See PRO, E 351/296 and 297. Lockhart received a privy seal dated 31 March 1639 for £40,000, unspecified use, according to PRO, E 403/2568, f. 93v. See also SRO, GD 406/1/1100, Vane to Hamilton, 8 May 1639.
168 L. Squibb, *Book*, p. 133.
169 Now preserved as PRO, E 402/4–344, according to W. Bryson (ed.) in L. Squibb, *Book*, p. 134, note 228.
170 Records of the manner in which Uvedale spent his money make up PRO, E 351/292 and 293. See also PRO, SO 3/12, ff. 22v, 27v, 30, Signet Office docquet book; PRO, E 403/2568, ff. 90v, 91v, 132v; PRO, IND 4225, Chancery, Patent Office docquet book (1638–41), f. 20v. Records of issues including weekly summaries were kept in PRO, E 403/2813.

heavy demand for imprests placed the tellers in difficulties, for they had to contend with the regular procession of holders of tallies queuing up to receive promised payment. In other words, the tellers disbursed money to two kinds of recipients, those bearing warrants to receive payment by way of imprest (immediate payment) and those holding tallies, like promissory notes, who had waited for their tallies to mature and now expected payment in full. By late August, the Crown contemplated postponing the reimbursement of royal servants who had given loans on the security of assignments of tallies; instead, these 'sympathetic' creditors would receive their cash in late 1641.[171] The order books kept by Pye disclose that during the Bishops' Wars the tellers sometimes found their reserves under severe strain.

Money flowed in methodically over a period of time, and the various paymasters and Ordnance Office administrators received their allocations piecemeal. Uvedale's accounts reveal a marked tendency towards delay and incomplete payment. Sir William latched onto the £24,000 remaining on the privy seal for the First Bishops' War on 14 November and 6 December 1639. A January 1640 privy seal had authorized periodic payments from the Receipt which would finance the new mobilization. But on 2 March the disbursement was not fully made, for the tellers were still amassing the last instalment of the £40,000 that had been due on 22 February. As it was, the 2 March disbursement was not completed until 11 March.[172] Uvedale collected £20,000 through a series of disbursements from March to May for the raising of four regiments of horse, comprising four troops of cuirassiers and twenty four troops of carabines. Throughout the spring the Receipt parcelled out enough money to go round to all the necessary receivers for the mobilization. Late and partial payments hampered the mobilization because large sums of money were required by the Lieutenant of the Ordnance (Heydon) and Master of the Armoury (Legge), to purchase armaments. Without cash they could place no orders.

Money also went to commanders and paymasters of the garrisons as they geared up for the summer's war: Byron and Walker at Carlisle, and Norton and Payler at Berwick (sometimes through Thomas Talbot, deputy Receiver General for Yorkshire) all received funds from the Receipt.[173] A new privy seal for £300,000 could not be issued until 20 August 1640, much too late to succour the army on the eve of Newburn. Uvedale had trouble

---

[171] Bodleian Library, Clarendon SP, XIX, f. 35v, Windebank to the King, 23 September 1640. The King apostiled this letter with a note that he had discovered a better way to raise money, dated 25 September 1640.

[172] PRO, E 403/2813, f. 33; Clarendon SP, XVIII, f. 269v, Windebank to the King, 28 August 1640.

[173] See PRO, E 403/2568, f. 91v, 26 March 1639, £5,000 to George Payler; also, PRO, IND 4225, f. 49v on Carlisle, f. 51 on Berwick, and ff. 38, 44, 45v, 47–8.

collecting £100,000 in late June 1640 and did not lay his hands on another imprest until a full two months later.[174]

Sir John Heydon drew heavily from the Receipt as well.[175] For example, on 11 April 1640 Uvedale's and Heydon's needs coincided. Uvedale sought money for four regiments of horse and Heydon demanded nearly £4,000 for match, equipment, and carts on three separate imprest orders.[176] The sums doled out (especially to a fen-drainer) on this date indicate that the tellers were reaching the bottom of the barrel.[177] On 18 April the tellers paid the £3,500 balance owed to Uvedale on the imprest of 31 March, but this denied Heydon full satisfaction of his £2,681 imprest. Throughout the summer of 1640, Heydon's claims conflicted with Uvedale's. As spring became summer, increasingly Harby, Heydon, Legge, Uvedale, and Irish Treasurer Sir William Raylton were in competition at the Receipt for hard currency. Each needed money to fulfil his responsibility, yet payment bottle-necked at the tellers.

When Uvedale received an order to take up £100,000 on 22 June 1640 he managed to collect only £28,000 by the month's end.[178] The remainder, it was feared by the mercantile community, would be issued from the Mint, where seized bullion was rumoured to be being coined. A two hour council meeting, attended by goldsmiths as well as English, Dutch, and Spanish merchants, dissuaded the King from paying his army with precious metals seized from the international mercantile community in the City.[179]

In effect, the organizers of the Bishops' Wars competed with one another for available cash. Of the initial allotments for commencing military preparations in 1639 and 1640 the largest sums were earmarked for Uvedale. But significant payments went simultaneously to the Lieutenant

---

174 PRO, E 403/2568, f. 132v; E 351/293, ff. 1v - 2v.
175 See above, pp. 91–5 and PRO, SP 16/407/64. Heydon's numerous entries in the issues can be found in E 403/2813 (issues books) and in the unfoliated entries in the issues books of the Pells (E 403/1752, from March 1638 to April 1639; E 403/1753, from April 1639 to April 1640; and E 403/1754, from April 1640 to July 1641).
176 See also PRO, E 403/1754, unfoliated, under 11 April 1640.
177 PRO, E 403/2813, ff. 44–5. The uncertainty of the outcome of the Short Parliament raised great anxiety at the Receipt. On 30 April Privy Councillor the Earl of Northumberland reported to the English ambassador in Paris, 'When I pressed my Lord Treasurer [Juxon] for your Lordships payments he tolde me [in] plaine tearmes that they had not a groate in the Exchequer for the satisfying any necessarie intertainements of Embassadours to be, nor doth he expect any but must come either from the parlament or by some other extraordinarie way.' Centre for Kentish Studies, De L'Isle and Dudley MSS., Sydney Papers, U 1475 C85/14, ff. 1–1v, to the Earl of Leicester, 30 April 1640. Although ambassadors were rarely paid punctually, the letter substantiates that payments not directly involved in the mobilization were being held up while Parliament deliberated.
178 PRO, E 403/2813, f. 60. Uvedale's collections from the tellers are summarized in E 351/293, ff. 1v–2v.
179 See above, pp. 119–20; HEH, EL 7842, EL 7843, Castle letters of 6 and 10 July 1640.

of the Ordnance, and to the Irish Treasurer.[180] Raylton conveyed at least
£50,000 into Ireland to Nicholas Loftus, who as deputy vice-treasurer
carried out Strafford's orders and prepared an army of 8,000 infantry and
1,000 cavalry, designed for use against the Covenanters. Raylton's account
verifies that he received £50,000 in two instalments in April 1640, and the
Exchequer records show that he continued to receive sums through the
summer, and into the autumn. The initial £10,000 was probably taken into
Holland, where Raylton purchased arms for the Irish army.[181] The Irish
contingent never landed, but the money was spent anyway. In fact, Raylton's fiscal acquisitions for the Irish forces interfered with the pay of the
English army by delaying full payment to Uvedale.

The inability of the Crown to wage war was in part financial, but not
simply in terms of the limitation of revenue sources; rather, the Receipt was
performing a task for which it was ill supplied. Given the absence of parliamentary subsidies to increase the flow of money into the Receipt, the tellers
were hard pressed to find sufficient coin to satisfy the imprests. Consecutive wars without parliamentary subsidies further compounded the
problem. Shortages of pay contributed to the failure to sustain important
units already in arms in Ireland. The Irish regiments, reasonably well
drilled and armed, sat idle at their rendezvous points awaiting the mobilization of the royal army in England. The Irish cavalry were not to proceed
to the general rendezvous until late July, 'due to want of monyes'. Wandesford told the commander of the horse that both cavalry and infantry were
to enter royal pay 'but whether we can provyde monye att that day to pay
you I knowe not'. They were still waiting for cash at the end of the month,
hoping for the subsidy money that had been voted by the Irish Parliament.
As yet no more than £300 had reached the army.[182] Whether an infusion of
cash from across the Irish Sea could have deployed these regiments on the
border at the crucial time remains unknown, but clearly the financial
pressure was felt on all fronts.

The transmission of funds within the army is not easily traced, for captains' accounts appear not to have survived (or were not kept). Uvedale
paid soldiers' wages directly to the colonels of the regiments, or their
respective paymasters, who disbursed pay every twenty-eight days, as was
the English custom. During the First Bishops' War the infantry was paid by

180 PRO, E 351/2662, 2663; E 403/2568, ff. 11, 72, 90; see also pp. 91, 98–100, 110, 171.
181 PRO, E 351/294, ff. 1v–2; E 403/2813, ff. 48v (£10,000), 53 (£2,000), 56v (£6,000), 57
    (£4,000), 58 (£3,600), 65 (£4,250, completing the old privy seal authorization, and £5,700
    on a new privy seal). Oddly, Raylton receives no mention in E 403/2568, a record of privy
    seal issues. On £10,000 for Dutch arms, SRO, GD 406/1/803, ff. 2–3, Strafford to Hamil-
    ton, 24 March 1640.
182 Bodleian Library, Carte MSS., I, f. 202v, Wandesford to Ormonde, 7 June 1640; f. 209,
    ditto, 12 June 1640; f. 211, ditto, 30 June 1640.

regiment, and the cavalry by troop.[183] In one case Uvedale paid Sir William Becher, who reimbursed the Lords Lieutenant for press money, hence the money went through the lieutenancy.[184] Uvedale also paid out to the artillery train, commissary, and medical establishments. The rate of pay was determined by the Privy Council.[185] Pay lists in 1640, such as for the Carlisle and Berwick garrisons, regiments of light horse, artillery train, and wagon master, were drafted by Strafford, Laud, Vane, Northumberland, Juxon, and other councillors, and then signed by the King. Charles participated in this process at least some of the time. Uvedale therefore could count on the personal involvement of the highest level of government in the matter of pay.[186]

No army in the mid-seventeenth century seems to have enjoyed regular pay and Charles's was no exception. The problem entailed more than putting coins in the captains' coffers at the outset of mobilization. Conveyance of ready money to the front had to proceed fairly smoothly so as to keep up morale. A company at Berwick in April 1640 'demanded every man fourten groats, which was for five dayes Conduct Money and for two dayes pay. They were disobedient to all command, putt themselves in Ranke and file and lightened their Matches.'[187] The men deserted after two were seized by officers. Sometimes pay would arrive when victuals were scarce, as in June 1639. 'Never till now was an armye heard of without Sutler or victualler till this, it is true they [the soldiers] are paid, but they cannot eate money.'[188] Should both food and shillings fail, officers began to worry. Sir Henry Mildmay lamented, 'I feare the want of monny will shortly fale out, breade and beere being all reddy twoe scarce in our army.'[189] The most drastic evaporation of ready money to pay the regiments came at the worst possible time: a few weeks before Newburn. Sixteen regiments were asked to give 'Creditt to his Majestie for 14 dayes Paie'. Some agreed unanimously to do so, such as the regiments of

[183] PRO, E 351/292. Evidence on the highest levels is also sparse. For example, when panic set in amongst the councillors in London as to how they would find moneys to keep the King in the field in May 1639, Windebank assured Charles that the anxiety over finances was communicated to him alone. Bodleian Library, Clarendon SP, XVI, f. 126v, 24 May 1639.

[184] PRO, PC 2/50, f. 196, c.27 March 1639.

[185] Ibid, ff. 215–19, 31 March 1639.

[186] PRO, SP 41/1, pay lists regarding the establishment of the army from May to July 1640, several of which are annotated by Windebank and endorsed by the King. See for example where Charles inserted allowances for horses for the provost marshalls on 8 May 1640 (folio marked '30' listing pay of the officers of the field) and for the allowances at Berwick (folio marked '12'), Charles's approval of a revision dated 8 June 1640. Strangely, some of Charles's signatures in this series have been defaced.

[187] PRO, SP 16/451/41, Conway to Northumberland, 27 April 1640.

[188] PRO, SP 16/423/15, Edward Norgate to Robert Reade, 3 June 1639.

[189] PRO, SP 16/423/67, Sir Henry Mildmay to Windebank, 10 June 1639.

Colonels Ogle and Wentworth; others not at all, such as those of Colonels Glenham and Lunsford. The latter's soldiers would soon come under fire at Newburn ford; how the dispute over pay affected their morale can only be guessed at. The other regiments divided, some officers agreeing to credit for a week's pay, others flatly refusing.[190] This sort of thing occurred regularly in continental armies, but for English citizen soldiers it was something new. It was bad enough to be pressed against one's will or pulled from the ranks of the trained bands; now the King wanted a soldier to fight the Scots gratis, risking his life against co-religionists in a war which Parliament had refused to endorse.

The fatal consequence of arrears of pay can be seen in the observation of Vice President Osborne, who told the commander of the English cavalry that it was better that the Scots advance a good way into Northumberland than that the unpaid English infantry be sent north.[191] On pay day, troops at Newcastle mutinied over the twopence deducted from their pay for the purchase and repair of arms. Troops purchased their own gunpowder at the rate of twenty pence per pound or higher. The shoddy condition of their firearms prompted some to pay as much as eight or ten shillings for the mending of their pistols (this seems to apply mostly, if not exclusively, to the calvary). Conway complained that 'the Pistolls have allmost all the stocks broken and glued that the breake with very little force, the locks were slight worke, and have been broken and mended slightly and breake in the pins and chaine in the hands of the skillfullest pistoleer; divers of the barrells are without holes'.[192]

Although Conway sympathized with the troops' grievances, he was in no position to tolerate disorder. When the mutineers voiced their complaints, Conway had the 'speaker for the rest' apprehended. On the next day, he sent for the prisoner. A group of more than a score of angry soldiers 'came very mutinously to my doore', he said. Conway had one of the protestors seized, and condemned him and the ringleader, taken the day before, to be hanged. Thinking that the execution of one mutineer would be sufficient to 'terrifye the rest', the two condemned men were allowed to throw dice; the loser died at the hands of a five man firing squad ('because I could not gett any to hang him'). Conway added, 'The Souldiers and Townesmen did thinke the one that I would not put him to death, the other that I durst not.'[193]

190 PRO, SP 16/465/77, August 1640.
191 Bodleian Library, Clarendon SP, XIX, f. 171, Conway's relation, letter dated 14 August 1640.
192 PRO, SP 16/454/30 I and 31.
193 Ibid. Hamilton had faced a similar situation at the end of the First Bishops' War, when a mutiny broke out amid his men, apparently over pay. He contemplated hanging several men, but (for the law's sake it would appear), referred the matter to the King, who in

Further mutinies over the failure of ready money to reach the rank and file occurred throughout the summer of 1640. Two companies belonging to Commissary General Wilmot's regiment, which also was engaged at Newburn, were dispatched to quell a mutiny and then broke into disorder themselves. When Conway had heard that his own cavalry might be called to extinguish the London uprising he suggested in all seriousness that the men be shown favour by relieving them of the twopence arms deduction from their regular pay. Conway also complained about the poor quality of the arms.[194]

The Wiltshire contingent protested over pay, and disorders erupted in Norfolk, Suffolk, Somerset, and Hampshire.[195] Units were hurried in to suppress mutinies, even at the risk of the malcontents inciting the enforcing troops. Two soldiers organized a revolt amongst the regiments stationed in Yorkshire that spread to 300 men. Astley brought in loyal companies from the Lord General's regiment and a troop under Captain Howard to quell them. In the aftermath both men cast lots and the loser was hanged along the highway, in view of the assembled regiments. In spite of his success, Astley pointed out that he could not induce the men to march without further pay.[196] The situation was not improved by reports that in his anger over the Wellington mutiny, discussed below, Charles decided to keep units a fortnight in arrears as a form of discipline.

The Exchequer was expected to perform a task which exceeded its capabilities at that time. The fact that the money *ultimately* was paid, however, demonstrates the resiliency of the institution and the tenacity of the staff. Where the Covenanters succeeded, on the other hand, was in enforcing the payment of taxes promptly by comparatively ruthless methods.[197]

return, referred it back to Hamilton. See SRO, GD 406/1/1177 and 1178, Hamilton and Vane correspondence of 20 and 21 June 1639.

[194] PRO, SP 16/463/93; SP 16/456/43; SP 16/454/30 (Laud and Northumberland); SP 16/454/31 (Vane); SP 16/454/32 (Windebank).

[195] PRO, SP 16/459/7; SP 16/456/33 (Norfolk); SP 16/456/42 (Suffolk); SP 16/457/50 (Somerset); SP 16/454/99 and 99 I (Hampshire) 16 May 1640; see also SP 16/459/7 for 'want of pay'; SP 16/459/64 and SP 16/456/43, faulty weapons.

[196] PRO, SP 16/463/93.

[197] See for example SRO, GD 406/1/1237, Nithisdale to the King, 5 April 1640; NLS, Crawford MS. 14/3/32, acts of the committee of war, 15 May 1639 and SRO, GD 112/43/1/6/30, articles four, eight, and especially article nine, dated 3 May 1639.

4

Reluctant lords and absent mercenaries

Nowhere is the traditional yet improvised nature of Charles's military plans more apparent than in the means by which he attempted to raise troops. The infantry of 1639 consisted of 'select' soldiers from the trained bands north of the Trent, supplemented by a press; the dragoons and cuirassiers were brought out by a feudal summons of the nobility, clergy, and gentry. In the Second Bishops' War the nobles played a minor role, called up very late in the campaign. In both Bishops' Wars, however, the King found mercenaries an attractive option. With no centralized militia system in Scotland, a small crack mercenary force supported by English trained bands could very well have won a pitched battle against the Covenanters. However, the financial weakness of the Crown made the hiring of mercenaries virtually impossible, and the King's machinations only cast further doubt on his motives for suppressing the Covenant by force.

THE SUMMONING OF THE NOBILITY

Before the Bishops' Wars, Charles conferred with Attorney-General Bankes regarding the Crown's authority to summon subjects to defend the border.[1] Some feudal tenures obliged residents of the northern counties to serve in a defensive capacity in case of a Scottish war, although some of this legislation had been repealed after the accession of James I.[2] The opinion given was that Charles could 'command all holding offices and lands in the posts adjoining Scotland' to arm themselves and await the King's command.[3] Many lords and gentlemen were instructed to return to their northern residences during the winter of 1638–9, although a formal summons was not

[1] See for example Bodleian Library, Bankes MS. 65/53, communications between Sir John Coke and Bankes, where it is argued that the Crown's 'ancient right' regarding service was restored by the resumption of Scottish threats (folio marked '110').

[2] Linda L. Peck, *Northampton: Patronage and Policy at the Court of James I* (London, 1982), pp. 191–2.

[3] HMC, Cowper, Coke MSS., p. 187, opinion of Bankes, endorsed by Secretary Coke, 1 July 1638; Gardiner, *History*, vol. VIII, p. 350.

issued until January. Letters were also sent to bishops and corporations to prepare to raise men for the royal army.[4]

In January 1639 Charles I called upon the English nobility to recruit and arm cavalry and attend the King's standard at York on 1 April. The King's letter explained, 'The late disorder in our Realme of Scotland begun upon pretence of Religion but now appearing to have been raised by factious Spirits and fomented by some fewe ill and traiterously affected particular persons ... Wee have reason to take into consideration the defence and safety of this our Realme.'[5] Because the Covenanters were striving to 'shake off all monarchicall government' and constituted a threat to England, the lords temporal were to perform traditional knight's service in order to *defend* England from invasion. The nobles were to reply within fifteen days of receiving the summons, specifying what assistance they were prepared to give their King. If a lord could not attend the standard personally, he might compound for a cash contribution, although this alternative was never explained clearly in the summons.[6]

Bearing in mind that the early Stuart nobility was militarily (though not politically) impotent, Charles's appeal to the nobility might appear to be little more than a fiscal expedient disguised as a feudal incident, like distraint of knighthood.[7] The summons did reap lucrative sums in some quarters: the Earl of Worcester tendered £1,500, while the Earls of Thanet and Winchester and Viscount Montagu each offered £1,000.[8] But a substantial motive for the summons lay in Charles's lack of horses, military equipment, and soldiers. Strong, healthy horses did not abound in northern England, and an adequate supply of the animals was necessary not only for the royal cavalry, but for the artillery train, supply wagons, and post-horse communication system as well. More than a thousand horses were needed to pull the carts and wagons that carried munitions, supplies, and arms.[9]

[4] PRO, SP 16/396, f. 61; SP 16/409/106, Council of War minutes, 17 January 1639.

[5] PRO, SP 16/396, ff. 94–5, Council of War entry book, 26 January 1639; SP 16/410/24, Charles to Lord Grey; there are numerous examples in the State Papers Domestic. For a similar summons in the time of Edward I found in the Attorney General's papers, see Bodleian Library, Bankes MS. 5/81, folio marked '175'.

[6] Charles also revived scutage, collecting £716 16s 8d during the Easter term 1640/1. PRO, E 405/285, unfoliated. Professor Russell kindly supplied this reference.

[7] Lawrence Stone, *The Crisis of the Aristocracy 1558–1641* (Oxford, 1965), chapter 5. While recruiting cavalry officers for the Second Bishops' War, the Earl of Northumberland remarked that 'many of them [are] young and inexperienced men. Your Lordship well knowes how little our nation hath beene accustomed to horse service', Centre for Kentish Studies, De L'Isle and Dudley MSS., Sydney Papers, U 1475 C85/7, f. 2, to the Earl of Leicester, 12 December 1639.

[8] PRO, SP 16/412/117 (Worcester); SP 16/413/25 (Winchester); SP 16/412/139 (Thanet); SP 16/412/67 (Francis, Viscount Montagu).

[9] PRO, SP 16/415/27, account of horses necessary for the artillery train and the baggage and equipment of infantry, etc., 23 March 1639.

The scarcity of hardy steeds forced Sir Jacob Astley to contemplate comandeering Durham pit-ponies for drawing ordnance.[10] The feudal summons would alleviate these shortages, and supply the King with 1,200 cavalry at little or no expense to himself.[11]

The depleted state of the Ordnance Office provided an additional motive for the summoning of the nobility. The lords would have to supply themselves and their 'retainers' with arms at their own expense. Although some weapons could be purchased out of royal magazines at Hull, Newcastle, and the Tower, most nobles equipped themselves from their own very modest arsenals, and the shops of local smiths and armourers. The Lord General had foreseen this need when he suggested to the Earl of Cumberland that he 'invite the nobility and gentry of the North to set on with country smiths to make plain pieces and pistols, with rests for muskets'.[12] The feudal summons also helped to swell the ranks of the royal army. Charles's antiquated summons, then, brought horses, arms, and men into his camp. Finally, the rally around the standard was a potent act of obedience that coerced the lords to demonstrate their loyalty and display to the Covenanters the authority of the King.

The precise number of horses that a given lord should supply was not specified. The summons directed each noble to bring along an entourage that befitted his station and zeal for the King's service. Calculating how many horse represented one's 'birth', 'honor', and 'interest in the public safety' (as the Council termed it) proved a laborious task for at least one noble family, the Montagus of Boughton, Northamptonshire.[13] The elderly Lord Montagu's son, Edward, met with his uncle, the Earl of Manchester, Lord Privy Seal, to discuss what constituted a sufficient contribution to the King's service. Manchester conjectured that the aged Montagu, now seventy-six years old, would be 'easily' excused of personal attendance at York by offering a sizeable donation. The King would accept money as readily as cavalry, though the final choice should be left to his Majesty. In short, the Earl advised, Lord Montagu 'had better send his

[10] Wedgwood, *The King's Peace*, p. 253. Astley had complained about the condition of northern horses; he described the mounts of the horsemen from Harbottle as 'litell nags'. PRO, SP 16/410/99, Astley to Windebank, 30 January 1639.
[11] Gardiner, *History*, vol. VIII, p. 384. Light horse as well as cuirassiers were to be raised. See Stafford RO, Jerningham Papers, D 641/3/D/2/55/4a; 4b; 4c. Archivist Jan Smith provided the reference to these manuscripts. Although the King might raise noble cavalry gratis, the lords received the King's royal pay once under the royal standard, as is evidenced in PRO, E 351/292, f. 12v.
[12] HMC Devonshire, p. 40, Arundel to Cumberland, 31 July 1638.
[13] E. S. Cope analyses Montagu's predicament in *The Life of of a Public Man, Edward First Baron Montagu of Boughton, 1562–1644* Memoirs of the American Philosophical Society 142 (Philadelphia, 1981).

Majesty 300 pounds than provide horses'.[14] Edward was of a different opinion; he suggested that if his father supplied steeds he might receive them back again at the end of the campaign. A £300 contribution he would probably never see again, for the King was not obliged to repay it. Manchester remained adamant, telling his brother to get on with paying the £300. Manchester's nephew still disagreed: £200, Edward reasoned, 'will be as well accepted as four horses, if you leave out in your letter besides those that attend you'. He added information about the contributions of other lords and courtiers so that his father might compare his offering with those of others. Certain judges were rumoured to be giving only £150, although the ambitious Lord Keeper Finch had presented £300 and the Lord Chief Justice £200. The Inns of Court were prepared, it was said, to donate £5,000, and the clergy 'they say will give liberally'. Edward closed, 'It is a very hard matter to provide arms for men and horses in London, they are so much employed; some send into the Low Countries.' Six days later, Edward's brother, William Montagu, informed their father: 'The benevolence for Scotland stops not at the noblemen, for the judges and serjeants have given £3000, and the four Inns of Court should give £5000, but they will not; only the King's counsel and the officers of courts, and some few great practisers give; the six clerks 100 marks a man; the City of London, 1,000 horse.'[15] For the Montagu family, these martial preparations boded ill. When Montagu's daughter Elizabeth, Countess of Lindsey, discovered that her father had been summoned to York, she became alarmed. William, being present, assured his sister that their aged father would not go galloping along the Tweed, sword unsheathed. He wrote: 'she understood it seriously, but I told her I thought it was meant only merrily, for I thought you would sooner send your younger sons than go yourself'. Nevertheless the Countess vowed to journey to York along with her father should he attend personally. She had little else to do since her husband had been appointed to the Council of War, and was now engaged upon a secret mission.

Initially, young Edward's advice prevailed; Lord Montagu decided to send four cavalrymen, pledging his personal attendance and willingness 'to lay down my life and all that I have'.[16] He explained to Manchester that if the King 'shall demand any certain sum of money (which as yet I cannot yield to in my thoughts), it must be far less' than the £300 Manchester had suggested. And even then, the sum could not 'be paid at once, but monthly', assuming 'the war hold out so long'. Was Montagu's situation that of one who could not raise hard currency overnight, or was it a case of

[14] HMC Buccleuch, Montagu MSS., I, p. 276.
[15] Ibid., p. 277.
[16] PRO, SP 16/413/22; HMC Buccleuch, Montagu MSS., I, p. 277.

a noble who suspected that Charles was crying wolf, hoping that donations to the war effort would finance the Personal Rule? In other words, did he think Charles would fill a war-chest only to make peace with the Covenanters at the last minute? He enumerated his reasons for responding as he did.[17] First, 'the King may think me a great moneyed man', if he offered a large lump sum. Second, it was more fit 'for the King to demand than for me to offer'. Third, 'It may be of a future ill consequence', thinking perhaps of future contributions, loans, or a reassessment of his county rates. Fourth, 'I do not know whether it shall be employed as I meant it'. (Did Montagu fear that these contributions would become a precedent, like ship money and become regular, or that their collection would make the future summoning of Parliament unnecessary?) Finally, 'if the war go not forward I shall have no money again, but my horse and arms may be returned safe again'.[18] Montagu hoped for peace, wishing that Charles would not actually follow through with the war. If Manchester suspected that his brother's heart was not in the war, his suspicions were soon confirmed. Montagu remarked, 'I would fain know of the wisest head that is, what good can come of this war.'[19] The Montagus' opinions, especially those of the father, show not only scepticism toward the war itself, but toward Charles's regime in general. They are the residue of the mistrust of the 1620s and 1630s.

More than one lord expressed confusion over the summons. John Egerton, Earl of Bridgewater, had been told that the King preferred a dozen cavalry to £1,000 and set about locating horses and arming his tenantry: 'Now is come a message by Sir W. Uvedale that the King is pleased to spare my horse, and expecteth to receive from me £1,000. Mr. Secretary, I cannot expend and disburse my moneys and have them ready lying to me. I have no mint or spring out of which moneys may flow into my purse or chest.'[20] In Bridgewater's case, the change of preference stemmed from the Crown's acute shortage of hard cash. Sir William Uvedale, Treasurer of the Army, was diligently searching for money during the spring of 1639. The Lord Treasurer had been paying out of the hands of the temporary receivers for some time, and liquid capital was hard to come by.[21] Sterling glittered more than armoured horsemen. Bridgewater requested credit for moneys

---

[17] See also Cope, *The Life of a Public Man*, pp. 158–70.
[18] HMC Buccleuch, Montagu MSS., III, p. 379, undated.
[19] Ibid., pp. 380–1, Montagu to Manchester, 18 February 1639.
[20] HMC Cowper, Coke MSS., p. 216, Bridgewater to Coke, 14 March 1639.
[21] C. M. Hibbard's investigation of Exchequer documents has revealed that, with regard to the clergy contribution of 1639, 'sizeable sums from the northern sees (perhaps as much as £6550) may have been diverted directly into the Army Treasury in the north. This would account for the absence of Exchequer receipts for three out of four of the northern sees', 'Episcopal Warriors', p. 165.

spent on arms already en route to Hull; £500 would be paid straightaway to Sir William Uvedale, and the balance as soon as possible. One wonders how noble contributions paid directly to Uvedale were accounted for. Certainly the moneys did not go through the Tellers of the Receipt, nor would they appear on his declared accounts, for the tellers did not give them out by way of imprest.[22] Since the rendezvous was to occur in a fortnight, the cash went directly to the Treasurer of the Army.[23] Coke's reply designated that Uvedale receive all sums.[24] These frantic financial demands, with Uvedale scouring for pennies, could only underscore the absence of Parliament and the fiscal support it could bring.

Those peers serving as Lords Lieutenant in their counties possessed far more onerous responsibilities than raising a personal contingent of horse. The lieutenants also supervised the selection of militiamen for the northern expedition as well as the conscription of foot soldiers. The Lords Lieutenant and their deputies were to encourage their neighbours to supply the King with money, men, and arms generously, and set an example in doing so. The Lord Lieutenant of Lancashire, Lord Strange, directed deputy lieutenant William Farington to assist gentlemen and freeholders in raising light horse. Strange provided Farington with a list of potential contributors. 'I shall therefore desire your paines and courtesty', he wrote, 'to consider of such as you thinke will be able, and move them in my name that 2 or 3 of them as yo shall thinke fitt, will joyne in the charge to furnish amongst them one Horse'.[25] The royal summons extended beyond the nobility and called upon the services and fortunes of gentlemen and freeholders. Strange's request was as traditional as the King's feudal summons to the peers. During the reign of Edward VI, Farington's ancestor had furnished a 'light horseman well harnised as apperteyneth, with a redde coate made of the Cassok fashion' for the English army that invaded Scotland in 1547.[26] But William Farington's duties were more burdensome than those of his ancestor, Sir Henry Farington, who had lived before the maturation of lieutenancy.[27] In March 1639 Farington also mustered and drilled the trained bands and enrolled the names of able-bodied males for the press. All of this placed onerous responsibilities upon individual Lords Lieutenant.

[22] PRO, E 351/292, 293, accounts of Sir William Uvedale for the 1639 and 1640 campaigns.
[23] HEH, EL 6608, Bridgewater to Coke, 16 March 1639.
[24] HEH, EL 6609, Coke to Bridgewater, 17 March 1639.
[25] S. M. Ffarington (ed.), 'The Farington Papers', *Remains Historical and Literary Connected with the Palatine Counties of Lancaster and Chester*, Chetham Society, 39 (1856), p. 58, Strange to Farington, 9 February 1639.
[26] Ibid., p. 123, Derby to Farington, 1 August 1547.
[27] Gladys S. Thomson, 'The Origin and Growth of the Office of Deputy Lieutenant', *TRHS*, fourth series, 5 (1922), pp. 150–67.

Of the approximately 115 summoned, how many lords responded favourably?[28] Peers, for the most part, attended or contributed cash. But as Montagu's letters show, a favourable response did not necessarily mean approval of the war or acquiescence in the full service demanded. Even Lords Brooke and Saye and Sele, who originally opposed the summons on legal grounds, attended as instructed. As events turned out, Charles would have been better off if the two had not appeared at all.[29] Responses are recorded to 77 of the 115 summonses. Thirty-three peers pledged some form of contribution, and the remaining forty-four declared their intention to be at York.[30] But most of the responses were not very enthusiastic. Those peers who escaped the long march, privation, and prospect of bloodshed were wounded instead in the purse. S. R. Gardiner's assessment of the nobility's sentiments is not far from the mark: 'Dragged against their will to the borders, and long deprived of the part in the Government which they held to be their due, the English nobles bore no goodwill to a war which, if it were successful, would place them more completely than ever at the feet of their sovereign.'[31] The Scots exploited these fears by telling the English that once the Covenanters were subdued Charles would turn his attention to the opponents of the Personal Rule in England: 'For when we're slain, this rod comes on your breech.'[32]

The display of loyalty and unity that Charles had hoped for failed to materialize. Since most of the nobles received the summons in early February, they had scarcely sixty days in which to raise the necessary cash or prepare themselves for war. At least a dozen claimed that 'shortness of time' prevented them from raising a proper contingent. Obviously, some lords were making excuses which might soothe the King's anger if they fielded a small or ill-armed group of soldiers. It is clear, however, that shortages of armour, firearms, and equipment hindered the preparations of many lords. Arms could not be manufactured overnight, especially in counties distant from the London arms market. William Montagu experi-

---

[28] PRO, SP 16/413/117, Nicholas's notes, undated. Russell in *CECW*, p. 165, points out that criticism was edited out by Nicholas. For the responses of some more notable lords: the Earl of Warwick asked to be excused because of his involvement in a West Indies venture, but pledged his son to attend with such equipage as his fortune would permit (no. 14). The Earl of Bedford expressed his willingness to attend with whatever horse and men he could raise under the circumstances, though in an earlier letter had pledged £500. Nicholas has written '£1,000' in the margin, next to Bedford's name (no. 33). See also *CSPD* (1638–9), XIII, p. 374, acknowledgement by Sir William Hewes, Clerk of the Cheque, regarding receipt of 115 summonses from Robert Reade, Windebank's secretary, 28 January 1639.

[29] Schwarz, 'Viscount Saye and Sele', pp. 17–36.

[30] PRO, SP 16/413/117; Schwarz, 'Viscount Saye and Sele', p. 19.

[31] Gardiner, *History*, vol. IX, p. 11.

[32] C. H. Firth, 'Ballads on the Bishops' Wars, 1638–40', *Scottish Historical Review*, 3, no. 11 (April 1906), p. 260.

enced just such difficulties in trying to secure arms for his father, and wrote angrily from London,

> It is a hard case when a necessity is accompanied by an impossibility as when things must be had but cannot be got. The King commands armour and pistols, and sets all the armourers and pistolers a-work for himself. The six cases of pistols were promised against Tuesday last, and upon Friday the King's warrant came to prohibit them to work for any but him, so that they could not be done to send this week; next week without fail. One case are sent now, which we had much ado to get; the locks are not fire-locks, but better; for besides the impossibility to get them, they are not mendable when out of tune [i.e. difficulty of repairing wheel-locks] ... As for arms [armour], Newman and I have searched again, but none to be found; here and there a mismatched suit, but none complete.[33]

The shortage of armour prompted some resourceful improvisations, like that of the Earl of Kingston, who had antiquated suits of armour converted into cuirassiers' armour. He told Sir Gervase Clifton, 'Many of the nobility have certified (as is sayd) the honourable secretaryes that they cannot provide armes, but will in their persons wayte of his majestie ... my servant Bowskill assured mee from the armourer of Nott[ingham] that two of myne armours with a little cost may be made good cuirashiers "à la moderne".'[34] Such objections would have been largely eliminated by better timing of the mobilization. Earlier notice would have deprived many lords of an excuse. Likewise it would have given the Privy Council more time to pressure the lords and gentlemen without unduly alarming the Covenanters, who would not have taken such a measure as seriously as, say, the garrisoning of Berwick or Carlisle.

The recusant Catholic nobility and gentry readily accepted Charles's call to arms against Presbyterian Scotland. However, Catholics such as Lord Brudenell were forced to purchase arms in the Low Countries because their weapons had been confiscated, for fear of a fifth column made up of conspiratorial papists.[35] A Protestant lord lamented, 'Recusants do extraordinarilily furnish themselves, and joy much at this business. It was wont to be the policy to disarm them; what it is now, to put them in such strength, I know not; it may prove of ill consequence. They and we, I am afraid, go not to a like end.'[36]

The careless manner in which the feudal summons was issued is demonstrated in the unlikely and unsuitable candidates who received the royal command to come to York. Ambassadors, aged peers, and royal wards were ordered to perform knight's service. Richard Forster, engaged in

---

[33] HMC Buccleuch, Montagu MSS., I, 14 March 1639, p. 282.
[34] HMC Bruce, p. 421, 1 March 1639.
[35] PRO, SP 16/412/141, 15 February 1639.
[36] HMC Buccleuch, Montagu MSS., III, p. 383, Montagu to Manchester. The role of the Catholics has been fully illuminated in Hibbard, *Charles I and the Popish Plot.*

diplomacy with the French King's agents, asked whether he should depart for York or remain at his post in London.[37] More exasperated was the Earl of Leicester, England's ambassador in Paris. He fumed,

I have lately received His Majesty's royal signature, not from any of the King's Ministers but from a private friend of mine in England ... My case differs from theirs to whom his Majesty hath been pleased to direct the like signatures, for I do not think that it was ever known that one who had the honour to be the King's ambassador should be recalled without his Majesty's recredential letters ... Yet I am commanded by the said royal signature to attend His Majesty at York by the 2nd of April next commencing, which all things considered is in a manner impossible ... I am in a great strait between the inobservance of affairs which are now in my hands only. Another article of the royal mandate en-joins me within 15 days after the receipt thereof (which a man that hath the sea to pass cannot be assured of) to certify unto one of the King's Principal Secretaries of State.[38]

Several nobles whose years made them poor choices for men-at-arms were also summoned to York. The Earl of Middlesex, sixty-four years old, who could not walk without a staff, promised to attend, should health permit. Conversely, twelve-year-old Lord Herbert asked to be excused on account of his age and because his arms were in the keeping of his guardian, the Earl of Warwick. Lord Dacre argued that royal wards were exempt from knight's service.[39] The 1639 summonses, then, exasperated the lords and to a degree discredited Charles's handling of the mobilization. And yet, they came. At least 810 horsemen appeared, at a total cost to the Crown of £9,720.[40] At £12 per cavalryman, the summoning of the nobility was a bargain, but it also had political implications, unifying the nobles under the standard of the King. In its political function the summons failed, for it only increased alienation without any substantial military advantage, at the cost of nearly £10,000 much needed elsewhere.

A slightly different approach to the mobilization of the nobility was used in the Second Bishops' War. In 1640, the Crown planned to utilize more extensively the military services of those who held lands along the borders. Strafford argued that Commissions of Array be sent out and that once the troops were on the borders with their lords, the King could instruct them to do as he wished, which included, presumably, sending them into Scotland on a massive invasion. 'In reason of state you have power, when they are there, to use them at the Kinges paie; if any of the Lordes [of the Privy Council] can shewe you a better way lett them doe it.' It was objected, probably by Northumberland, that the 'Towne [London, was] full of

[37] PRO, SP 16/410/147, January 1639 (?).
[38] HMC Cowper, Coke MSS., p. 213, Leicester to Coke, 25/15 February 1639.
[39] PRO, SP 16/413/106 (28 February 1639); SP 16/412/115 (13 February 1639) and SP 16/412/61 (7 February 1639).
[40] PRO, E 351/292, f. 12v, account of Sir William Uvedale.

nobility whoe will talk of it'. Strafford retorted, his contempt for the lords conspicuous, that he would 'make them smarte for it'.[41] Ultimately, it was only on 20 August 1640 that the formal order to perform knight's service upon the borders was issued.[42] As was the case for the 1640 mobilization in general, the nobles were called up too late in the summer to figure in the outcome of the war. Perhaps Charles hoped that the fiscal crisis of August 1640 might be somewhat mitigated by fines paid by lords in lieu of personal attendance. But fining nobles at this juncture could only strengthen the 'Scottish party' (on both sides of the borders) by alienating a constituency which the King needed. Those lords that did muster could reinforce New-castle.[43] In neither Bishops' War did Charles coax much military support from his nobles. The gauntlet through which they had run (the 1639 summons, the Short Parliament, and the tardy call-up of August 1640) simply served to increase their suspicions of Charles's political agenda and kingly abilities.

The comparative security enjoyed by Tudor and Stuart rulers owed much, it has been said, to the taming of the nobility. But the peers had rarely been adversaries to royal government. Buttressed by loyal nobles, an English King could accomplish many things, such as the invasion of France. Charles I, however, had alienated many of his English and Scottish lords.[44] Moreover the narrowing of orthodoxies in church and court further disrupted the Crown's relations with the nobility. The 1630s saw distancing between most ancient families and the Caroline centre. The Privy Council was dominated by the court, and the Court by Charles's intimates. On the one hand, this was good for the Crown, for the King did not not have to fear that an upstart over-mighty subject might champion the reformed religion and topple his regime.[45] But on the other hand Charles I did not have a loyal and militarily potent nobility upon which to draw. This had not mattered a lot in the brave show he planned for 1639; the nobles needed only to look good. In 1640, however, battle appeared unavoidable which accounted for the relegation of the nobles to an aux-iliary role and a late call-up at the end of August 1640. The summons,

[41] PRO, SP 16/441/83, 10 January 1640.

[42] Larkin (ed.), *Stuart Royal Proclamations*, vol. II, p. 732; Gardiner, *History*, vol. IX, p. 188.

[43] Bodleian Library, Bankes MS. 27/10. A proclamation to summon all such as hold of his Majesty by grand sergeantry, escuage, or knight's service, to do their services against the Scots, according to their tenures. Printed in Rymer, *Foedera*, vol. XX, p. 433. The phrase 'already begun his Journey, towards the Northern Parts of this Kingdom' is substituted by Bankes in this copy for 'purposed within a short time to be at the town of Newcastle upon Tyne', p. 433, lines 7–9.

[44] Maurice Lee, Jr., *The Road to Revolution. Scotland under Charles I, 1625–1637* (Urbana, Ill., 1985), pp. 223–44.

[45] However, see the Essex 'toasting incident' in Fissel, *'Bellum Episcopale'*, pp. 304–5.

however, had forced each noble to weigh his allegiance to the King against
the political and religious issues of the day. Charles drew them one and all
into the political fray through military service and contributions.

MERCENARIES: POLITICS AND MONEY

Without a bellicose and martially experienced nobility to stiffen the royal
army, Charles looked at the possibility of hiring mercenaries. Like other
employers of mercenaries during the era of the Thirty Years' War, Charles
I negotiated with whomever was available, regardless of religion or nation-
ality. The King explored the possibilities of recruiting Spanish, Danes,
Dutch, and Irish, and so jeopardized the trust of his subjects by using
foreigners to enforce his rule. Again the historian is faced with a case of
Tudor 'success' and Caroline failure, for the Tudors (Henry VIII and
Edward VI principally) had brought in foreign mercenaries to fight the
Scots and stamp out rebels. But the political and religious context of
1638–40 made Englishmen mistrustful of foreign intervention, even in the
royal service. The attempt to inject foreign troops into an Anglo-Scottish
crisis places in context Strafford's celebrated remark about 'an army in
Ireland'. The matter was to be settled peaceably by English-speaking, Protestant brethren, not by foreign troops. Clearly there were political considerations which made such a practice in England quite abominable.

Those royal subjects most skilled in the art of war served foreign princes
on the continent, by permission of the King. English units fought in Flanders, British brigades reinforced the Dutch, Scots served the French, and
Irishmen filled the ranks of the Spanish Army.[46] In August 1638 the Condé-
Duke de Olivares asked ambassador Hopton about the likelihood of
obtaining further levies from Ireland. Hopton countered that Irishmen conscripted by the Spanish later proved traitors to their King. The curt reply
did not dissuade Olivares, who importuned again, suggesting secret
recruitment so that the French would not make a similar demand. On 12
August he formally requested between 4,000 and 6,000 infantrymen.[47] At

---

[46] 'British' recruits were valued. See the articles of the Spanish ambassador circa May 1637
in O. Ogle and W. H. Bliss, (eds.), Calendar of the Clarendon State Papers Preserved in
the Bodleian Library, p. 132, item viii, no. 3. After 1621, the number of British levied for
foreign wars climbed, especially under Charles, who used recruiting as part of his foreign
policy. I. R. Bartlett, 'Scottish Mercenaries in Europe, 1570–1640: A Study in Attitudes
and Policies', The Scottish Tradition, 13 (1986), p. 20.

[47] Louis XIII was not to be outdone, for a levy of a thousand troops for French service was
permitted in Scotland in October 1638. One suspects that Charles was content to deplete
the number of would-be soldiers in that kingdom. SRO, GD 406/1/734, commission to
Alexander Erskine, 24 October 1638 and GD 406/1/988, Traquair to Hamilton, 5 January
[1639]. According to Bartlett, 8,000 soldiers were pressed for the French King between
1639 and 1642. See his 'Scottish Mercenaries in Europe, 1520–1640', p. 22.

that moment the King of Great Britain faced military problems of his own. It occurred to Charles and his councillors that fellow princes might assist each other in time of military need. Why not swap several thousand raw recruits for a smaller professional force?

The first such 'exchange' scheme was apparently hatched in a conversation in Brussels between Colonel Henry Gage, serving in the Spanish Army, and Prince Thomas. Prince Thomas's favourable reaction prompted the colonel to contact his brother, George, who was a royal 'messenger' at the papal court, and Secretary Windebank. All parties involved were Roman Catholic. The English ambassador at Madrid, Sir Arthur Hopton, already enmeshed unwillingly in negotiations to enlist several thousand veterans of the Army of Flanders to serve in the First Bishops' War, was drawn in, though he was kept in the dark about the ultimate goal of the plan.

Gage's design grew out of quarrels over recruiting which erupted among British regiments in the pay of the King of Spain during the winter of 1638–9. Sir William Tresham complained to Secretary Windebank regarding the recruiting, especially in London, of men for Gage's regiment, particularly by one Captain Pavier. Gage heard of Tresham's complaints through Sir Balthasar Gerbier and a Sergeant-Major Shaw and protested to Windebank.[48] The disruptive effect upon royal favour of their unseemly row elicited comment from Secretary Windebank in his dispatch to the ambassador. He also told Hopton that Colonels Tyrone and Tyrconnell had been recruiting in Ireland without royal approval, and that another 1,000 men were en route to the British regiments.[49] His dearth of English officers, commissioned and non-commissioned, forced Charles to look to the very same pool of talent recruited by the Covenanters: British continental veterans.[50] That Gage and Tresham were at each others' throats made the transfer of one of those commanders that much more attractive. The mobilization of a royal army against Scotland fired Gage's imagination and ambitions. Certainly Gage understood the premium placed on military leadership in the late 1630s.[51] The tenuous movements toward an Anglo-Hispanic alliance and the military and diplomatic dealings (true and alleged) between France and Scotland, made the placement of an experienced English 'mercenary' commander at the head of a foreign army a reasonable solution to the Covenanter revolt. On 1 February 1639 Windebank proposed that George Gage be dispatched to his brother's side on the

---

[48] Bodleian Library, Clarendon SP, XV, ff. 86–87v, letter written 8 January 1639 from Brussels.
[49] Bodleian Library, Clarendon SP, XV, f. 105, Windebank to Hopton, 22 January 1639.
[50] Furgol, 'Scotland turned Sweden', p. 136.
[51] J. H. Elliot, *Richelieu and Olivares* (Oxford, 1987), pp. 130–1.

pretence of a devotion to the Queen in order to negotiate an exchange of substantial levies to keep up the strength of the English and Irish regiments in Flanders in return for the use of 6,000 'crack' troops.[52]

Windebank contemplated a lightning stroke which would snuff out resistance at the very centre of Covenanter opposition. He planned to embark the 6,000 veteran Spanish infantry and 400 cavalry at Dunkirk and clandestinely ship them north, through the Firth of Forth, where they would descend upon Edinburgh Castle. Colonel Gage would embark '6000 foot and 400 horse, all ancient soldiers and ready armed, to be transported from Dunkirk' into Scotland, and have 'surprised the Castle of Edinburgh; which would have given the covenant a deadly blow, and His Majesty had mastered that rebellion by that time he sholde have arrived at Yorke'.[53] The utilization of Catholic soldiers against Protestants would certainly have raised eyebrows in England, and one must wonder if the cure would not have been worse than the disease. But the development of the plan sheds much light on Charles's strategy for the King personally authorized Gage's mission, once it had begun, and on his sentiments about using foreign troops from Catholic countries.

The undated proposal for this project drafted by George Gage states unequivocally that the King's 'ill-affected subjects should not dare to budge nor would a farre greater army of our owne men awe the subject haulfe soe much as a fewe forran forces'.[54] Originally, George Gage envisioned an invasion force of 10,000 with a dual command shared between a subject of Charles I and another in the service of Philip IV. The army's pay would be supplied by their co-religionists, the English Catholics and the Pope. His Holiness's contribution would be rewarded by abrogation of the recusant laws. True, those laws were statutory and a Parliament would be needed for their repeal. But, Gage asserted, the Emperor Charles V possessed an army whose presence coerced the Diet to elect him Emperor. Charles I could do likewise, 'having a forran army on foote, subdue the Scotts therwith, and at the same instant soe keepe the Parlament in awe, that his majesty might easily make them come to what condicions hee pleased'.[55] With allusions to the 'reconciliation' of Henry IV of France, Gage advocated that a 'stowt spirited Preist' be sent to Rome to mediate through a Dr Houlden and bring the Pope into the design.

Clearly the Gages acted on their own scant authority, although Winde-

52 Bodleian Library, Clarendon SP, XV, ff. 121–121v. Windebank memo of 1 February 1639.
53 Bodleian Library, Clarendon SP, XVI, ff. 18v, 20, Windebank to Hopton on 15 March 1639, after the failure of the design.
54 Bodleian Library, Clarendon SP, XV, f. 76. The attack on Edinburgh Castle may have been the brainchild of Secretary Windebank.
55 Bodleian Library, Clarendon SP, XV, f. 76v. Gage's knowledge of Hapsburg history was a bit spotty.

bank's sponsorship ultimately won Charles's personal approval. On 4 February, only three days after Windebank's memorandum proposing George Gage be sent to his brother, Colonel Gage approached Prince Thomas in Brussels. Although the Spanish remained apprehensive of the Hollanders and French, they might have released 4,000 infantry and 400 cavalry in return for annual levies from the British Isles that would keep their three Irish and two English regiments at 2,000 men apiece.[56] Upon the same day in London Windebank drafted instructions for Colonel Gage exchanging annual recruitment for 6,000 infantry – 4,500 being harquebussiers and the rest pikes – along with 400 cavalry, to be embarked at Dunkirk on Spanish vessels but under English pay.[57] Their destination was the York rendezvous on 1 April. Perhaps initially Windebank planned to land them at Hull and march them to York, though such a design, to disembark foreign troops in an English port, would have triggered all sorts of rumours. There is no mention to Gage of what was probably their true terminus – the Firth of Forth and Edinburgh. In order to cloak these actions from the Covenanters the story was to be given out at Dunkirk that the men were bound for Biscay, Italy, or somewhere else in the world.

Colonel Gage presented to the Cardinal Infante the royal request for the exchange. Unfortunately for Charles, the Spaniards had suffered several reverses which discouraged the deal. Most seriously, at Dunkirk the Dutch damaged the Spanish fleet. Other setbacks at Cambrai and Breisach placed Philip IV on the defensive.[58] Disappointed, the Gages sought an alternative course. George reiterated his nomination of his brother for a royal command, and Colonel Gage suggested that the two English regiments (comprising under 4,000 men) could be transferred to the borders under his command. He pledged, 'I will pawne my life to effect it with our owne men, which may be raised and embarked for Yorke with much lesse noise, and daunger of discovering the designe'. Like Windebank, he believed that the war could be won quickly and wished to participate: 'I am ready to lay it [his life] downe in this action of Scotland'.[59] In the meantime, he was worried that Spanish confidence in the exchange might erode, as the Spaniards had inquired whether Lord Deputy Wentworth could send troops from Ireland without express royal approval. The same questions reached the ears of his brother, also in Brussels.[60] Although negotiations

---

[56] Bodleian Library, Clarendon SP, XV, f. 128v, Colonel Gage to George Gage, 5 February 1639.
[57] Bodleian Library, Clarendon SP, XV, ff. 130–2, Gage's instructions, 5 February 1639.
[58] Letters from Colonel Gage to Windebank, in Bodleian Library, Clarendon SP, XV, ff. 140–41, 16/26 February 1639; described in detail by Col. Gage to Windebank, XV, f. 171, 2/12 March 1639 and again, XV, ff. 177–177v, 5 March 1639.
[59] Bodleian Library, Clarendon SP, XV, f. 178, dated Brussels 5 March 1639.
[60] Bodleian Library, Clarendon SP, XVI, f. 5v, George Gage to Windebank, 5 March 1639.

continued, including a Spanish proposal that in return for veterans Charles
would use his ship money fleet to convoy and protect Spanish vessels on
the Flemish coast, the mercenary transaction failed to materialize. Had the
Spanish exchange succeeded, Charles would perhaps have committed his
next gargantuan political blunder. The disembarkation of notorious
enemy troops at the invitation of the King would have confirmed the worst
fears of many Englishmen. Charles I had betrayed his people to a popish
conspiracy. The Spanish veterans were certainly a match for the Covenanters. In that event, however, the Covenanters would become England's sal-
vation, for only the Scottish party would be able to dislodge the oppression
of mercenaries.[61]

Besides 'put not your faith in princes', perhaps Strafford's most memorable reputed line is 'you have an army in Ireland which you may use to
conquer this kingdom'.[62] The mercenary plots of 1639–40 explain the
context of that celebrated, fatal remark. A full year before Strafford's
observation, Charles I had condoned such a policy by sending recredential
letters to Colonel Gage at Brussels. The notion of using Catholic troops to
eradicate a Calvinist rebellion was anything but new in spring 1640. If fear
of Spanish invaders persisted, the greatest terror of English countrymen
was the Irish plunderer. Although the army maintained by the English
government in Ireland was largely Protestant and hence politically safe, the
very idea that troops whose place of origin was Ireland might be quartered
or deployed in England was loathsome in itself. It was believed by at least
one of Charles's nobles that the Irish should be subject to more stringent
restrictions for departing from that island. Irish emigrants specialized in
three occupations: scholarly pursuits, soldiering and begging. The 'scholl-
ers' ended up in the service of popery, the soldiers fighting for 'forrein
princes and by both these professions they learne to be lesse affected to the
Crowne'. Such sentiments about the seditious nature of the Irish make
understandable the popular incredulity regarding the King's invitation of
Irish troops into England to participate in a war against Protestants.[63]

In 1639 Lord Deputy Wentworth's force in the Pale comprised a loyal
force which would suit the King's needs. But its removal from Ireland
would prompt Catholic revolt. Since the mobilization for war against Scotland demanded his full resources, Charles could not risk a second front in
Ireland. The incessantly plotting Windebank toyed with the logistically
challenging strategy of pitting the Irish army against the Covenanters, then

---

[61] C. Russell, 'The Scottish Party in English Parliaments 1640–1642 or the Myth of the
English Revolution', Inaugural Lecture in the Department of History, King's College
London, 29 January 1991, pp. 11–16.
[62] See pp. 47–9, 171.
[63] Centre for Kentish Studies, De L'Isle and Dudley MSS., Sydney Papers, U 1475 Z 47/9.

returning the force to Dublin before Catholic resistance coalesced in Ireland.[64] At this time, late October 1638, Wentworth was readying forces clandestinely, with Charles's approval, in anticipation of a meeting of the Irish Council of War on 21 November. These troops, for example Ormond's newly commissioned troop of heavy cavalry, would serve shoulder to shoulder with English forces.[65]

On the eve of the First Bishops' War, the Lord General, Arundel, commissioned the Earl of Barrymore to raise 1,000 Irish infantry, both volunteers and conscripts. He was to cooperate with the Lord Deputy and find means of transporting them into England, and conduct them to the rendezvous at Selby.[66] The Earl of Barrymore's regiment never arrived in England, however. On 24 April, Sir Patrick Curwen wrote from Carlisle, informing the Lord General that the Irish soldiers would not arrive until at least the end of May.[67] By then, it was too late.

Another court-hatched scheme for enlisting Irish soldiers centred around Randal MacDonnell, Earl of Antrim, who proposed to attack the Kintyre peninsula in western Scotland. Antrim enjoyed the good graces of the Queen and Archbishop Laud, as well as Charles. Married to the widow of the assassinated favourite, the Duke of Buckingham, the earl had been recommended by Hamilton as a potential force for countering the Covenanters.[68] In addition to possessing extensive lands in northern Ireland, he claimed as inheritance holdings in western Scotland which now lay under the control of a rival clan, the Campbells, headed by the Earl of Argyll. When Argyll elected to subscribe to the Covenant, Antrim perceived an opportunity to recover 'his' lost inheritance in Kintyre.[69] Talk of bringing clan rivalries into an already bitter religious quarrel only served to increase distrust and rebelliousness in Scotland. Antrim's MacDonnells and their allies, the O'Neills, were of the Roman Catholic faith, while their rivals on

---

[64] PRO, SP 16/400/65, memo by Windebank, 20 October 1638; above, p. 37. There is no overt evidence that Ireland was ripe for revolt, only the historian's knowledge of the subsequent events of 1641, which of course must be seen in the context of that fateful year. Perhaps Wentworth was too worried and Windebank not so fanciful.

[65] Bodleian Library, Carte MSS., I, f. 169, Wentworth to Ormonde, *circa* 17–26 October 1638, probably the former date.

[66] PRO, SP 16/414/60, Arundel to Barrymore, 8 March 1639.

[67] HMC Cowper, Coke MSS., p. 223, Curwen to Arundel, 24 April 1639. Barrymore did ultimately command Irish regiments. See PRO, E 351/292, f. 14 for the First Bishops' War. In the Second Bishops' War, see E 351/293, f. 7.

[68] SRO, GD 406/1/10775, f. 3, Hamilton to the King, 15 June 1638. The best discussion of Antrim's abilities is J. H. Ohlmeyer, *Civil War and Restoration in Three Stuart Kingdoms. The Career of Randal MacDonnell, the Marquis of Antrim, 1609–1683* (Cambridge, 1993), pp. 77–99. Dr Ohlmeyer kindly shared her page proofs with the author.

[69] Clarke, 'The Earl of Antrim', pp. 108–15; Wedgwood, *The King's Peace*, pp. 224–6; on the MacDonnells and Scottish 'mercenaries' see Cyril Falls, *Elizabeth's Irish Wars* (New York, 1970), pp. 76–7.

the western coast of Scotland, the Earl of Argyll, Lord Luce and the Campbells, were Protestant. The Scottish lords' fears of a royally inspired Catholic attack took on a degree of credibility when it was reported that Irish Catholics were being encouraged to invade western Scotland. Antrim's choice of a commander reflected very poor political judgement: Colonel Eoin O'Neill (known as 'Don Eugenio' in Flanders) of the notorious O'Neill clan, who served in the Spanish army. Wentworth thought him a traitor. Antrim proposed to assemble an army of 4,800 to 6,000 infantry and light-horse in Ulster and transport them aboard thirty long-boats to the Kintyre peninsula, harass the Campbells, and divert Scottish forces from the borders.

Considering the Crown's lack of weapons and ready cash, the expedition would be feasible only if Antrim and his cronies footed the bill. He requested muskets, pistols, pikes, armour, building supplies, and boats. The bulk of Antrim's supplies would have to come from the stores of Thomas Wentworth, Lord Deputy of Ireland, who possessed a keener eye than Antrim in military matters. Wentworth understood that Antrim was incapable of delivering what he had promised. The young man carried a sizeable debt, had no credit, possessed no naval or military expertise, and had allies of very dubious loyalty.[70] Antrim demanded 1,200 barrels of powder even though the royal stores in Dublin contained only 528.[71] In addition he asked for £20,000. Finally, although Antrim said he would finance the construction of the thirty long-boats, he expected to cut wood from the royal forests in County Londonderry. Antrim later found that masts could not be produced by felling trees and nailing them to a deck. Discovering that his craftsmen were unable to make masts, he took measurements and ordered them from the royal naval store in Dublin. When the masts arrived, they did not fit; Antrim's servants had erred in their calculations.[72]

The King had intimated to Wentworth, 'I should be glad if you could find some way to furnish the Earl of Antrim with arms, though he be a Roman Catholic; for he may be of much use to me at this time to shake

---

[70] Bodleian Library, Clarendon SP, XV, ff. 167–8, to Secretary Windebank, 2 March 1639; SRO, GD 406/1/652; see also Wentworth's distaste for the 'Glandonnells' in Sheffield City Library, Strafford MS. Xa, ff. 168–70, to Lord Lorne, 28 August 1638. Although Wentworth's military knowledge is indisputable, J. H. Ohlmeyer has argued that Antrim was not as ill-informed about martial matters as Wentworth and the historians have judged, *Civil War and Restoration*, pp. 84–5. Antrim's selection of Owen Roe O'Neill does evidence the choice of an able commander, as the latter's rout of Monro at Benburb in 1646 testified. I am grateful to Jane Ohlmeyer for this point.

[71] Bodleian Library, Carte MSS., XLIV, f. 341/257.

[72] Ohlmeyer, *Civil War and Restoration*, p. 85; Clarke, 'The Earl of Antrim', p. 112, n. 21; Wedgwood, *The King's Peace*, p. 529.

loose upon the Earl of Argyle.'[73] The Lord Deputy found Charles's carelessness in this appalling, and he minced no words. To arm so many native Irish was dangerous. Worse, Antrim's regiment consisted of 'habituated Traitors, or those that have in the former times of Rebellion heere have been rebells themselves, and had their hands in the innocent blood of many good subjects, and who once so united might perchance not prove so well natured to law [lay] down their Armes'.[74] The vigour of Wentworth's language conveyed his frustration. How could Charles and Windebank be so near-sighted as to arm men more dangerous than the Scots rebels?

On 2 March 1639 Wentworth reported that Antrim's 'forces are noe readier than I formerly advertised' and that the Earl would cause more harm than good: 'in naked truthe, (as I feared) rather to awaken, then beate, an ennimy'.[75] Although served with the feudal summons, belatedly on 1 April when the rest of the nobility had supposedly already arrived at York, Antrim remained in Ireland. He appeared before the Irish Privy Council to give an account of his preparations for the invasion of Kintyre. On 11 April the King instructed Wentworth to authorize Antrim to recruit and transport soldiers to Scotland. However, the Irish Council's scepticism had grown. Antrim's hope was to draw them into his preparations in order to share responsibility. The suspicious Privy Councillors declined, stating that only Antrim was fully qualified to proceed with the project, since he knew all the details and had been in direct communication with the King. Antrim's next tactic was to make 'exorbitant demands' of the council, who then out-manoeuvered the Earl by agreeing to his demands, knowing that Antrim would ultimately capitulate and confess his impotence. After much delay, the young earl admitted that initially he had believed that the Scottish disturbances amounted to no more than a storm in a teacup, and had decided to exploit the situation by promising to embark upon a campaign that might win the King's favour as well as restore the Macdonnell lands held by the Campbells. He never actually thought the King and the Scots would come to blows. Antrim confessed his poverty and that his preparations were at a standstill. 'The failer was onley in himselfe.' Later he tried to place the blame on the King's government, and the Irish Council implored Secretary Vane to set the Earl straight. Antrim, like his royal master, had underestimated the resolve of the Scottish nation, and both blustered their way into a perilous

---

[73] Halliwell, *Letters*, pp. 311–2, 25 January 1639, citing W. Knowler (ed.), *The Earl of Strafforde's Letters and Dispatches* (London, 1739), vol. II, f. 275.

[74] Bodleian Library, Carte MSS., XLIV, f. 341/257. One must wonder if Wentworth knew of Charles's negotiations with the Gage brothers.

[75] Bodleian Library, Clarendon SP, XV, ff. 167–168, to Secretary Windebank, 2 March 1639.

situation.[76] As in his encouragement of the Gages, Charles's support of Antrim and the Clan Donald threatened to ignite a conflagration like the Thirty Years' War throughout his kingdoms. Charles simply could not fathom the religious and xenophobic fears which would have arisen should Gage's Spaniards or Antrim's Irish have marched under the royal banner through the byways of rural England. In his father's reign the religious divisions were acknowledged; men were to 'remain both protestant and loyal to the British King'.[77] Charles, who never really understood this 'wars of religion' business, seemed oblivious to the political consequences (domestic and international) of importing Romanist troops into the midst of his kingdom, an intervention which could only strengthen English sympathy with the Covenant.

Royal sponsorship of Antrim's activities in 1639 blurred the distinction between Irish Catholic and Irish Protestant troops. The ethnic, religious, and social distinctions of Caroline Ireland were inscrutable in English eyes. Probably rumours about the arrival of soldiers from Ireland did not distinguish loyal Protestant Irish, or 'Old English', from those Irish who practised Roman Catholicism. The King's use of all types of soldiers further muddied the waters. In the Second Bishops' War Strafford supervised Irish recruitment. Eight thousand infantry would be raised, entering royal pay on 18 May 1640, and then be transported into England for an incursion into Scotland at the end of June. They would be assisted by 2,000 English foot and 500 cavalry.[78] With Strafford's departure to England, the organization and mobilization of the Irish army fell into the able hands of Christopher Wandesford, his kinsman, who appears to have done an admirable job but succumbed to the deadly effects of the King's delay of the rendezvous in England. The Irish soldiers were not to be transported there until they could link up with Charles's main army. The political failure of the Short Parliament had disrupted Wandesford's timetable.

The putting of [off] the meting of the Army was grounded on the other side [in England] upon no other reason certaynley but the loss of tyme which the King was at in expecting the success of the parlament, so that the levyes of foot was so long

---

[76] Bodleian Library, Carte MSS., XLIV, ff. 340/256–340v/256v. The traditional view of Antrim's utter incompetence has been criticized by J. Ohlmeyer, who points out the sporadic and inconsistent directions given to Antrim by the King and his ministers as well as Wentworth's unequivocal opposition to all of the Earl's endeavours, *Civil War and Restoration*, pp. 86–93.

[77] Bartlett, 'Scottish Mercenaries in Europe', p. 16. Men could, if they maintained their religious and dynastic allegiances, fight alongside Roman Catholics on occasion, as did Sir Roger Williams in the 1590s.

[78] SRO, GD 406/1/803, ff. 1–2, Strafford to Hamilton, 24 March 1640. A detailed army list including captains, lieutenants and ensigns is found in Bodleian Library, Carte MSS., I, ff. 181–187v. However, J. Ohlmeyer suggests that this army was 'largely composed' of Catholics: *Civil War and Restoration*, p. 94.

deferred there that they coulde not be ryddy to mete at there [their] Rendezvous at Berwick before the last of July.[79]

The effort in fashioning the Irish army of 1640 must be appreciated. By far the most formidable problem faced was that of supply. Weapons, wagons, tents, and horses had to be purchased and collected from England and elsewhere. The logistical hurdles overcome, the army contended with delay and shortages of pay. Throughout the summer orders postponed the march to Carrickfergus to await transport. Regiments stood down in their temporary quarters in the localities, drilling and wondering when they would be shipped to England. As it was, the order never came, for the Covenanters' preemptive strike against the royal forces in late August was accomplished before all the English regiments were in place and the Irish troops could be summoned.[80]

The quality of the Irish troops may well have been superior to that of the English forces. The men were reported to be in good order and there is no evidence of a substitution clause diluting the press.[81] If the Irish forces had been sent regardless of the preparedness of the English army, the Second Bishops' War might have turned out differently. They were the only force in Britain capable of facing the Covenanters in midsummer. Had they been deployed in the North, Leslie would probably not have advanced with impunity. The reason they were not shipped east does in fact have a lot to do with the need to coordinate the movement of the Irish regiments with the royal army's migration into the north. But one must remember that the slowness of the march in England was due to lack of pay (not to mention arms). The want of money most certainly did affect the Irish regiments as well, for shortages of pay made the Irish Council wary of sending the men off without sufficient funds to keep them in the ranks. Ironically, just as in the case of their English comrades-in-arms, the longer the Crown held up the mobilization for the arrival of more money from the Exchequer, the larger grew the arrears of the soldiers. Had the Irish regiments arrived, disciplined and armed but unpaid, the disorders of summer 1640 would have been worse. Charles did indeed have an army in Ireland, as Strafford had reminded him at the council table. But the King dared not use it. It may have been the one correct decision he made that year.

Protestant powers, too, received Charles's requests for soldiers. William of Orange was approached in February 1639 by royal letter and a secret briefing from Charles's agent, Boswell. The imminence of the Spanish

---

[79] Bodleian Library, Carte MSS., I, f. 194, Wandesford to Ormonde, 16 May 1640.
[80] Bodleian Library, Carte MSS., I, ff. 179–179v, and 194 for logistics; ff. 202v–203, 204, 209, 211, 218, 239v–240, for the suspension of the mobilization.
[81] Bodleian Library, Carte MSS., I, ff. 214–214v, 231–231v, where William St Leger boasts of the discipline and expertise of the soldiers awaiting transport at Carrickfergus.

threat prevented the Dutch from considering the offer with any serious-ness.[82] William would not have been wise to trust his troops and con-fidence to a monarch who, within the year, would be sheltering, and supplying powder to, the Spanish enemy. Apparently the King reckoned that troops, whatever their source, were in effect generic and therefore uncontroversial. Commanders were another matter, for they were promi-nent and could evoke comment. When a foreign duke, possibly Ulrich, the son of Christian IV of Denmark, sought a command in the Second Bishops' War, Charles declined because of 'the dangerous consequence of bringing in strangers for the Kingdomes service in busynes of war'.[83] Danish common soldiers, however, were another matter, especially as the military situation worsened.

In summer 1640 a scheme to enlist two regiments of Danish cavalry was touted. On the last Sunday in June, Charles sent General King, a veteran of the Thirty Years' War, back to Hamburg, reportedly with confidential instructions and a ring valued at £1,000. John Castle reported to the Earl of Bridgewater that the 'wizards of the court' conjectured that 3,000 Danish cavalry would be deployed against the Covenanters. But should peace come in the interim, then these Danes would be used to 'bridle and bring under the stubborn dispositions of the Commons of this kingdom, who in these times of his majesty's necessity have shewed too much disaffection'.[84] In fact the rumour contained much truth. The Venetian ambassador too had intelligence of King's errand, and informed the Doge that King had been ordered to raise two regiments of Danish horse immediately. He claimed that the Lord Treasurer had been instructed to issue £50,000 to King. But the Exchequer found no merchant willing to make up the letters and there was no ready money in the Treasury.[85] Accurately, Giustinian prognosticated that the affair would come to naught due to the Crown's 'lack of credit, a result which generally dogs the proposals of this court'.[86]

General King arrived at the Danish court on 11 July and met the follow-ing day with Christian IV, who expressed willingness to aid Charles but wanted a written proposal. The King could not, for secrecy's sake, comply. In a subsequent royal audience on 18 July, Christian offered some of his own troops and permission for levies, at English expense. Charles would

---

[82] BL, Add. MS. 12,093, f. 15, Charles to the Prince of Orange, 18 February 1639; Berkshire RO, Trumbull MSS., LXI, Weckherlin's diary, 22 February 1639; and G. Groen van Pansterer, *Archives on correspondence inédite de la Maison d'Orange-Nassau*, 2nd series, vol. III (Utrecht, 1859), pp. 144–5. I owe these references to Peter Donald.

[83] A. J. Loomie (ed.), *Ceremonies of Charles I. The Note Books of John Finet, Master of Ceremonies, 1628–1641* (New York, 1987), p. 57.

[84] HEH, EL 7841, Castle newsletter, 1 July 1640.

[85] See pp. 47–9, 146–8, 294–5.

[86] *CSP Venetian* (1640–2), XXV, pp. 61–2, n.89; Wedgwood, *The King's Peace*, pp. 225–6.

also have to supply the ships to transport these men. The Danish King volunteered soldiers, but not money or vessels.[87] On 6 August 1640, the Danish king authorized his ambassadors Ulfeld and Crabbe to accept the Orkneys, if sufficient cash were unavailable.[88] Throughout August rumours circulated in London about the landing of the Danes, perhaps (in a curious parallel from the previous year's campaign) upon the Scottish coast, while the Marquis of Hamilton attacked the opposite side of the island. The size of the force was calculated at 6,000 infantry and 300 horse under General King's command. As late as 24 August tales still foretold the arrival of the Danish ambassador with a contingent under General King. The plan came to nothing because Charles had no money and was unwilling to cede the Orkneys.

The supposed advantage of using Danish troops was that they could ride roughshod over disorderly native troops and keep discipline in the royal army. But the same financial weakness that prevented Charles from purchasing the services of mercenaries prompted the sort of disorder that the presence of mercenaries might have prevented. The solutions which Charles pursued in fact contributed to his problem, namely his powerlessness. The nobles had had the prospect of war thrust in their faces in a very personal way. The broad net that the King had cast for mercenaries in various quarters raised suspicion about his respect for the rule of law, the safety of his subjects, and his commitment to the maintenance of peace in the realm. In the era of the Thirty Years' War Charles's actions carried a foreboding that was peculiar to his time. Lords had been summoned for border service for centuries. But was this a raid on disorderly Scots or the extension of the bloodbath of religious war to peaceable Britain? Solicitation of mercenaries was nothing new. But could the arrival of Irish or Spanish troops be the vanguard of a popish conquest and a massacre of Protestants? Ironically, the monarch had empowered the shires to defend themselves, ostensibly against foreign aggressors. The perfect militia had contemplated neither an expedition against Scotland nor the alternative, turning its collective back on the King. Like the summoned noble in 1639, the weary creditor, and the harried members of the Short Parliament in 1640, the English militiaman had to choose. Would he fight for the King or not? He was placed in this dilemma because he comprised part of the only substantial military force in England.[89]

[87] SRO, GD 406/1/1146 and 1147, King to Hamilton, 19 July 1640. Peter Donald kindly supplied these references.
[88] Gardiner, *History*, vol. IX, p. 176, note 1.
[89] Russell, 'The Scottish Party in English Parliaments', pp. 6-9.

5

The perfect militia

Since the Middle Ages no monarch had tackled the problem of creating a trained military force for the defence of the realm with as much vigour as the young Charles I. During the war years of 1625–9 he aimed at fashioning an 'exact' or 'perfect' militia in England. Had he established a standing army or mobile regiments of trained-band soldiers, the civil wars might not have occurred. But he did not. Instead he reinvigorated tradition rather than innovated, by demanding that the trained bands fulfil their potential. However, the existence of the perfect militia did not hinder the Scots from crossing into England in 1640, nor did the trained bands flock to the royal standard in 1642.

Two questions dog any inquiry into the mobilizations of 1639 and 1640. Was the English militia capable of fighting the Covenanters? Tangentially, why did the King excuse trained soldiers from the expedition by allowing the substitution clause? This chapter argues that militia service, like military charges, was determined by the political relationship between the localities and the central government. Given the political and religious controversy surrounding the Scottish mobilizations, Charles could not make unqualified demands upon the military resources of the shires, especially as regards taking the militia out of the shire. Although the auxiliary role played by the trained bands in the Bishops' Wars was a direct result of the way in which the King mobilized his forces, the liability of the militia for such campaigning had developed over the centuries.

The nature of militia service

Placing militia service within historical perspective poses problems of definition which are best solved by describing what it is not. Feudal levies, based upon homage, scutage, and tenurial obligation are regarded as distinct from militia service, which is more communal in that the obligation stems from one's citizenship within borough, shire, or village. Militia bands were comprised of 'freemen', answering to their community, bound to no one but their collective interest to defend their liberty by force of arms. Obligation lay to the community, either the discrete locality or the realm at large, not to a lord (save the King, as father of the realm). Under a strong monarchy, ambiguity clouded the obligation. Was one obliged to the King *personally* or to the realm in general? Prior to the seventeenth century military obligation was very often defined and remitted according to the sovereign's wishes. The extent of a King's political strength determined how flexibly he could interpret and enforce militia service.

Militia service differed contractually from impressment. The common law drew a line between royal soldiers and militia which became even sharper when the expanded military obligations of Tudor statutes expired after 1604, giving the common law restrictions on service greater force based upon earlier medieval custom and legislation. Trained-band soldiers were not under the King's regulations; they served the local community. As freeholders they were defending their own property. Having picked up their arms without taking the King's shilling, no contractual obligation compelled them to cross the shire's boundaries. Common law restrictions on the use of the militia persuaded the King to devise an indenture placing the trained bands under royal pay and regulation, as was done in East Anglia in 1639.[1] Impressment was more explicitly contractual than militia service.[2] A specific contractual relationship was formed when a conscript (militiaman or not) accepted the King's shilling. 'Subcontractors' serving as royal officers did the pressing with the assistance of the locality.

The Crown often struggled to obtain from the shires well-armed able men in time of military exigency. Although it often succeeded in getting the troops, training remained a problem, and the military revolution of the sixteenth century exacerbated the problem by making training that much more essential in fielding an army quickly. The solution was the trained bands of the 1580s, created by the implementation of the principle of selection in 1573. The 'nation in arms', once simply divided into 'furnished' and 'unfurnished' categories, was superseded by a type of county military elite, who received (theoretically) an unprecedented ten days' training per annum. With selection and training came increased purchases of arms, powder, shot, and match. In time the county communities procured pikes and calivers, replacing bills and bows. In each shire the trained band set about drilling seasonally in order to learn the art of war. The demand for infantrymen, coupled with the increased complexity of formations and

---

[1] For a contract for militia service see the Kentish indenture in PRO SP 16/419. For a comparison of Suffolk indentures for raw levies and militiamen, see University of Minnesota Library, Phillipps MS. 3836, ff. 122–122v.

[2] N. B. Lewis, 'The Recruitment and Organization of a Contract Army, May to November 1337', *BIHR*, 37, no. 95 (May 1964), esp. p. 7.

weaponry, meant that the most adept and stout men (aged sixteen to sixty and of reasonable substance) were selected out of the eligible untrained militia to be honed into an effective fighting force. The military revolution had barely reached Elizabethan England so that Charles had to create a new breed of militiamen.[3]

The social structure of Tudor and Stuart England helped shape the development of the trained bands. Local gentry had emerged in their own right as powerful interest groups within each county community.[4] The nobility retained its influence, but increasingly in alliance with gentry factions based upon combinations of familial and religious affiliations. Coalitions of lords and gentlemen meant that military leadership in each shire was no longer the preserve of a local magnate and his hangers-on; gentry participated actively in county-level military organization through the institution of lieutenancy. Lieutenancy and the trained bands pushed local gentlemen deeper into the business of county government. This constituency viewed Caroline government with some suspicion, for the 1620s brought conflict at Westminster between King and Commons and the 1630s witnessed the isolation of many of the gentry from church and court.

The freeholders of the militia regarded local gentlemen as their natural leaders in both civil and military matters. Deputy lieutenancy bestowed military responsibility upon many of the gentry. Armies of infantry drew upon their resources. In this sense the Crown's direct control over the military resources of the shire decreased as authority settled on the county community, mediated through local governors and lieutenants who voiced the concerns of the local inhabitants as well as implementing the policies of the central government. The King had to summon a community, not an individual.[5] It also meant that sometimes the trained bands spoke for themselves in a way that was unusual in the feudal host, for the militia's allegiance was communal or civic (in the case of the towns) rather than personal, or a distinctively English amalgam of the two. A lord might couch his reservations towards his personal military obligation to the King within the terms of a personal contract. A community spoke in legal terms, too, but grounded more upon principle and custom rather than upon individualized contract. And principle and custom were seemingly ignored by the Crown in the 1630s, with no outlet for expressions of concern which the gentry might wish to utter. Those ties that *were* personal stemmed from

---

[3] Lindsay Boynton, *The Elizabethan Militia 1558–1638* (London, 1967), p. 113.
[4] A. J. Fletcher, *Reform in the Provinces. The Government of Stuart England* (New Haven, Conn., 1986), pp. 282–373.
[5] Though there are of course numerous medieval examples of communities rendering military service, this is strictly my own interpretation.

familial allegiances grounded in county society, and the patronage of the Lord Lieutenant.

The accession of James I blunted whatever military preparedness existed on the English side of the borders. The first Stuart King aimed at pacifying the Anglo-Scottish frontier, and the Union of the Crowns meant that future conflicts between these English-speaking Protestant nations would be coloured by their Britannic and Stuart identities. The expiration of the 1558 statute requiring musters, horses, and armour implied that Scot and Englishman would now live in fraternal harmony.[6]

When Charles and Buckingham tried to restore military ardour in the 1620s, it was done so tactlessly that for many 'military' and 'arbitrary' became synonymous. Regardless, Charles did much to prepare his subjects for war by promoting the perfect militia and the ship money fleet in the 1630s. The statutory ambiguity of the King's military programme associated the issues of militia rates and muster-master pay with the grievances of the 1620s. By 1638, suspicion of anything military was great indeed. Common law restrictions on using the nation's militia against Scotland raised the charge of illegality, already hotly debated within the context of 'defence of the realm' in Hampden's Case. The Bishops' Wars in fact were not a true measure of the organizational and institutional efficacy of lieutenancy and the trained bands, for a real test of the system in actual combat did not come about in 1639 or in 1640.

Uncertainty about deployment of the militia beyond the community's borders (and its terms of service) revolved around whether it was a royal army or a local defence force. A mere levy, to be disposed as the King saw fit, was qualitatively (if not always legally) different from a force specifically charged with defending a certain corner of the realm. Royal leadership often defined the nature of the force; the King's presence transformed a shire levy into an appendage of the royal army. The monarch's person made 'national' what was customarily local. Charles I seems to have understood this fully, at least in theory. The ancient militia could be welded together as a 'national' army out of components selected from provincial bands[7]. Domesday Book evidenced that the fyrd, the Anglo-

---

[6] Boynton, *Elizabethan Militia*, p. 209, citing 1 Jac. I c.25; see also John Thornborough's *A Discourse Plainely Proving the Evident Utilitie and Urgent Neccessitie of the Desired Happie Union of the Two Famous Kingdomes of England and Scotland* (Oxford, 1604) and *Ioiefull and Blessed Reuniting of Two Mighty and Famous Kingdomes, England and Scotland into Their Ancient Name of Great Brittaine* (Oxford, 1604). Sir Thomas Craig's *De Unione Regnorum Britanniae Tractatus* (London, 1605) blamed calamities that had befallen Britain throughout the centuries upon the separation of Crowns. His emphasis on religion as the foremost bond in reuniting England and Scotland was particularly prophetic after 1637.

[7] Michael Powicke, *Military Obligation in Medieval England; A Study in Liberty and Duty* (Oxford, 1962), pp. 7–9, 14.

Saxon military force of the localities, was liable for service 'everywhere' in extraordinary circumstances. However, inherently it comprised a local defence force, especially on the coast, being absorbed into the King's army only in the event of a significant threat to the realm. The key was royal pay. There lay Charles's weakness. He had set in motion the apparatus of the militia without a stock of money. The King's shilling made them his; without it, they remained a militia, restricted to (or safe within) the shire. The yoking of the local institution to royal policy forced definition of the relationship between Crown and subject, making it a political issue.

THE POLITICAL AND HISTORICAL CONTEXT OF MILITIA SERVICE

The medieval origins of militia service

Militiamen often helped the Crown to victory. The Battle of the Standard (1138) enabled cavalry raised through knights' service with an infantry of Yorkshire militiamen to defeat a formidable Scottish force. Local militia survived because of the utility and affordability of local foot-soldiers. A loose collection of local defence forces took on the definition of a 'national' militia through the initiative of the King.[8] Henry II's Assize of Arms did not discriminate between feudal and non-feudal obligation but divided those ' "well-established" freemen and the general levy'. Social rank determined one's military obligation. The arms requirements were apportioned by levels of wealth, not tenure, which injected fiscal criteria that moved the militia beyond the bounds of the feudal system. The 'national levy' saw wholesale impressment or selection of militiamen. Still, local forces served in a defensive posture, mostly to repel mercenaries. The Assize's new writs may have been innovative, but the principle was traditional.[9] The militia emerged as an elite force of sorts, but that distinction lay in its training and weapons rather than in its social standing.

A precedent occurred when militia bowmen dispatched to the Welsh wars in 1265 received pay from the Exchequer once across the shire's border. Edward I further mixed forces of knights and shire infantry, with increased use of a cash nexus and indentures. It was precisely this that

[8] Noyes, *Commissions of Array*, p. 15.
[9] For service against Scotland, sheriffs' writs were issued in 1244 and service *sum toto posse* in 1255, according to Powicke, *Military Obligation*, pp. 65, 67; on the variety of writs, see Noyes, p. 19. Also see F. M. Powicke, *The Thirteenth Century, 1216–1307* (Oxford, 1962), pp. 91, 181.

Charles I would attempt with the militia in the Bishops' Wars. By around 1277 written and verbal contracts increasingly clarified terms of service.[10]

Edward I's 1296 Scottish campaign, like the initial plan for 1639, comprised 30,000 infantry including shire forces. In both cases that number failed to materialize. Given the size of the projected army and the use of contracts to raise levies, Charles's army did resemble that of Edward I – a noble contingent buttressed by militia and conscripted (contracted) infantry. The 1298 writs of summons called for levies of 29,000 infantry, drawn from Wales, Shropshire, Cheshire, Lancashire, and the northern counties, which was not unlike the 1639 call-up. The size of these levies, though the full numbers were not realized, meant that the modestly trained and/or well-equipped foot of the localities were greatly diluted by raw, impressed tenants of the nobles.[11] Charles I's armies, then, were best served by the medieval model because they needed reinforcements from the shires. Charles's problem with unskilled men was unique only in that warfare now demanded greater training than in Edward's day. The centralized and national military system of the post-Marian militia statute still resembled the armies of the Middle Ages.

The Statute of Winchester (1285) fits nicely into the common law tradition that obliged freemen to defend their community, while the system of defence – the keeping of weapons – was formalized via statute.[12] By classifying men according to wealth and the arms they should possess, Crown and Parliament imposed a paradigm upon the localities. Nowhere did they state that the boundaries of the shire were to be crossed. The payment of local forces when called beyond the shire and the arms-and-armour formula of the Statute of Winchester resembled custom and in effect limited the military obligation.[13] In the Scottish campaigns of 1307, 1310, 1319, and 1322 the Crown reached into the local communities for

[10] Powicke, *Military Obligation*, pp. 93–4; the earliest surviving example, enrolled in Chancery in 1287, is discussed by N. B. Lewis, 'An Early Indenture of Military Service, 27 July 1287', *BIHR*, 13 (1935), p. 85, note 7; see also Powicke, *Military Obligation*, p. 97.

[11] Michael Prestwich, *War, Politics and Finance Under Edward I* (London, 1972), pp. 93–5 and J. E. Morris, *The Welsh Wars of Edward I* (Oxford, 1901), pp. 284–5, 298. The 1299–1300 expedition mustered only 2,500 (out of the 16,000 demanded from the northern counties, including Derbyshire, Staffordshire, Shropshire, and Nottinghamshire), who then deserted. See also Joan Wake (ed.), *A Copy of Papers Relating to Musters, Beacons, Subsidies, etc., in the County of Northampton A.D. 1586–1623*, Northampton Record Society, (Peterborough, 1935), p. xxxv.

[12] The 1285 statute 'gave for the first time parliamentary sanction to a system of compulsory arming, but had no clause imposing compulsory service', according to Wake (ed.), *Musters, Beacons, in Northants*, p. xxxvi.

[13] Prior to the Scottish campaigns of the early 1300s, the Crown issued Articles of Inquiry (1306) to evaluate the enforcement of the Statute of Winchester, according to Charles M. Clode, *The Military Forces of the Crown; Their Administration and Government*, I, pp. 345–6.

infantry, and purchased their services outside the shire by giving out royal pay at general muster or once across the county boundary.[14] The militia had acquired a dual identity – as a local defence force serving at its own cost with its weaponry defined by the Statute of Winchester, and as a recruiting ground exploited by royal officers empowered by Commissions of Array to levy for national service.

A tradition of obtaining troops from towns and shires for northern expeditions had clearly emerged.[15] It was to this tradition that Charles I resorted. But he overlooked the importance of drawing the locality and Parliament into the preparations. The locality's sense of identity (and grievance) was more closely defined through repeated demands upon the community's money and manpower. Military obligation, parliamentary procedure, and the collective interest of the community were brought into focus more sharply. The tripartite of military obligation (feudal summons, militia service, and impressment via Commission of Array) became increasingly distinct. In 1327 Edward III issued the feudal summons in its entirety while the general obligation for all men was implemented separately; the North undertook full-scale mobilization while select militia units came from Nottinghamshire, Derbyshire, and Staffordshire under local commanders bearing Commissions of Array.[16]

The indenture system destined to evolve into impressment flourished. The statute 1 Edward III c.2 reacted against Edward II's presumptions in commandeering the militia and proliferating Commissions of Array. The fifth clause reiterated the common law doctrine that one could not be compelled to serve beyond the shire boundary, except in cases of clear danger such as an actual foreign landing. The seventh clause accepted that expeditionary forces would continue to be fielded but demanded the King should pay the bill. This latter clause made a useful precedent for the collection of coat-and-conduct money under the Tudors and Stuarts, though common law tradition could be interpreted as that men should be supported by the county until they actually crossed the border, at which time they were formally in the King's pay.[17] Charles's predecessors, therefore,

---

[14] R. W. Kaeuper, *War, Justice and Public Order* (Oxford, 1988), pp. 24–5. Between 1311 and 1313 Edward II fashioned an army from northern lords who performed border service and paid contingents of southern shire militia. Experiments with the recruitment of heavy infantry occurred during the 1314 mobilization, including the impressment of Yorkshire's entire infantry, financed by the localities (vills). See Powicke, *Military Obligation*, pp. 140–2.

[15] Powicke, *Military Obligation*, pp. 156–7.

[16] Albert E. Prince, 'The Army and Navy', in J. Willard and W. Morris (eds.) *The English Government at Work, 1327–1336* (Cambridge, Mass., 1940), vol. I, pp. 344, 346.

[17] Further clarifications of the procedure of impressment, necessitating the written contract or indenture, followed in the fifteenth clause. Clode, *Military Forces of the Crown*, p. 346. See Richard Cust on Charles's inflexibility, *The Forced Loan and English Politics*, p. 321.

had been forced to wrangle with their subjects' military obligation. The difference was that most monarchs were at least willing to negotiate with Parliament.

Michael Powicke wrote, 'the right of consent to taxes and customs was used by the commons to secure legislation reinforcing the limitation set by the statutes of 1327 on the use of their military forces outside the realm'.[18] Whether or not a Scottish or Welsh war was 'outside the realm' depended upon whether it was intended as an offensive or defensive operation. The implications for the Bishops' Wars are clear – was the aggressor the King or the Covenanters? Previously, any action beyond the county boundary was foreign, 'and "foreign" simply means outside the county'.[19] The Scottish campaign in the summer of 1335 included forces from a score of counties, including far-away Wiltshire, Dorset, and Somerset (though Devon and Cornwall were excused). Charles I, too, drew the West Country into his 1640 campaign. Clearly border campaigns, even if they ventured inside Scotland, could be construed as defensive and within the limits of the royal prerogative.

Impressment and militia service, still intertwined and at times indistinct, relying upon citizenship rather than land tenure and homage, had superseded feudal service. Modified contracts for military service took their place alongside the feudal contracts, and increasingly large segments of society faced weapons assessment and soldiering by the time of the Stuarts.[20] The systems of militia service and impressment overlapped, based upon a general allegiance and a more specific contractual bond with the sovereign. Charles I therefore tapped the militia system by selecting trained-band members and endeavoured to place them within the impressment relationship by forcing them to take the royal shilling, hence contracting trained bandsmen through the traditional indenture. Similarly in 1344 Edward III had considered fighting Scotland with shire levies only, though 'pardoned felons' would reinforce the county forces.[21] The same year saw statutory definition of service outside the realm at the King's expense via a system designed to supersede the Statute of Winchester. Formulae based upon goods and lands determined what military support a given citizen would tender to the Crown. A national system of military taxation was planned; a survey of 1344 enrolled the names of all substantial citizens and ranked them by wealth. Henry VIII and Wolsey

---

[18] Powicke, *Military Obligation*, p. 182.
[19] Wake (ed.), *Musters, Beacons, in Northants.*, p. xxxvi. The mobilizations of 1346 and 1355 comprised the latter, and 'county and urban levies made up the whole army, with the exception of a few household or garrison troops', Powicke, *Military Obligation*, p. 185.
[20] Lewis, 'A Contract Army', p. 5 and Prince, 'The Army and Navy', pp. 351–2.
[21] See R. Nicholson, *Edward III and the Scots* (Oxford, 1965), p. 167.

ventured a similar arrangement in 1522. As a contractual system centered upon a cash nexus, such a scheme was desirable if the King was to maintain his war policy. For example, in the Scottish campaign of 1347 nobles received royal pay for their tours of duty. Unpaid feudal cavalry service had been eclipsed by a pay schedule. Along with this system came an allowance for substitutes. This loophole attempted to lessen parliamentary and popular protest in the face of intense military burdens, and with it came a statute of 1348 forbidding service abroad at county expense. In 1640 the Short Parliament appears to have considered similar legislation on the eve of its dissolution.[22]

Parliament intruded increasingly on mobilization in reaction to the expansion of the Crown's military demands. In contrast, the reign of the second Stuart is striking in the total absence of a relationship with that institution which had financed royal wars in the past, even when simultaneously striving to limit the military obligation through definition. In 1350, the statute 25 Edward III c.8 drew recruitment and military obligation even more closely within Parliament's jurisdiction; this was followed by the statute of 1355, which made clear that the raising of troops contrary to tenure was illegal without parliamentary sanction. Parliament had interposed itself in the recruitment process. However, statutory limitation did not lessen military demands any more than debate over the means by which to conduct war constituted a refusal by Parliament to assist the King.[23] Partnership in recruitment, like cooperation in military finance, ultimately enhanced royal authority through parliamentary assistance. The composition of Charles's armies resembled those of the Middle Ages, yet the techniques for securing funds and the obligations of his subjects did not. To adapt medieval models to the 1630s Charles would have had to establish a relationship with Parliament.

The sporadic utilization of militia in royal armies was partly a consequence of the terms of service. At a time when the Scots recruited through a general levy, the English fielded conglomerate armies of feudal contingents and local forces (which could be classified as militia or impressed soldiers depending upon *who* was chosen from the community and the

---

[22] Powicke, *Military Obligation*, pp. 188, 194–7; A. R. Myers (ed.), *English Historical Documents 1327–1485* (New York, 1969), IV, pp. 85–6; see also p. 208; Fissel, 'Scottish War and English Money', pp. 206–8.

[23] J. H. Leslie (ed.), 'Statutes and Acts of Parliament – Army', pp. 219–20. The 1355 Scottish expedition drew heavily on the shires, and the Crown declined to reimburse pay and supplies spent in the mobilization. As the Crown increasingly thrust the responsibilites for pay upon the localities, Parliament fought to redress the situation, ideally reverting to the arrangements under Edward I. Powicke concluded: 'the statute against finding men according to the value of one's lands was more effective than the one against money levies to support county troops'. See Powicke, *Military Obligation*, pp. 202–9.

contractual status of the indenture). In the case of local defence, the militia owed unpaid service up to forty days, without contract. Impressment cost the Crown money. Summoning substantial citizens who kept weapons according to the Statute of Winchester was cheaper and faster than assembling a rag-tag army of conscripts. The crux of the matter was as much the *expense* of prolonged campaigns as the violation of shire boundaries.[24]

Scottish conflicts forced statutory definition of the military obligation, which then led to assessment of the relation between ruler and subject. For this reason, military demands following the controversies of the 1620s and 1630s placed Charles I's government in a suspicious light. But clearly a stronger militia had not guaranteed the localities the right to define their role and place in the military organization of the realm.[25] In fact, the expanded use of Commissions of Array issued under privy seal to the magnates threatened to make communal forces simply an auxiliary to be used at will, under indenture for prolonged campaigns or gratis in Welsh or Scottish wars. Only magnates possessed sufficient influence to protect the border counties. Shire militia alone could never have maintained peace on the frontier with Scotland. Communal forces were better placed under a lord armed with a Commission of Array.[26]

The militia under the Tudors

Certainly, however, the taming of the nobility strengthened the linkage between Crown and shire forces. Under Henry VIII Commissions of Array

[24] In 1383 the 'North Trent' counties and the towns of Lincoln and Hull faced general levies of shire forces in John of Gaunt's campaign against Scotland. In 1384 the 'commons petitioned against recent arrays of men (*gentz*) of their counties to go to Scotland at their own cost or the cost of their counties and secured re-enactment of the statute 1 Edward III', Powicke, *Military Obligation*, p. 245. 'Henry IV's Welsh and Scottish armies were largely composed of fee-holders summoned by chancery writs addressed to the Sheriff', and the same held true for French expeditions in 1406–7 and 1415–20, according to Powicke, *Military Obligation*, p. 214. The Commons protested at Henry I's use of local forces without pay in the Welsh campaign. Later, the militia restrictions of 1327 were enshrined in a 1402 statute. In 1404 a new form of Commission of Array 'for use when pay for service outside the county was not required', came into use because of the repeated development of militia levies against Scotland and Wales.

[25] In the fifteenth century the King and nobles drew upon the militia in times of civil war as well as in fear of invasion. Under Henry VI Commissions of Array were used for 'defence and civil war'. In 1437 and 1442, the Statute of Winchester was reissued. The Wars of the Roses dragged in 'county and town militia which reveals itself in writs of array, accounts by chronicles, and in muster rolls', according to Powicke, *Military Obligation*, pp. 220–2. Commissions of Array were issued in York in 1485 and as far south as Suffolk, Norfolk, and Essex in 1486 in preparation for a Scottish threat.

[26] Noyes, *Commissions of Array*, p. 38; R. L. Storey, 'The North of England', in S. B. Chrimes, C. D. Ross, and R. A. Griffiths (eds.), *Fifteenth Century England* (Manchester, 1972), pp. 131–3.

helped field forces at Flodden.[27] Moreover, Henry exercised greater control over the military apparatus along the borders by reconstituting the Council of the North and by his imposition of an early form of lieutenancy. Thomas Cromwell carried the business further in his proposal 'for the ordering of the manred of this King's realm', which aimed at creating a system which drew in uniform manner upon the resources of the localities.[28] The deputation of authority inherent in Cromwell's design presaged the creation of lords lieutenant later in the century.[29]

Centralization demanded uniformity, a sentiment also entertained by Charles I. In spite of occasional attempts (such as in 1511) to enforce the Statute of Winchester, border counties were as slow to report their militia strength in 1522 as in 1638. In fact, Cumberland, Westmorland, Northumberland, Lancashire, Yorkshire, Nottinghamshire, and a segment of Derbyshire (all counties involved in border defence) failed to submit returns by the end-of-the-year deadline.

Henry VIII's 1542 campaign against Scotland probably incorporated militia units. His army resembled medieval hosts, as did that of Charles I in that it was based upon county contingents and personal commissions to his nobles. The latter resembled lieutenancy commissions more than the quasi-feudal summoning of the nobility, though in the Bishops' Wars the lords reinforced the levies and in 1542 the opposite seems to have been true. The companies taken from Yorkshire and Durham in 1542 and held in reserve on the Borders were probably militia units[30]. Under the regimes of Somerset and Northumberland the former's policy of garrisoning precluded the use of militia, and the political instability under both regimes discouraged putting large numbers of civilians in arms. As a result, Somerset spent £351,251 on troops and Northumberland experimented with a modest standing army of cavalry.[31] None of these options was feasible during Charles I's Personal Rule.

The Marian militia statutes strove to bring into being the 'national militia' of the Tudor imagination. From landed men worth £1,000 to £5 freeholders, subjects knew what horse or bills or pikes to provide, as did the local communities. All answered to the royal commissioners of musters, who were new and potentially powerful administrators. It was an ambi-

---

27 Noyes, *Commissions of Array*, pp. 43, 46.
28 J. J. Goring, 'The General Proscription of 1522', *EHR*, 86, (1971), p. 687.
29 J. A. Guy, *Tudor England* (Oxford, 1988), p. 168.
30 *Letters and Papers, Foreign and Domestic, of the Reign of Henry VIII* (1542) (London, 1900), vol. XVII, nos. 764 (Privy Council to Norfolk, 10 September 1542), 778 (instructions for the York Commissioners, 13 September 1542), 786 (Norfolk to PC, 14 September 1542), 794 (Shrewsbury to Scudamore, 15 September 1542), pp. 422, 428–9, 432–3, 438, respectively. For musters see no. 882, pp. 492–511.
31 Guy, *Tudor England*, pp. 202, 216.

tious if stillborn attempt at administrative reform. One can only wonder if, under different political circumstances, the Marian establishment might have evolved into a sort of standing army by the time of the Stuarts. Substantial landed men, nobles and gentry, continued to be responsible for providing servants, tenants, and dependents in time of war. 'Quasi-feudal' recruitment could no longer produce the troops needed. Households were smaller, social mobility greater, and tenants less willing to submit themselves to outmoded forms of personal military service based on land tenure. The realm required a 'national' shire militia. The nature of service was thus transformed from a personal, contractual relationship (that transformation gradually evolved from traditional tenurial service to indentured retinues, expanded use of Commissions of Array, and the anti-retainer legislation of the later Middle Ages) to a county system where communal identity with the shire – or even the parish, wapentake, or hundred – responded directly to the central government's demands via commissioner or deputy lieutenant. Thus a system often described as 'national' in reality reinforced county identity and increased solidarity among the inhabitants of the county community.[32]

Early in Elizabeth's reign nationwide musters occurred roughly every four years, as the administrative effort and disruption of the workforce made annual musterings well nigh impossible. Ideally, the cooperation between Crown and localities in recognition of the universality of the defence of the realm would induce the hundreds and wapentakes to arrange some drilling in the interim. Although the central government experimented with printed certificates and strove to instil uniformity in the militia system, the institution ultimately functioned through the efforts of local governors: 'Everything depended on the energies and abilities of the commissioners'.[33] Charles I was no less dependent on the efforts of the commissioners. The 'national' took precedence over the 'personal' system of recruitment.[34]

The rebellion of the northern earls in 1569 erupted amid extensive mustering and review of the nation's militia and offers some measure of how well the new system responded to military threats in the north.[35] Several tithings integrated gunners and pikemen into their ranks so that the skilled infantry were nearly equally distributed amongst the four categories of weapons: bills, bows, calivers, and pikes. A greater number, though, obtained a 'token' caliverman as evidence of the militia's 'modernization'

---

[32] J. J. Goring, 'Social Change and Military Decline in mid-Tudor England', *History*, 60, no. 199 (June 1975), pp. 188–90.

[33] C. G. Cruickshank, *Elizabeth's Army* (second edn, Oxford, 1966), p. 134.

[34] Goring, 'Social Change and Military Decline', p. 194.

[35] PRO, *State Papers Domestic, Elizabeth* 12/50; 51; 52; 53; 54; 55; 56; 57.

while the majority of soldiers retained their bows and bills. One wonders about animosities between hundreds and tithings which had gone to the expense of introducing arquebusses, calivers, and pikes and those adamantly, or surreptitiously, avoiding their duty. Perhaps resentment against laggard hundreds accounts for the vitriolic complaints about the heaviness of assessments.

The autumn 1569 mobilization, with its ensuing incursion into Scotland, convinced Elizabeth that her military establishment was inadequate for the perilous world of the 1570s. Shortages of trained men, horses, armour, pikes, and calivers dogged the royal forces. The Queen's commanders hesitated to confront the rebels, fearing themselves outnumbered as well as badly equipped. In these straits, theories about military obligations were cast aside. Conveniently, muster certificates drafted only a few months before disclosed England's martial readiness. The thin ranks of the militia of the northern counties needed to be fortified by men from the south. Elizabeth understood that major military actions in the north could not be waged solely with the military resources of that region.[36] Similarly, Charles I would use East Anglian militia for Hamilton's assault force in 1639 and lean heavily on the West Country for recruits in 1640. In 1569 commissions were issued to lords lieutenant to levy from the furnished (and, with luck, trained) men of the southern counties and march north. Sussex, Elizabeth's Lord General, described how he had 'raised all the forces in all the wapentakes near this city, and chosen out of them so many able men as have any kind of weapon'.[37]

It was reckoned that an expeditionary force of 20,000 foot and 2,500 horse could be raised in Berkshire, Oxfordshire, Hertfordshire, Essex, Bedfordshire, Buckinghamshire, Wiltshire, Norfolk, Suffolk, Somerset, Middlesex, and London. In the end, though terribly slowly, the Crown obtained 12,000 infantry, the majority of which came from the southern counties.[38] Again, the size of the force and the slowness of its mobilization paralleled the Bishops' Wars. The suppression of the 1569 rebellion not only revealed weaknesses (weaponry, administrative sluggishness) but also showed that emergencies such as insurrections or invasions could force the suspension of statutes.

In an emergency the statutory limitations of service for county defence and maintenance of the integrity of shire boundaries were disregarded. The

---

[36] Wake (ed.), *Musters, Beacons, in Northants.*, pp. xxxvii.

[37] *CSPD Addenda, Elizabeth*, p. 111, no. 30, Sussex and four of the Council of the North to the Queen, 20 November 1567.

[38] London had a modern contingent of 4,000 foot, half of which carried calivers, 1,500 shouldered pikes, and the remaining 500 carried bows. PRO, SP 12/59, pt. II, ff. 212, 216–217v; PRO, E 351/229, ff. 7–11v.

men levied south of the Trent in 1569, and in the north for that matter, included fully equipped militiamen. When the earls retreated into Scotland, the southern militia became engaged in a foreign war. Even if the Crown pleaded 'border service', that obligation did not apply to the men from south of the Trent. All this makes Charles I's exactions in 1639–40 seem rather traditional, if ill-advised in the context of the seventeenth century.

During the general musters of 1569, deputy lieutenants emerged, whose jurisdiction made possible the shire-based trained force in the 1570s.[39] The commissions varied according to the tasks assigned. With the assistance of justices of the peace and a muster-master, deputy lieutenants served as royal agents for military affairs. They supervised training, investigated arms borrowing, and pressed more rigorously than could an outsider. Recruited from among the gentry, they reflected the increasing involvement of the gentry in military activities.[40] They displaced the sheriff as the means by which levies were selected, accounted and marched away to the royal army. The deputy lieutenant determined eligibility for trained-band service and impressment. He exceeded commissioners for musters in the scope of his powers, yet remained as much a part of the community as an extension of the Privy Council.[41]

The principle of selection predated the 1573 trained-band legislation. 'Selection' comprised the further maturing of the categories used in Elizabethan muster certificates. Some commissioners, such as those of Devon in 1560, separated the men aged sixteen to sixty into three groups. 'Pryncipall' men were best suited for soldiering, those of the 'seconde' rank had some promise, and the remainder were classed as 'unable', meaning physically inferior rather than infirm;[42] 10 to 30 per cent achieved 'pryncipall' ranking. Hence a crude system of ranking existed more than a decade before the inception of the trained bands. Although not every county described the condition of its men as anything more than 'furnished and unfurnished', the specific weapons shouldered by the bands were regarded as essential information which the certificate had to convey.

New administrative arrangements were matched by modernization of the tools of war and the sustenance of the forces. The cumulative effect of Elizabeth's military charges (purchase of powder, match, and shot, replacement of bills and bows with pikes and calivers, and repair and maintenance of corslets) came on top of the charges associated with

---

[39] PRO, SP 12/59/57–62, lists of deputy lieutenants in 1569.
[40] This is based partially upon Thomson, 'The Origin and Growth of the Office of Deputy Lieutenant', pp. 154–5.
[41] Stater, 'War and the Structure of Politics', pp. 88–9.
[42] This is my own interpretation of PRO, SP 12/13/18.

impressment, specifically coat-and-conduct money. Each decade saw more men sent overseas; by 1603 it seemed as if England was perpetually upon a war-footing.[43] The central government clamored for improvement of trained-band equipment, allowing reductions only if the more manageable number were more 'throughlie furnysshed'.[44]

Most indicative of the need for reliable infantry was the inclusion of trained-band infantry in overseas levies, for example to France in the 1590s.[45] Once again, the Tudors made greater demands upon the militia than did Charles I, prior to the Civil War. In Elizabeth's reign, Crown and Privy Council dictated whether or not the situation required trained-band infantry or not. Utilization of the militia for overseas duty, legal or not, served to season the levy with a percentage of trained men and to lessen the demand on the counties for additional weapons (since the trained-band soldiers already possessed theirs). Elizabeth's government also seems to have thought the militia reinforcements sent to Normandy in 1593 less likely to desert.[46] The need for skilled, armed soldiers prompted the Queen to violate custom if not statute (as had her father and his predecessors). Trained calivermen, and later, musketeers, were prized. They proved themselves against the rebels in 1569 at the Gelt crossing, and commanders often begged for more 'shot'.[47]

Assuming that Elizabethan government had provided sufficient impetus for the creation of a skilled military elite, did the county communities bring the militia to a peak of readiness? The answer is a dismal 'no'. Had Spanish *tercios* disembarked in 1588 they would probably have trounced the trained bands.[48] Muster certificates in 1588 and afterwards 'showed marked deterioration'.[49] The reasons for England's chronic martial anaemia in the 1590s were similar to those under Charles I: lack of money and overworked local government. The stresses of the musters and levies of

[43] See below p. 220 and the tables in Cruickshank, *Elizabeth's Army*, pp. 290–1.
[44] Boynton, *Elizabethan Militia*, p. 95, citing PRO, SP 12/167/14. Strategically positioned counties required stringent mustering. Maritime counties, especially Kent, were supposed to keep their forces at a comparatively high pitch of readiness. County communities were arranged by location into six, grouping for the supervision of training and assessment. J. N. McGurk, 'Armada Preparations in Kent and Arrangements Made after the Defeat (1587–1589)', *Archaeologia Cantiana*, LXXXV (1970), esp. pp. 71–7, 91–3. See also Boynton, *Elizabethan Militia*, p. 96.
[45] See for example Somerset RO, DD/PH 220, lieutenancy book, f. 26, deputy lieutenants to Lord Lieutenant, 16 July 1591.
[46] R. B. Wernham, *After the Armada. Elizabethan England and the Struggle for Western Europe 1588–1595*, p. 291. The Rouen relief force included militia from Essex and Hertfordshire, p. 381, note 36. On Normandy, pp. 462–3.
[47] Training directions are discussed in Thomson, 'The Origin and Growth of the Office of Deputy Lieutenant', pp. 159–63; Boynton, *Elizabethan Militia*, pp. 113–23.
[48] G. Parker, 'If the Armada had landed', *History*, 61 (1976), pp. 358–68.
[49] Boynton, *Elizabethan Militia*, p. 173.

the period from 1585 to 1601 were quite similar to those of the 1620s. The predominant strand of continuity, however, was the unwillingness of local communities to carry an increasingly heavy, and ill-defined, military obligation.

Combat use of the trained bands was avoided in 1588 (as in 1639–40), making assessment of the militia difficult. The cockpit of an Anglo-Spanish confrontation would have been Kent, divided into east–west halves and prepared to meet an invasion force on her northern, eastern, or southern boundaries, or to dispatch 4,000 militiamen to Sussex (if the Spanish beachhead were established there). Of the 10,000 foot of the Kentish militia, fewer than 3,000 were trained. Two thousand elite trained men of Kent sheltered the Queen at St James's.[50] In this national emergency, the best soldiers did not defend the county *per se*, but flocked around the monarch. Charles I's expectations in 1639, when he gathered militia around himself at York, seemed reasonable enough to himself, though one must question whether Alexander Leslie had intentions similar to those of the Duke of Parma. Although Kent was the most vulnerable shire, where the Spanish were expected to land, the focus of the nation's defence became the protection of the sovereign and to this end the statutory prohibitions on military service beyond county boundaries were cast aside.

Regarding the pay of the Kentish trained bands, however, the troops received their coating and conducting at the expense of the shire, receiving royal pay only upon arrival at the rendezvous. Most if not all counties paid out coat-and-conduct money without reimbursement from the Elizabethan Exchequer, though upon dispersal a modest amount covered the soldiers' return to their localities.[51] The shires learned during the late Tudor and early Stuart period that the Crown expected the localities to shoulder military charges without compensation. After decades of such exploitation, it is not surprising that Kent proved uncooperative during the Bishops' Wars. Charles ordered that the deputy lieutenants receive 'a sharp reprehension'.[52]

Grievances about the cost of the Elizabethan militia and accompanying charges resemble those of the 1620s and 1639–40. William Lambarde, in a confidential letter of mid-December 1587 to the Lord Lieutenant of Kent, Lord Cobham, assessed the impact of fifteen years of military charges revolving around the training of select militiamen. The strength of the

---

[50] McGurk, 'Armada preparations in Kent', pp. 80–1, 84.

[51] For Northamptonshire coat-and-conduct money in 1588, see Wake (ed.), *Musters, Beacons, in Northants.*, p. 21. The Northamptonshire men received ten shillings a man for conduct, and coats valued at fifteen shillings apiece, which was rather expensive.

[52] Bodleian Library, Clarendon SP, XVI, ff. 68–68v, Windebank to the King, 13 April 1639, and apostiled by Charles at York on 16 April. See also SRO, GD 406/1/812 and GD 406/1/938.

trained bands could indeed be increased. But the multiplicity of charges
had to be considered. Landlords forced up rents, impoverishing farmers
and confounding the rural economy. The central government had compounded this distress by a series of taxes raised in 1581, 1582, 1585, 1586,
and 1587. A trained infantryman could not be taken from his livelihood
and exercised for less than 12d a day, a horseman 20d.[53] Given the regimen
of training, each trained soldier cost his community a minimum of £1 per
annum. The mounting cost of coats, powder, and bullets would have to be
spread over a community disgruntled with the expense of military preparedness. If the substantial men of the militia were taxed, wouldn't this be
an 'unequall distribution'? To exempt them placed the entire burden on the
less affluent, who would reel from the weight of taxation. These groans
had accompanied the principle of selection since its inception. The most
common response was to petition for reduction of the county forces.

   Elizabeth, like Charles after her, brushed aside protests and fielded the
local forces. Whether the troops at Tilbury would have prevailed over the
enemy remains conjectural, but spokesmen from diverse viewpoints, Burgh-
ley for the government and Sir John Smythe as a critic of the court and
times, expressed grave doubts about the quality of the militia.[54] Those
deputy lieutenants who certified in the 1580s that their bands had reached a
peak of excellence meant that an appropriate percentage of firearms had
been introduced, that the men knew how to handle their weapons and keep
in rank. Once pitted against veterans, as appeared imminent in 1588, the
truth would be seen. It was one thing to keep the peace and protect the
shire from uprising or incursion, quite another to square off against professional soldiers from the continental wars. One could say the same of the
perfect militia of the 1630s.

THE EARLY STUART MILITIA

In its English context, the military revolution meant that fighting wars was
no longer primarily the affair of a distinct social class – the nobility.
National defence, first thrust into the hands of the commissioners of
musters, then in to the steadier grip of the deputy lieutenants, made military administration, in the guise of defence (the militia) or offence (levies
for overseas service), a community obligation. No longer simply a matter
of the magnate insisting on personal service based upon individual ties of
tenure or indenture, mobilization now affected entire communities. Local

---

53 McGurk, 'Armada Preparations in Kent', p. 77.
54 See Morris, *Musters, Beacons*, pp. civ-cvii; also Sir John Smythe, *Instructions, Observations, and Orders Military . . .* (London, 1595).

allegiances served national interests, and did so at the direction of gentlemen as much as of lords.[55]

In 1639 Charles I would find that ancient landed families could still put horsemen in the field, but in paltry numbers and with some reluctance. Arguably, the best cavalry came now from the militia horse bands.[56] The most formidable military presence in the realm lay in the counties, administered by the local governors, and serving as the county community's first line of defence. The gentry ultimately controlled the local military establishment and had supported the militia largely for their own security. Charles's reform of the trained bands in the 1630s threatened to alter the militia's function, at least as the gentry saw it, and the campaign of 1639–40 confirmed fears that the trained bands could be made a tool of royal policy.

From the Crown's point of view, little more had occurred than the delegation of authority. In truth, the justices and deputy lieutenants had become masters of the countryside: 'the lieutenancy fulfilled the same function as retaining: it could be seen as a way of keeping horses and armour at the cost of the county and in formal partnerships instead of uneasy truce with the Crown'.[57] These partnerships were forged between the monarch and collective bodies of local governors, men who considered themselves obligated to community interests as well as obedient to the Crown.[58] Dealing with a community was sometimes more difficult than coercing an individual. The King might humble an upstart lord and elevate the obedient, but had little alternative to browbeating local governors. He could replace one amateur with another, but that would not be likely to remedy the disaffection of the county community.[59]

The forces created to protect the realm, it was alleged, bankrupted the counties when the cost of a militiaman ranged from 17s to above £2 in some cases. The ascendancy of the Elizabethan gentry permitted them to spread more broadly the increasing cost of the military establishment, in spite of the central government's paternalist desire to spare the potentially disorderly poor. In effect they allied with the nobility to place the burden on their inferiors by extending the rating system to the lower orders. Contrary to the government's wishes, the county elite shifted a portion of the

---

[55] Goring, 'Social Change and Military Decline', esp. pp. 188–92, 198.

[56] On county militia horsebands see Boynton, *Elizabethan Militia*, pp. 76–88; on the need for horse troops, see the entry of 2 December 1569, *CSPD Addenda, Elizabeth*, p. 132.

[57] Fletcher, *Reform in the Provinces*, pp. 291–2, citing J. P. Cooper, *Land, Men and Belief: Studies in Early Modern History* (London, 1983).

[58] See Fletcher, *Reform in the Provinces*, p. 355 and Stater, 'War and the Structure of Politics', pp. 87–106.

[59] Stone, *The Crisis of the Aristocracy*; more recently, Robert Lachmann's *From Manor to Market: Structural Change in England, 1536–1640* (Madison, Wisc., 1987).

burdensome rates in an 'extension of taxation to lower incomes'.[60] Because militia rating lacked statutory sanction, the government hesitated to alienate the social stratum from which local governors were drawn. The Crown's 'failure to devise an equitable rating system produced a sense of grievance which ... undermined militia efficiency'.[61] The conjunction of arms assessment under the 1558 statute with militia assessments created an atmosphere in which the county community declined to give perfection of the militia their full support. The equity of ship money in the late 1590s was as often hotly debated as militia rates. As was the case in the 1630s, local governors would have to sort out which received priority, the collection of ship money designed to protect the realm from foreign invasion, or the honing of the trained bands whose role was more geared to local defence.

The similarity with Charles I's perfect militia is apparent. Elizabethan and Caroline England saw the introduction of veteran muster-masters for drilling, along with increased imposition of military charges, some of which stemmed from impressment. Both monarchs were concerned with the improvement, modernization, increase, and uniformity of weapons, and the cultivation of a trained cadre (after 1573 the trained bands and after 1629 the perfect militia). Both systems experienced abortive tests, in 1588 and 1639-40 respectively.

The decline of trained-band strength in Cumberland, Westmorland, and Northumberland accompanied the disarming of the Anglo-Scottish marches. The pacification aimed at minimizing the boundary between Scotland and England, or 'North Britain' and 'South Britain' as James would have liked them to be called.[62] The King strove 'utterlie to extinguishe as well the name, as substance of the bordouris'.[63] The creation of pacific 'middle shires' made sense in that the borders had become difficult to defend on either side. Building costs, the rapid evolution of fortifications in the 1500s, and the inherent fiscal weaknesses of both central governments meant that neither Scots nor English could achieve affordable security.[64]

From an early Stuart point of view, the 'enemy' was no longer national, but familial and territorial. The 1605 commission created an administra-

---

[60] Boynton, *Elizabethan Militia*, p. 94; Cruickshank, *Elizabeth's Army*, p. 133.

[61] A. Hassell-Smith, 'Militia Rates and Militia Statutes, 1558-1663', in P. Clark, A. Smith and N. Tyacke (eds.), *The English Commonwealth, 1547-1640, Essays in Politics and Society presented to Joel Hurstfield* (Leicester, 1979), p. 94.

[62] See G. M. Fraser, *The Steel Bonnets* (London, 1971), p. 315.

[63] Quoted in S. J. Watts, *From Border to Middle Shire Northumberland 1586-1625* (Leicester, 1975), p. 204.

[64] Colvin, Ransome, and Summerson, *King's Works*, vol. IV, pp. 607-13. On the garrisons of Berwick and Carlisle, see pp. 13-16.

tion that would extirpate border lawlessness. Force was applied to banditry and feuding. Constables and commissioners were the order of the day, not muster-masters. In fact, the borders were 'de-militarized'. Restrictions on weapons and fortifications were promulgated and disorderly persons sent off to fight in continental wars.[65] The government worked at stabilizing the six border counties rather than arming, mustering, and drilling a perfect militia of Borderers. Inhabitants of the borders had grown accustomed to banditry, raids, and feuds. However, in the era of Anglo-Scottish warfare, 1296 to 1560, they disliked having their insular and comparatively barren world pierced by royal armies of either side. Now peace was imposed from above by a Crown that did not trust either side. The border country mentality of separateness from the nation meant that the armies of the Bishops' Wars were more safely recruited outside the borders. With a negligible militia, there was little else to do.

When James did get round to assessing his military strength in 1605, the counties were allowed to forgo training. Then, on 30 June 1608, the system geared up again; Gloucestershire and Essex lurched into action, enrolling able men and reviving the trained bands, while other shires, such as Somerset and Wiltshire, remained rather languid.[66] In 1612, the tempo quickened, and the militia system emerged from its 'long vacation'.[67] The decade 1613 to 1623 witnessed marked improvement in the condition of the trained bands, culminating in the issue of *Instructions for Musters and Armes, and the Use Thereof: By Order from the Lords of His Majestie's most Honourable Privy Counsayle* (1623).[68] James declined to erect statutory authority for militia activity by allowing the expiry of the 1558 statute. An already murky military obligation was immersed in greater darkness. His government reversed itself between 1613 and 1623. Rumours of German wars prompted refurbishment of the county military. This entailed more than oiling armour and buying match and powder. The ranks of the trained bands had to be filled. During the next five years military rates escalated and new firearms were purchased.[69] Muster-masters toured the shires. The clergy enforced more stringently the military obligation of tenants and servants. Uniformity was set forth as an ideal, with regular drilling according to identical manuals, standard bore muskets, etc. and promulgations from a central body: the Council of War.

[65] Fraser, *The Steel Bonnets*, pp. 316–19.
[66] For Essex, see A. Clark, 'The Essex territorial force in 1608', *The Essex Review*, 17, no. 66 (April 1908), pp. 98–115. W. P. D. Murphy (ed.), *The Earl of Hertford's Lieutenancy Papers 1603–1612* (Devizes, 1969), pp. 8–9.
[67] Boynton, *Elizabethan Militia*, p. 212.
[68] On this official militia manual, see Barnes, *Somerset 1625–1640*, pp. 248, 347.
[69] Calivers were banned in 1618. See Boynton, *Elizabethan Militia*, p. 238.

The same spirit enfused the 1630s with 'thorough', Arminianism, and Caroline centralization.

The Elizabethan discretionary policy of selection based upon social utility characterized the 1620s: the able-bodied untrained went overseas, and the militia mustered for defence. By 1639, customary practice had taken on some aura of legality. The principle of selection was revived by a central government which needed skilled soldiers, and the localities which were weary of arming, mustering, and enrolling selected and unselected men.[70] But the refinement of the trained bands coincided with Charles I's continental campaigns. Consequently the commissioners for musters, the justices of the peace, the constables, and the lieutenants tried to create within their communities an effective home guard while dispatching impressed levies, with the attendant responsibilities for billeting, collecting coat-and-conduct money, and administering martial law. The advent of the forced loan during the war years made resistance to Caroline military activities even more acute than the war-weariness and militia rating controversies of the 1590s.[71]

Generalizations regarding the early Stuart militia are qualified by regional variation, particularly in northern counties where the arduous tasks of creating a perfect militia met with disappointment. The recalcitrance of Cumberland and Westmorland extended to loans, impressment and ship money as well as musters. In spite of urgings between 1625 and 1628 to achieve an 'exact militia', the border counties declined to muster their assigned contingents of horse and foot as late as November 1628. Cumberland's deputy lieutenants could match the 40 horse and 250 foot reputedly raised in Westmorland, but no increase (especially in cavalry) could be achieved without the clergy, who of course had their own assessment. Although the modest contingent was armed, the lateness of the harvest and time of year discouraged any general muster. In Northumberland the militia rates stirred unrest so that the full number of trained soldiers certainly could not be achieved except by 'charging the lands at the old rents', which had been attempted with some success, but most citizens refused to pay 'excepting against its legality'. Westmorland neglected even to produce a certificate, though verbal reports indicated that their militia was in readiness. Westmorland's chronic tardiness in submitting accounts of her preparedness, the predictable shortages of horses in the north, rural poverty, and the borderers' innate mistrust of central government indicate

---

[70] See for example Fletcher, *Sussex*, p. 182. For an interesting departure from the norm, see the general muster list for Buckinghamshire compiled on 24 September 1618, which includes some labourers. The laxity in allowing labourers to infiltrate the ranks may reflect years of peace and a landlocked county: HEH, STT Military Box 1 (7).

[71] Cust, *The Forced Loan and English Politics*, pp. 1–12, 150–85, 316–37.

that at least during the early Stuart era the northern trained bands were the worst and weakest in the realm.[72]

The King's reluctance to fortify the borders and reinforce the Carlisle and Berwick garrisons in 1639 was influenced by the lack of information on the strength of the militia in Cumberland, Westmorland, and Northumberland. Charles dared not make significant military preparations on the borders if the militia could not secure the area against a Scottish counterstroke. The three shires' returns were conspicuously absent in the profile of the trained bands compiled in 1638, eliciting the footnote that on 10 July 1626 these counties had received orders to ready their trained bands, 'But noe Accomp haveing been hitherto given, nor any Muster Rolls returned from the said three counties and towne of Newcastle'.[73] Durham seemed rather better, if only because Bishop Neile personally oversaw the general muster in summer 1626. The Bishopric's trained bands numbered more than a thousand foot and several score horse.[74] The musterers, Captain Hilton and Mr Ward, had exercised the bands. Outdated armour and weapons were being rooted out and replaced; Roman Catholics had been disarmed and excluded from the ranks. A provost marshal had been appointed, powder laid up, and the able-bodied not of the trained bands enrolled. In short, Durham lay in a fairly good state of readiness. Given the comparatively large militia of Yorkshire, certainly above 10,000 infantry, one can see that northernmost border defences were rather 'soft',[75] but that a firm 'second line' existed in Durham, Yorkshire, and Lancashire.

THE MILITIA IN THE BISHOPS' WARS

In 1638, the fifty-two counties of England and Wales, along with the Bishopric of Durham, Bristol, the Cinque Ports, London, and Newcastle, accounted for trained forces totalling 93,718 infantry and 5,239 cavalry.[76] Contingents of 'private arms', remnants of the old armed but untrained militia, persisted in many counties, particularly the Midlands. Gentry and substantial yeomen formed themselves into 'freeholder bands', distinct

---

[72] *CSPD* (1628–9), p. 374. See also *CSPD* (1625–6), p. 420, where Cumberland declined to give the Crown its full quota of the 'voluntary gift' but would 'contribute according to their subsidy so that they may be freed from the greater charge of arms'. Northumberlandshire responded in similar fashion, begging not to be included with Newcastle in providing warships. And, as usual, Westmorland made no return.

[73] PRO, SP 16/408/162; SP 16/381/66, f. 3 and Bodleian Library, Clarendon SP, XV, f. 80.

[74] In the 1638 returns, which seem to approximate to the quotas of the 1620s, Durham had 532 musketeers, 500 pikemen, and 60 cavalry. Bodleian Library, Clarendon SP, XV, f. 80; PRO, SP 16/34/80, Neile's report.

[75] PRO, SP 16/34/80, Neile's report; on garrisons, see pp. 13–16.

[76] PRO, SP 16/381/66; SP 16/409/216; Bodleian Library, Clarendon SP, XVI, f. 80; HEH, EL 7682.

from the trained bands proper, and were instructed by the Crown to stockpile weapons which might then be distributed to untrained men who would be formed into companies and drilled. Although their origins in some counties may lie in the Elizabethan volunteer cavalry of the 1590s and the untrained militia under James I, Charles I did much to formalize their structure through orders issued in 1626 and 1635. As the private forces approximated in size to the shire forces in some areas, the King may have assumed that these units could reinforce the militia. It was not an unreasonable idea. The Covenanters did quite well in mobilizing privately owned weapons in the creation of a national army. One has to wonder if a fair number of arms, some of which may have been taken from recusants, lay in the homes of local gentry. Moreover, the private bands resided in a strategic area, the northern and midland shires. The weakness of the idea of employing freeholder bands in the Bishops' Wars was that they were even more susceptible to parochialism than the trained bands, were more protective of their privately owned weapons because they considered their arms exclusive, and the command of the units was very much personalized by the gentry who supervised weapons' distribution and training. The same factors which made deployment of the perfect militia difficult made use of the freeholder bands next to impossible.[77]

Mobilizing the northern militia posed problems. Cumberland and Westmorland had been slow in reporting their strength, some certificates showing blanks, Cumberland's trained forces amounted to no more than 250 foot and 100 horse, with Westmorland of identical weakness. Northumberland fielded only 500 infantry and 100 cavalry.[78] The militia was not geared to repel Scottish incursions but rather coastal invasions, especially from the south. Reversing this configuration was no easy matter. The captains sent into the north were outsiders without the personal connections which could facilitate coercion of the locals. Arundel, the Lord Lieutenant for Cumberland and Westmorland, was urged to intercede with his tenants, especially in the matter of increasing the militia by a third. Those, such as at Burgh, who petitioned against military charges, were to be quieted.[79]

Arguably, the trained bands had attained their highest level of proficiency by 1638. That seems to have been the case in southern counties such as Sussex.[80] A general if uneven improvement in training and equipage had

---

[77] Brian Quintrell very kindly supplied a great deal of information on the 'private arms' question. Anthony Fletcher and Thomas Cogswell also assisted, though the interpretation set forth here is my responsibility.

[78] PRO, SP 16/409/216, and Arundel Castle, autograph letter 377.

[79] Arundel Castle, autograph letter 377.

[80] Fletcher, *Sussex*, p. 182.

occurred throughout the years of Personal Rule, so that by 1638 the militia was at least as well prepared for service as during the peak years of Elizabethan invasion scares. Generalizations are undermined by local variation. Certainly the border militia remained pitiful in 1638, but Hamilton's mobilization in East Anglia showed that some units, for example those of Suffolk, were presentable. There had been lapses and some negligence during the Personal Rule, as T. G. Barnes has shown for Somerset. In terms of the maintenance of local arsenals and at least occasional drilling, the Caroline militia received more weaponry and instruction than the men the Covenanters called to arms. On the eve of the Bishops' Wars, then, the perfect militia should have been superior if not equal in readiness to the Covenanters' troops.[81]

In the summer of 1638 Sir Jacob Astley surveyed the militias of the West Country, an area of great importance given the thousands of trained soldiers available there. Astley encouraged standardization of weapons and other improvements. On the surface his circuit appeared to be 'business as usual', but as one of the King's key military advisors he knew full well that these substantial militia units might be deployed in the north within the year.[82] Yet one must wonder if the reality matched the ideal. Satisfying one's muster-master by shouldering the appropriate weapon and appearing for muster to drill at the appropriate time was not quite the same as being prepared for combat. The entire thrust of the latter half of the Personal Rule had been to create an international military force – the ship money fleet. Naval power, not land forces, had received the most attention. The perfect militia was a second line of defence, designed to intercept any landings which might have evaded the royal navy. A successful ship money fleet should have meant that the expertise of the trained bands would never need to be tested. The collection of ship money therefore took precedence over enforcing muster attendance. The outbreak of the 1637 rebellion not only forced the Privy Council to look in the opposite direction, it also changed the kingdom's defence priority, from sea to land.

On the borders, the Council of War turned, appropriately, to a prelate, the Bishop of Durham, to muster the trained bands of the bishopric 'and to have them in readiness upon any occasion to drawe near to assist the Towne of Newcastle'. Similar orders were sent to the President and Council of the North at York, where no muster of the Yorkshire militia had taken place, flouting the orders of the Privy Council.[83] Citizens who

[81] See the discussion in Fletcher, *Reform in the Provinces*, pp. 286–92.
[82] On Astley see pp. 10–12.
[83] PRO, SP 16/396, f. 9, Council of War entry book; PRO, PC 2/49, ff. 424–5, Privy Council register, 16 September 1638. Procedurally, the Council of War initiated the order through the Privy Council; on the Yorkshire militia see Sheffield City Library, Strafford MS. Xa, ff. 158–9; 160–1; 198–204.

failed to provide their allotment of weapons or horses were called before
the Council, like ship money defaulters. On 30 September, the London
militia was instructed to hold annual musters between 31 March and 20
April 1639.[84] The first of these dates coincided with the formation of the
King's expeditionary force. The recent military activities of the London
militia were more ceremonial than substantial. On 25 August 1638, Londoners converged on Finsbury Field to watch militiamen and others
compete in an archery contest, staged to promote the shooting of the
longbow. The London trained bands also served as an honour guard
during the procession welcoming Queen-Mother Marie de' Medici in
October.[85]

On the day the London militia received an order to prepare for a spring
muster, similar letters were sent to the Lords Lieutenant of the counties
north of the Trent. The Crown had shipped powder, match, and shot to
Kingston-upon-Hull and Newcastle; these munitions would be made available (at a cost) to the local militia. The Privy Council hoped to circumvent
the excuses that too little ammunition remained in the county magazines to
supply a general muster.[86] Equipment shortage was in fact a serious
problem, created by a dearth of arms manufacturers in the north and
chronic defaulting by those obliged to present arms at musters.[87] Astley, Sir
Thomas Morton, and six captains rode north to organize and review the
trained bands.[88] Astley and his men reviewed the militia of Leicestershire,
Nottinghamshire, Derbyshire, Staffordshire, Lincolnshire, Rutland, the
West Riding, Northumberland, Hull, and Newcastle. Sir Thomas Morton
and his captains bore responsibility for Durham, the East and North
Ridings, Cumberland, Westmorland, Cheshire, and Lancashire. Trained-
band soldiers' names were enrolled, their weapons inspected, and defects
remedied, if necessary, from supplies at Hull. Astley and Morton assisted
in organizing regiments (usually 1,000 men, but to be increased to 1,500 if
possible) and the names of the infantry and cavalry were to be enrolled. No
one was to be excused or substituted for 'without speciall cause. Where any
of the Trained Bands have been hired for any Towneship, those men that
have been soe hired and Trained shall not desert the Service without Leave,
and if they shall, then they are to bee severely punished.'[89]

[84] PRO, PC 2/49, ff. 421–2; see also f. 703, index of muster defaulters; PRO, SP 16/399/42;
    PRO, PC 2/49, f. 438, order of the Privy Council.
[85] Corporation of London Records Office, *Journal of the Court of Common Council*,
    XXXVIII, f. 134, Lord Mayor's proclamation; ff. 164v–165, Lord Mayor to the captain of
    the trained bands, 28 October 1638. This event is splendidly recorded in an engraving of
    Marie's arrival in Cheapside, with militia attendant, preserved in the Museum of London.
[86] PRO, PC 2/49, f. 443.
[87] PRO, SP 16/396, ff. 63–4, shortage of armourers in Yorkshire. See also ff. 64–6.
[88] PRO, SP 16/396, ff. 34–5, SP 16/404/68; Oxinden, *Oxinden letters*, pp. 141–3.
[89] PRO, SP 16/396, ff. 39, 45.

The captains' reports render a fair portrait of the strength of the trained bands at the beginning of the Bishops' Wars.[90] From Cumberland and Westmorland we find an account of the activities of Captain Waites. In Lancashire, Captain Thelwall bestowed his approval of the militia infantry, though the horse bands failed to meet his standards.[91] The Privy Council thought fit to 'spare' the counties under Astley and Morton's jurisdiction for 'all the Men and Forces of those Shires (being nearest to Scotland) should bee reserved for a Second Army if there should be occasion'.[92]

I doubt ther is a mistake in Sir Jacob Astleyes Liste of the number of souldiers charged uppon Nottinghamshire, for therin are butt 407 mentioned wheras ther charge is 1050, the like may be in many other Countyes within his List, as is very probable, seinge the nine next adioyninge to us are chared in his list [nine counties adjacent to Yorkshire supplied less than half the number fielded by Yorkshire] butt with 6000, and this county with 12240 and yett one of those nine (namely Lincolnshire) hath above 60 parishes more then all Yorkshire. I could wish this particular were a little inquired after by the Mustermaster Generall, for in truth Sir if ther be this mistake in many (as I beleeve ther is in Nottinghamshire) we shall hould ourselves much agreived to be all drowne outt and nott the halfe of some other countyes.[93]

On 18 November 1638, all English and Welsh counties were instructed to muster their trained bands and keep them in readiness.[94] Throughout late November and December 1638, the lieutenants and justices of the peace found themselves engaged in military preparations unprecedented since the 'brief flurry of activity in 1635'.[95] From the countryman's point of view, the King could not have picked a worse time (save, perhaps, at harvest) to exercise the trained bands. Few if any Englishmen relished trailing pikes in the snow. The unseasonable muster was necessary because the council's orders had not 'been soe exactly observed as these times require'.[96] In addition to drilling and reviewing, the deputy lieutenants were to increase their regiments by a third. Exemption from county rates and military obligation was to be denied to those who might plead privilege according to their 'Lande' or 'by reason of his service or Attendance on Us or on any of our Courts or Offices of Justice'.[97]

---

[90] For example, Thelwall in PRO, SP 16/410/102.
[91] D. P. Carter, 'The "Exact Militia" in Lancashire, 1625–1640', *Northern History*, 11 (1976 for 1975), p. 89, citing PRO, SP 16/410/102.
[92] PRO, SP 16/409/148 and 148 I; SP 16/396, ff. 72–3.
[93] BL, Coke MS. C60/15, Sir Edward Osborne to Coke, 26 January 1639.
[94] SRO, GD 406/1/10794, Vane to Hamilton, 18 November 1638.
[95] PRO, PC 2/49, ff. 542–5; Barnes, *Somerset 1625–1640*, p. 271.
[96] PRO, SP 16/396, f. 47.
[97] PRO, SP 16/396, f. 48.

Who served in Charles's trained-band contingents?

Charles's prospects for victory hinged in some measure on the quality of the soldiers he could field. Since training was crucial during the era of the military revolution, the deployment of the perfect militia against the Scottish levies might have won the war. The question remains, however, as to how many royal soldiers were trained militia and how many were raw recruits. Because indentures do not make clear if the recruits were untrained unfortunates or selected militiamen, it is difficult to ascertain the type (and training) of the soldiers Charles levied. One limited but illuminating method is to examine the occupational identity of the pressed soldiers in the light of assumptions about the social differentiation between militia and pressed levies.

Of the 1,200 Suffolk militiamen dispatched to Harwich in early April 1639 as part of Hamilton's amphibious expedition, the occupations of a score of pikemen are recorded. The dozen trained pikemen from the southern Suffolk townships east of Ipswich, including Sudbury, Brent Eleigh, Acton, Assignton, Boxford, and Nayland were roughly divided between agricultural workers and clothmaking artisans.[98] Acton supplied a pair of pikemen described as husbandmen, as did Moux Eleigh. Sudbury provided a pikeman who earned his living as a gardener. Apart from Simon Arnold, a tanner from Wiston, pikemen were drawn from the cloth 'industry', including two weavers, a feltmaker, cordwainer, and shearman. Suffolk gentlemen were sponsors, not trained-band members. Better to rate a gentleman than enrol him, so that he could contribute financially. Gentlemen possessed servants and dependants, and could assemble private contingents. They customarily 'sponsored' a neighbour, tenant, or employee in the militia by providing the man's weapon and accoutrements, or by paying a rate. Consequently, many muster rolls and returns listed trained-band soldiers both by locale or under the names of resident gentlemen. The pikemen sponsored by local men of standing were overwhelmingly clothworkers. Of the eight listed, six were skilled in the clothmaking trades: three weavers, a pair of shearmen, and a comber. The only exceptions were a cooper named Thomas Vale, from Groatan, and Bartholomew Marsh, a husbandman supplied by Christopher Scarlet of Nayland. The thirty-six musketeers sponsored by private parties were pre-

---

[98] Southern Suffolk suffered depression in the cloth trade, and the economic adversity of the times made many gentlemen, especially clothiers, lukewarm to the idea of expending money on a war with distant Scotland. East Bergholt, for example, was the scene of widespread resistance to coat-and-conduct money, with clothiers being particularly unable, and unwilling, to pay the military tax. PRO, SP 16/456/451, Suffolk (East Bergholt) coat-and-conduct money return, 8 June 1640.

dominantly clothworkers (especially weavers) and husbandmen.[99] These Suffolk trades, agriculture and clothmaking, were then protected by enrolling the workers in the trained bands.

Labourers, who made up the bulk of the early seventeenth-century levies were generally rare in the ranks of the militia.[100] As for clothiers, the wealthiest paid subsidies and supplied weapons. Smaller clothiers, who might employ only a handful of men, were excellent candidates for the trained bands. If a man employed others, he sustained the community. By including him in the militia, he was immune from the press, and remained in the hundred. Likewise, a substantial clothier might protect his most productive employees. As S. J. Stearns has argued, the protection of the local economy and its more valuable members was as important, if not more important, than providing the central government with soldiers. However, the vagueness of the term 'labourer' bedevils a full assessment of the social composition of early Stuart armies. It is clear that labourers, be they agricultural workers or not, made up the bulk of the levy. It is possible, though, that part-time agricultural workers and the lesser tenants (such as cottagers) of the manor would be pressed before the yeomen and husbandmen and that these less substantial members of the community were classified as 'labourers'. In this sense, the absence of yeomen and husbandmen may not indicate that *all* husbandmen were exempted, only the more affluent.

How great a proportion of yeomen and husbandmen existed in the overall economic community of the various (and diverse) counties of England? What per centage of the community at large can be described as labourers? Two extraordinary manuscripts, one from 1608 and another from the eve of the First Bishops' War, give occupational information regarding the community at large. The first is the famous Smith of Nibley survey of Gloucestershire in 1608.[101] The second is a list of the able-bodied men of the eastern division of Northamptonshire in late 1638.[102] The

---

[99] BL, Add MS. 39,245, f. 179v/396, Wodehouse Lieutenancy papers.

[100] On labourers see pp. 226–31 below. Boynton states that the Caroline trained bands were 'inundated by husbandmen and labourers', *Elizabethan Militia*, p. 245. Husbandmen were in fact encouraged to serve. Labourers did sometimes account for significant numbers of military as in Buckinghamshire in 1618, HEH, STT Military Box 1 (7). See also Barnes, *Somerset 1625–1640*, p. 250.

[101] J. Smith, *The Names and Surnames of all the Able and Sufficient Men in Body fit for His Majesty's Service in the Wars, within the County of Gloucester Viewed by the Right Hon. Henry, Lord Berkeley, Lord Lieutenant of the said County, by Direction from His Majesty, in the Month of August, 1608, in the Sixty Year of the Reign of James the First, Compiled by John Smith of North Nibley, in Gloucestershire* (London, 1902, facsimile Ann Arbor, Mich., 1972).

[102] PRO, SP 17E, box of miscellaneous parchments from the reign of Charles I, 'A List of Enrollment of untraned men of able bodyes within the East division of the County of Northampton fitt for his Majesty's Service in the warrs' comprised of six sheets of parch-

Gloucestershire census is a muster roll intended to provide the names, residences, occupations, and approximate age of men capable of bearing arms. Individuals charged with subsidies and the provision of arms are also listed. Militiamen are designated with the code 'tr', denoting them as 'trained' soldiers. Weapons are also described. The Northamptonshire document excludes ratepayers and trained-band soldiers, listing untrained, able-bodied men.

The able men of Gloucestershire, according to Smith's survey, numbered close to 20,000. Nearly half of these were engaged in agriculture, whereas 11½ per cent possessed no occupational designation. Labourers likewise amounted to 11½ per cent.[103] However, Buchanan Sharp has demonstrated that Smith probably underestimated the number of Gloucestershire labouring poor. Smith analysed each hundred by manor; but rural poor, such as cottagers and artisans who lived on waste areas beyond the boundaries of the manor, were probably overlooked. Consequently, Smith underestimated the number of labourers.[104] Stephen Stearns has conjectured that 'in Gloucester at least the levy bore down particularly harshly on the rural landless to supply the army'.[105] The 1608 Gloucester muster roll distinguishes the occupations of trained band soldiers from those of the untrained able-bodied, revealing a sharp distinction between the kinds of men that served in the militia and the candidates for impressment. This is to be expected, of course; since the establishment of the trained bands, it was assumed that the more substantial citizens should serve in the militia. According to Tawney's analysis 46 per cent of the Gloucestershire workforce was involved in agricultural production. Labourers made up 11½ per cent. As many of those who would have been categorized as 'labourers' escaped notice, we may assume (very roughly) that in reality that amounted to perhaps 20 per cent, at most 25 per cent, of the inhabitants of Gloucestershire. Indentures from the Bishops' Wars and the expeditions of the 1620 contained 30 to 55 per cent of labourers, with some skilled craftsmen and a smattering of husbandmen, some yeomen, and the occasional gentleman (except in the case of Leicestershire in 1640).[106]

Tudor and Stuart military theorists often speculated upon whether it was nobler to trail a pike than to shoulder a musket. If choice of weapon

---

ment of varying size. Sir Rowland St John was primarily responsible for the compilation of this document.

103 A. J. Tawney and R. H. Tawney, 'An Occupational Census of the Seventeenth Century', *EconHR*, 5, no. 1 (October 1934), p. 31; S. J. Stearns, 'Conscription and English Society in the 1620's', *JBS*, 11, no. 2 (May 1972), pp. 6–7.

104 B. Sharp, *In Contempt of All Authority, Rural Artisans and Riot in the West of England, 1586–1660* (Berkeley, Calif., 1980), pp. 187–8.

105 Stearns, 'Conscription and English Society in 1620s', p. 7.

106 See pp. 230–1.

reflected social status, data in the Gloucestershire muster survey of 1608 suggests that occupation had little to do with the type of weapon carried in the trained bands. Pikemen made up roughly 40 to 50 per cent of the militia, the others bearing firearms. For the husbandmen, 39 per cent were pikemen, 25 per cent carried calivers, and 24 per cent served as musketeers (12 per cent of the husbandmen listed as militiamen did not designate their weapon). Among the yeomen, the statistics are similar (40 per cent pikes), although the musketeers far outweigh the calivers (39 per cent to 16 per cent), illustrating, perhaps, the sturdy English yeoman's ability to lug about the heavier firearm (or, perhaps, afford one). Tailors, weavers, clothiers, and gentlemen (who rarely toiled in the field) were most likely to be calivermen or musketeers. Skilled craftsmen were more likely to possess the dexterity needed to handle the new-fangled guns. Those with strong backs – husbandmen, labourers, and yeomen – fielded a goodly number of pikemen. But the proportion and types of weapons would appear to be more reflective of the availability of weapons and the needs of the militia rather than established on strict occupational or status lines.

The Gloucestershire trained bands were composed overwhelmingly of husbandmen, with a sizeable segment of yeomen. The Gloucester authorities owed consideration to their neighbours as well as to the Crown. How efficient were the trained bands of Gloucestershire during the Bishops' Wars? The historian of that county quotes 'a man who knew them well' in 1640. There was

> Gross ignorance and supine neglect of military discipline, there being no ground for the study and exercise of arms that might keep the body of the state in health and vigor. Nor is it unlikely that extreme vassalage was the end of that long sluggish peace ... The trained bands, accounted the main support of the realm and bulwarks against unexpected invasions, were effeminate in courage and uncapable of discipline, because their whole course of life was alienated from warlike employment; insomuch that young and active spirits were more perfect by the experience of two days' service.[107]

An amateur army, husbandmen, craftsmen, and tradesmen had their own livelihoods to think of, and did not want to spend weeks drilling and training. When Charles decided to deploy militiamen against the Covenanters, removing them from their shire, families, and trades, he violated the early Stuart custom of employing the trained bands as 'bulwarks against unexpected invasions'. Men of quality regarded themselves as free from the

[107] William B. Willcox, *Gloucestershire 1540–1640, A Study in Local Government* (New Haven, Conn., 1940), citing John Corbet, *An historical relation of the military government of Gloucester, from the beginning of the Civill Warre between King and Parliament, to the removall of Colonell Massie from that government to the command of the western forces* (London, 1645), pp. 10–11.

press.[108] In the towns, tradesmen and craftsmen were in no position to neglect their work and go north. Nor could agricultural workers abandon their fields for several months and play soldiers. One notes the recalcitrance of the Kentish trained bands in 1640: 'all are yeomen and farmers that Say they must be as assuredly undone by going, as by refuseing'.[109]

Late Elizabethan and early Stuart militiamen were drawn from substantial men below the gentry. In the spirit of the Statute of Winchester each social rank made its contribution. While the nobility and gentry shouldered their own military and administrative burdens, the townsmen, tradesmen, skilled workers, and productive husbandmen and yeomen served as trained-band soldiers. In June 1625 the Essex lieutenants made certain that 'trayned men be chosen of freeholders or their sonnes and householders, sparinge others for forreigne employments'.[110] Although the old tripartite of untrained, select unarmed, and select armed had been superseded, still some lesser yeomen and craftsmen managed to gain entry into the militia through the 'reserve' system. But for the most part, the militia in 1638–40 was comprised of yeomen, and their urban counterparts, skilled craftsmen. When Charles set about mobilizing those men, he was attempting something that had rarely been done by the Stuarts, only intermittently attempted by Elizabeth I and Henry VIII (when French wars demanded it), and accomplished systematically only in the Middle Ages.

In Derbyshire the Lord Lieutenant, the Earl of Devonshire, set about drilling and inspecting the arms of the trained bands and described their condition in December 1638.[111] Simultaneously, he attended to the untrained able men of the shire, compiling through the petty constables a comprehensive list numbering 17,308.[112] The dual classification reflected the exemption of the trained bands from the pool of men available for the press. He wrote, 'I have also herewithall sent to your Lordships [the Privy Council] according to your Commandment a List of the names of all the men in this county able and fitt for the warres, (except the Trayned Bands)'. On 18 March 1639, Derbyshire pressed its contingent of 200 raw men, which was conducted to Selby by Captain Edward Lower.[113] Derbyshire's 400 trained-band soldiers were commanded by Lower and Captain Thomas Milward, which might indicate that Lower was escorting his 200 militiamen northwards.

The Council of War had granted the lieutenancy the option of dispatch-

[108] PRO, SP 16/40/104, Herts deputy lieutenants.
[109] PRO, SP 16/453/11.
[110] Cited by A. Clark, 'Essex Territorial Force 1625–1638', *The Essex Review*, 18, no. 70 (April 1909), p. 68.
[111] PRO, SP 16/409/1 I.
[112] PRO, SP 16/405/II.
[113] PRO, SP 16/409/1; SP 16/396, f. 140.

ing entire companies or of selecting men from a variety of units.[114]
However, occupations in the 1639 indenture suggest that these 200 were
pressed from the able men, and that naturally a trained-band captain
would be the logical choice for a conductor. That notion is confirmed by
the inclusion of Derby on a list of shires from which trained-band soldiers
were drawn, the thirteen 'northern' counties where the Crown wished to
keep the trained bands intact.[115] The indentures for the Bishops' Wars are
most often rolls indented tripartite, virtually identical to those used for
overseas expeditions in the 1620s. Of course, the forty-two counties not so
near the borders *did* receive orders to select men out of the trained bands.
But are these the same units which are documented by the indentures?
Militia were converted into a royal army through receipt of the King's
shilling, recognized by an indenture. Yet, although the Tudors (Henry VIII
and Elizabeth) sometimes deployed trained soldiers in this fashion, 1620s
indentures make clear that under the Stuarts the exemption of militia from
such service had become the rule.

Given the qualifications for membership of the militia, the indentures
containing occupational information discourage the interpretation that the
lists include the names of militiamen only, for far too many labourers are
included.[116] Indentures for the Bishops' Wars, like those of the 1620s, are
made up of roughly 30 to 55 per cent of labourers. It is of course possible
that the mention of artisans, tradesmen and the occasional 'gentlemen'
documents the inclusion of trained soldiers. But none of the indentures for
the Bishops' Wars or any other Stuart campaigns designates any pressed
soldier as coming out of the trained bands. The document written up by
Sir Rowland St John in Northamptonshire, providing occupational information about the able men in the eastern division of Northamptonshire,
gives us a sense of the social stratum from which men were pressed.[117]
Coupled with the famous Smith of Nibley survey for Gloucestershire in
1608, the evidence shows clearly that the categories of occupations found
in indentures are far too low on the social ladder to be those of militiamen.[118]

Evidence, however, that virtually all the indentures are exclusively
untrained men appears in the different indenture preambles recorded by
the Suffolk deputy lieutenants in their book. Unfortunately, there do not
seem to be any corresponding indentures, listing individual soldiers. But

---

[114] PRO, SP 16/396, f. 161; SP 16/409/106, 17 January 1639.
[115] PRO, SP 16/396, f. 133.
[116] Fletcher, *Reform in the Provinces*, p. 294, last paragraph; Boynton, *Elizabethan Militia*, pp. 220–1.
[117] PRO, SP 17E.
[118] The sole exception I have found is the Buckinghamshire militia roll of 1618, HEH, STT Military Box 1 (7).

the existence of the 1639 Kentish trained-band indenture provides a companion piece which illustrates two different recruiting formulae.[119]

In 1639, Essex, Suffolk and Kent fielded contingents of pressed men and homogeneous companies of militia (made up of two-thirds muskets and one-third pikes).[120] The Suffolk indenture, drafted by Sir William Plater, Sir William Harbie, Sir Roger North, Edmond Poley and William Waldegrave, deputy lieutenants of the county of Suffolk on the one hand, and Colonel Sir Nicholas Byron on the other – 1,200 'treyned soldiers' together with their arms complete – indicates that the regiment was selected from the 'treyned bands'. But Suffolk was unusually obedient. Hamilton made it clear that the troops from Essex, Cambridgeshire, and Kent were almost entirely untrained and improperly armed. If the rest of England had responded as Suffolk did, Charles might have won the First Bishops' War.[121]

The striking difference between begrudging but obedient service in 1639 and the 1640 army that became 'the greatest law enforcement problem in living memory' was occasioned by the changed political context of royal demands on the nation's militia.[122] The bulk of Charles's 24,000 infantry came from levies of untrained men.[123] Charles excused most of the nation's militiamen in 1639 (by design or substitution) because his strategy aimed at frightening the Scots into a surrender. The northern militia was to be mobilized during the First Bishops' War, so that select elements could be called upon from the 'North Trent' area and from comprehensive 'call-ups' in Cumberland, Westmorland, Northumberland, the Bishopric of Durham,

---

[119] See pp. 211–14.

[120] On the Kentish indenture, see PRO, SP 16/419, box of indentures from spring 1639; on Essex see Bodleian Library, Firth c.4., Essex letter-book, f. 609 and SP 16/396, ff. 132–3.

[121] University of Minnesota Library, Phillipps MS. 3863, end of f. 122v; SRO, GD 406/1/939, Hamilton to Windebank, 23 April 1639. For more on the Suffolk mobilization see BL, Add. MS. 39,245, ff. 177v–190. 1640, however, was a different matter. The pressed soldiers in Suffolk mutinied and sequestered their officers, according to PRO, SP 16/456/77, Suffolk deputy lieutenants to the Privy Council, 12 June 1640.

[122] Barnes, Somerset 1625–1640, p. 277.

[123] The Exchequer documents distinguish between unclassified (presumably raw) troops and those comprised of 'Trayned Souldiers', as in PRO E 351/292, ff. 8–8v where militia regiments from Yorkshire, Northumberland, and Durham are listed under Sir William Savile, Sir William Pennyman, John Hammond, Charles Vavasor, and Sir Henry Vane. In terms of size, for example, Savile's Yorkshiremen numbered 819 and were grouped into six companies. As the rendezvous was within their shire, they could not begrudge their service, though an invasion of Scotland would have altered the terms of service. See also PRO SP 16/396, ff. 129–32, which lists the shires which were to contribute trained soldiers, f. 133, instructions to leave the northern and central militias intact, ff. 133–4 the selection of trained bands from East Anglia for Hamilton's expedition, and ff. 139–40, the shires' pressing of raw soldiers. See also SRO, GD 406/1/938.

and above all, Yorkshire.[124] Further trained-band contingents were selected in the East Anglian counties as the basis of Hamilton's force. There is also evidence that West Country militia were to be utilized in the First Bishops' War. Lord Poulett's regiment was to be made up of 1,200 infantry and 500 cavalry from the 'Trayned Bands', though he apparently argued that local officers should be allowed to choose, conduct, and command the contingent. Reading between the lines one senses that Poulett wanted some latitude in substituting raw men for militia.[125]

The militia in the Second Bishops' War

In 1639, Charles thought Covenanter resistance would disintegrate by the time his army massed at the borders. In 1640, though, actual warfare was more likely, so trained-band soldiers from *all* counties, including the far south, were to be sent against Scotland. Although the evidence is sparse, it would appear that in 1640 as many if not more than in 1639 of the overwhelming number of militiamen escaped service, sending raw men in their stead. The militia Charles expected to deploy in 1640 chose not to fight, thanks to the 'substitution clause' discussed below.

The bulk of the trained bands, the hub of royal administration, the repository of wealth, and the storehouses of weapons (from abroad and the Ordnance) lay in the south of England. In 1640, Charles therefore gathered his expeditionary force from South Trent. When the 24,000 infantry and 6,000 cavalry were mobilized, the Crown left the forces of the thirteen northern counties in place; they were not immediately incorporated into the royal army.

As planned in March 1640, the royal army was to number around 30,000 infantry organized into twenty-five regiments.[126] The design called for 10,000 foot to be sent by sea from the ports of Gravesend, Harwich, Yarmouth, and Grimsby. The allocations comprised Sussex (600), Surrey

---

[124] For example, on 17 May 1639 the Lord General called up elements of the Yorkshire militia, who were to be given advance pay from the Treasurer at Wars. BL, Add. MS. 18,979, f. 52, Arundel to Lord Fairfax.

[125] Avon Reference Library MS. B 28176, Buckingham to Poulett, 7 March 1639. That the militiamen drawn from the West Country were a minority of the soldiers taken is borne out by notes ostensibly written prior to the mobilization of 1640. Half of the 4,000 weapons owned by the shire (either Wiltshire or Somerset – it is not clear) were loaned to pressed troops, with the clear implication that those sent in 1639 from this rendezvous were *not* of the trained bands. Bristol RO, Ashton Court Collection, Smyth MS. 36074 (56), undated. This may well have been the son of Lord Poulett who had in fact received a temporary commission for Poulett's militia regiment in 1639. See Smyth MS. 36074 (132B), 7 March 1639.

[126] PRO, SP 16/448/11, Council of War, 16 March 1640. See also discussion of mobilization plans of 26 March 1640 in PRO, PC 2/51, ff. 392–400, which is confirmed by PC 2/52, f. 473.

(800), Kent (700), Cinque Ports (300), Middlesex (1,200), Hertfordshire (650), Essex (700), Buckinghamshire (500), London (1,200), Huntingdonshire (400), Suffolk (600), Norfolk (750), Cambridgeshire (300), Bedfordshire (400), Lincolnshire (200), Nottinghamshire (300), and Derbyshire (400). This force was modelled upon the Hamilton expedition of 1639, though the levies were spread among a greater number of counties, rather than demanding entire regiments of 1,200 from the counties of East Anglia. Like the 1639 amphibious expedition, there was to be 'very good choice made of the men oute of the Trayned Bands'.[127] Identical terms applied to the 17,600 infantry scheduled to march overland for Newcastle. The quotas were: Berkshire (600), Brecknock (200), Bristol (200), Cardigan (150), Carmarthenshire (250), Carnarvon (160), Chester (500), Cornwall (1,600), Denbigh (200), Devon (2,000), Dorset (600), Flint (80), Glamorgan (200), Gloucestershire (1,500), Hereford (300), Leicestershire (400), Merioneth (100), Monmouth (250), Montgomery (200), Northamptonshire (550), Oxfordshire (600), Pembroke (300), Radnorshire (100), Rutland (60), Somerset (2,000), Southampton (1,300), Stafford (300), Warwick (500), Worcestershire (600), and Wiltshire (1,300), with an additional 4,000 to be taken from London.[128]

During the Second Bishops' War, the Crown resorted to the medieval practice of pressing the local militias by Commission of Array. In effect, the government expanded the practice that had been implemented successfully in 1639 for the Marquis of Hamilton. Like ship money collection, now a greater range of shires would provide for defence. But though precedents existed, the context of spring 1640 was inhospitable to encroachment on the common law restrictions against taking militia beyond the county boundaries, Commissions of Array and indentures aside. The deputy lieutenants and constabulary resisted, sometimes refused, to deploy the trained bands under the tumultuous circumstances of summer 1640. The reluctant cooperation of 1639 became outright refusal in 1640.[129] The change of heart can be ascribed to the dismal and pointless First Bishops' War, and to the military issues before the Short Parliament, elected, assembled and dissolved in the midst of these preparations. The MPs had before them a bill which would have placed statutory restrictions on the deployment of the trained bands out of the shire. The dissolution left the matter unresolved, with the deputy lieutenants attempting the enforcement of a policy deemed illegal.[130] The Hertfordshire deputy lieutenants told

127 PRO, PC 2/51, f. 397.
128 There are numerous examples of indentures and instructions. For example see the Rutland indenture, HEH, HA Military Box 1 (28); for instructions, see PRO, PC 2/51, f. 400, confirmed 3 May 1640, PC 2/52, f. 470 and PRO, SP 16/452/17 I.
129 C. A. Clifford, 'Ship Money in Hampshire', pp. 91–105.
130 Fissel, 'Scottish War and English Money', pp. 206–11.

their Lord Lieutenant frankly: 'we find no power given us to raise moneys for the pay, coating and clothing of the soldiers or to deliver them over to such commanders as shall be appointed to receive them out of the county ... or to impress the trained bands to this service if they shall refuse to take press money'.[131]

A week later, as Parliament was assembling at Whitehall, the deputy lieutenants further explained the resistance of the Hertfordshire militia. Whereas the Council wanted them to press the cream of the trained bands, these 'men of better quality' regarded themselves as privileged from impressment. The Crown's orders flew in the face of tradition and, consequently, the would-be conscripts had 'grown cunning and bold in their conceived rights'.[132] The disposition to question the Crown's design to build an elite fighting force from the best of the trained militia affected virtually every county. The 'national' reaction may have stemmed from the fact that many of the gentry and nobles who served as lieutenants (and later, also as colonels of regiments[133]) conceived of resolving these issues on a national level through the institution of Parliament. This concerted pressure bore on the King. Charles, who so often vacillated when he should have stood firm and stood firm when he should have shown flexibility, made a critical error the day after the Short Parliament opened. Six regiments of militia had been demanded of Yorkshire. The shire would comply, but suggested some modification of the government's orders. As the trained bands were composed largely of 'men of good abilities, and estates of their own', if obedience was to be expected, their local colonels should have remained in command; however, during the First Bishops' War they were officered by strangers or men of inferior rank.[134]

Another lesson learned in 1639 was the enormous cost of hiring substitutes. The lieutenancy allowed those with many children, large farms, or substantial trades, or those charged with private arms, to hire their own servants or others in keeping with the substitute clause, for they 'conceived it prejudicial to the commonwealth to send such men in person'.[135] Charles, preoccupied with the Short Parliament, gave way. Taking a phrase or two from the plea of Sir Edward Osborne, vice-president of the Council of the North, he acknowledged that 'diverse old and infirme Men are found and sondry very good Farmers of Husbandry or Tradesmen are necessitated to goe in our service which is ... preiudiciall to the comon

---

[131] HMC Salisbury, pp. 309–10, deputy lieutenants to Earl of Salisbury, 10 April 1640.
[132] See PRO, SP 16/450/104.
[133] In Yorkshire the mobilization was delayed because many of the colonels were 'Parliament men'. See PRO, SP 16/448/66 and SP 16/450/35.
[134] PRO, SP 16/450/92.
[135] PRO, SP 16/450/92. The question of substitution is dealt with on pp. 241–63.

wealth'.[136] Wholesale substitution now received the royal blessing. Of
course, the council had allowed substitution all along, but the decision
regarding Yorkshire's six regiments came from the royal pen itself. Charles
understood the substitution clause, for he rationalized its implementation.[137]

Suffolk, which had cooperated magnificently with the Crown in 1639,
reacted with some surliness in 1640. The trained bands had been assembled
and press money offered to 600, who refused, 'sayeinge they never knew
the trayne to marche out of their County'. Accepting the King's shilling
was not only illegal in their eyes, but insulting as well. Militiamen were not
riff-raff to be hired out at 8d per day. They protested their loyalty to the
locality and the King's person. They bore no cowardice in defending the
shire, for that was their responsibility. They told the lieutenants they 'conceive themselves allwayes prest (and ar still ready and willing)'. The deputy
lieutenants threw up their hands, reporting 'we have used all the power
wee can with eache severall captain to persuade their soldiers to accept
presse mony, but they can prevaile nothinge with them'. One can surmise
that in these straits, the lieutenants resorted to wholesale impressment of
the untrained able-bodied to fill their quota.[138]

In midsummer 1640, the mayor and burgesses of Boston complained to
the Privy Council that the Lord Lieutenant of Lincolnshire had ordered
them to have the trained bands in full readiness to march to York. There
are several fears expressed in the Boston petition. First, with the militia *en
route* to York, the port was vulnerable to assault by sea, from Covenanters,
the French, or pirates.[139] Second, unruly inhabitants of the fens could seize
upon the occasion and riot, while the families of the militiamen remained
defenceless. Finally, the trades and livelihood of the trained soldiers would
suffer in their absence: 'most of the traynd souldiers in Boston are Tradesmen and the livelyhood of them and their familyes depends upon their
presence to manage their trades'.[140] Although an amphibious attack was
far-fetched, the other fears were reasonable. The contention that prolonged
absence from their trades would adversely affect the families of tradesmen
serving in the militia was also correct.

The deputy lieutenants, Sir William Thorold and Captain Robert
Markham, encountered a recalcitrant constabulary whose foot-dragging

---

136 PRO, SP 16/450/109.
137 See also *CSPD* (1640), XVI, pp. 95–7. On the fatal consequences of the substitution
clause, see pp. 241–63.
138 PRO, SP 16/451/5, 20 April 1640.
139 The signet letters for the militia of nine counties south of York did not go out until 25
August.
140 PRO, SP 16/461/71, petition to the Privy Council from the inhabitants of Boston, July
1640.

prompted them to complain to the council: 'wee feare unlesse there be some Course forthwith taken for the suppressing of Mutenous and rebellious ill affected people allready prest, and yet by the neglect of Constables to raise. Wee shall not be able to rendere soe good an account.' The constables claimed that they could not fulfil their duties because the most able-bodied men had fled into the forests to avoid being taken. Consequently, the only men remaining were 'Lame Sicke and unserviceable men'. Meanwhile, 'all other men more able in their towneshipps doe forsake their habitations, fly into woods and there Arme themselves with pitch forks and other weapons to defend themselves from the said Constables'. Warrants had been issued, but no one would, or could, serve them. For example, the chief constable of the wapentake of Boothby-Graffoe discovered that a pair of his constables 'would neyther obey him nor his Warrant'. The Lincolnshire constables who did not shirk their responsibilities were stymied not only by the prospective conscripts, but by the citizenry at large. When the deputy lieutenants met with the constables at Seaford, constable Lawrence Bennett reported that the inhabitants of his community had refused outright to contribute anything to the military preparations, particularly coat-and-conduct money. Meanwhile, the soldiers were very much aware of the war's unpopularity, desertion thinned the ranks daily, and those that remained became restless. Captain Markham expressed the belief that 'some example must be made by death, or the distempers of the souldiers will breake into violence'.[141]

In Kent, that shire of 'refactory' behaviour, the lieutenants could not coerce the militia to serve:

Sir Humfry Tufton did winne upon the Soldiers, until the latter part of the day, when an unlook'd for Silence, and after that a stubborne Sullennesse, possest the rest of them, and infected the former to the defeate of our better expectations. The breife is, we find a confusion. Some will not goe beyond their colours, others will not goe into Scotland, all are yeomen and farmers that Say they must be as assuredly undone by going, as by refuseing.[142]

The denuding of defences in the south to launch another war against Scotland must have seemed folly. If the Scots were so hell-bent on invasion, why had they not crossed in 1639? The pointless Pacification of Berwick, followed by the ruptured Short Parliament, made general mobilization of the southern militia seem absurd.

Regional variation there was. In Northamptonshire, where constable

---

[141] PRO, SP 16/454/49.
[142] PRO, SP 16/453/11, deputy lieutenants of Kent to the Lord Lieutenant, the Earl of Pembroke and Montgomery, 11 May 1640. The soldiers involved were members of the trained bands who were to be sent against Scotland and wished to send untrained impressed men in their places.

Plowright had been pressed in 1639 and William Pargiter had tested the legality of coat-and-conduct money, the divisions were divided in their respective responses.[143] In the east, the trained bands were ready to accept prest money and the inhabitants willing to pay their coat-and-conduct assessments. Not so the western division, in which the militia refused unanimously to cooperate 'refusing utterly . . . to be either dissiplind, or to bee delivered up to any other captaine except their owne'.[144]

A confluence occurred in most shires, joining protest against coat-and-conduct money and unwillingness to allow the militia to march against Scotland. On 19 August 1640 the King ordered the lieutenants of Leicestershire, Nottinghamshire, Derbyshire, Staffordshire, Lincolnshire, Cheshire, Lancashire, Yorkshire, and Wales to have trained bands in readiness for a rendezvous.[145] The coercion of the militia to engage in service beyond the boundaries of the shire increased as the Crown's military situation worsened. A series of Commissions of Array were issued during the summer. The statute 5 Henry IV c. 13 provided Charles I with a precedent, according to which royal lieutenants had authority to organize soldiers within the shire and deploy them outside of the county, using the form of a writ enshrined within that statute. Commissions of Array had provided a model for the indentures used for pressing during the 1500s and early 1600s. When the Attorney General perused the precedent in company of the King and Privy Council, none there could know that this issue would be debated in the Long Parliament during the struggle over the militia ordinance and later over the legality of the Commissions of Array that began the Civil War. The King and his councillors decided around 1 July 1640 that the Lord Keeper was to use Commissions of Array for raising forces against Scotland, for they did not compromise extant commissions of lieutenancy.[146]

Commissions of Array stiffened the authority of commissions of lieutenancy, particularly in the northernmost counties. On 26 August 1640 the absence of the Earl of Arundel, Lord Maltravers, the Earl of Northumberland, and others prompted the Crown to send out Commissions of Array for those mobilizing the north in the absence of the Lords Lieutenant. Sim-

---

143 On Plowright, see pp. 232–8 and the article by V. Stater, 'The Lord Lieutenancy on the Eve of the Civil Wars: The Impressment of George Plowright', *The Historical Journal*, 29, no. 2 (1986), pp. 279–96. On Pargiter, see p. 133.

144 PRO, SP 16/454/44, 21 May 1640; SP 16/452/95, 9 May 1640.

145 PRO, SP 16/464/33, 34.

146 Rushworth, *Historical Collections*, vol. III, p. 1201. Yorkshire responded to this procedure rather strongly, probably because of the size of its trained bands as well as being the main staging area for both wars. Whereas the King had proclaimed his intention to 'lead on the Trained Bands of this County to the Frontiers of the Same', they could not afford to mobilize such a large force, consisting of 12,000 foot and 400 horse, especially after spending £100,000 on the 1639 war.

ultaneously, the Privy Council executed Commissions of Array for the nine counties of South Trent nearest to Yorkshire. Because the Scots had now passed the Tweed, the entire trained bands of the nine counties were to be ready to march at twenty-four hours' notice.[147] The fact of invasion along with the authority of the Commissions would commit the militia against the Scots.

How extensively did the militia participate in the Second Bishops' War? The March mobilization plans envisioned the selection of the better-armed and better-trained militiamen from throughout the counties of England and Wales, except those on the Border, which were to remain intact. The survival of the substitution clause meant, however, that local authorities retained the choice of conscripts. Any militiamen chosen could put another man, trained or untrained, in his place. Outright bribery by captains, so common in 1639, was banned. Pragmatically, the Council must have realized that only a few if any, of the trained soldiers would actually march.

Charles got his army, but its quality and expertise did not constitute a perfect militia. The lieutenancy could not prevail against men from the trained bands who refused press money. This failure was symptomatic of resistance to Caroline rule in general. The Hertfordshire militia wished to maintain tradition, exercising their customary exemption from foreign service and strange officers. There had been pressing of militiamen in 1639, for example when the East Anglian bands were transported by sea to the Firth of Forth. It did not occur to them that this exemption had not been enjoyed by their Tudor grandfathers. They protested their loyalty to the Crown in words and style identical to those voiced by the members of the Short Parliament. Like that assembly, they gathered historical precedents to buttress their case. In 1588 local militia had gathered around the Queen's person at Tilbury 'and no further'. During the Essex conspiracy trained-band soldiers had ringed the gates of Whitehall, refusing deployment elsewhere in London. In a crisis, they had proved loyal to the Crown, though within limits. 'We are not, as we conceive, to be broken or disbanded until we be utterly dissolved.' As the militia was the chief strength of the realm, they were not be deployed except in dire emergency. Certainly in a great kingdom such as England other soldiers could be found. It was folly 'before one blow be struck to press the trained bands as if we were the meanest and basest of the King's subjects'.

A dangerous precedent had occurred in the First Bishops' War. If half of the militia were deployed, the remainder also became subject to the press, as did the officers and gentlemen of Hertfordshire. They proclaimed

[147] Ibid., pp. 1232–4.

loudly, 'we are as free born as any of the gentry of this kingdom, and in this respect we know no privilege they have above us'. To strip the county of the natural leaders of society was to invite disorder and sedition. The men of the trained bands carried on the principal trade of the market towns, tilling the soil that sustained the realm. These freeholders were the 'heart's blood of the country'. Nothing short of the destruction of the trained bands was threatened by the pressing of the militia.[148]

---

[148] *CSPD* (1640), XVI, pp. 95–7, petition of the militia, undated though compiled during the sitting of the Short Parliament. On this matter as an issue before the House, see Fissel, 'Scottish War and English Money', pp. 206–8. The Privy Council deemed the constables responsible for the petition and ordered their prosecution by the lieutenants. Hertfordshire constables may also have been responsible for protests and petitions against coat-and-conduct money in 1640. See above, pp. 132–5, including the connection between coat-and-conduct money petitioning in Middlesex and resistance to impressment of husbandmen, PRO, SP 16/453/52.

6

Impressment and the substitution clause

As the nobles had abdicated their military function by the 1600s, so the militia during the Bishops' Wars shunted military service to their social inferiors. Charles I had to search lower on the social scale in order to find recruits. Conscription of civilians has always been a difficult task. The military revolution greatly increased the difficulty for European states; although population rose in the 1500s and early 1600s, the bloated size of armies outstripped demographic growth. Faced with increased demand for recruits, citizens sought definition of liability for impressment.[1] In England the unpopularity of impressment, with its coercion and danger, stemmed also from the shallow fiction that receiving the King's shilling entailed a contract freely entered into by both parties, subject and sovereign. Originally the term 'prest' (probably of French origin) meant 'ready'. Hence a 'prested' soldier had taken the ready money of the recruiter and become instantly available for royal service, having entered a bond by accepting the coin. However, this meaning was eclipsed by an English term which more accurately depicted the coercion involved, 'pressed', or forced.[2] The recruit was compelled to enter the contract.

The justification for taking a free man forcibly into the armed forces was quite familiar in the reign of Charles I: the defence of the realm. Just as the militiaman was obliged to protect the community in which he lived, or the shires to pay for ships to protect the coast, so the pressed soldier (unable to contribute financially) did good service by toiling in the ranks wherever his King had need of him. Charles I interpreted 'defence of the realm' in the broadest terms, of course. Inland counties paid ship money and in the 1620s Englishmen were pressed to fight the King of Denmark's battles (though in the latter case one was defending global Protestantism). In fact, the extensive impressment of the 1620s did much to make impressment the grievance of the lower orders, as ship money and coat-and-conduct money

[1] I. A. A. Thompson, 'The Impact of War' in P. Clark (ed.), *The European Crisis of the 1590s* (London, 1985), p. 261.
[2] See J. R. Hutchinson, *The Press Gang Afloat and Ashore* (London, 1918), pp. 9–11.

215

were those of their social betters. Broad definition of 'defence of the realm' in 1638–40 further united social groups in resistance to military charges and obligations in 1640.

THE POLITICAL AND HISTORICAL CONTEXT OF IMPRESSMENT

In the Middle Ages there existed 'a mixture of social condition in the lowest rank of militia organisation'.[3] In historical perspective, the intermingling of social rank at the lowest level made the distinction between impressment and militia service rather muddy because service was determined by criteria other than social status. Since medieval rulers regarded weaponry as the primary criterion for calling up men, the militia was often deployed simply because it was better armed. The Statute of Winchester had been silent on the duty owed while being explicit on the arms to be kept. Monarchs therefore called up categories of weapons, not always types of men.

Edward III's penchant for contracting large armies made the concept of impressment increasingly distinct from militia service. The individualized nature of the indenture along with the cash nexus placed the conscript in a relationship unique from that of the *armati* or militia dragooned by the King. 1 Edward III, statutes 2, 5 and 7, dictated that levies be paid from the King's purse. The parliamentary protests of 1344 pressured the King to honour these contractual relationships.[4] Given the scarcity of able-bodied men after 1348, there was no great surplus male population to herd into the ranks (at least in the countryside). Selection of troops from the shire militia cannot be described as a summoning of the militia, for the latter were (at least in theory) subject to a general muster. The Commission of Array, specifying certain types of soldiers from the shire forces for a specific service mentioned in an indenture, constituted impressment. Significantly, the first instances of impressment came from the ranks of the militia, not the untrained.[5] In tracing the evolution of the press, one is struck by the way in which the militia had ultimately exempted itself by the time of the Stuarts.

Tudor and Stuart population increases presented new alternatives as well as challenges for local governors. With real wages distressingly low and unemployment high, county authorities now had idle men on their hands, including those classified as 'sturdy rogues' or 'masterless men',

---

[3] W. Hudson, 'Norwich Militia in the 14th Century', *Norfolk Archaeology*, 14 (1901), p. 291.
[4] See for example 18 Edward III stat. 2; on the connection between 1327 and 1344, see Prince, 'The Army and the Navy', p. 361.
[5] Prince, 'The Army and the Navy', p. 358 and Powicke, *Military Obligation*, pp. 189–190.

who were perceived as threats to the social order. Local magistrates, by pressing at the lowest levels of the male population, could deal with the problems of the chronically unemployed and the troublemakers of the parish: petty criminals, drunkards, philanderers (who left bastard children dependent upon the parish), and others deemed undesirable. Unemployed men from Surrey and Sussex were sent to the Low Countries during the late 1580s and reinforced English forces in Picardy in 1597. In Elizabethan London 'masterless' men and householders not supporting families were ordered to be pressed on 30 March 1589. A few days later London aldermen were told to apprehend strangers. Unemployed men were rounded up that autumn as well.[6] One hundred and fifty troublesome Grahams found themselves shipped off to the Low Countries Wars during the pacification of the borders in 1605. The Danish levies of King Charles's subjects in 1627 targeted 'strong and sturdy beggars and vagabonds, masterless men and idle loiterers, who want [sc. lack] trades and calling and competent means to live upon [sc. the unemployed]'. All would be taken by force if necessary.[7]

Once the misfits had been recruited, their survival was doubtful. The attrition rate for English soldiers fighting abroad was staggering. The campaigning in Normandy over the three years from 1589 to 1591 cost the lives of 11,000 English common soldiers, only a tenth of whom were combat fatalities.[8] The mortality rate explains the reluctance of Tudor and early Stuart regimes to send manually skilled, able-bodied men on foreign expeditions. Using parishes as sources of manpower for armies could cripple local communties by killing off able men, especially if the impressment became extensive. Demographic analysis of Swedish parishes *circa* 1621–39 demonstrates the horrendous effect of sustained impressment on local society.[9]

The inequity of the military obligation sometimes made local inhabitants more aware of social grievance and 'class distinction'. Impressment, in that it forced decisions as to who remained safe within the county community and who left for an uncertain and possibly terrifying journey, not only caused tension among the lower orders, but also caused resentment against

[6] Corporation of London Records Office, *Journal of the Court of Common Council*, XXII, f. 278; f. 304, 15 August 1589; f. 328, 25 September 1589. R. Mark Benbow kindly supplied these references.
[7] Fraser, *The Steel Bonnets*, pp. 318–20; G. Parker, *The Military Revolution: Military Innovation and the Rise of the West, 1500–1800* (Oxford, 1990), pp. 49, 175.
[8] Wernham, *After the Armada*, p. 407.
[9] Parker, *The Military Revolution*, pp. 52–4, especially note 30 on p. 177 which suggests Bygdea was representative; on wastage see also Geoffrey Parker's *The Army of Flanders and the Spanish Road, 1567–1659. The Logistics of Spanish Victory and Defeat in the Low Countries' War* (Cambridge, 1972), and Myron P. Gutmann, *War and Rural Life in the Early Modern Low Countries* (Princeton, N.J., 1980).

those social betters who were the agents of impressment. By the early 1600s impressment was an issue which generated social conflict and class stratification of a sort within the normally unified county community.

The Welsh War of 1282–3 had provided a model of regional recruiting. Men were drawn from nearby counties and the Marches in ways which helped to define the procedure and terms of impressment. The 'practice of pressing promiscuously' was institutionalized when the King appointed captains to select soldiers from the quotas of men raised by the sheriff. The sheriff, like the constable and deputy lieutenant later, rounded up his number, meaning that he made a selection. One is tempted to conclude that even at this early stage in the history of impressment the problem for the local official was identical to that during the Bishops' Wars: the sheriff would supply the King's officer with those the community could spare while the freemen, acting as a 'militia' under the Assize of Arms, stayed at home. Those pressed then received the King's pay 'at our wages' (*ad vadia nostra*), and a contractual relationship was born.[10] The procedure became formalized under Edward I, as Commissioners of Array created companies of conscripts from the shires. Still, though, the regional location determined the patterns of impressment under Edward I. From Edward II on, however, the principle that the realm at large required support from a broad spectrum of counties became more explicit. Sometimes for purely fiscal reasons, such as the cost of transportation or scarcity of conduct money, levies drew most deeply from the most convenient recruiting ground. A functional division grew out of the allocation of troops north of the Trent for border service, with the counties south of the Trent performing coastal and continental service.[11]

In 1322 'the first year of a levy from all England' occurred. In the half dozen county levies from July 1322 to July 1338, the principle of 'national' obligation was applied often regardless of the type of soldier or his destination. For example, when pressing infantry for Scotland in July and August 1322, horse-archers for the siege of Dunbar in December 1337 and March 1338, and foot-archers for the Flanders service in June and July 1338, Lincolnshire, Northamptonshire, Leicestershire, Warwickshire, Wiltshire and other shires provided the King with soldiers for all six presses. All types of weapon were liable for continental and border service.[12] 'The

---

[10] Noyes, *Commissions of Array*, p. 25; Morris, *Welsh Wars*, p. 92; Powicke, *The Thirteenth Century*, p. 422.

[11] 'Occasional compulsory service in France was only laid on counties south of Trent', according to Wake (ed.), *Musters, Beacons, in Northants.*, pp. xxxvii–xxxviii.

[12] J. E. Morris, 'Mounted Infantry in Mediaeval Warfare', *TRHS*, third series, 8 (1914), table on p. 96 which shows that counties south of the Trent were liable for Scottish expeditions. However, the omission of the border counties conceals whether or not they contributed to the Flanders service, which seems unlikely.

practice gave rise to controversies over the legality of demanding service outside the counties in which the chosen men lived, over the expenses of equipping such men, and over the date or point from which the "conscripted" men should be paid.'[13] The 'national' obligation was 'universal' but now men claimed exemption based on general usefulness, social rank, or membership of the county defence force.

When the 'cash nexus' intervened and Scottish service became paid, did that mean that the militia became exempt, since they served for little or no pay in defensive wars? The 'conductor' of the fourteenth century was the 'arrayer'. Like his Stuart descendant, he entered the shire for the purpose of pressing a given number of men and with local assistance made the decision as to who was eligible and who was exempt. Arrayers reviewed the men and 'arrayed' them. The soldiers received clothing, equipment (horses if specified), and the King's pay. From thence they were either conducted under an officer to a rendezvous or held in readiness.[14] Although the sheriffs and arrayers coordinated the levies, the nobility provided a means to exercise influence. Commissions of Array empowered lords as agents of the Crown, whereas before they acted as individuals within the feudal system. The full weight of the monarchy fell behind the nobleman once he had grasped the King's commission. One can connect the practice of Commissions of Array with the later system of commissions of lieutenancy, wherein impressment, militia service and peacekeeping could be institutionalized through the installment of a nobleman to oversee the affairs of the shire while avoiding the perils of the overmighty subject.[15] 'The feudal lords retained, and possibly increased, their leadership in matters of war. Not only did they receive privy seal letters to array troops for important campaigns, but also they received an overwhelming majority of commissions for the array of communal troops against invasion.'[16]

A broader, more national system of impressment continued under the Tudors, though unsteadily. Henry VII countered Scottish invasion threats through Commissions of Array for York and as far south as East Anglia, again illustrating that though regional defence was the norm, the defence of the realm could draw upon the entire kingdom.[17] The extent to which the soldiers were either militia or pressed levies is unclear, though probably the former. What was already broad geographically could be made wider socially. By statute, all Englishmen were to rally to the King in time of emergency regardless of the time of year, and those possessing fees, offices

[13] H. J. Hewitt, *The Organization of War Under Edward III* (Manchester, 1966), p. 36.
[14] Ibid., p. 37.
[15] See Noyes, *Commissions of Array*, p. 1, note 53.
[16] Powicke, *Military Obligation*, p. 214.
[17] Noyes, *Commissions of Array*, p. 43.

or annuities owed a personal allegiance not only to defend the realm but also the sovereign's person. A wider interpretation followed, calling upon those who held lands, honours and lordships under letters patent, to serve at royal pay. Henry VIII's Scottish and French campaigns used impressment on a wide scale with little regard for customary niceties. Trained soldiers were embarked for French service. A merchant who refused a forced loan found himself pressed for the Scottish War.[18]

Commissions of lieutenancy began to replace Commissions of Array, almost imperceptibly, for their composition compared closely.[19] Under Edward VI, subjects' 'bounden duties' and service 'both within this realm as without' received further statutory sanction which coincided with increased use of lieutenancy.[20] Mary consolidated military obligation, particularly militia service. A statute now distinguished the militia from the simple able bodied: 'the Law attempted to establish a national military force to be paid for by the subjects according to the amount of property held'. The implication was clear. If one lacked the status or wealth to contribute to the Marian military establishment, then by default one's body might be called upon. By closely defining militia service, those not so designated became targets for the press. The Marian Act buttressed the monarch's customary right to press soldiers with the force and definition of statute.[21]

Elizabeth increased the authority of the lieutenancy, improved the militia, and relied upon national levies, except in those counties bordering on Scotland. Between 1585 and 1602 she pressed a minimum of 68,331 soldiers for Ireland, France and the Netherlands.[22] But exemptions proliferated, based on geography, rank, or utility. Not until the genesis of the trained bands in 1573 did clear guidelines emerge, though the Crown reserved the right to press whomsoever it chose.[23] The Bishops' Wars, apart from their unique political and religious context, were simply another Tudor–Stuart mobilization. What made the Bishops' Wars different was that uncertainty regarding the Crown's ecclesiastical agenda and its political policies prompted scrutiny of the purpose of the mobilization more closely than usual. As the militia was the predominant military power in the kingdom, Englishmen wished to be assured that the trained

---

18 11 Henry VII c.18, where each subject is 'bounden to serve' and 19 Henry VII c.1; Noyes, *Commissions of Array*, pp. 44–7; Hale, *War and Society in Renaissance Europe*, p. 78.
19 Noyes, *Commissions of Array*, p. 48.
20 Clode, *Military Forces of the Crown*, vol. I, p. 352.
21 Noyes, *Commissions of Array*, p. 50.
22 Cruickshank, *Elizabeth's Army*, p. 291.
23 Somerset RO, DD/PH 220, a Somerset and Wiltshire lieutenancy book, contains numerous entries which show that the Crown clearly chose whomever it wanted from the localities, at least during the period 1585 to 1601.

bands would not be misused or squandered in a dubious cause in a time of danger. If the King embarked on a substantial military adventure, it would be for him to use pressed men.

In pressing troops, the line of least resistance was to ensnare 'outsiders' – petty criminals. Those whose actions placed them on the periphery of useful society could be prevented from disrupting society by serving to defend it. Since sturdy rogues and vagabonds and petty criminals were conscripted, it is hardly surprising that military service could be conceived as a fitting punishment for some offenders. Prisoners from Newgate, for example, reinforced the siege of Le Havre in late May 1563. Physical stature was weighed along with criminal record in ascertaining which prisoners qualified for pardon by way of service. A stout fellow guilty of theft was the ideal candidate. A puny lad in his early twenties and a sixty-year old burglar remained gaoled, while tall horse thieves were accepted. Habitual criminals, regardless of build, were rejected as incorrigible, as in the case of William Cleppett, a common cutpurse.[24] Of thirteen prisoners destined for overseas service in 1563, twelve had been committed for house-breaking and robbery; the exception was John Cundall, a gentleman convicted of manslaughter after a killing. Eighteen criminals from Middlesex included robbers, burglars, and housebreakers, like Thomas Redman, who stole 'a brasse branch and a booke called Jewells work' from St Clement Danes' Church. George Lewes had been convicted of manslaughter in the killing of William Sharpe. Anthony Ellis and Humphrey Harecourt fought and wounded a constable and his officers. Ellis was fined £100, and Harecourt a lesser amount, and received sentences of a year and a day in gaol.[25] Conscription even proved the equivalent of a 're-trial'. Thomas Longe had been condemned for taking a purse which contained eight shillings and five pence. However, 'the Evidence was not cleare', and he had no prior criminal record. Longe had been indicted, arraigned, and given sentence of death, but 'the Evidence uppon his Tryall was doubtfull, and that it could not bee made to appeare before us that hee was ever detected of any other Crime, and for that hee is an able person fit for imployment in the warres'.[26] When in 1587 Kentish clothworkers conspired to plunder grain from the homes of the well-to-do, a commission of oyer and terminer decided that the would-be rioters should be employed as soldiers: 'the commissioners did not find that the offense "touched the

---

[24] PRO, SP 12/28/63, 27 May 1563.
[25] PRO, SP 14/170/28 I, list of Middlesex prisoners, July 1625; PRO, SP 14/170/28 II. Thomas Redman, the church-breaker with a taste for Bishop Jewel's writing, was charged with 'Sacriledge in robbing' St Clement's. I assume the 'brasse branch' is a type of candlestick.
[26] PRO, SP 14/170/71, information regarding Thomas Longe, 28 July 1625; SP 14/170/71, certificate by the 'Commissioners of Gaole Delivery'. See also SP 14/170/70.

lives" of the four suspects who were tried and found guilty; taking a cue
from their original charge of punishing deserters from the army, they sen-
tenced the clothworkers to military service in the Netherlands'.[27]

The impressment of offenders, whether violent criminals or petty
thieves, malefactor knights or penniless rogues, implied opportunity for
atonement. If one offended society, then one could be removed from
society, in one sense as punishment, in another as a form of rehabilitation
in the guise of 'community service'. Honourable performance on the field
of battle could balance the ledger. The notorious Folvilles of the 1300s
obtained pardons by serving against Scotland and later fighting in Flanders. During the 1344 campaign, Edward reinforced militia units with 'pardoned felons'.[28] If the offender survived, indeed distinguished himself in
war, then fortune had smiled and he was redeemed. When at the Queen's
behest the London sheriffs released a pair to the Earl of Warwick, the royal
reprieve aimed at giving the men an opportunity 'to recompenc their
offenc' by serving abroad. Prisoners were released from a Buckinghamshire
gaol in summer 1625 for service in the Low Countries.[29] James I reasoned
that many prisoners had been convicted but reprieved due to 'speciall
causes', and those of strong body might by their future good behavior
redeem themselves by fighting in 'forraigne parts'.[30]

EARLY STUART IMPRESSMENT IN THE BISHOPS' WARS

Given the medieval precedents, Charles I's demands on his subjects were
entirely reasonable, and the tasks assigned to Attorney General Bankes and
others in searching out precedents indicate that the King was aware of
them. Given the recent history of the relationship between impressment
and militia service, the Crown's demands were impolitic and gave an
impression of illegality. Without powerful nobles, foreign mercenaries or
skilled militia at the core of his army, Charles I was heavily reliant on
pressed troops. Ironically the most powerful man in the kingdom was
forced to rely upon his meanest subjects for the success of royal policy. But
impressment was more a punishment than an honour and the pathetic
recruits could not master the tools of the military revolution in a fortnight.
The King chose the wrong men to do his fighting.

[27] Sharp, *In Contempt of All Authority*, pp. 45–6; P. Clark, 'Popular Protest and Disturbance in Kent, 1558–1640', *EconHR*, second series, 29, no. 3 (August 1976), p. 367.
[28] E. Stones, 'The Folvilles of Ashby-Folville, Leicestershire, and Their Associates in Crime,
1326–1347', *TRHS*, fifth series, 7 (1957), pp. 128–9; Nicholson, *Edward III and the Scots*,
p. 167.
[29] PRO, SP 12/24/41, 20 September 1562; PRO, SP 14/170/17, Sir Thomas Denton to the
Council of War, 18 July 1625.
[30] PRO, SP 14/170/28, the King to the Keeper of Newgate, 21 July 1625.

The haphazard methods of early Stuart impressment led to inequity. Men were conscripted entirely by accident, or by misfortune, like the poor Dutchman seized while strolling to a London theatre.[31] Others were taken because they had offended their landlord or the local constable, some due to their social status: they were neither affluent enough, nor in possession of the kind of personal connection necessary to gain admission to the trained bands, and were thus subject to the press. Even with regard to reprieved criminals there was little equity in the system. Poor Thomas Longe of Northampton might very well have been unjustly accused of theft, and because of the authorities' doubts about his guilt was sent off to the Low Countries with men whose crimes were quite blatant, such as criminals who had been convicted of manslaughter. Whether the crime was suspicion of cutting a purse, as in Longe's case, or manslaughter, the punishment was the same: servitude as a common soldier in the Thirty Years' War.

The most notorious complaint about impressment in England was not so much the inequity of selection but the bribery of conductors and sergeants, compounded by malicious recruitment. Reluctant conscripts were allowed to buy their way out of the ranks, an expensive alternative, but safer than desertion. The practice debased the system of impressment further and only the most unfortunate, and generally unskilled, found their way into the royal army. In Michaelmas 1628, a Cambridge deputy lieutenant, Sir Simeon Steward, was fined £50 because he had released a butcher named Spencer for twenty shillings. 'Simeon further said to Spencer, that if he would not leave the town of Ely and give up his trade (being a butcher) that then he would be taken at the next press.' The Attorney General concluded, 'this sin of Sir Simeon goes generally to all the deputy lieutenants of England'.[32] The motive could be either malice, as in Steward's case, or profit. An unscrupulous conductor who had orders to press 100 men might 'overpress', and conscript 110. The ten who offered the highest 'reward', sometimes amounting to several pounds, could purchase their release. The captain then departed with a full contingent and a hefty purse.[33]

In Berkshire in 1625 Morris Tuffey of Buscott accused his landlord of

---

[31] Sergeant-Major Leigh's report, PRO, SP 16/4/160. See also Stearns, 'Conscription and English Society', pp. 8–9, especially notes 30 and 31.

[32] Star Chamber case against Steward, Michaelmas 1628, based upon Harvard Law School MS. 1128, no. 48. T. G. Barnes kindly supplied a translation from the legal French. The episode is detailed in 'Deputies not Principals, Lieutenants not Captains: The Institutional Failure of Lieutenancy in the 1620s' in Fissel (ed.), *War and Government in Britain*, pp. 63–6. See also Barnes, *Somerset 1625–1640*, p. 255, and Stearns's 'Conscription and English Society', p. 12.

[33] Ibid., pp. 11–23; cf. particularly note 45

'commaunding the Constables to presse him' in spite of the fact that he was sixty years old and had a wife and family. Ralph Hatt of Stamford claimed 'that Sir Robert Knowles caused him to be prest because he went a fishing in a common poole'. Nicholas Palmer of Abingdon alleged 'he was pressed for malice, for that a Boucher dwelling neare his house made means to have him prested thereby thincking to obtaine his house'.[34] In Stafford, Francis Everton asserted that the 'Constables owing him some ill will', he had been approached by the deputy lieutenant, Sir Simon Weston, who proferred Everton press money. Claiming to be a gentleman, Everton refused the money, telling Sir Simon he would go voluntarily if he so decided, but would never be pressed. Wiborne Johnson of Spentrice, Kent, insisted that he had been pressed because he was involved in litigation with Sir Ralph Boswell. Sir Thomas Walsingham told him 'because he had suite with the said Sir Ralph he should goe. Notwithstanding he offered to put a lusty able man in his roome [place] and to give money to him for a reward.'[35] This latter abuse was particularly objectionable, since it could be said that impressment could be used to defeat an adversary without recourse to the law, and that the due process of the law could be circumvented by pressing litigants or witnesses. Such allegations increased the aura of illegality surrounding Caroline military demands.

By 1638, some Englishmen could recall impressment as a fate worse than death, inflicted in the company of the most despised elements of society. The Personal Rule had dimmed that memory, for after the 50,000 pressed in the 1620s, the peace of the 1630s spared the communities. Endemic vagrancy and economic dislocation (caused largely by depression in the clothmaking sector) coupled with continued population increase meant that numerous able men were available for impressment.[36] The existence of surplus men in the community along with the increasingly marked distinction between militia service and pressed service meant that the most substantial citizens, accustomed to a decade of peace as well as exemption from military liability, felt relatively secure from such service on the eve of the Bishops' Wars. Conversely, the less affluent and the poor found themselves highly vulnerable in 1639. The years of peace had protected them, but war spelt the end of their immunity.

The Crown's scouring of the countryside, coupled with increased demand for men due to the changing nature of warfare (the military revo-

---

[34] PRO, SP 16/4/160, the report of Sergeant-Major Leigh. I have used the numbers from the upper right-hand-corner of the pages for foliation. The report is divided up according to county, and cases are numbered individually. For the Berkshire cases of malicious impressment, see f. 244, nos. 4, 5, and 9; Stearns, 'Conscription and English Society', p. 9, no. 34.

[35] PRO, SP 16/4/160, Leigh's report: Staffordshire, f. 242, no.5; Kent, f. 264, no. 4.

[36] See for example PRO, SP 17E, Northants certificate.

lution), and the increased incidence of conflict (the wars of religion) was comparatively thorough. The classification of men as volunteer militia shrank the pool of potential recruits, so that the less fortunate found themselves more likely to be pressed. The importance of social distinction based upon means and militia service, from the Statute of Winchester to the exemption of trained-band soldiers from paid expeditionary service, meant that over the centuries militia service took on the characteristic of privilege (though mustering and muster-masters remained perennially unpopular) and impressment a punishment for being unemployed, poor, an outsider, or a criminal. Thus service that had been intermingled became polarized. In the Bishops' Wars, the pressed men complained of impressment and the militia grieved that they were being used like pressed men.

Charles put little faith in pressed soldiers, probably because of the military failures of the 1620s. In 1639, the initial levy of untrained able-bodied infantry was set at 6,000, only a quarter of the proposed army of 24,000. Subsequent presses, however, especially in the thirteen northern counties, could be anticipated. Charles for the most part hedged his bets on the select trained bands and personal contingents of the nobility and gentry, which he hoped might comprise 75 per cent of the royal army. As the King ultimately raised between 15,000 and 20,000 men, raw levies ultimately made up one-third to one-half of the English forces. In 1640, little or no pressing was planned initially. Select militia units primarily, and secondarily 'volunteers' from the elite, were to fight the Second Bishops' War. As it turned out, companies were fashioned from untrained soldiers anyway. The percentage of raw men was much higher than anticipated, largely due to the substitution clause. The wholesale exploitation of that loophole especially in 1640 produced an army quite different from that which had been planned.

Contingents of raw men were grouped into regiments of 1,200, based upon region. Barrymore's regiment was fashioned from Welshmen. Lord Grandison drew upon Leicestershire, Worcestershire, and Gloucestershire.[37] When men were conscripted for military service, the 'conductors' (the officers in charge of inspecting, enrolling, and accompanying the troops) fashioned an 'indenture', which listed the recruits and sometimes their home parish and occupation. Two virtually identical indentures were drawn up, usually upon parchment – originally from a single piece then divided by a jagged cut so that the pair could be re-fitted to assure veracity. One copy remained with the conductor, while the other was sent up to the Council in London.[38] Supplemental data was often included along with the

[37] PRO, SP 16/462.
[38] For example, the government's roll of the 600 men pressed in Rutland on 10 June 1640 is SP 16/462, while the lieutenants' copy is HEH, Hastings MSS., HA Military Box 1 (28). Those indentures preserved in the PRO (SP 16/419; 462) were the Privy Council copies

soldiers' names, for example their places of residence and occupations. No indentures with occupational data appear to have survived from the six northern counties for the Bishops' Wars. Nor are there any for Norfolk, Essex, Kent, Sussex, Hampshire, Dorset, Devon, or Cornwall. The bulk of evidence on the background of English soldiers comes from central England. Inclusion of occupational data in lists of soldiers is not unique to England. The covenanting armies, too, provide some evidence of social background. The Earl of St Andrews's armed tenants included a 'couper', 'meillmaker', 'taylor', and a 'mason'. More distinguished professions are represented among those providing muskets and pikes, namely, a doctor, a minister, and a barrister.[39]

If the English trained bands were comprised mostly of yeomen, husbandmen, skilled craftsmen, and tradesmen, what of the able-bodied men who did not enjoy exemption from impressment? A glimpse at their social status and occupations can be had from examination of the eastern division of Northamptonshire in 1638. The list of around 918 able men is dominated by husbandmen (227), labourers (156), and servants (109), accompanied by various craftsmen such as tailors (46), masons (43), carpenters (42), and weavers (26). Men of quality are scarce: no gentlemen and only fifteen yeomen are enrolled (40). When the local authorities selected men from this pool, they invariably took those without valued skills, and protected the useful, including those engaged in agriculture.[40] The largest category is that of husbandmen, interesting in that labourers consistently made up the bulk of early Stuart levies, while husbandmen were often wholly exempted from the press. In Northamptonshire, of 100 men conscripted for the 1625 Cadiz expedition, 34 were labourers and only 5 were husbandmen.[41] But although husbandmen and sturdy farmers no doubt possessed the sturdy constitutions and stamina requisite for good soldiers, they were too valuable to society in their food-producing efforts to be made prey to the press. Consequently, husbandmen were generally taken only as a last resort.

In the Derby levy of 1639, only a single husbandman can be found amongst 200 soldiers. In contrast, of the 230 Warwickshire men pressed for the First Bishops' War, 35 were husbandmen. Again, the largest category was that of labourer, nearly half of the levy (110 men out of 230).[42]

---

and those found in private papers and local record offices those of the conductors. The procedure is confirmed in BL, Harleian MS. 4014, Cambridgeshire militia papers, f. 36.
[39] NLS, Crawford MS. 14/3/49, f. 2, men and arms from the parish of Kilconquhar, 1639.
[40] PRO, SP 17E, 'A List of Enrollment of untrained men of able bodyes within the East division of the County of Northampton fitt for his Majestys Service in the warrs.'
[41] PRO, SP 16/2/101 (original parchments); BL, Add. MS. 34,217, ff. 15–15v (manuscript copy).
[42] PRO, SP 16/417/40, indenture of early April 1639 for Lieutenant Moses Treswell to escort the 230 pressed Warwickshire men to Selby.

However, a perusal of the Warwickshire indenture for Count Mansfeld's 1624 expedition finds not one husbandman. The contingent was made up entirely of labourers and skilled craftsmen, such as basketmakers, card-makers, bellowsmakers, pewterers, and haberdashers. Interestingly, in the levy consisting overwhelmingly of labourers, two yeomen and a gentleman, Thomas Byddle of Bashford, were included.[43] The relative absence of husbandmen might be explained by S. J. Stearns's research: 'The council apparently gave some credence to these complaints raised about the impact of the levy on agriculture for, in one agitated county at least, Hampshire, they explicitly urged Secretary Conway, in his capacity as Lord Lieutenant, to press more heavily from the town "to spare hus-bandry".'[44] One would think that for a winter campaign, as Mansfeld's was, a few husbandmen might have been available for military service due to the fact that there were no crops in the field, but the indenture indicates that none were taken. The inclusion of the yeomen (and Mr Byddle) remains a mystery. Extensive enclosure, assuming it forced men off arable land and diminished employment opportunities in agriculture, could increase the number of husbandmen available for military service by diverting them into the ranks and lessening the burden on the parish.

Nearly three-quarters of Derbyshire's 1639 contingent of 200 conscripts were 'labourers', the remainder possessing some vocation, excluding seventeen for whom no occupation is given. Among the regional and occu-pational variations, the contingent from Derby town was composed entirely of craftsmen: a chapman, a tailor, a blacksmith, a brickmaker, a feltmaker, and a pair of drapers. Unlike the rural areas, the township did not supply labourers. Of twenty-two men pressed in Reppingdon and Gresly hundreds, seventeen were labourers. Likewise, the hundreds of Mortaston and Litchurch combined to enroll twenty-two labourers in their quota of twenty-five men. The other hundreds had similar proportions, although the northwestern region of Derbyshire, rich in lead, provided twelve miners, and, interestingly, the only husbandmen in the entire levy.[45] Labourers also predominated in the 1627 levies from Derbyshire, thirty-six out of fifty. The remainder were craftsmen such as shoemakers, a slater, a milner, etc. Lead miners were also conscripted, a trio being taken from the northwest of Derbyshire. The composition of the 1627 press was similar to that of the First Bishops' War, the only difference being that Derby town's

---

43 PRO, SP 14/178, tripartite indenture from Warwickshire.
44 Stearns, 'Conscription and English Society', p. 6, citing PRO, SP 16/73/65.
45 PRO, SP 16/419. The Derbyshire indenture of 1639 is also interesting in that it includes the names of men pressed from Melbourne and Ticknall, the site of enclosure rioting during the summer of 1639: Robert Meadcalfe of Melbourne, a labourer, and John Holland of Ticknall, a potter. On the Derbyshire riots see p. 277.

contingent comprised three labourers, and no skilled craftsmen.[46] In the same year, 1627, one hundred Derby men were recruited to serve the King of Denmark.[47] Almost half were labourers (forty-eight), and there was a sizeable group of miners as well (fourteen), mostly drawn from the hundred of High Peak, a forest area. The strangest characteristic of the 1627 Danish press was the presence of a constable and two clothiers, categories of men rarely conscripted. William Greatrax of Wirkesworth hundred found himself pressed in spite of his holding the office of constable. Two High Peak clothiers, John Hage and Robert Blackshaw, ended up shouldering arms with the miners and labourers. In the context of the Danish press and forced loan, the impressment of the constable and clothiers might be instances of malicious or punitive conscription, these men being, perhaps, loan refusers. Even more curious, of the twenty-three men pressed in High Peak, except for Greatrax, Hage, and Blackshaw, all were either labourers or miners. There were no skilled craftsmen or artisans.[48]

As may be seen from the case of Derbyshire, regional and occupational variations existed, even though labourers made up the bulk of the levies. Besides geographical diversity, the *terminology* of the indentures complicates generalization about conscription on a national scale. The most frustrating problem is defining precisely what is meant by a 'labourer'. Even the Tawneys' impressive analysis of the Gloucestershire militia survey of 1608 found an adequate definition of the term impossible. They separated labourers in the Smith of Nibley survey into two categories: those dwelling in the major towns, Gloucester, Cirencester, and Tewkesbury, were classified as engaged in non-agricultural employment, a reasonable assumption. All the others, living in rural areas, were then considered to be agricultural workers, though they were quite likely to be supplementing their work in the fields with simple, semi-skilled crafts. The Tawneys conjectured that many of the inhabitants of the Forest of Dean and the surrounding areas who were labelled 'labourers' were in fact forest miners:

> The number of coal miners and ironworkers in the Forest of Dean appearing in Smyth's lists is so small that it seems to us probable that some workers in these categories were entered as labourers, a procedure which was the more natural because a good many of both had some other occupation and were not employed in the industries in question throughout the year. With that exception, persons appear normally to have been described as labourers only when there was no specific occupation, other than agriculture, to which they could be assigned.[49]

[46] PRO, SP 16/46, box of parchments.
[47] PRO, SP 16/72/11, indenture dated 26 July 1627.
[48] On forest miners in general, see Sharp, *In Contempt of all Authority*; on loan refusers, see Cust, *The Forced Loan and English Politics*, p. 57.
[49] A. J. Tawney and R. H. Tawney, 'An Occupational Census of the Seventeenth Century', pp. 31–3. See also Keith Wrightson's *English Society, 1580–1680* (New Brunswick, N.J., 1982), pp. 40–51.

The high percentage of labourers residing in the Forest of Dean encouraged this interpretation. However, they continued, 'Against this view must be set the fact that labourers are not specially numerous in the other group of mining hundreds, Langley and Wineshead, Puckelchurch, and Barton Regis, which supplied workers to the Bristol coal-field.' 'Labourer' and 'miner' could be used interchangeably because Smith's survey was undertaken in 1608, while the real exploitation of the iron ore resources in the Forest of Dean did not start until 1611–1612.[50] In the High Peak district in 1627 the local authorities distinguished miners from labourers. If the distinction was not clearly drawn in the Forest of Dean section of Smith's survey, due probably to irregular employment, the delineation is quite clear amongst the lead miners of northwestern Derbyshire. The indentures for the Rhé expedition and the First Bishops' War from High Peak separate 'myners' from 'labourers'.[51]

The question as to whether or not a given labourer was an agricultural worker or an unskilled workman engaged in labour unrelated to growing and harvesting makes the analysis of indentures risky. One cannot clearly distinguish between agricultural and non-agricultural employment because labourers were unskilled, or semi-skilled at best. Their lack of training in a specific craft separated them from the tradesmen and craftsmen, the shoe-makers, blacksmiths, carpenters, butchers, and bakers. Although a distinction can be made between labourers and craftsmen, the categories of artisan and labourer often overlapped. Many rural landless pursued non-agricultural employment in the countryside, particularly 'cottage industries', and could be described either as artisans or labourers. In short, although a labourer might not possess specialized skills, he could still work in a manual trade involving the use of cloth, wood, or iron. His marginal employment, depending very heavily upon the cloth export market and local markets, put him in a precarious position. Should his manually produced items find no market, he might temporarily seek work in agriculture. In short, these labourers and artisans, being semi-skilled and at the mercy of the market, could quite conceivably work at both non-agricultural *and* agricultural labour, depending upon the situation and the season. Siphoning off such individuals into the military caused virtually no disruption of the shire community. As these people rarely had fixed employment, their

[50] Buchanan Sharp kindly pointed out this fact. Any errors in the interpretation of the Smith of Nibley survey are, of course, my own.

[51] PRO, SP 16/46 (1627) and SP 16/419 (1639), boxes of indentures. The Tawneys' theory is supported by Buchanan Sharp, who writes: 'There are a number of examples in Exchequer and other legal records of a Dean Forest inhabitant being called a laborer on one occasion and miner or woodworking artisan on another. In Dean, as in other forests, there was no clear dividing-line between artisans and laborers', *In Contempt of All Authority*, p. 187. High Peak, like Dean, was populated by forest miners.

temporary (or possibly, permanent) removal did not threaten the some-times fragile economy of the locality. An unemployed, semi-skilled man seeking work wherever he might find it could well be described as a labourer, given the diversity and temporary nature of his employment. Thus the labourer was generally landless or at best a smallholder, margi-nally employed, often capable of working in either an agricultural or a non-agricultural capacity, susceptible to the effects of poor harvest and fluctuations in markets like that for cloth, and often only partially visible to the local authorities if he did not live within a manor. His economic and social marginality made him an excellent candidate for impressment.

Another midland county for which there is ample evidence, Leices-tershire, exhibits a roughly similar pattern of impressment. Data on the social composition of the 1624 and 1627 presses survive, as well as the entire levy of 400 soldiers for the Second Bishops' War. In 1640, more than two-thirds of the soldiers were labourers, the remaining third being com-prised mostly of craftsmen: eighteen tailors, sixteen cordwainers, seven weavers, etc. A solitary husbandman and a gardener were the only men involved in the tilling of the soil. Like Hampshire and Warwickshire, Leicestershire declined to take men from agricultural pursuits. Fifteen men described as 'gentleman' are scattered through the indenture, though five are bunched together, listed consecutively. Of these latter, four have appar-ently Irish surnames: O'Brien, MacSweeney, O'Connell, and MacSweeney again.[52] Given the relatively common practice of pressing strangers, it seems very possible that some visiting, and perhaps unwelcome, Irishmen were deemed fit to serve His Majesty in the war against Scotland. The fact that 'Mr Holland' and David Clarke are likewise listed without mention of a home hundred or parish lends weight to the theory that at least some of these 'gentlemen' were either visitors or newcomers to Leicestershire. It is striking though that the 'gentlemen' outnumber the 'husbandmen' fifteen to one.

Comparing the 1640 indenture with two from the 1620s, the first Rhé expedition levy contains four yeomen (one from the town of Leicester) and a solitary husbandman, out of approximately 120 soldiers. Apart from shepherds and the usual large contingent of labourers, the remainder are craftsmen. Once again, it appears that husbandry was spared, so to speak.[53]

---

[52] Dennis Gorban of Husband Bosworth; William Granger of Broughton Ashley; John Langton of Barleston; Morris Obryon of Stawston; Owen Mackswynny of Ashley; Jeffrey Okennell (no residence given); Edmund Mackswynny (no residence given); John Harbert (no residence given); William Palmer of Barkby; William Lary of Dadlington; Mr. Holland (no residence given); Tighe Swilleman of Harborowe; Charles Chartey of Staple-ton; David Clark (no residence given); Edward Blunditch of Ratsby. PRO, SP 16/462.

[53] PRO, SP 16/46/10, indenture for the levy of 150 infantry (only about 120 are listed, however), 7 April 1627.

The 1624 indenture tells a very different story, however. Of the roughly 182 soldiers whose names appear, 52 are labourers, but 61 are described as husbandmen! A gentleman is included for good measure.

Why should husbandmen dominate the 1624 press when they are almost non-existent in the 1627 and 1640 levies? The answer may lie in the season. Mansfeld's press occurred during the winter, while the Rhé levy took place in spring, and the press for the Second Bishops' War in the summer. In other words, the Mansfeld levy was conducted *after* the harvest, when husbandmen were not as essential, unlike the 1627 and 1640 levies. Charles had arranged the levy for the First Bishops' War for early spring 1639. The Second Bishops' War press was conducted in summer, even closer to the harvest than the levy of the previous year. No doubt local authorities in counties with substantial amounts of ground under cultivation would be concerned about depleting the agricultural workforce. Besides reducing the workforce at harvest time, the cost of pressing soldiers, particularly coat-and-conduct money, forced farmers to expend capital on military charges when that money was needed to pay labourers to bring in the harvest and when they were short of coin, having invested in their crops but not yet reaped their profits. In the neighbouring county of Rutland, no husbandmen or yeomen were conscripted in 1640.[54] In 1624, however, five husbandmen were conscripted along with fifteen labourers, a gentleman, two yeomen, and twenty-three craftsmen.[55]

Occupational data in the indentures suggest that the men pressed for the Bishops' Wars, like the expeditions of the 1620s, were untrained men from the lowest social stratum. Certainly it is possible that some militia units were represented by indentures that did not contain occupational designations, or served without formal contract, and without press money. If our generalizations about a basic distinction between the types of men who served in the trained bands and those pressed from the less skilled work force are correct, then the indentures bear out that Charles I received large contingents of poorly trained men. As for the perfect militia, it does not seem much in evidence based upon the fragmentary sources extant. The substitution clause, discussed below, accounted in large part for the absence of militiamen in the English army. The process of impressment further undermined Caroline authority when it was subverted by local officials to rid the community of undesirables or to harass their enemies.

A press provided occasion for weeding out the marginal types from the community. It was not difficult to make the transition from those who were of little use to those who had incurred the professional or personal odium

---

[54] HEH, Hastings MSS., Military Box 1 (28) and PRO, SP 16/462, identical Rutland indentures dated 10 June 1640.
[55] PRO, SP 14/178, box of indentures from the Mansfeld expedition.

of the constables, justices, or deputy lieutenants. Grudges and local rivalries sometimes determined who was taken and who remained. In 1639 Bartholomew Vere, the constable of Reepham in Lincolnshire, maliciously pressed Robert Beech, a servant of the local parson and militiaman as well. Sixteen to twenty able men were available for conscription, but the constable chose Beech anyway. The council took note of this illegal action and ordered the deputy lieutenant to investigate and report back.[56]

The 'malicious' impressment of constable George Plowright in 1639 by deputy lieutenant Sir Rowland St John also required the mediation of the Privy Council.[57] T. G. Barnes has stressed the importance of personal disputes and rivalries in local politics, and it was such a conflict that provided the impetus for 'Plowright's case'. Mr Thomas Bacon and constable Plowright had been in dispute in Burton Latimer, Northamptonshire, over issues such as religion, forced loans and ship money. When Plowright brought his ship money returns to the sheriff at Northampton, Bacon was supposed to have instigated the town's bailiff to requisition Plowright's mount for post-horse duties, even though Plowright was performing the King's service and other steeds were available. Adding injury to insult, Plowright later discovered that his horse had been lamed.

Normally, the Privy Council paid little heed to animosities between Northamptonshire gentlemen. However, when the press for the First Bishops' War was conducted in March 1639, the deputy lieutenants pressed constable Plowright, who protested that he had been conscripted at the instigation of Thomas Bacon so that he would be at York with the royal army when his Star Chamber suit against Bacon appeared before the Attorney General. On 28 April the Privy Council instructed Plowright to produce witnesses, including Dr Sibthorpe, a former justice of the peace in Burton Latimer, who stated that 'the said Bacon had procured that trouble of being prest a Soldier to bee brought upon him [Plowright], for haveing presented the said Bacon in his Majesties Court of Starr Chamber'.[58] Earlier, in 1624, Bacon had resorted to malicious impressment when he conspired to impress one Shrive, clerk of a local church. In 1639, Sibthorpe believed that Bacon saw the impending campaign against Scotland as an opportunity 'to ridd the towne of Plowright'. Sibthorpe declared to the Privy Council that Bacon wished to 'ridd That Knave Plowright out of the town', but that 'Plowright was a Freeholder, and would not be blasted out

---

[56] PRO, PC 2/50, f. 367, Privy Council register, to deputy lieutenants, 19 May 1639; PRO, SP 16/421/97, council to deputy lieutenants, 21 May.
[57] See Stater, 'The Lord Lieutenancy', pp. 279–96.
[58] PRO, PC 2/50, ff. 310–11, 28 April 1639.

of the towne'.[59] The council also summoned Sir Rowland St John, the chief deputy lieutenant of the eastern division of Northamptonshire, to answer these serious charges.[60]

There was some reason to think Bacon might very well have initiated the pressing of Plowright. 'Mr. Bacon was served with process to heare Judgment in Starchamber about 5 daies before Plowright was prest, and Plowright was Commaunded to Attend Mr. Attornie about that Cause which is to bee heard the 10th Maie.' On the day before the press, a friend of Bacon's overheard that 'if but two went for Souldiers out of that towne, Plowright should be one of them'. Popular opinion held that 'it was done to service Mr. Bacon's turne. And that if [Plowright] had not prosecuted Mr. Bacon in Starchamber, this troble had not bene'.[61] Sir Rowland St John and the other deputy lieutenants told a different tale. Being informed that Bacon had been committed for persuading the lieutenants to press Plowright, St John notified the council that during the preparations for, and execution of, the press, there was no communication whatsoever with Mr Thomas Bacon, who resided in the western division of the county. Bacon knew nothing of the press in Burton Latimer. Plowright's accusation not only lacked justification, but charged the lieutenants with dishonest

---

[59] For the harassment of Plowright, see 'Circumstances and probably reasons that Mr Bacon had a hand to have George Plowright prest for a Soldier', PRO, SP 16/409/2. This undated document is calendared with another document, a certificate by Sibthorpe and twenty-four others commending Plowright's character, dated from the 1 January 1638/9 (SP 16/409/2 I). The undated document is miscalendared, since the press occurred in spring 1639. The certificate by Sibthorpe probably relates to a Star Chamber case which was pending prior to the press. For Sibthorpe's 'official' account of his conversation with Thomas Bacon, see SP 16/420/67, and for the Privy Council's order to Sibthorpe to divulge information concerning the dispute, see PC 2/50, ff. 310–11 and SP 16/418/82, order of the Privy Council dated 28 April 1639. While vicar of Brackley in February 1627 he preached a sermon later published as 'Apostolike Obedience. Shewing the Duty of Subjects to pay Tribute and Taxes to their Princes, according to the Word of God . . .', which justified the forced loan. In the 1630s he conducted a mild witch hunt against notable 'puritans'. For Sibthorpe's correspondence, which reveals the background to the Plowright case, see HEH, Stowe MSS., STT 1876 to 1895.

[60] PRO, SP 16/418/81, directions to St John, 28 April 1639.

[61] This document is PRO, SP 16/409/2, and is miscalendared under the date 1 January 1638/9. The 'guiding spirit' behind this manuscript's composition is Dr Robert Sibthorpe, although he is mentioned in the third person in item 2, and the document is not in his hand. V. Stater suggests Sibthorpe's authorship as well. Sibthorpe took action to free Plowright from military service during the first week of April, and it was the good doctor who organized the drafting of SP 16/409/2 I. The discussion which follows reinforces this point. The relationship between 2, 1 and 2 is made clear in item 2 of SP 16/409/2, where the certificate is 'annexed' to the 'Circumstances'. Either Sibthorpe misdated the certificate, or it had been drafted shortly after Christmas 1638 for another purpose. The reference to the upcoming Star Chamber hearing on 10 May 1639 would suggest that the 'Circumstances' were compiled between 6 April and the first week of May 1639. For Sibthorpe's other Star Chamber adventures, see Stater, 'The Lord Lieutenancy', pp. 286–7.

practices. The constable had been pressed because he had misused his office. He had pressed the servants of gentlemen, strangers of quality, and detained them without cause, so the lieutenants had taken Plowright himself. Far from using the King's press to further a personal vendetta, St John had disciplined Plowright for dereliction of his duties. Plowright had received a warrant from the chief constable of the hundred to press three men from the township of Burton Latimer. Rather than press his neighbours, however, Plowright collared 'divers straungers of other townes and amongst the rest a servant of one Mr Glapthorne of Whitlesey a Justice of peace in the Isle of Eley whom hee detayned allmost three dayes till the sayd Mr Glapthorne sent his letter to Sir Rowland St John for the release of his servant'. The chief deputy lieutenant set the servant at liberty. On the following day, Plowright presented three conscripts to the deputy lieutenants. One was judged unfit, another with wife and children, and the third claimed to be a resident of a neighbouring town and subject to their press. Plowright had not brought a single fit man from Burton Latimer. 'Here upon the deputyes haveing pressed divers other constables for such like miscaryages or neglects, did geiuve him prest money but with libertye as all the rest had to retourne that night to provide fitter men against the next morning.'

Instead of hurrying out to find sufficient men, Plowright seems to have conferred with Dr Sibthorpe, for he appeared in the deputies' chamber with one of Sibthorpe's servants, who brought a request to excuse Plowright because he was to appear before the Star Chamber. Sir Rowland then 'moved that the sayd Plowright might be Spared from the Journey and bound to answeare his misdemeanor at the next Sessions'. Given the confusion, the deputy lieutenants retained Plowright on the roll of pressed soldiers, but gave him leave to procure a substitute to be approved by Sir Lewis Watson, who was preparing to depart for the rendezvous at York. In the morning Plowright returned accompanied by two candidates. Watson found neither man satisfactory. Again Plowright went searching for a replacement. When he returned, now four days after the press, he presented to Watson a letter from Dr Sibthorpe reiterating the plea that Plowright be excused because of the Star Chamber suit. St John was about to take horse to meet with other deputy lieutenants in order to draft the final indenture that would be sent to the Lord Lieutenant. He sympathized, but needed a man to take Plowright's place. In order to present the allocated number of men, St John agreed to delay a little longer; Plowright hurried back with James Basford, a substitute he hired for £10.[62] Sir Rowland accepted him,

[62] HEH, Stowe MS. STT 1877, Sibthorpe to Lambe, 15 April 1639; Basford resided in Burton, but was not listed among the available able bodied. HEH, Stowe MS. STT 1878, Sibthorpe to Lambe, 19 April 1639 and PRO, SP 17E, box of miscellaneous documents

and 'having the Roles then in his hand erazed out Plowrights name and inserted the other and instantly not sturing from the place writt a letter to the conductor to receive him and rattifie the Role'.[63] Mr Bacon had nothing whatsoever to do with Plowright's predicament. As for Plowright, he got off easily and never had to journey to York. Apparently, Plowright did choose to journey at least part of the way to Selby, ostensibly to ensure that James Basford would be accepted as a substitute.[64]

The Privy Council committed Plowright to the Gatehouse prison and Bacon was discharged.[65] Plowright reminded the council of his poverty, having to pay Bacon, St John, and Mulsoe's charges of £13 3s 4d, and having expended considerable sums during the four years he had been embroiled in his Star Chamber suit with Bacon. He requested that this punishment be mitigated somewhat, and he be given reasonable time to pay. On 31 May 1639, George Plowright was freed. On 10 June, the constable entered a bond of £100 to ensure that he would apologize publicly to Sir Rowland St John at the next Assizes, and beg his pardon.[66]

Lurking beneath the personal animosity of this quarrel are two larger political issues: ship money and religion. When Dr Sibthorpe urged Richard Kilvert to aid him in freeing Plowright from military service, he reminded him that the constable of Burton Latimer had performed good service in obtaining ship money from the 'English Puritans' of Northamptonshire, but was now faced with perishing at the hands of the 'Scottish Puritans'. He also complained that one of the conscripts from Burton Latimer had been released through the intercession of Edmund Sawyer, a 'Puritan'.[67] The conscription of the constable was even more disgraceful, since larger and richer towns than Burton Latimer had not been burdened with supplying three men. Worse, the sturdy, disorderly young men that merited impressment had evaded the pressmen. The inhabitants of Barton

from the reign of Charles I, 'A List or Enrollment of untrained men of able bodyes within the East division of the County of Northampton fitt for his Majestys Service in the warrs', f. 23, left column, under Huxloe hundred.

[63] PRO, SP 16/421/44, 'The true cause and manner of proceeding in the presting of one George Plowright Constable of Burton Lattimer in the Countye of Northton to have been sent for a Soldier in the northerne Service', 17 May (?) 1639.

[64] Plowright may have wished either the Captain's or even the Colonel's approval in addition to that of St John, the chief deputy lieutenant. HEH, Stowe MSS. STT 1876 and 1878, Sibthorpe to Lambe, 12 and 19 April 1639 respectively.

[65] PRO, PC 2/50, ff. 35–9, Privy Council register, 7 May 1639. PRO, SP 16/421/43, order of the council, 1 May 1639. Bacon's name appears alongside St John's but has been struck out. SP 16/421/109; PC 2/50, f. 359, Privy Council register.

[66] PRO, SP 16/422/3, Plowright's petition to the council, undated. PRO, PC 2/50, f. 400, Privy Council register; SP 16/422/107, warrant to release Plowright. See also SP 16/423/73.

[67] This could be Sir Edmund Sawyer, auditor of the Exchequer. HEH, Stowe MS. STT 1880, 28 April 1639. Stater's description is pp. 289–91. Kilvert was a Middle Temple lawyer, according to Stater, 'The Lord Lieutenancy', p. 287.

Seagrave, 'a Common receptacle of disorderly persons', were excused from supplying any soldiers. When the warrant from the high constable had been delivered to Plowright, it had come from a third party, opened, so that 'all idle and young fellows' who dreaded military service had disappeared.[68] Thomas Bacon was not described as 'Puritan', but the list of accusations against him did refer to him as a 'Factious man and a Favorer of inconformable persons'.[69] He had been locked in a dispute regarding ship money payments with Plowright since around 1635.[70]

Larger political issues had invaded local communities. Stater describes it as an 'ideological intransigence that was gradually taking hold in the shires'. This politicization was a result of the Personal Rule, as Sibthorpe's letters illustrate. Even as early as the forced loan of 1627 he perceived that the Crown was struggling against wicked men. In the 1630s he defended Arminianism and ship money. It was the supporters of Caroline government who, along with the King, 'gave English political life an increasingly hard and uncompromising edge', while the allegedly 'Puritan' faction upheld lieutenancy and strove to keep politics out of the business of local government.[71]

If Charles's military demands were not all unreasonable in the light of medieval and Tudor precedents, why then was there such restiveness? Respect for governmental legitimacy was sufficient to mobilize an army in 1639 (and again in 1640), yet mistrust of the King's policies undermined the quality of those armies. Charles, who cared so much for outward appearance, got what he deserved: the form of an army, but without the fighting spirit needed to win. The politicization of mobilization continued through 1640, accelerated by the meeting of the Short Parliament. Yet even in 1640, when murder and riot accompanied the mobilization, deputy lieutenants whose sympathies often lay with the muster defaulters and coat-and-conduct money refusers still did the job. For example, Sir Guy Palmes, who had introduced into the Short Parliament legislation to limit the Crown's ability to take soldiers out of the shires, continued to discharge his duties in pressing troops for the Second Bishops' War. But his heart was not in it, for

---

[68] PRO, SP 16/417/47, Sibthorpe to Kilvert, 6 April 1639; HMC Cowper, Coke MSS., p. 219.
[69] PRO, SP 16/409/2, 'Circumstances'; for dating see above, n. 61.
[70] PRO, SP 16/422/3, Plowright's petition to the Council, undated.
[71] Stater, 'The Lord Lieutenancy', pp. 286–7; on the highly political viewpoint of Sibthorpe see HEH, Stowe MS. STT 1880, f. 2, where he says that his opponents have, quite literally, inbred and become mighty, to Sir John Lambe, 28 April 1639. See also the postscript on f. 4, dated 29 April, regarding Mr Crewe's refusal to pay ship money. For further examples of Sibthorpe's fusion of local and national politics with the religious controversies of the 1630s see also STT 1876, 1884, and letters of 27 May, 3 June, 7 June, 17 June.

he and his colleagues protested their inability to coerce their neighbours to serve.[72]

To return to Dr Sibthorpe's perceptions in 1639: he reported with disgust to Sir John Lambe that many of the Northamptonshire soldiers had deserted; these included three from Burton Latimer. The constables refused to report the whereabouts of the deserters to the deputy lieutenants, so Sibthorpe had sent out a warrant. He proceeded to name the localities whose pressed troops had deserted, and complained that one deserter had sold his arms on the way home. Worse, no one seemed willing to question whether the men were 'lawfully discharged', having deserted the King in the face of the enemy, leaving Charles to face the Covenanters with diminished forces. One can only guess at the outrage Sibthorpe felt fifteen months later, after the Short Parliament, the disorders of summer 1640, and the rout at Newburn.[73]

Neither contemporaries nor historians have explained Burton Latimer's difficulty in supplying three pressed soldiers for the First Bishops' War. Thirteen men were classified as available for the press.[74] Although one cannot say for certain why Plowright was foolish enough to accuse Thomas Bacon falsely of malicious impressment, it is apparent that he was reluctant to press his fellow townsmen. According to the documents that supported Plowright's character in the struggle with Bacon, his family had been freeholders in Burton Latimer for more than a century.[75] George Plowright had served in local government in a variety of capacities: overseer of the poor, sidesman, churchwarden, then one of the three constables for Burton Latimer. He enjoyed substantial support in the community, particularly from the clergy.[76] In this sense, the constable was the man in

[72] See HEH, Hastings MSS. HA 10623 and HA 10624, Hastings correspondence (box 16), Rutland deputy lieutenants to the Earl of Huntingdon, 5 September and 12 September 1640, regarding defects in the militia. By this time, of course, the war was lost.

[73] HEH, Stowe MS. STT 1893, 17 June 1639.

[74] Richard Pell (husbandman), William Parsons (shepherd), Martin Falkner (tailor), Richard Smith (husbandman), William Key (husbandman), William Hewitt (labourer), Thomas Stacy (servant), Henry Infeild (servant), William James (carpenter), Thomas Wallis (husbandman), John Green (servant), Thomas Lee (husbandman), and Bryan Bellamy (labourer). PRO, SP 17E, 'A List or Enrollment of untrained men of able bodyes within the East division of the County of Northampton fitt for his Majestys Service in the warrs', f. 23, left column under Huxloe hundred.

[75] According to J. Wake (ed.), *The Montagu Musters Book A.D. 1602–1623*, Northampton Record Society, 7 (Peterborough, 1935), Edward Plowright served in the trained bands for Burton Latimer in 1613 and 1614 (pp. 75, 86, and 105) and Robert Plowright in neighbouring Adwincle in 1619 (p. 200). There was also a Plowright serving as a bailiff in nearby Kettering in 1613 and 1614. According to SP 16/409/2, George Plowright was a 'Freeholder as his forefathers have bene in the same towne this 100 yere'. On Plowright's viewpoint see HEH, Stowe MS. STT 1582, to Sir John Lambe c. 1639 and STT 1583, to the Privy Council c. 1639.

[76] PRO, SP 16/409/2 I commends George Plowright, yeoman, for serving the community for nine years in the above-mentioned posts, describes him as 'dutifull honest and Carefull

the middle. Keith Wrightson has written, 'Mediating between the national legislative ideal and ambivalent local realities was the whole apparatus of Tudor and Stuart government.'[77] Plowright had to discharge his duties as directed by the government, yet as an important member of the local community, he had to implement orders in the face of opposition from his neighbours and friends.

The constable, like the justice of the peace and the deputy lieutenant, was the conduit between the distant, closed council chamber, and the people of England. Sometimes the gulf between the ideal and the real world could not be bridged. The council instructed the local authorities to press sturdy young men. Military theorists advocated that the most physically (and morally) endowed men should be enlisted. But, from the countryman's point of view, these were precisely the kind of men who were needed to bring in the harvest and to labour in the villages. From the beginning of the division between trained and untrained men a wedge was driven between theory and practice because the Crown asked of the localities more than the county could afford: her best young men.[78]

Freeholders' sons were exempted from the press because they were seen as valuable to the community. During the electioneering prior to the Short Parliament, Mr Elmes, who had served as a Northamptonshire deputy lieutenant in the 1639 mobilization, found his candidacy troubled by allegations that he had pressed a freeholder's son and then released him for £8. The rumour's maliciousness stemmed as much from the inappropriateness of pressing the son of a freeholder as from the charge of bribery.[79] The episode demonstrates how the elections to the Short Parliament accelerated political division and, arguably, political consciousness.[80] Elmes's associ-

and a diligent Promoter of his Majestys and the Churches Service' and is signed by twenty-nine civil servants and clergymen. See Stater's profile in 'The Lord Lieutenancy', on p. 283.

[77] K. Wrightson, 'Two Concepts of Order: Justices, Constables and Jurymen in Seventeenth Century England', in John Brewer and John Styles (eds.), *An Ungovernable People, the English and their Law in the Seventeenth and Eighteenth Centuries* (London, 1980), p. 26.

[78] See Hale, *War and Society in Renaissance Europe*, pp. 127–78.

[79] Bodleian Library, Bankes MS. 18/5, deposition of Thomas West, 5 May 1640, and 44/13, notes on individuals involved in the Elmes Case, drafted around May 1640.

[80] The literature on this matter is extensive. The two essential works are D. Hirst, *The Representative of the People? Voters and Voting in England Under the Early Stuarts* (Cambridge, 1975), and M. Kishlansky, *Parliamentary Selection. Social and Political Choice in Early Modern England* (Cambridge, 1986), especially p. 32, n. 34. See also pp. 18, 33, 35, 47, 109–11, 118–21, 130. For comparison, see J. K. Gruenfelder, 'The Spring Parliamentary Election at Hastings, 1640', *Sussex Archaeological Collections*, 105 (1967), pp. 47–55; 'The Election to the Short Parliament, 1640', in H. Reinmuth, jr. (ed.),*Early Stuart Studies. Essays in honor of David Harris Willson* (Minneapolis, 1970), pp. 180–230; 'The Election for Knights of the Shire for Essex in the Spring, 1640', *Transactions of the Essex Archaeological Society*, third series, 2, part 2, (1968), pp. 143–6, and his major work, *Influence in Early Stuart Elections 1604–1640* (Columbus, Ohio, 1981).

ation with the war in general and the impressment of a freeholder in particular earned him the emnity of the community and, ultimately, the intervention of the King himself. The politicization of the shire elections drew Whitehall into the localities. On Sunday, 3 May 1640, when London was buzzing over the protests voiced in the Short Parliament, Charles himself presided over a council meeting of seventeen of his most influential servants (including Laud and Strafford) wherein he ordered that thirteen Northamptonshire men, including the vicar of All Saints, answer charges for allegedly slandering Elmes.[81] While the King and Attorney General scrutinized Northamptonshire politics, Northamptonshire MPs had come to Westminster and were elevating local protest over Caroline rule to the level of a national political issue. Sir Gilbert Pickering, the MP who had been elected in Elmes's place, put forward his county's petition against charges associated with mobilization ('armie monie, waggon monie, horse monie, conduct monie') as well as innovations in religion and other Personal Rule grievances.[82] In the meantime Sir John Crewe, the other shire member whose opposition to ship money had so infuriated Dr Sibthorpe, became chairman of the committees for grievances and religion.[83] Clearly, as political issues became more coherent and national in scope, the centre and periphery grew increasingly indistinct and intertwined. The factions of Northamptonshire and the policies of Whitehall were now tangled up in a truly national political debate made vocal in the Short Parliament.[84] This political context made impressment all the more difficult, especially on the eve of the Second Bishops' War.

In the spring of 1640, the Lord Mayor of London informed Secretary Vane about the City's progress in pressing its allotment of 200 men to reinforce Berwick garrison. On 3 March the King ordered Lord Mayor Henry Garway and the Common Council to conscript 'able and serviceable men' from the wards.[85] Three days later, the Privy Council reminded the Lord Mayor and Aldermen that 'above all things there must be an especiall care had in the choice of the men that they be of able bodies of yeares meet for this imployment, and well-clothed, but none of the said

For a work which conflicts with the interpretation set forth here, see P. R. Seddon, 'The Nottinghamshire Elections for the Short Parliament of 1640', Transactions of the Thoroton Society of Nottinghamshire, 80 (for 1976, published 1977), pp. 63–8.

[81] Bodleian Library, Bankes MS. 42/55, Privy Council notes by Secretary Edward Nicholas.

[82] PRO, SP 16/40/25; Cope and Coates (eds.), *Proceedings of the Short Parliament*, pp. 17, 275; Maltby (ed.) *Aston's Diary*, p. 10.

[83] Ibid., pp. 5, 148. Both were Committees of the Whole House.

[84] For further evidence of the politicization of Northamptonshire, see A. N. Groome, 'Higham Ferrers Elections in 1640. A Midland Market town on the Eve of Civil War', *Northamptonshire Past and Present*, 2, no. 5, (1958), pp. 243–51.

[85] Corporation of London Records Office, *Journal of the Court of Common Council*, XXXIX, f. 61v, the King to the Common Council, 3 March 1640.

men are to be taken out of the trained bands'.[86] In Garway's letter to Vane, written in early April, he states quite frankly that the aldermen had issued a precept 'to take upp all Idle persons that weare to bee found in Tavernes Innes and Alehouses' and that one hundred such fellows had been apprehended and locked up in Bridewell since 'Midnight last'.[87]

One might wonder if drinking establishments were the logical place to find the 'able and serviceable' men the Crown demanded.[88] It is clear that taverns and public houses harboured a great many adult males, so it was the most convenient recruiting ground, in London at least. The aldermen may not have wished to advertise their penchant for scouring alehouses for soldiers; a copy of Garway's order of 23 March 1640, instructing the aldermen to press 200 men, and written on a single sheet, apparently for the perusal of the Privy Council, directs the aldermen to find able men within their wards.[89] The entry of the same date that is enrolled in the journals of the Court of Common Council contains additional information not included in the copy: the aldermen were advised to press able men, well-apparelled for the season, 'especially hostlers Tapsters Chamberlins and such like', who were to be sent off to Bridewell. Not only could the parish be rid of idle men who frequented pubs, but some form of control over illegal or disorderly alehouses might be exercised.[90]

Taverns also served as a refuge for deserters. On 11 April, Garway notified the aldermen that the 'greatest parte' of the pressed soldiers 'have of late escaped and run away by reason of the negligent government of some Officers to whose care they were committed. Theis are in his Majestys name streightly to make a carefull and dilligent search in all and every Innes Allehouses victualinghouses and other houses and places within your ward that you shall suspect to harbour any of the said prestmen', and to hold the re-captured men at Bridewell.[91] It was no simple matter to detain several hundred men in an urban area such as London, where an escaped

---

[86] Corporation of London Records Office, *Journal of the Court of Common Council*, XXXIX, f. 63, Privy Council to Lord Mayor and aldermen, 22 March 1640.

[87] PRO, SP 16/450/26, Lord Mayor Garway to Secretary Vane, 4 April 1640(?).

[88] Hale on the 'society of soldiers' in *War and Society in Renaissance Europe*, pp. 127–78.

[89] PRO, SP 16/448/70, order of the Common Council of London sitting in special session, 23 March 1640.

[90] Corporation of London Records Office, *Journal of the Court of Common Council*, XXXIX, f. 68v, Lord Mayor Garway's instructions to the aldermen, 23 March 1640. The quotas for each ward follow (original spelling): Broadstreete 5 (men), Langborne 6, Billingsgate 8, Coleman-streete 5, Cordwainer 6, Cripplegate within and without 15, Chapel 8, Tower 10, Hintney 6, Breadstreete 6, Faringdon within 15, Faringdon without 25, Queenhith 7, Limestreete 2, Cornhill 6, Walbrooke 5, Aldersgate 8, Candlewicke 5, Bridge 6, Dowgate 6, Bassieshawe 2, Algate (blank), Bishopsgate 15, Castlebaynard 9, Portseaken 10.

[91] Corporation of London Records Office, *Journal of the Court of Common Council*, XXXIX, f. 70v, Lord Mayor Garway to the aldermen, 11 April 1640.

soldier might hide in the populous city. For this reason, the aldermen utilized Bridewell prison as a 'holding area' until the men were delivered to the Crown authorities at Tower wharf. Another obvious advantage of keeping the conscripts at Bridewell was the presence of imprisoned vagrants and sturdy rogues. It was common practice to search out masterless men and incarcerate them in Bridewell and Newgate. With conscripts held in prison it was relatively easy to include rogues and thieves in the levy if the need arose to obtain more soldiers. Fewer prisoners would crowd the filthy gaol. The Elizabethan tradition of pressing London criminals quickly revived.

In May 1638, Thomas Gardiner, the Recorder of London, had responded to the request of Secretary Windebank to transport convicted criminals then imprisoned in Newgate for military service in Colonel Tresham's forces in Flanders. He recommended the following offenders: Jonathan Johnson and William Spilstead, who had broken into the home of Sir John Jacob and purloined 'dyvers and parcells of plate'; Edmund Fordham, a convicted horse-thief; Daniel Baldsin, who was, in American parlance, a 'cattle-rustler'; Samuell Sparrowtt, indicted for stealing a pewter pot valued at 18s and some sugar; Islip Adson, convicted of breaking and entering with intent to steal; Susan Austin, a female horse-thief; and Raphe Combey and Steward Baker, who had stolen sheep.[92] London's burgeoning population and social problems ensured that riff-raff were always available for the press.

THE SUBSTITUTION CLAUSE

The local community had no ready source of potential recruits such as the Londoners had in Newgate. In the local context, impressment could be a very personal process. Competition to avoid the press could be quite keen, favours could be solicited and special consideration sought. Men tried to escape the net through bribery. During the Bishops' Wars, the bribery of conductors and captains plagued the recruitment of a royal army as it had in the 1620s. Trained men as well as conscripts busied themselves with hiring substitutes which legitimized negotiation over candidacy for forced service. A report compiled during the summer of 1640 confirms the bribery of conductors for the release of soldiers in Warwickshire, Essex, Berkshire, the Isle of Ely, Norfolk, Cambridge, Kent, and Leicestershire. There were additional examples from other locations, but only a portion of the report

---

[92] PRO, SP 16/389/33, Gardiner to Windebank, 3 May 1638. Susan Austin was probably transported, but not to a military unit. See Parker, *Military Revolution*, p. 175, note 20.

survives.[93] For example, Lincolnshire had seen its share of corruption during the preparations for the First Bishops' War. Attorney General Bankes inquired personally into the matter, demanding letters of the Council and lieutenants investigating 'the abuses of divers officers that tooke money to discharge souldiers'.[94] Charges of misconduct in the administration of military preparations were convenient ammunition in the skirmishes among the gentry. George Smith of Boston, a gentleman who had been appointed 'Prestmaster', initiated a suit in the Civil Law Court of Chivalry against a merchant, John Camacke, who had referred to Smith as 'a bribery fellow'.[95] Constable Henry Browne of Grantham, however, found the hiring of substitutes an unprofitable business. While conducting the men of his locality to Great Coates, where they were to be handed over to the captains, Browne was made aware that many of the soldiers desired to purchase substitutes. Like their compatriots from Norfolk, they wanted no part in Hamilton's expedition. Because of their 'great families and charge at home' they asked Browne to approach Captain Hammond and arrange for the hiring of substitutes, to which Hammond agreed, provided that the Lincolnshire men came up with sufficient funds. Allegedly, Hammond agreed to locate the replacements, and collected money from the soldiers and Constable Browne who had lent certain sums to his men.

Brown's predicament illustrates the difficult situation of the constabulary, caught between service to the Crown and a neighbourly concern for the men he was conducting. Months after the episode, several soldiers still had not reimbursed Browne. Whatever monies he had received had been given to the Captain. His intentions had not been corrupt; he protested that he was 'not one peny in purse a gainer' by the transactions. Browne 'had done his neighbours good service and had not transgressed the lawe'.[96] Yet the King still did not get the good soldiers he needed. By 1640, resistance to forced service caused a major tactical error due to the unreliability of pressed soldiers.

The poor quality of recruits for the 1640 levy caused serious problems for Astley and Conway, who struggled with logistical and financial problems that were deleterious enough in their own right. In July, Conway's

---

[93] PRO, SP 16/461/102, undated, probably late summer 1640. The first page is missing. References indicate that at least six pages made up this report. Its author and purpose are unknown.

[94] PRO, SP 16/432/65, Bankes to the clerk of the council, 16 November 1639; see also SP 16/427/71, Lincs deputy lieutenants to the council, 20 August 1639.

[95] G. D. Squibb (ed.), *Reports of Heraldic Cases in the Court of Chivalry, 1623–1732*, printed by the Harleian Society (London, 1956), p. 49, citing 'Cur. Mil., Boxes 5/108, 109', 5 July 1640, 'a cause of scandalous words provocative of a duel'.

[96] PRO, SP 16/445/8, affidavit of Henry Browne, 11 February 1640. See also PRO, E 403/2813, f. 29 (in Star Chamber).

forces were far below strength, lacked money for wages and provisions, and were dangerously uninformed of the whereabouts of the Covenanter army. He did not expect immediate assistance from Sir Jacob Astley's infantry at Selby, for his forces also were smaller than anticipated and drastically short of cash. Nor could Conway rely on the trained bands of Yorkshire. As was noted above, the Yorkshire gentry were largely disaffected with Charles's new war and the royal army gathering within their county. A pair of colonels had been dismissed, due to their lack of enthusiasm for the *bellum episcopale*, leaving only two to command the militia. In addition to a dearth of officers, many of the weapons of the militiamen had been lost in the First Bishops' War and not replaced. Trained soldiers had apparently fled, too, so that new, untrained men had been taken into the ranks.[97] Conway summed up his predicament:

I am teaching Cart-horses to manage, and making men that fitt for Bedlam and Bridewell, to keepe the ten Commandements; soe that Generall Lesley and I keepe two schooles, he hath scholers that professe to serve God, and he is instructing them how they may safely doe injury and all impiety. Mine to the uttermost of their power never kept any Law either of God or the King.[98]

By 1640, even those pious Covenanters resorted to conscripting riff-raff. 'Adulterers, furnicators, thieves, murderers, drunkards [and] sabbath breakers' were designated by the parish minister in appropriately Calvinist fashion and organized into two regiments for the Second Bishops' War.[99]

As for defending Newcastle, Conway was again hampered by inadequate funds, as well as by a lack of cooperation from the inhabitants of Northumberland and Durham, especially the residents of Newcastle-upon-Tyne.[100] The fortifications and defences prepared for the campaign of 1639 had hardly been extensive.[101] Conway met with the oligarchy of the town to discuss a defensive posture. Because Newcastle lacked a formidable garrison, Conway suggested that a number of able-bodied men be armed at royal expense. So great was the Newcastle town-leaders' mistrust of the King's military exactions that they balked at Conway's suggestion. They feared that the creation of such a force would establish a precedent for a municipal militia, which might have to be maintained indefinitely. There were other disquieting possibilities. If the General of Horse issued royal

[97] PRO, SP 16/463/103, Osborne to Conway, 14 August 1640; David Dalrymple (ed.) *Memorials and Letters relating to the History of Britain in the Reign of Charles I* (Glasgow, 1766), pp. 93–4; Cliffe, *The Yorkshire Gentry*, p. 320.

[98] PRO, SP 16/455/38, 28 May 1640.

[99] Parker, *Military Revolution*, pp. 52, 177, citing S. Reid, *Scots Armies of the Civil War 1639–1651* (Leigh-on-Sea, Essex, 1982), p. 12.

[100] R. Howell, Jr., *Newcastle Upon Tyne and the Puritan Revolution: A Study of the Civil War in North England* (Oxford, 1967), p. 120, no. 2.

[101] PRO, MPF 287, Sir Jacob Astley's map of Newcastle's defences, 1639.

weapons to the Newcastle men, could they then be regarded as part of the King's army? The Lord General was also the Lord Lieutenant of Northumberland; could the lieutenancy summon citizens to the borders to perform a defence of the country, which might ultimately become an invasion of Scotland, or a stalemate on the borders? The reluctance of the Newcastle men stemmed from their uncertainty about their military obligation and the Crown's designs. It is revealing, however, that initially the civic leaders imagined they had more to fear from Charles's schemes than the guns of the Covenanters. Ultimately, Conway convinced them to raise some musketeers and pikemen for the sake of their own defence.

Astley and Conway could not gather sufficient military support from Yorkshire and Newcastle. The entire weight of the military enterprise fell upon the shoulders of the impressed soldiers of summer 1640. The 'seasoned' militia were not as numerous as had been hoped. Conway's reports make clear the unreliability of these raw levies. Their lack of training, their surliness over pay, and the absence of sufficient officers hamstrung the war effort. When the first blow fell, at Newburn Ford, it was a group of 'west country clownes', part of Lunsford's contingent of rowdy Somersetshire men, that sustained it. The poor quality of infantry raised by the 1640 press was a major factor in the defeat at the Tyne.

In Scotland, Alexander Leslie possessed no 'perfect militia'. The dichotomy of trained bands and raw levies did not exist there. The absence of a national system of defence placed the Covenanters at a distinct disadvantage. One can understand Charles's optimism, that a nucleus of 'perfect' militiamen, reinforced by raw levies of horse and foot, and supplemented by volunteers, could scatter the untrained tenants of rebellious lairds. However, the self-reliance that characterized the Scottish nobility under the early Stuarts enabled the Covenanter lairds and gentlemen to build, within presbytery and parish, a national military system in a matter of months. Citizens mustered in the parishes because the orders of the central government at Edinburgh emanated in orderly fashion through the levels of authority linked by committees. By virtue of administration and mentality, the Scots created a national army from private means.[102]

Able men aged between sixteen and sixty faced military service, as was the case for their counterparts in England. But military obligation was another facet of the broad jurisdiction of the landed aristocracy, and often tenants' highest allegiance was paid to their landlord rather than to the state. Since some nobles rejected the Covenant, an alternative form of national military service, based upon the civil and religious administration of the realm, supplemented traditional service based on land tenure,

[102] Furgol, 'Scotland Turned Sweden', p. 138.

though the latter persisted, as when Hamilton recruited his tenants to serve the King in 1639.[103] Now Scotsmen would be asked to defend themselves, their families, and God's church: 'defence of thair religioun lyves and all is derrest'.[104] They did not, however, tarry in the locality until the English appeared at the parish church, but prepared themselves for border service. Their logistical problem resembled that facing Charles: local men had to be coerced into leaving their community to defend the borders. The contrasts in manipulation, persuasion and coercion illuminate the nature of the armies of the Bishops' Wars.

The Covenanters began by commanding rolls of all the able-bodied in each parish, compiled by not only a local commissioner (whose function resembled an amalgam of an English justice of the peace and a deputy lieutenant) but the parish minister as well. Church and state joined to assemble an accurate list of all men capable of defending kirk and country. As they did not have to deal with the English distinctions between trained and untrained, armed and unarmed, they settled upon a single criterion – those physically suited for combat would be levied. The community itself, coerced by the firm hand of the Covenanters, demanded that duty be done. Those who were thought fit to go must not refuse, for they should be chosen 'of the most personable men and that may be best spaired'.[105] After readying themselves, the committee of war would send in veterans to train and drill them.[106] Weapons would be provided from the community, purchased if need be by gentleman and landlords. The lairds and gentlemen of the locality were to take the lead in gathering arms and designating the men. The committee in Edinburgh would send word when they were needed at the borders.[107] The committees (of presbytery or shire) examined the rolls, intermediating between Edinburgh and the parish and enforcing policy closer to the community. For example, the committee at Perth disapproved the returns from the parishes of Kenmore and Killin as incomplete. The landlords (heritors) and their household servants were to be listed first, then the respective tenants enrolled. No 'worthie' man was to be deleted.[108]

---

[103] SRO, GD 406/M1/95/7–10.
[104] SRO, GD 112/39/774.
[105] NLS, Crawford MS. 14/7/43, raising of foot in Fife, *circa* 19 March 1639. For examples of these rolls see Crawford MS. 14/3/48, parish of Kilconquhar 1639, 383 men capable of bearing arms, 174 as musketeers, 154 as pikemen, and 14/3/49, booklet for parish of Kilconquhar 1639.
[106] SRO, GD 16/52/19.
[107] See for example the letters to Sir Colin Campbell, SRO, GD 112/39/772 and 774, where he was to help equip and organize men between sixteen and sixty, in anticipation of their summoning to the Borders. If local weapons could not be found, they were supplied in Edinburgh. GD 112/43/1/6/30, article 5.
[108] SRO, GD 112/39/736.

An incomplete roll was inequitable, for since the entire community was threatened, all should rally to its support.

The Covenanters succeeded in creating institutions and procedures for impressment, whereas the Crown could not bring in the quality of men desired. One recalls the Scottish remark that a smaller force of Covenanters could rout the English because the former were willing to fight, being 'volunteires'.[109] Volunteers or not, the Scots coerced men to serve. Could Charles have hoped to have won the Bishops' Wars with the type of soldiers he possessed? A 'balanced' army, with personal units unified by loyalty to a gentleman or noblemen most certainly could have spearheaded a major force where 'perfect' militiamen provided expertise and leadership to a roughly equal number of raw men, and should have stood up against Covenanting armies similarly composed.[110]

In February 1639, while the English nobility prepared to raise soldiers from their tenants and servants and captains inspected the trained bands of the northern counties, the Privy Council ordered the selection of militiamen from midland and southern shires for the Scottish expedition. Exempted from county military contributions were the most substantial members of society. The clergy and nobility possessed their own unique relationship with the Crown, and their contribution to military service was independent of the lieutenancy. Wealthy gentry were rated to supply

---

[109] PRO, SP 16/448/18 I, news from Edinburgh gathered by William Roberts, secretary to Lord Ettrick, 17 March 1640. Volunteers, of course, lacked discipline, as remarked Lieutenant Colonel William Johnstone, who was trying to rally royal forces in Aberdeen. He asked for trained (presumably English) soldiers who would obey his commands. See SRO, GD 406/1/859, to Hamilton, 10 June 1639.

[110] See for example the apparently uncoordinated groups sent to the front armed with archaic weapons, as in SRO, GD 112/43/1/6/32, Breadalbane muniments, 7 June 1639. Edward Furgol analyses how weak in fact were the Scots on the eve of the Bishops' Wars in 'Scotland Turned Sweden', pp. 134–7. Analysis of the Scottish mobilizations of 1639 and 1640 lies beyond the scope of this book. But one cannot help but be impressed with how the Covenanters raised troops with a less-centralized system of recruitment than that of the Crown (given that the Scottish localities were very much part of the decision-making process) and managed to arm themselves without a national arsenal. On the raising of forces see for example SRO, Breadalbane muniments, GD 112/40/2/2/86; 88; 96. On the scarcity, irregularity, and agedness of Scottish weapons, see SRO, GD 406/1/755, f. 3, where Huntly describes to Hamilton the 'great defect of defensive armes amongst the Gentrye', 17 February 1639. This weakness plagued the King's supporters as much as the Covenanters and may have helped discourage the formation of a royal party in Scotland, for who could fight for the King without weapons? See also GD 112/40/2/2/ 95 (arrows with 'forked heads'); 119 (manufacture of iron bullets); 74 (targets). See also the receipt of the motley assortment of arms in GD 112/43/1/7/50, gathered from private hands. That the Scots were inferior in equipment and numbers of men was generally true from the early Middle Ages to Culloden. The difference in 1639 and 1640 is that they got what they needed and deployed themselves in the right places.

money, armour, and horses, and their servants sometimes served in the trained bands.[111] But for the lesser tradesmen, craftsmen, artisans, agricultural workers, unskilled labourers, the alternatives were either serving in the trained bands with their more affluent neighbours, or being considered untrained but able-bodied men available for the press. England's able-bodied males between the ages of sixteen and sixty were classified as either potential conscripts or militiamen. The advantage of serving in the militia was the Crown's policy of exempting trained-band soldiers from impressment.[112] The social inequity is clear: the yeoman, tradesman, and skilled craftsman might save face *and* avoid service for a few shillings but woe unto the poor, particularly deserters. Such a system of conscription and substitution encouraged tensions between those degrees of people subject to military service.[113]

On 18 February the Lords Lieutenant received instructions to select able bodied, trained soldiers complete with arms from their jurisdictions. For example, the Earl of Suffolk was to choose 400 Cambridgeshire militiamen as well as 1,500 from Suffolk and 700 from Dorsetshire.[114] These soldiers, already armed and possessing some familiarity with their weapons, would form an experienced nucleus around which the conscripts and 'retainers' of the nobility would rally. The county communities faced a dual drain on their manpower for levies of untrained men coincided with the selection of trained-band soldiers. The call-up fell fairly evenly, at least in design, upon the realm, for this was a 'national' war. While the military forces of the thirteen shires most proximate to the borders remained intact, the others would help to provide the royal expeditionary force, which it was hoped would number 24,000 foot and 6,000 horse when finally mustered at York. A goodly number of men were expected from the lords, the exact number being unknown for the nobles' returns were still being tallied in February 1639.[115] Another 6,000 infantry and 1,000 horse would be pressed outright, while a further undetermined number would be taken out of the trained bands: 'that the Foot bee all taken out of the Trayned Bands of every County by quall proporcons and numbers, but where any Trayned Man shall bring an able person to serve in his place it shalbee left to the discrecon of the Lord Lieutenant and deputy lieutenants to accept of him'.[116] The

---

[111] Rating is explored in Hassell-Smith, 'Militia Rates and Militia Statutes', pp. 93–110.
[112] See Fletcher regarding the social status of the militia in *Reform in the Provinces*, pp. 294, 298.
[113] Fissel, '*Bellum Episcopale*', pp. 390–1.
[114] BL, Harleian MS. 4104, ff. 32, 36v–38, 39, 40–40v, Cambridgeshire militia papers. The King later trimmed the Cambridgeshire contingent to 300 men. See also University of Minnesota Library, Phillipps MS. 3863, f. 90v and BL, Add. MS. 39,245, f. 178.
[115] See p. 158.
[116] PRO, SP 16/396, ff. 105–6, the King to Arundel, 9 February 1639.

lords lieutenant might accomplish this by designating entire companies for Scottish service or selecting men from various companies.[117] The great flaw in these plans was the substitution clause, the loophole by which the selected militiamen could gain exemption quite legally, thereby providing opportunities for corruption and favouritism while debasing the perfect militia. For example, the City of London received its instructions:

where any trayned Souldier desirous to stay at home shall offer another as able to serve with his Armes in his place in this Service Wee leave it to you in such case to enterteine and list the person offered by such trayned man soe he be able and not otherwise. And likewise where you shall finde any belonging to the trayned bands that is unable or unfit by reason of his Chardge or otherwise to be sent in this ymployment Wee require and authorize you to cause some other sufficient man of that City (fitter to be spared) to be ymployed ymprested and armed at the charge of the partie soe excused and Listed to serve in his Roome The bringing and conducting the said three thousand men to the said Rendezvous is to be performed by some persons fit for Conduct as you shall thinke good.[118]

The Suffolk lieutenants were instructed,

where any Trained Soldiers desirouse to Stay at home shall offer another as able to Serve with his Armes in his place in this Service wee leave it to you or your Deputy Lieutenants in such Case to Entertane and List the person offred by such Trained Man soe as he be able and not otherwise. And Likewise wher you or your Deputy Lieutenants shall find any of the Trained Bands that is unable or unfitt by reason of his Chardge or otherwise to be sent in this imployment we require and authorize you to cause Some other Sufficient Man of that County (fitter to be Spared) to be impressed and armed at the Chardge of the partie soe excused and Listed in his Roome The bringing and conducting the said Man to the said Rendezvous is to be performed by some such persons fitt for to Conduct as you shal thinck good to appointe to take Charge therof who are to deliver the Said Soldiers over upon Muster.

The deputy lieutenants passed on the orders to the captains:

And if any traned Souldier desirous to stay at home being unable in boddy or unfitt by reason of their chardge for this imployment shall offer unto you some other sufficient man (of the same County) to be impressed and armed at his chardge, that then you excuse the trained Souldier and list the person soe offered unto you, if you thinke him *evry* waies able and sufficient in his roome. This business is in it Self soe weightie, as we doubt not, but your extraordinary care and diligence wilbe soe wateing (?) as when ever his Majestie Shall comaund these Souldiers, they shalbe in such readynes as noe blowe may fall either on you or us.[119]

---

117 PRO, SP 16/396, f. 61, 17 January 1639.
118 Corporation of London Records Office, *Journal of the Court of Common Council*, XXXVIII, ff. 217–217v.
119 BL, Add. MS. 39,245, ff. 174v/386, 18 February 1639. Also for Suffolk, see University of Minnesota Library, Phillipps Ms. 3863, ff. 90–2.

Militia service by proxy had been practised early in the development of the trained bands. Elizabethan men of substance had excused themselves from martial rigour while maintaining their militia eligibility by sending sons, tenants, or friends in their stead. In the case of influential husbandmen, substitutions aided the bringing in of the harvest. In autumn 1588 farmers drilled instead of toiling in the fields, with 'disastrous' results.[120] The preservation of agriculture encouraged substitution, giving it an economic as well as a social justification.

The substitution clause also rested upon the assumption that not every Englishman was suited for combat. Personal military service could be avoided honourably by a contribution to the Crown's war effort. If a man lacked strength or spirit, it was better for him to supply his King with a reliable recruit. Thomas Hobbes recognized this in *Leviathan* when he wrote that although a sovereign was justified in executing those who refused his command to go to war, still the subject 'may nevertheless in many cases refuse, without injustice – as when he substitutes a sufficient soldier in his place, for in this case, he deserts not the service of the commonwealth'. Thus the pacific tradesman might fulfill the social contract, to Hobbes's satisfaction at least, by hiring a burly peasant to shoulder his pike. For the poor conscript, however, no honourable avenue of escape existed, for 'he that enrolls himself a soldier, or takes impressed money, takes away the excuse of timorous nature, and is obliged not only to go to the battle but also not to run from it'.[121] Whom did that soldier serve? Hobbes specified 'the commonwealth', whereas a man like Clarendon would have said 'his sovereign'. As we have seen, the militia served both community and monarch, which on occasion caused tension between centre and periphery.

From November 1638 to March 1639, all English and Welsh trained bands received orders to muster and drill. Obviously, if the preparation of the militia was imperative enough for midwinter musterings, the release of those trained soldiers in the spring made little sense. By allowing militiamen to hire untrained substitutes, the council undermined efforts to perfect the trained bands. The substitution clause was self-defeating. 'If the King intended that his army should be an expert fighting force, it was a sad commentary on his "perfect militia" that he considered a strong-backed yokel the equal of a trained band soldier'.[122] The authorization of substitutes was designed therefore to appease angry militiamen and their families.

---

[120] Boynton, *Elizabethan Militia*, p. 110.
[121] Thomas Hobbes, *Leviathan*, (ed.) H. Schneider (Indianapolis, 1958), part II, chapter 21, 'Of the Liberty of Subjects.'
[122] Barnes, *Somerset 1625–1640*, p. 272.

One can trace the genesis of the substitution clause from the council chamber, through the lieutenancy, to the county communities themselves. The Council of War had anticipated a lukewarm response to the Crown's military preparations in some quarters. Memories of the campaigns of the 1620s, with their extensive presses and military charges, coupled with a decade of resentment towards the Personal Rule, created the hostile climate in which the King mounted a war against the Covenanters. The council's awareness of the potential unpopularity of the war prompted the suggestion that the King abolish certain fines, monopolies and commissions in an effort to curry favour with the public.[123] The substitution clause was fashioned for the same reason. As we have seen, most citizens of Caroline England believed that the militia was *not* an expeditionary force. Nor did the statutory basis of the rates for the financing of the trained bands rest upon very solid ground.[124] Since utilization of the shire military depended upon goodwill and cooperation from the more substantial members of the community, it was necessary that a conciliatory clause excuse those adamant about militia service against Scotland, giving captains and deputy lieutenants the latitude to avoid outright refusals.[125]

The substitution clause compounded the inherent weaknesses of the Stuart military system, the amateurishness that stemmed from irregular drill, untrustworthy officers, and the poor quality of arms. The admission of untrained substitutes into the ranks of the selected trained bands further diluted skill and training. The chronic problems of rusted armour, shortened pikes, and muskets of varying bore remained, and perhaps became worse, as those rated with supplying arms were quite reluctant to provide costly new weapons to the bumpkins who replaced the trained militiamen.

The Stuart military system, both central government and localities agreed, was to be two-tiered. Militiamen were to 'bee oft the Gentry, freholders, good farmers or ther sonnes that are like to bee resident in the country and that the meaner sort oft people and servants' left as fodder for the press.[126] Substantial members of society deserved the distinction of toting weapons; indeed proper breeding somehow inculcated martial prowess. The obverse revealed a fear of poor and disorderly persons organizing and becoming skilled in the use of arms. Weapons cost money, and the comparatively affluent could afford to buy and maintain them and devote several days to training. Those who employed others (clothiers),

123 See pp. 68–70.
124 Hassell-Smith, 'Militia Rates and Militia Statutes', pp.93–110.
125 For background on this dilemma during the 1620s, see Barnes, 'Deputies not Principals, Lieutenants not Captains', pp. 58–83, and Stater, 'War and the Structure of Politics', pp. 87–106.
126 Bodleian Library, Tanner MS. CLXXVII, f. 5, Norfolk deputy lieutenants to Captain Sir John Holland, 5 November 1628.

those that gathered the harvest and raised animals (husbandmen and yeomen) should remain within their community while the marginally employed, semi-skilled, strangers, newcomers, and rogues were intended to fill the ranks of the expeditionary forces. Between 1585 and 1602, the central government impressed at least 105,810 English and Welshmen for overseas service. Fifty-thousand Englishmen were pressed during the 1620s, leaving bitter memories and fear of impressment amongst the common people.[127] Levies for Mansfeld's doomed expedition of 1624 were to 'bee of able Bodies and yeres ... But none of them taken out of the trayned Bands'.[128] T. G. Barnes observes that in Somerset the 'activities of the constables in pressing men for the Rhé expedition flooded the trained bands with men who took refuge in the local company to avoid the pressmen'. With the admission of these 'lower orders' into the militia, much ill-feeling resulted in 1639 when Charles 'selected' members of the trained bands for service upon the borders. Many militiamen felt betrayed. As trained-band soldiers, they should have remained in the community, pursuing their trades and supporting their families.[129]

Henry VIII, when raising men for France in 1544, did not distinguish conscript from militiaman. He compelled the lords and gentlemen of the locality to make the selection.[130] Elizabeth's inconsistent utilization of the trained bands in the 1590s twisted the role of the militia. She wrenched units out of the trained bands, placed them under 'outsider' captains and embarked them to distant battlefields. The political and financial drawbacks of Elizabeth's methods (in that loyal subjects were aggrieved and productive members of the community removed from the economy) prompted the mitigation of this policy, so that later presses, as into Brittany, spared the militia.[131] Charles, too, relented.

Local authorities may have had latitude in choosing or exempting trained-band members (or 'unarmed militia'), as in the 1602 Irish press of 100 foot from Northamptonshire. The Queen ordered the commissioners to muster and levy sufficient men, but, as the council's instructions make no mention of militiamen, the sturdy fellows who received coat-and-conduct money and had their names entered on 'Rolls tripartite Indented'

---

[127] Based on tables in Cruickshank, *Elizabeth's Army*, p. 290. Stearns, 'Conscription and English Society', p. 5.

[128] University of Minnesota Library, Phillipps MS. 3836, f. 1v, the Privy Council to the Earl of Suffolk, 31 October 1624. See f. 2v for a militia exemption clause.

[129] Barnes, *Somerset 1625–1640*, p. 250. Stone, *The Crisis of the Aristocracy*, p. 100. C. Russell, *The Crisis of Parliaments: English History 1509–1660* (Oxford, 1971), p. 31 and Wernham, *After the Armada*, pp. 17, 20, 281, 381, 417, 463, in which cases of Elizabethan use of the militia for overseas duty are cited.

[130] See *Letters and Papers Henry VIII* (1544), 19, pt. 1, pp. 149–66.

[131] See for example Somerset RO, DD/PH 220, f. 13v.

were probably raw men, though they could have included militiamen.[132] Perhaps, since Northamptonshire was a landlocked county, the Crown did not feel anxiety in siphoning off a few trained soldiers. This was in direct contradiction of the practice under James of forbidding the pressing of trained men, though in 1624 the example comes from more vulnerable Suffolk.

The utilization of the trained bands was dictated by national considerations which ultimately grated against the geographically localized interests of the county communities. But local governors decided who qualified for trained-band service, and they manipulated the odds of an individual's being pressed or remaining within the community. Those who did the pressing, the deputy lieutenants, were assisted by those who kept the peace, the justices, so that a linkage between military obligation and social control existed in practice, if not explicitly in theory. Military service, they reckoned, should not rend the social fabric nor compromise the defence of the shire. Naturally, the interests of the local gentry took precedence over the Crown's needs and the destinies of the poorer sort. When influential members of the trained bands purchased a substitute to serve in their place the consequence was a degree of 'class tension', animosity towards the wealthier militiamen, and above all, the Crown, who had created this unjust state of affairs. The ironical notion that militia status somehow bestowed immunity from serious military service grew as the trained bands were increasingly exempted from expeditionary service under the early Stuarts. When the commotion in Scotland precipitated unexpectedly a massive 'defensive' campaign, many militiamen panicked to find a suitable substitute. In most cases a cash nexus determined the replacement. These ill-advised methods of raising troops not only failed to produce a satisfactory army, but alienated and angered all levels of society against Charles's Personal Rule and the war against Scotland.[133]

Another advantage in using the trained bands was that the perfect militia possessed its own weaponry.[134] While many resisted expeditionary service, militiamen were equally reluctant to loan their arms. The unwillingness of the trained bands either to loan their arms or to serve in the ranks confounded the central government. More than a week after the rendezvous at York had begun in 1639, the supposedly expert Kentish troops earmarked for the Hamilton expedition had not materialized. One of the officers came up to Drury Lane and called upon Secretary Winde-

---

132 Wake (ed.), *Montague Musters Book*, pp. 214–15.
133 See the Suffolk situation in Fissel, *'Bellum Episcopale'*, p. 246. Also, note Suffolk's cooperation in 1639 in SRO, GD 406/1/821.
134 Hamilton's men, especially substitutes, were examined at Yarmouth as to the condition of their weapons. PRO, WO 49/69, ff. 90v–93v.

bank in person. He complained that the soldiers and arms were 'utterly unserviceable'. Straightaway Windebank went down to Whitehall in search of the Lord Chamberlain, the Lord Lieutenant of Kent. Not finding him he located Northumberland, who as Lord Admiral advised a stern letter signed by the Lords Lieutenant, rebuking the deputy lieutenants. It was all Windebank could do. Ultimately the situation prompted the intervention of the King himself.[135] At a rendezvous on the eve of their departure for the north in 1639, a contingent of pressed troops refused to surrender the 2,000 weapons they had borrowed from the arsenal of the local militia. Rather than cross the shire boundary unarmed, they chased away the deputy lieutenants. Similar abuses plagued the lieutenants of East Anglia. If arms were to be entrusted to pressed men, the loaned weapons should not be the finest pieces in the country. The best should be kept by the militia for defence, for borrowed weapons were very often 'pawned' or 'spoyled'.[136] Consequently, the hired substitutes, who were no better than untrained, pressed soldiers, were often badly armed. Although one might pay as much as £15 to escape military service, countrymen rarely displayed liberality in purchasing arms for the unfortunates who went in their stead. Complaints about faulty weapons were more numerous than criticisms about the fitness of the men. One captain, disappointed with the quality of weapons presented, singled out a soldier and commended him for shouldering a fine musket, remarking that he wished all the firearms were as good. The musketeer replied that his master had purchased the gun in question because no cheaper one could be found. 'My master sought to have found a worse musket, hee could find none in all the towne, if hee could, I should have had it.' Some muskets lacked touch-holes, while others had touch-holes so large that a man might turn his thumb in one.[137] Certain pikes had so rotted that they crumbled when handled. Harcourt's men also found themselves equipped with old ship-muskets, too heavy for infantrymen, as well as old-fashioned body armour and pikes of unequal length.[138]

The Marquis of Hamilton's expedition suffered most from the substitution clause. Gathered from East Anglia, the amphibious force was bolstered by trained soldiers because they might encounter immediate

---

[135] They were reluctant for good reasons. Suffolk's arms were returned greatly damaged and Cambridgeshire's pile seems to have disappeared. SRO, GD 406/1/868, 29 July 1639. On the men, see GD 406/1/938. On Windebank's response to the Kentish defects, see his letter to Hamilton, GD 406/1/812, dated 9 April 1639. The King's response is Bodleian Library, Clarendon SP, XVI, ff. 68–68v.

[136] Bristol RO, Ashton Court Collection, Smyth MS. 36074 (56), f. 1, notes by Thomas Smyth (?).

[137] PRO, SP 16/417/110. Hamilton to Vane, 7 May 1639, see SRO, GD 406/1/1200; Gardiner (ed.), *Hamilton Papers*, pp. 78–80.

[138] PRO, SP 16/418/1, Harcourt to Windebank, 18 April 1639.

resistance from the Covenanters upon landing on the Scottish coast. When Hamilton's colonels inspected their troops they discovered that few, if any, of the soldiers were 'of the trained bands'. Reporting on the quality of the recruits at Yarmouth, Sir Simon Harcourt wrote: 'Neither are they the men of the old trained bands of the county, but almost all hyred, raw and inexpert in the use of their armes and consequently unfit.'[139] In Hamilton's own words, 'The greatest cause of these misfortunes as I conceave is in regard of that claus in the Counsailes letters, which gave libertie to the lord Lieutenant, when they found any just reason to spare a trained man if they should take some able man in his place.'[140] But the fault lay not with the Lord Lieutenant, or even the deputy lieutenants, but rather with the constables and the justices of the peace. The constabulary and justices did the picking. Upon receipt of a warrant from the deputy lieutenants, the constables were to pick out a set number of men from the militia. In 1639, they were in many cases simultaneously pressing raw men for the infantry destined for York. So it was an easy matter to press a few extra untrained fellows and, at the no doubt strident protests of the selected trained-band soldiers (who saw little difference between 'impressment' and 'selection'), substituted as was allowed in the letters of King and council. The government trusted that the constabulary and justices would, having the lieutenancy to oversee the matter, not employ the clause to the detriment of the King's service. Such faith was rewarded in Suffolk but disappointed in Kent and Essex for the most part.[141]

The Kentish men, not too keen on denuding coastal defences for a Scottish expedition, declined to give Hamilton the best of the trained soldiers and equipment. The men and arms were judged 'utterly unserviceable', yet the departure to York of the Lord Lieutenant, the Earl of Pembroke and Montgomery, made the direction of the deputy lieutenants rather difficult in trying to remedy the situation: 'Essex, Suffolk and Norfolk had a stronger sense of resentment about the exact militia than any other part of England. In the first place their burden was heavy: 13,495 foot soldiers and 950 horse in all in 1638.'[142]

That 'sense of resentment' in 1639 could still be overcome by a zealous

---

139 PRO, SP 16/417/72, Morton to Windebank; SP 16/418/1, Harcourt to Windebank, 18 April 1639.

140 SRO, GD 406/1/820, f. 2, Hamilton to Windebank, 19 April 1639, and GD 406/1/909, where he estimated that only 50 of the 1,000 Kentish soldiers ever held a musket, to Laud, 13 April 1639. See also GD 406/1/11/44, 19 April 1639.

141 See for example BL, Add. MS. 39,245, f. 179, warrant to chief constables from deputy lieutenants, 28 March 1639. Even though Suffolk acquitted itself well in 1639, the petty constables were warned during the preparations for the Second Bishops' War to find better men than they had in 1639: f.190, letter dated 10 April 1640.

142 Fletcher, *Reform in the Provinces*, pp. 301–2; Bodleian Library, Clarendon SP, XVI, ff. 68–68v.

lieutenancy. While Essex and Cambridgeshire turned out poor men, defective arms, with not a little contempt from the lieutenants, Suffolk in contrast cooperated, providing Colonel Byron with good men and weapons, with the deputy lieutenants discharging their duties with diligence.[143] The effectiveness rested upon the lieutenants, for the recalcitrant Cambridgeshire deputy lieutenants and their obedient Suffolk counterparts served under the same Lord Lieutenant, the Earl of Suffolk. The mixed reaction of the East Anglian shires demonstrated the crucial role of the high constables and deputy lieutenants in securing the cooperation of the localities.

The Essex and Suffolk lieutenancy books contain the council's instructions to investigate abuses; the deputy lieutenants were to 'finde out what monyes hath beene taken from any trayned men to free them and put others in theire Roome'.[144] The council reminded them that it was the King's special care and goodness that had allowed 'such trayned souldiours as should bee found unfitt or unable by reason of theire Charge or otherwise' to utilize the substitution clause. They deplored 'greate and intollerable exaccions taken for exemptinge of divers of the trayned men'.[145] The deputy lieutenants delegated the responsibility of selecting the men (hence posing the situation which led to substitution) to the captains, who as gentlemen of quality knew the soldiers personally.[146] 'Negotiations' regarding the release of soldiers could be entertained while the men were marching from their place of recruitment to the rendezvous point. In several instances, travellers upon the highway were seized to replace men who had bought their way out of the service.[147] It was more efficient, however, to solicit bribes before the march.

In Southampton during May 1639, one Captain Tucker almost systematically excused several able men for cash. Utilizing his 'Agents', Anthony Howard, Moses Bradley, and Anthoney Cleeter, Tucker collected tidy sums from reluctant soldiers: John Warner paid £3, William

---

[143] SRO, GD 406/1/821, Hamilton to Windebank, 23 April 1639; on the performance of the Suffolk deputy lieutenants, see University of Minnesota Library, Phillipps MS. 3863, ff. 85–122v and BL, Add MS. 39,245, ff. 170–179v.

[144] The preparations for Hamilton's campaign are easily traced because lieutenancy books for Essex, Suffolk, and Norfolk survive. The Essex lieutenancy book is preserved in the Bodleian Library (Firth MS. c.4); Suffolk in the British Library (Add MS. 39,245) and the University of Minnesota Library (Phillipps MS. 3863); Norfolk in the Bodleian Library (Tanner MS. CLXXVII), with a copy entered in the King's MS. 265 in the British Library. Lieutenancy books, actually letter books, consist of transcriptions of correspondence received from King, Council, and Lords Lieutenant usually arranged in chronological order. For Suffolk, see especially Phillipps MS. 3863, ff. 118–118v.

[145] Bodleian Library, Firth MS. c. 4, ff. 618–19.

[146] University of Minnesota Library, Phillipps MS. 3863, ff. 118–118v.

[147] Note that Captain Parker, discussed pp. 258–60 below, recruited for Hamilton's expedition.

Glaspoole 20s, John Cozens 20s, John Coale £3, Ralph Hide 20s, and Robert Gammett 10s, amongst others.[148] Evidence regarding bribes received for the release of conscripts and militiamen is fairly extensive because the central government demanded of the counties information about such abuses.[149] Attorney General Bankes and the Council intended to make examples of such offenders at the Assizes or in the Star Chamber.[150]

In Norfolk, Captain Thomas Parker of Tunstead hundred demonstrated that entrepreneurial skills, combined with a few confederates, could earn a captain quite a few pounds. Captain Parker managed the spring muster and selection of trained-band soldiers as if it were a family business. His son, Thomas, acted as 'Ancient', a sort of senior clerk and administrator, while his other son, Gilbert, served as lieutenant. Several local citizens were employed as intermediaries between the Captain's family and those who proffered bribes. The Parkers used a variety of schemes to extort money from reluctant recruits. For example, when Robert Steward was selected for Hamilton's army, he approached one of Captain Parker's sons and informed him that he would consider the young man a friend if a substitute were accepted. This friendship had to be purchased, however. Steward would have to tender £5. Steward handed over 'Twenty Nobles' as payment to the substitute as well.[151]

Robert Everard found exemption a little more complicated. His son had been chosen from the trained bands and he wished the young man to stay at home. When Everard produced a substitute, Captain Parker refused to accept the fellow. Discouraged, Everard spoke with one William Debnam, who 'advised' him to contact Thomas Martins, the conductor. Martins agreed to see that a substitute was enrolled in place of Everard's son, but stipulated that £10 be given him 'for his paines'. Not entirely satisfied with £10, Martins also extorted thirty-five shillings from the young man's mother, along with the promise of an additional five shillings. The considerate Debnam received a gift of ten shillings, as well, from the grateful

---

[148] PRO, SP 16/442/43, Privy Council's response to the petition of Leonard Dare, 1 January 1640.

[149] PRO, SP 16/427/117, minutes taken by Sir William Becher of matters discussed in Council. Restitution was also contemplated. See item 5.

[150] See for example PRO, E 403/2813, f. 29, where Robert Johnson, a messenger of HM Chamber, delivered writs from the Star Chamber to Lincolnshire for the investigation of constable Henry Browne's alleged solicitation of bribes in exchange for substitutes. It is not clear if these were militia or pressed men who purchased exemption. For constable Browne see p. 242; for corresponding information regarding London, see the *Journal of the Court of Common Council* in the Corporation of London Records Office, XXXVIII, ff. 217–217v.

[151] PRO, SP 16/426/8 VI, the information of Robert Steward, 24 May 1639.

Mrs Everard. Having greased enough palms, the Everards' son escaped service.[152]

When examined by the deputy lieutenants, Debnam assumed the role of the helpful, concerned neighbour. He had aided Robert Bell in keeping his son-in-law from being sent off to fight the Covenanters. While the trained soldiers were being chosen on the Tuesday before Easter, Debnam was watching ('as a Spectator') when Bell approached him and asked if he would go to Captain Parker and request an exemption for Robert Tracy, his son-in-law. Bell offered forty shillings to anyone who could engineer Tracy's release. He handed Debnam twenty shillings, and said another twenty would be forthcoming. Supposedly, Debnam went to the captain, who referred him to Lieutenant Gilbert Parker, who then sent him on to the Ancient, young Thomas Parker. Debnam ultimately came to negotiate with the conductor, Martins, who took the twenty shillings, and agreed that the remainder would be accepted when Tracy was discharged. Apparently, the young man harboured doubts about the arrangement, for he sent Debnam back to Captain Parker to inquire if his release was imminent. Parker promised that Tracy would indeed be discharged. However, when Tracy reported to the conductor, he discovered that there was no order for his release. Tracy demanded that either the twenty shillings be returned or he be let go immediately. Martin countered by telling him that he must wait until they had arrived at Yarmouth. Tracy's fate is unknown.[153]

Debnam is a minor character when compared to Captain Parker's son Thomas, the company's 'Ancient', who handled most of the bribes and extortions personally. James Carr of Smallbrough testified that Thomas employed Richard Shalder to draft 'divers Bills and Bonds' to be utilized in the exemption process. Shalder admitted that he had witnessed some transactions, and had been paid forty-six shillings for drafting bills and 'coppyinge out of the Rolls'. When Woolston Steward desired to procure a substitute, Parker consented. However, 'sixe or seaven dayes' later, Thomas appeared at Steward's home in Beeston and informed him that the substitute had not been approved at Yarmouth. A warrant had been drafted, and Steward summoned to Yarmouth, with armour and weapons. Parker confided, however, that a gratuity of £5 might alter the opinion of the captains at Yarmouth. Steward gave Thomas £3 and assured him that more money would be delivered soon.[154]

In addition to William Debnam, the Parkers employed Edward Draper, who had collected the bribe from Robert Tracy and been instrumental in

---

[152] PRO, SP 16/426/8 I, the information of Robert Everard, 10 July 1639.

[153] PRO, SP 16/426/8 IX, the information of William Debnam, 5 July 1639.

[154] PRO, SP 16/426/8 II; SP 16/426/8 IV, the examination of Richard Shalder; SP 16/426/8 V, the information of Woolston Steward, 21 May 1639.

the release of Thomas Lacy. The elder Lacy, of Dillham, Norfolk, requested the discharge of his son on the grounds that the lad was his sole assist-
ant in farming. The substitution clause had been designed to alleviate such
problems. When young Parker was approached he told the father that his
son could not be spared for so meagre a sum as forty shillings. Lacy sought
out Draper, who had been the intermediary in gaining the discharge of
Robert Lacy. Draper arranged the transaction, informed Lacy that £5
would satisfy Parker and that he would handle the cash. Lacy then presented him with £4 and a promise of another twenty shillings, provided
that the substitute, Edmond Feen, would not require payment. Draper
pointed out that the gratuity given to Parker was separate and distinct from
the money provided for the substitute, and Lacy was compelled to pay an
additional £5, making his total expenditure £9.[155]

The Tuck brothers of Worstead likewise discovered that the Parkers
were a crafty lot. Robert Tuck was charged with providing a musket, while
his brother John served as a lighthorseman in the trained bands. John was
attending muster a few days before the militiamen were to be selected for
the Scottish campaign. During the exercising, he was thrown from his
horse and dislocated a shoulder. Although John Tuck was injured days
before the militiamen were selected, and in spite of the fact that Robert
Tuck was untrained, rated with supplying a musket only, Captain Parker
decided that Robert would be a fine choice for a soldier and ordered him to
serve in his brother's place, with his own arms and equipment. No doubt
surprised by this unexpected development, Robert Tuck was not at all
enthused at the prospect of soldiering and enlisted a substitute, a consideration 'he saw granted to other men'. Tuck struck a bargain for £5 with
Robert Jolly, a former trained-band soldier more experienced than himself.
On the day of the final choice of militiamen Robert was approached by
Henry Baspoole, who inquired what Tuck was prepared to do in order to
have Jolly accepted. Robert replied that he would give forty shillings to
Thomas Parker the Ancient. Baspoole retorted that a forty shilling gratuity
was 'as good as nothing', and that he must offer more. Tuck responded
that he would satisfy Parker. Three or four days later, Parker rode up to
Tuck's home in Worstead, but found him absent. After searching the
nearby town, Parker returned to Tuck's house and encountered him upon
the road. Parker announced that he had come for his money and expressed
surprise that Tuck had not yet delivered the sum. Tuck asked how much
would please him. Parker demanded £5. Tuck denied that he had promised
so large an amount. On the contrary, Parker countered, Mr Baspoole had
said that Tuck guaranteed a payment of £5. No, Tuck argued, he had

155 PRO, SP 16/426/8 VIII, the information of Edward Draper, 23 May 1639; SP 16/426/8
VII, the information of Thomas Lacy, 5 June 1639.

offered forty shillings, not £5. Parker refused the lesser amount, claiming that he was but a servant and could not reduce the charge (when asked to whom he was accountable, he specified his brother Gilbert, who, as captain, conducted the soldiers). Parker pointed out that if Tuck joined the army at Yarmouth, it would cost him a great deal. Exemption, too, was an expensive business. In the end, they settled for £4, Parker telling Tuck that for the sake of his landlord, he would not insist upon the additional twenty shillings.[156]

William Nuttal of Witton, a tailor who served in the trained bands, was reluctant to participate in Hamilton's expedition, as he needed to work in order to pay off the debt on his new dwelling. He asked Parker the Ancient if forty shillings would suffice in the hiring of a substitute. Parker replied that it 'would doe noe good'. After some negotiating, Nuttal escaped, but paid out more than £3.[157]

Receiving bribes in return for release was not confined to the eastern counties. In Devon, Degory Doole of North Petherwin claimed to have given £9 18s to one George Yeo, 'the Captain's Brother', who in turn paid the second son of Sir Lewis Poland (Pollard) so that he might escape military service. Doole added, however, that as far as he knew, the deputy lieutenants were unaware of the transaction. Thomas Jeffrey of Mankorhampton proffered a bribe of £6 to Lieutenant Hugh Pollard, in addition to hiring a substitute. The Privy Council also discovered that John Tellerd of Marlborough was 'guilty of Exaction of both the Sums viz. Eight Pounds and ten Shillings of Edward Stretch, and Fifteen Pounds of John Avent, both of the Parish of south-milton'. The Privy Council agreed to direct the Attorney General to prosecute the culprits in the Star Chamber.[158] Complaints about bribery, extortion, and abuse of the 'substitution clause' prompted the Privy Council to order the deputy lieutenants of all counties to investigate. On 9 May 1639, letters were issued, stating that:

his Majestie of his Special grace and goodnesse was pleased to give authority and liberty to you the Deputy Lieutenants to entertaine others in the place of such Trained Souldiers as should bee found unfit or unable ... under colour of that Clause ... there are great and intollerable exacions for exempting of divers of the Trained Men ... enquire and find out what Summ or summs of money or other consideracion hath been taken or required from any Traned Men.[159]

---

[156] PRO, SP 16/426/8 III, the information of Robert Tuck, 9 June 1639.

[157] PRO, SP 16/426/8 X, the information of William Nuttal, 19 July 1639. One of Thomas Parker's 'extortion letters' survives as SP 16/426/8 XI.

[158] PRO, PC 2/50, f. 684; PRO, SP 16/429/95, memo signed by the deputy lieutenants George Chudleigh and Thomas Drew, entitled 'The Complaints of the North devition taken at the Generall trayning this year 1639'; Rushworth, *Historical Collections*, vol. III, pp. 974–5; PRO, E 403/2813, f. 35v, writs delivered around Christmas.

[159] PRO, PC 2/50, f. 344, Privy Council register. These letters were sent round to Berkshire, Kent, Essex, Suffolk, Norfolk, Cambridge, Lincolnshire, Devonshire, and Southampton.

Young Thomas Parker's activities also came under government scrutiny. Parker was committed by the Norfolk authorities, and in November 1639, the council ordered the justices of the peace to examine him, and 'cause a proceeding to bee had in such a course as you shall iudge to bee most effectuall against the said Parker for his exemplary punishment.' Parker remained in custody throughout November.[160] In at least one county, deputy lieutenants were authorized to re-assemble regiments in the aftermath of the Pacification of Berwick and ask if any bribes had been solicited by the captains. If so, the complaint was to be put in writing and brought to the attention of the authorities.

When preparations for the Second Bishops' War were undertaken in spring 1640, the council made it clear that the abuses and corruption of the previous year would not be tolerated. The deputy lieutenants were told to make good choice out of the trained soldiers. Substitutions would be allowed, but only under certain conditions. The Privy Council empowered the lieutenancy to substitute able men for freeholders or unsuitable recruits at the lieutenants' discretion. But no money was to change hands, as had occurred in 1639. It is notable that the government continued to accept the substitution of untrained men for militiamen in 1640; bribes, corruption, and extortion were to be eliminated, not the substitution clause itself. Given the complaints of the Marquis of Hamilton, that of the 5,000 soldiers that made up his army only 200 possessed even the most rudimentary familiarity with musketry, such shameful lack of training forced Hamilton to pursue a very cautious strategy when his amphibious force reached the coast of Scotland. He dared not risk a raid or invasion when his men were raw and poorly armed. The fact that substitution was allowed after the financial and organizational failure of 1639 illustrates the Crown's predicament in soliciting soldiers, arms, horses, carts, and money in the 'country'. Military charges were almost uncollectable when resistance to exactions intensified. Local and national political sentiment demanded a concessionary policy regarding militia service, especially in 1640 when the issue had been raised in Parliament. Therefore, some loophole had to exist through which those freeholders, tradesmen, and yeomen who served as militiamen, might escape being sent out of the county.

As noted above, p. 255, note 144, the lieutenancy books for three of the counties, Essex, Suffolk, and Norfolk, are extant and thus give account of the receipt of the council's letters and the subsequent action upon them. See also PRO, SP 16/420/112.

160 PRO, PC 2/51, f. 24, 8 November 1639 and f. 95, 29 November 1639. Parker was ordered to remain in custody after his appearance earlier in the month. On 7 May 1640, a Thomas Parker was summoned before the council with a Francis Taylor, who had been a messenger. Whether or not it was the Thomas Parker of 1639 is unknown. PC 2/52, f. 474.

In 1640 a Devonshire fellow encountered the Norfolk pressed soldiers on the open road. The man was seized so that Captain Dibney, the conductor, might set free Edward Buds, a man of able body and 'a good drummer'. Buds paid the Captain twenty shillings, and the Devonshire man was handed twelve pence for press money, a lucrative transaction for Dibney. John August was journeying to London when Captain Levesy's group of Cambridgeshire men passed by. August was taken and pressed in place of a fellow who had offered the Captain £5 for his release.[161] The Bishops' Wars witnessed opportunities for corruption inherent in the late Tudor and early Stuart system of conscription. The veniality and lack of fair play that characterized the Personal Rule made these exactions all the more odious, especially considering the political and religious objections to the war. In spite of the council's pronouncements, charges of questionable exemptions, bribes and extortions plagued both wars. In Wales, the conductors pocketed 'good summes of money', and 'exposed the soldiers ... to begging and much misery'. In Essex during 1640, a Lieutenant Barnham offered exemption from his company at the price of £5, though bargains were struck for a lesser sum. Problems arose regarding exemption, pressing, and collection of coat-and-conduct money in virtually all the counties of England and Wales throughout 1640.[162]

The substitution clause, however, engendered resentment because it pitted neighbour against neighbour. Worse, it demoralized the soldiery, particularly when on march or being mustered. As one English officer recommended, 'no soldier [should] be admitted to Exchange after they come to the place Rendesvouz for this (by experience I find) will begett a murmurre, if not a muteny in a Regiment.[163]

Wentworth alluded to the absurdity of substitution in his advice to Lord Clifford, who was preparing to defend the north in 1638–9. The very men who escaped service would make the best combat troops. He cautioned Clifford about allowing substitution without his personal knowledge: 'Suffer those men not to be changed with other new men without your expresse warrant of yourselfe, or other such Principall officer imployed under you'. What point in rigorous training if only to excuse them in a crisis? Anyway, the type of citizen protected by the clause was precisely the man best suited to defend the community of the realm. 'Take that all your Trayned men be house-keepers or at least the sonnes of some good yeomen

---

161 PRO, SP 16/461/102 and Fissel, *'Bellum Episcopale'*, p. 272.
162 PRO, PC 2/51, f. 202, Privy Council to the Earl of Bridgewater, 22 December 1639; PC 2/52, f. 510, council to Lord Mayor, 27 Mayor 1640; see PC 2/52, ff. 542–62 for the pervasiveness of corruption and the resistance to military exactions.
163 PRO, SP 16/450/35 I.

men, which may have more settled placs of Aboade, then hired servants which are commonly once a year flitting from one Maister to an other.'[164]

Given the longer view of military obligation, both militia and impressment, Charles I's demands were within tradition. Where legality was on his side, political considerations should have dissuaded him. Precedents existed which argued both for and against the deployment of the trained bands outside of the shire. His father's reign had seen a deliberate break with traditions he now wished to resuscitate. Recent custom consigned a defensive role to the militia, a clear division being established between those eligible for expeditionary service and those safely within the ranks of the trained bands. But just as many precedents, and earlier ones at that, made clear that Charles could call upon the full resources of the kingdom in order to defend it. The decline of border defences certainly made a persuasive case for the mustering of all shires, including South Trent. Since border military strength was unprecedentedly weak, the threat from the north constituted an emergency.

But if Charles's requests were legal, did he get the armies he wanted in 1639 and 1640? His formula was not as foolish as might appear. Edward I and Edward III had done very nicely with amalgamized forces which combined feudal, militia, and impressed components. However, all three elements failed to live up to expectations in 1639–40. Many nobles were alienated from royal policy and all were of little military use. The militia, especially in 1640 after the constitutionality of deployment of the trained bands had been raised in the Short Parliament, regarded the security and sanctity of the locality as more important than Covenanter revolt and so resisted the selection of militiamen and the borrowing of their weapons. The impressed soldiers were drawn from the lowest levels of society and were likewise regarded as more of threat to public order than the Scots. In 1640, they proved it. One can only wonder if the shortage of arms in 1640 was entirely through force of circumstance or if many communities were simply afraid to arm the pressed soldiers. The patterns of impressment under the Stuarts guaranteed that the worst men would be levied and that they would have little or no military discipline.

Most serious was the failure to create a dozen or so solid regiments from the pooled strength of the trained bands. After the failure of 1639, the government pursued such a scheme in 1640, when irregular numbers of militia were to be drawn from Wales and the central and southern shires of England. The 30,000 trained soldiers out of the more than 79,000 militiamen available could join with the 15,773 trained men of Anglesey, Yorkshire, Lancashire, Durham, Newcastle, Northumberland, Cumber-

---

[164] Sheffield City Library, Strafford MS. Xa, miscellaneous correspondence, f. 160, Wentworth to Lord Clifford, 18 August 1638.

land and Westmorland.[165] This comparatively gargantuan army of more than 45,000 militia would have exhausted the resources of the Exchequer unless they served at their own cost, perhaps on the authority of the precedent which claimed that militia could provide thirty to forty days of unpaid service. The political situation and memory of the 1620s worked against any such solution.

The substitution clause shielded able men from the press, diluted the quality of the militia companies raised, and gave ample opportunity for corruption and favouritism which cast a bad light on the Crown's dealings. One must seriously doubt if the disorders of 1640 would have occurred if the regiments had been comprised of trained men drawn from the more respectable levels of English society. Hence the King never got what he wanted, partly due to the ill-conceived nature of the mobilization (especially the substitution clause) and partly because military demands were felt to be grievous in Tudor and Stuart England. The parliamentary debates of the 1620s and the spring of 1640 made the constitutional objections more potent and the religious context of the Bishops' Wars made recalcitrance appear right in the sight of God. Thus although structurally and bureaucratically it was exceedingly difficult for Charles to make war, the troops did in fact arrive in the north. The poor quality of these men stemmed from a badly managed mobilization and an unwilling public. But the role of the King in this business should not be overlooked. The mobilization followed his personally chosen timetable and the unwillingness of his subjects stemmed from a widespread belief that the war was pointless. When defeat came at Newburn and the retreat followed, it stemmed largely from the fact that these men were too raw, too badly equipped and led, to be deployed. Such troops would rather ignore royal authority than uphold it.

[165] PRO, SP 16/41/116.

7

Riot, iconoclasm, and murder amongst the soldiery

The Bishops' Wars aimed at buttressing the monarch's religious and political authority. The disorders of the common soldiers made a mockery of royal authority, for mutinies and violence perpetrated by instruments of royal policy made clear the enormous gap between Charles's notions of absolutism and the political failure which made its enforcement impossible. How could a King expect the obedience and loyalty of his subjects while his own soldiers ran amok? Worse, these low-born troopers questioned the lofty theological and ideological arguments which the Crown made against the Covenant. The religious context of the war, in a campaign accompanied by acts of iconoclasm, brought the political question of the purpose of the war to the forefront. Although the campaign of the previous year had seen the disorder that customarily accompanied early modern armies (such as brawling, theft of livestock, etc.) the violence of 1640 was more pronounced and of a different character. Most riot in summer 1640 focussed upon property, secular and ecclesiastical, and was symptomatic of political collapse. Enclosure railings were dismantled in Derbyshire and Staffordshire. Communion railings were destroyed in Essex and Hertfordshire.[1] The disturbances of 1640 reached their zenith in cruelty toward alleged Catholic officers.

Iconoclasm: godly religion or simple riot?

Dr Barkham, the parson of Bocking, presented Captain Rowlston's company with fifty shillings and a barrel of beer after muster on the morning of 22 July 1640, at Braintree, Essex. Barkham's gift may have been an expression of clerical charity or a bribe made in the hope of preventing

---

[1] The proximity of outbreaks of violence, both against property and people, seemed to spark similar occurrences in neighbouring areas. Although one is struck by the iconoclastic and personal nature of the 1640 violence, there persisted the same sort of mischief that had gone on in 1639. Reports of deer poaching and the pursuit of a 'witch' were in the same vein as the arson and livestock thefts of the 1639 campaign. PRO, SP 16/458/18; SP 16/459/36.

disorders. Either way, he soon regretted his generosity. Breaking open the keg and sampling its contents, the men became bad tempered with drink. In this condition they fell into discussion of religion. Although theology was not seen as the business of infantrymen, the soldiers were concerned about the purpose of the war that they had been told to fight. When Rowlston's soldiers had drunk enough, they proceeded to thank the gracious parson by going to Barkham's church and ripping out the communion rails. 'They went to his Church and pulled up the Rayles about the Comunion Table in the Chancell and brought them before their Captain's Lodging and there burn't them.' These 'reforms' must have pleased the soldiers, for they launched a similar attack upon another church in the locality. It is significant that they not only broke down the rails, but ignited them on the doorstep of Captain Rowlston.[2] The lighting of a pile of communion rails in front of an officer's quarters might appear to be nothing more than drunken vandalism; and yet, this episode casts light upon the soldiers' attitude towards both the rails and their commanding officer. Was the pyre of rails a display for Rowlston, reminding him that the soldiers would not tolerate popery? Rowlston had complained about 'divers Disorders' committed by his men and the soldiers made a collective statement by choosing to light the fire at Rowlston's lodgings.

The drunken attack upon the communion rails was followed by more acts of violence against churches, which inspired similar disorders. Sir John Maynard observed that the insolencies of the troops billeted in Essex 'doe every day increase'. The soldiers even dared to strike during services! The rampaging troops were going about 'to reforme churches and even in tyme of divine service to pull down the Rayles about the Communion Tables'.[3] The Archbishop of Canterbury lamented, 'In Essex the soldiers ar verye unrulye, and nowe beginn to pull up the Railes in Churches and in a ma'ner to saye they will reforme since the Lawes euerye whear broken.'[4] Episodes of destruction spread to adjoining counties. The Earl of Salisbury wrote from Hertfordshire that 'the soldiers heere in the cuntry begin to follow the example of theire neyghbours of Essex in pulling downe the railes about the Comunion Table. At Haddham where Dr Pashe is the incumbent they have pulled downe a windowe lately built by him.'[5]

One of the instigators in the Hertfordshire rail-breaking was a glazier and self-styled captain, Edmund Aylee, of Bishops Stortford. He and seven

---

[2] PRO, SP 16/461/25 I, information of Captain Rowlston before the Essex justices, 25 July 1640 and SP 16/461/25, Warwick to Vane, 27 July 1640. According to Rushworth, the rails were burnt at the *minister's* door: *Historical Collections*, vol. III, p. 1232; commissioners were appointed to try the Essex offenders.

[3] PRO, SP 16/461/24, Maynard to Privy Council, 27 July 1640.

[4] HMC Morrison, p. 432, Laud to an anonymous lord.

[5] PRO, SP 16/463/90, to Windebank, 13 August 1640.

other soldiers entered the church at Rickmansworth one Sunday, 'after Sermon and service ended in the forenoon [and] did there riotously and suddenly pull downe and breake in peeces the rayles about the Comunion Table, and also in the afternoon of the same day, did also riottously and suddenly breake downe and defaced part of the cover of the font'. That night Aylee, drinking in the White Hart, a public house, boasted that 'he was the Captaine of those unruly Souldiers that did pull downe the Rayles in our Church'. Aylee claimed to be a veteran of sixteen forays against communion rails, having torn 'downe and broken with his own hand' offending railings in seventeen Hertfordshire sanctuaries. Aylee bragged that he commanded 500 men and paid them to destroy 'all the alters [railed communion tables] in Hartford sheare untill this 23 of Agust'. At that time, 'Captain' Aylee would march his men north in search of the King and rebel Scots. Should Charles be fighting the 'Papists, they would fight on his side, and if the Scotts fought against the Papists, they would fight on the Scotts side'. If the civil authorities captured him, he could summon his 500 soldiers within a day. Aylee claimed that Mr Thomas Conesby had jailed him at Hemstead, 'but he was brought out of prison by the souldiers by force'.[6]

Regardless of whether the good 'Captain' could really muster 500 men, Rickmansworth church no longer had communion-table or altar railings in its chancel. Why did some English soldiers find communion rails so objectionable? It is unlikely that most of the soldiers who participated in the rail-breaking of 1640 possessed sophisticated theological justifications for removing the rails, be they altar or communion table railings. The Protestant conviction that celebration of communion commemorated Christ's sacrifice contrasted greatly with the Roman Catholic doctrine of transubstantiation which claimed that the elements became, quite literally, the flesh and blood of Christ. Protestants rejected this magical transformation.[7] No area of the church, nor any piece of furniture or image was considered sanctified by the physical presence of God or Christ. If transubstantiation were rejected entirely and consubstantiation viewed with suspicion by some, the communion table deserved no extraordinary reverence. It was no more holy than the bell in the belfry. With the puritan emphasis upon preaching, the communion table was not as important as the pulpit. Kneeling before the table made it seem altar-like and reminiscent of popish superstition. And kneeling before receiving the eucharist was as efficacious as bowing at the name of Jesus, or praying before the image of a saint or

6 PRO, SP 16/466/23, examinations of Edmund Aylee and John Passill, in conjunction with William Briggs, 23 and 29 August 1640. Rickmansworth had experienced similar violence the century before. See Margaret Aston, 'Iconoclasm at Rickmansworth, 1522: Troubles of Church Wardens', *Journal of Ecclesiastical History*, 40, no. 4 (October 1989), pp. 24–52.
7 John Phillips, *The Reformation of Images: Destruction of Art in England, 1535–1660* (Berkeley, Calif., 1973), p. 143.

the Virgin Mary. The Arminian emphasis upon ceremony and the 'beauty of holiness' conflicted with a puritan concept of the eucharist. It is significant that in both Essex and Hertfordshire doubt was expressed about the purpose of the war. Aylee's remarks indicate some uncertainty as to who was fighting against popery. Certainly, many Englishmen saw the Bishops' Wars within the context of the European conflict of the Thirty Years' War. All the planet, it seemed, was involved in the cosmic struggle between Roman Catholicism and the reformed religion, or the forces of evil and good. These suspicions were evident in the actions of the soldiers who demanded that their commanders take communion with them and, in the case of the Worcestershire soldiers, pledge that the campaign was in the interest of the Protestant faith.[8] The struggle against Satan took precedence; there should be no contradiction between serving God and obeying the King. In the case of the religious and political struggles of the 1630s, fear of popery overcame deference. This unrest focussed upon the microcosm of the communion table.

Because the body of Christ deserved the utmost respect it was important to ensure that the communion table, where Christ's sacrifice was commemorated and glorified, be respected and sanctified. According to the canons.

> experience hath shewed us how irreverent the behaviour of many people is in many places, some leaning, others casting their hats, and some sitting upon, some standing [upon], and others sitting under the Communion Table in time of Divine Service, for the avoiding of these and the like abuses it is thought meet and convenient by this present synod that the said Communion Tables in all chancels or chapels be decently severed *with rails* to preserve them from such worse profanation.

The railings were not popish, and the positioning of the table was considered to be a matter of indifference:

> Because it is generally to be wished that unity of faith were accompanied with uniformity of practice in the outward worship and service of God, chiefly for the avoiding of groundless suspicious of those who are weak, and the malicious aspersions of the professed enemies of our religion; the one fearing the innovations, the other flattering themselves with the vain hope of our backslidings unto their Popish superstition, by reason of the situation of the Communion Table ... the standing of the Communion table sideway[s] under the east window of every chancel or chapel is in its own nature indifferent.[9]

The breaking of communion rails did not originate during the Bishops' Wars, nor did it end with them. The soldiers carried on as some civilians

---

[8] See also p. 285.
[9] The Canons of 1640, printed in J. P. Kenyon (ed.), *The Stuart Constitution, Documents and Commentary* (Cambridge, 1973), pp. 170–1 (my italics).

had done in the late 1630s.[10] In midsummer 1638, in All Saints, North-amptonshire, some culprits had 'very lately cut the rail ... that was about the Lord's board in pieces, and brought down the Lord's table into the middle of the chancel'.[11] The notion that communion rails revealed the growing influence of popery within the English church was reinforced when those rails bore images which seemed conducive to idolatry. The parishioners of All Hallows Barking, London, complained that the new baptismal font and communion table railings displayed 'certain carved images, the picture of the Holy Ghost and a cross'. This complaint was made during the year of the First Bishops' War, and although the railings remained in place, the 'imagery was taken down'.[12] Soldiers burst into a church at Radwinter, near Maldon, and broke down a statue of Christ and various other 'graven images', such as cherubim and seraphim, which were burnt in the street. It would appear that these images were products of the refurbishing of churches in the 1630s.[13] Iconoclasm, coupled with fear of popery, combined to make church furniture and images seem diabolical to the puritan eye. The result was the paradoxical viewpoint of the protestant who considered 'the image of Christ in the roodloft as a picture of the Devil'.[14] The 1630s witnessed a considerable number of innovations: new railings, new fonts, new windows, new surplices, and a new service book. They had not yet acquired the acceptance which tradition and familiarity bestowed and to some seemed to be unholy trespassers in the parish church. In the wake of the announcement of the canons of 1640, drawn up and approved by a Convocation which sat while the Short Parliament had been dissolved, the new trappings were a novelty and seemed incongruous with the extant church.

Archbishop Laud surmised that the soldiers rioting in Essex had torn down the communion rails because 'they will reforme since the Lawes euerye whear broken'. The troops were carrying out a reformation on their own, often with the consent of local civilians. The belief that they were embarking upon a crusade in the name of 'Reformation' was as fervent among the soldiers as it was among parliamentary armies two years later. During the summer of 1642, parliamentary troops from London 'reformed'

10 This fact is not recognized in Aston, *England's Iconoclasts*.
11 Cited in P. S. Seaver, *The Puritan Lectureships: The Politics of Religious Dissent, 1560–1662* (Stanford, 1970), p. 261, quoting *CSPD* (1637–8), XII, p. 518.
12 Cited in Phillips, *The Reformation of Images*, p. 172. Phillips refers to the ninth volume of the Privy Council register. I have searched PC 2 unsuccessfully.
13 PRO, SP 16/461/32, Rossingham newsletter, 17 July 1640. Buchanan Sharp kindly pointed out the signficance of this episode. The Daventry mutineers would not fight against the gospel or be commanded by papists, according to SP 16/460/5, report of Sir Nicholas Byron, 14 July 1640.
14 Keith Thomas, *Religion and the Decline of Magic: Studies in Popular Beliefs in Sixteenth and Seventeenth Century England*, p. 477.

churches in the same general area through which royal soldiers had rampaged during the Second Bishops' War. The day after arriving at Acton, the men entered a church and 'defaced the auntient and sacred glased picturs' and burned the communion rails. The following day, the troops heard a sermon by 'Mr Love' and made a pyre of communion rails taken from Chiswick.[15] Attacks on the homes of Dr Duck (a crony of Laud) and the Earl of Portland were prevented by the officers. Some of the soldiers planned to enjoy their third consecutive day of communion rail burning, but discovered that the rails at Hillingdon were missing. They contented themselves with shearing the minister's surplice into handkerchiefs.[16]

Religion alone cannot explain all the acts of iconoclasm, of course. For example, before ascribing 'Captain' Aylee's motivation to puritanism or anti-Arminianism, one should consider the case of another rail-breaker, with a very similar surname, one John Ayly of Kelvedon, Essex. In September 1640, with the Scots occupying the north of England and Charles's government in disarray, rioting erupted, including an attack on a church in the parish of Kelvedon. John Ayly had participated in the destruction of the communion rails at Kelvedon. His criminal record, however, merits examination: 'The younger Ayly's misdeeds included absence from church, failing to pay church fees, not rendering an account of his parents' goods after their decease, fornication and standing excommunicate. On one occasion he achieved the unusual distinction of being presented jointly with his father for adultery with the same woman.'[17] Such a man probably possessed neither a tender conscience nor reasoned theological objections to communion rails. Kevin Sharpe concludes that:

Not even in the most elastic definition of that much-stretched word can Ayly be described as a Puritan; his attack on the rails probably sprang not from a reasoned disquiet at the implications of Arminianism, but rather from a conviction that they represented an acceptable target for a man who must have born considerable resentment against the intrusions of the Anglican church in its attempts to produce a godly and disciplined society.

Popular anti-popery and scepticism of Arminian innovation were not necessarily synonymous with 'puritanism'. The iconoclasm of the Bishops' Wars was more focussed than that of the civil war. Where image-breaking and the like encompassed objects old and new after 1642, as had been the case during the time of Edward VI, the destruction of religious objects in 1640 concentrated upon innovations made during the Personal Rule.

---

[15] This may have been Christopher Love, the Presbyterian. Conrad Russell made this suggestion.

[16] *CSPD* (1641–3), XVIII, p. 372, Nehemiah Wharton to George Willingham, 16 August 1642.

[17] J. A. Sharpe, 'Crime and Delinquency in an Essex Parish 1600–1640', in J. S. Cockburn (ed.), *Crime in England 1550–1800* (London, 1977), p. 320.

Although the focal points for desecration were quite clear (recently installed rails, Arminian surplices, new decorations incorporating images), the powerful sense of resentment and fear that fuelled the vandalism remained unformulated. Much of the violence stemmed from a general fear of Catholicism. Anti-popery, 'the lowest common denominator of English politics', provoked a visceral reaction especially amongst the ill-educated.[18] The ubiquitousness of the imagined Catholic threat prompted people to strike reactively, with little thought. Feeling beset and besieged, they struck out at whatever seemed ominous or new. Novelty was par-ticularly unsettling, for it was a product of the dangerous times.

In addition to striking down objects like communion rails and baptismal fonts, the soldiers also attacked individuals. These unfortunates repre-sented institutions against which troopers felt compelled to vent their spleen: clergy and local law enforcement officers. Clergymen had been threatened and forced to flee in Essex and Cambridgeshire. The rumour that Bishop Wren was at Wisbech Church sparked off a riot when a mob of soldiers surrounded the building.

There was a Commission of sewars held att Wisbige, where the Bishop of Ely was to be present, but being desired by Sir Charles Harbert not to come by reason of some soilgers there billited, he foreboare; when the other Commissioners were new satt, they perceived some redcoats peepinge in att the windoe, and others att the doare, whereupon they sent to see whatt was the matter, and they found 200 of them att the gate, where upon they shutt it, until such time as they had made a hole in the back wall for the conveiance of 6,000£. They had there of the Kinge's for dreaninge matters; but all this while a great clamour was without, 'give us Wren, that damned bishop Ely, wee will have him, or else fyer the towne and cut the throats of all the Commissioners'.[19]

Some fought back. In Warwickshire, the officer who a year later would be known as 'Lunsford the Butcher' admitted that he and his fellow officers had killed some of their own men in self-defence. The soldiers deserted in swarms, and the local population did more to egg them on than to dis-courage them. Pursuit was useless. Lunsford and his fellow officers were 'daily assaulted by sometimes 500 of them togeither', and in response 'hurt and killed som' to protect themselves.[20] The Warwickshire disturbances were severe enought to merit a royal proclamation.[21] The Somersetshire authorities blamed the rowdiness on delays in the dispatching of the

[18] B. Sharp, 'The Place of the People in the English Revolution', Theory and Society, 13 (1984), p. 101.

[19] HMC Rutland, p. 522, Francis Fane to Rutland, 8 August 1640.

[20] PRO, SP 16/457/91, Lunsford to Northumberland, 22 June 1640; Gardiner, History, vol. IX, pp. 160–1.

[21] PRO, SP 45/10 and in the Corporation of London Records Office, Journal of the Court of Common Council, XXXIX, f. 100v. It is printed in Rymer's Foedera, vol. XX, p. 13 and Larkin (ed.), Stuart Royal Proclamations, vol. II, pp. 716–18.

soldiers and the county's unwillingness to provide adequate funds.[22] Material considerations – pay, food, and living conditions – also animated disorders. Food and shelter were often of the worst quality. Officers penned warnings to the council, predicting dire consequences if armed and hungry men were not paid promptly and fully. Even willing recruits could not fight the Scots on empty bellies. Soldiers quartered in Norfolk told the lieutenants that they were loyal to the King but would not march without sufficient provisions.[23] The miserable conditions in which conscripts were forced to live made absurd tales believable. Having marched his men from Berkshire, Captain William Lower led his company into Northamptonshire through the town of Brackley. There they encountered several of the Daventry mutineers, who filled the ears of the Berkshire men with tales of slavery and forged commissions:

those mutaneers had soe possessed them with their base lyes that they would heare noe reason: they tould my men that they were goinge to be shipd and sould for slaves, that the officers had false commissions, that the King gave them noe authoritye, that they should be used like dogges, that all was peace in Scotland, and that was only a pretence to carry them some other where, that we were all papists, and that my Lord Generall himselfe was one.

Lower assured the troops that they would not take a single step outside the kingdom, but the men refused to believe him and threatened to beat out their captain's brains.[24] As in the case of the anti-popish outrages against churches and clergy, the soldiers responded to fear. Collective paranoia and uncertainty about their officers' intentions (and suspicion of church and state) provoked them.

For example, at Wisbech, Wren, the quarry of the most vocal of the soldiers, was not inside the meeting hall. However, £6,000 *was*. This large sum had been designated for one of the King's draining projects. The commissioners found it prudent to pierce a hole in one of the walls and hide it. Obviously, we do not know whether or not the enlisted men's intelligence-gathering capability, which was good enough to discover that Wren was supposed to be there, had learned of the £6,000; but it is a possibility that some of the men knew of its presence. In reporting Lieutenant Evers's murder, Nathaniel Fiennes related how troopers demanded that their officer take communion with them. But he also included a curious tale: that the soldiers' real intention in killing their officer was to steal the pay: 'it was discovered that they had resolved among themselves to kill all their officers in their march and to sease upon the kings mony'. This story, repeated by Rossingham's newsletter (which was not unusual, as they seem

22 PRO, SP 16/459/7, 1 July 1640.
23 PRO, SP 16/459/95, Sir Thomas Jermyn to the council, 13 July 1640.
24 PRO, SP 16/461/5, to Windebank, 24 July 1640.

to have shared or copied information) has no foundation in the archival sources, including the examinations of the assailants and witnesses.[25] But it is still somewhat disturbing, for there might well have been those who could see some advantage in killing their officer under pretence of religion, seizing a satchelful of coins, and deserting.

A survey of the disorders in the English army of 1640 reveals that the apparent causes of mutiny and violence were three: religion, discipline (or lack of it), and pay. The prompt payment of the soldiers' wages was the most apparent, especially with the army while in the north. The main complaint from men such as Astley and Conway was that lack of pay caused most of the unrest. Perhaps the most memorable quote of 1640 comes from Lord Conway, upon whose shoulders fell the command of the army: 'I feare unpayde souldiers more than I doe the Scots and the Divell to boote; God keep you from all three.'[26]

Why was the popular violence of 1640 more daring than in 1639? With the nation mobilizing for war and the elite deeply divided, situations occurred which held potential for violence (soldiers marching into communities, taxes being collected, large numbers of men being gathered together and given an opportunity to discuss their mutually held grievances). This occurred at a time when dissension within the governing classes removed some restraints on violence. Local law enforcement was incapable of suppressing soldier riots. Enclosure riots are the best example. Quarrels amongst gentry, lords, and Crown fuelled unrest while simultaneously diminishing the ability of those groups to quell disturbances from below, particularly soldiers, who were armed and possessed a peculiar kind of solidarity. 'Army service followed a separation from civilian society that generated its own risky brand of defiance.'[27] That defiance challenged authority. An unarmed individual is less likely to assert himself than an armed individual surrounded by comrades also bearing weapons, as was demonstrated in 1640 by soldiers in challenging gaols.

In Marlborough, several Wiltshire militiamen had been imprisoned for refusing to pay coat-and-conduct money on the grounds that their service exempted them from the assessment. Their comrades broke open the prison, and freed the refusers. The local authorities

had sent out their warrants for the leavying of coate and conduct mony, that many men had paid their proportions but some obstinate, they had committed to the Gaole these being of the traine bands when some belonging to the traine bands had

[25] HMC Rutland, p. 522, Francis Fane to Rutland, 8 August 1640; Huntingdonshire RO, Manchester MS. 32/5/17, Nathaniel Fiennes newsletter, 11 July 1640; PRO, SP 16/460/56, f. 1, Rossingham newsletter, 21 July 1640.
[26] Fissel, *'Bellum Episcopale'*, p. 404.
[27] Hale, *War and Society in Renaissance Europe*, p. 172.

tumultously consorted together, and had forceably broken open the prison doores and lett forth those men.[28]

At Wakefield the soldiers paused long enough to attack the House of Correction, 'breakinge the windowes of that house, wheeles, and other ymplementes used there'.[29] At Selby, Sir Jacob Astley, who bore the responsibility for supervising the rendezvous, discovered upon his arrival that the soldiers had simply rescued their imprisoned compatriots. Prisons had been attacked, and officers and civilians threatened. Astley sequestered a house and converted it into a gaol. A trench was dug around the place, and a garrison of forty installed. Having established a well-fortified gaol-house, he utilized 200 of Sir William Ogle's company as military police, who patrolled the town and cleared the streets at curfew.[30]

The pressed soldiers who broke open the prison at Cirencester were not reluctant to recruit from the legal profession. If anyone needed a good lawyer, it was a mutinous soldier who went about freeing prisoners from local gaols. When the troops smashed open the prison doors, an incarcerated lawyer informed his would-be liberators that he was imprisoned only upon a contempt charge and would be released soon enough. Should he join up with the mutineers his ultimate penalty would be much greater and he would probably never again practice law. However, the soldiers insisted that he accompany them upon the march, acting as legal counsel. They offered to make him their 'Attorney General'. According to Rossingham, the young man, a bachelor and free spirit, consented, and departed along with the mutineers. In contrast with those soldiers who simply freed all prisoners, the troopers who forced their way into Derby prison inquired into each captive's offence to determine who merited liberation. A debtor and a left-over deserter from the First Bishops' War found themselves at liberty by the grace of the soldiery.[31]

Such episodes demonstrate that gaol-breakings were chaotic but not entirely anarchistic. They shared a common characteristic – the conviction that authority had been misused. Implicitly, government had been subverted, order undermined, and the men were restoring a justice. If attacks on rails and clergy reflected contempt for the contemporary church, prison breakings (be they to liberate internees or simply to damage the structure) struck against authority, certainly local though possibly central. Rage and resentment found these targets convenient, as they could represent different

---

[28] PRO, SP 16/456/44, Rossingham newsletter, 8 June 1640.
[29] John Lister (ed.), *West Riding Sessions Records, Yorkshire Archeological Society Journal*, 54 (1915), p. 230.
[30] PRO, SP 16/458/62, Astley to Conway, 30 June 1640; SP 16/459/64, Astley to Conway, 9 July 1640.
[31] *CSPD* (1640), XVI, p. 45, Rossingham newsletter, 4 July 1640.

things to different rioters. Still, few crimes were committed against private property; anger vented itself on property which symbolized church and state. These outrages, so public and violent, threatened the government, in that an impotent central authority could not expect unqualified obedience from its subjects during the mobilization.[32] Enforcement, when possible, was therefore swift and equally public. One of the gaol-breakers was caught and brought to the capital, where he 'was hangd drawne and quartered, his heade is an ornament to London bridge, and his quarters to the 4 gates of the Citye'.[33]

One aspect of the increasing polarization of English society in the late sixteenth and seventeenth centuries was that violence became increasingly a plebeian pursuit. The gentry and yeomen distanced themselves from the tumults of their social inferiors, while the latter indulged in violence on an unusually extensive level. Apart from the trained bands allegedly freeing coat-and-conduct money refusers, riots and rebellions – spontaneous outbreaks of violence – no longer had the instigation or leadership of disaffected yeomen or gentry. The polarization of society had a lot to do with respectability. Men *could* sort out their differences in a more civilized fashion, such as litigating themselves into indebtedness. The failure of society's natural leaders to reach a consensus made the situation appear increasingly extraordinary in popular eyes. The more extraordinary it seemed, the less applicable were the customary rules of behaviour. Those elements of society which should have been allies and integral parts of an organic polity which comprised the state had inexplicably fallen out. The breakdown had, to some extent, legitimized conflict. Social bonds were loosened. It did not matter whether cobblers, tinkers, and tanners understood the political and religious issues, the fact was that 'the law is everywhere broken'.

Those members of society who indulged themselves in rioting, including the soldiers of the Second Bishops' War, had a somewhat different view of time and space than did the literate and socially influential. E. P. Thompson's suggestion that common folk had very little in the way of a 'predictive notation of time', that opportunity was grabbed as occasion arose, explains the spontaneity and intensity of the riots of 1640. In such bursts of activity, there was no need to analyse the purpose of action; rather, one plunged into things, the end of that action being whatever one imagined it to be. Here the symbolism and other-worldliness evoked in Keith Thomas's work helps to explain the attacks on churches. Removal of new

[32] One is reminded of Conrad Russell's remark that 'Authority is necessarily threatened by disorders it cannot control', in *Parliaments and English Politics*, p. 337.
[33] Bodleian Library, Tanner MS. LXV, f. 78, Robert Crane to Sir Robert Crane, 29 May 1640, from Whitehall.

furniture from a church could symbolize many things: rejection of the conservative moral discipline of puritan Christianity, the exorcism of the demon of popery, protest over the incursion of the central government's ecclesiastical hierarchy into the traditional and settled realm of the parish, or simply the exhilaration of loosening the social bonds. As the three basic religious currents in this period (puritanism, Arminianism, and Roman Catholicism) did not, apparently, have a tremendous impact upon the lower orders, perhaps localities retained their own autonomous views of religion, behaviour, society, and the world. This parochial, almost 'folkish' perspective made the ideological divisions of the opposite pole of society, the gentlemen, prosperous yeomen and lords, rather rudimentary, though in fact they were better formulated than popular concepts. Thus it was possible for them to attack Dr Barkham's church and simultaneously conceive themselves as rejecting the enforced conservative morality of the ecclesiastical hierarchy, while others believed they were combating a form of diabolical idolatry, and still others were having good sport at the expense of their betters.

Impressed soldiers were conscripted from the lowest levels of English society, most having earned their living as labourers or artisans. Soldiers and civilians were often at odds, but common social grievances could unite them in opposition to a common enemy. The inhabitants of Needwood Forest in Staffordshire 'seized upon the opportunity of the two Bishops' Wars with the Scots to settle grievances over enclosure'.[34] The Crown's policy of disafforestation antagonized the lower orders of rural society. Local folk found themselves excluded from land they regarded as common. When a royal forest was enclosed, these people were denied access to a source of fuel, food, and building materials. In response, rural people sometimes joined forces with the King's soldiers to destroy enclosures. A survey undertaken during the reign of James I discovered that Needwood yielded 'no tangible benefits' to the King, and that the 'fees of the forest officers and the widespread destruction of the woods were a drain on royal revenues'. Disafforestation was recommended. Between 1635 amd 1637 a variety of commissions devised plans to divide the Uttoxeter ward of the forest, the Crown receiving one half, and the inhabitants the other in compensation.[35] The local population would retain their half of the forest ward 'in free and common socage', while the Crown leased its half. Apparently, the inhabitants did not approve of this arrangement, for a series of enclosure riots occurred in 1639. When a group of Staffordshire soldiers returned to Uttoxeter to be discharged, they attacked the Needwood Forest enclosures, which were 'throwen downe and destroyed in a very ryotous

[34] B. Sharp, *In Contempt of all Authority* p. 221.
[35] Ibid., p. 221–2.

manner'.[36] Civilians and troopers had cooperated in this attack, rallying to the beat of a drum. The Privy Council instructed the justices of the peace and the judges of assize to proceed against the perpetrators.[37]

When Charles's government embarked upon the Second Bishops' War in 1640, the Privy Council reminded the Staffordshire lieutenancy that the newly levied soldiers were to be prevented from demolishing the royal enclosures as they had done the previous summer. The warning was issued in vain: 'when the 300 men raised for this service from the surrounding hundreds assembled at Uttoxeter on July 1, 1640, a number of them marched out and destroyed the enclosures in the forest'.[38] The men rampaged for several days, in spite of the efforts of local authorities to calm them.[39] On the evening of the day of the rendezvous, the constables had busied themselves with billeting arrangements (always a delicate matter) and the raising of a small force of townsmen capable of extinguishing any disorders. The troops' conductors retired to supper. As they were finishing their meal around nine o'clock, the constables alerted them that the soldiers were gathering with the intention of breaking down the rails at Uttoxeter Wood. The conductors and constables, reinforced by forty or fifty townsmen (armed with halberds and whatever else they could find) 'made after them'. Following closely upon the soldiers' heels ('soe neere them at the first settinge fourth, as that we were withing hearinge of them'), the local authorities arrived at the scene, only to find the rails already aflame and the soldiers defiant. It should be noted that the rioters were local men, having been pressed from the hundreds of Seisdon and Cuttleston. The troops succeeded in pulling down 'som tenne Roodes of Rayles and had made two fiers'. When the soldiers refused to desist, several were seized by the officers and placed in custody of the armed townsmen and constables. At this moment, another contingent of soldiers appeared and rescued their comrades. Outnumbered and poorly armed, the conductors, constables, and townsmen fled. The next night the soldiers returned to the forest and resumed the burning of enclosures. The disturbances continued until 5 July.[40] As happened several times during the Second Bishops' War,

[36] SRO, GD 406/1/1249, Bagot, Hasley, and Compston to Digby, 3 July 1640; PRO, SP 16/458/95, notes regarding disturbances in the Uttoxeter ward of Needwood Forest, undated.

[37] PRO, PC 2/50, f. 28, Privy Council register, 19 July 1639; Sharp, *In Contempt of all Authority*, p. 222.

[38] Ibid.

[39] Ibid., PRO, SP 16/460/8, Stafford deputy lieutenants to the council, 15 July 1640; G. Wrottesley (ed.), 'The Staffordshire Muster of A.D. 1640', *Proceedings of the William Salt Archeological Society*, 15 (1894), pp. 201–31, which is an edited version of SP 16/460/8, with some analysis.

[40] PRO, SP 16/460/8, Stafford deputy lieutenants to the council, 15 July 1640. The names of the rioters can be found in SP 16/460/8 II and PRO, PC 2/52, ff. 680e–f.

local authorities responded too slowly and without sufficient force to overawe mutinous soldiers. The fact that these rioters were Staffordshire men made the problem of enforcement that much greater, as was the case when the Devon lieutenants were asked to proceed against their neighbours in the aftermath of the murders of Lieutenants Mohun and Evers.[41] The harried constables and conductors were obliged to call upon villages and towns within a five mile radius.

The King was not the only one who found his enclosures burned. In Derbyshire, Sir John Beaumont led his contingent of 1,200 troops into the town of Ashby. They were not Derbyshire men, but had been conscripted in the West Country, predominantly from Somerset, Wiltshire, and Bristol. They marauded through the Derby hills, broke down enclosures, set fire to the mill belonging to now-retired Secretary Sir John Coke, and dug up the mill dam. Coke's son could not 'prevail with them' when he tried to stop the disorders. Nor were any officers to be found. Coke encountered two of 'inferior rank', but neither was willing or able to suppress the rioting. When the soldiers threatened to burn down Coke's manor house, he began to fortify the place. A drummer appeared 'upon the hill above the Charnels, as if they were drawing' near to Coke's manor at Melbourne. The attack upon his residence was merely a bluff, however. They did succeed in putting the Cokes on the defensive, making suppression of the rioting that much more difficult.

Coke complained that the inhabitants of Calke and Tickenhall had 'mightily provoked' the soldiery 'to set upon us'. Coke also accused the troops' commander, Sir John Beaumont, of having condoned the attack upon the Derby enclosures and Coke's mill. An anonymous neighbour claimed to have seen Beaumont drinking at a local house during the rioting. Sir John was mounting his horse to ride off in search of his men when 'one of Ashby came openly to him and desired to drink another cup of wine with him, for that the soldiers had not done their exploit yet; whereupon he returned again into the house'. The soldiers, 'being animated by the commission of this insolency', proceeded to commit other crimes. Robberies had been perpetrated. Beaumont and Coke, whatever their differences, were threatened with murder, and arson was reported in some villages.[42] The episode compares with the Staffordshire enclosure riot in that the soldiers were not natives of the county, yet were still encouraged by the local residents, particularly those of Tickenhall and Calke, who allegedly exploited the disturbances to settle a score with the Cokes.

The most vicious instances of soldier violence, the killings of Lieutenants

---

[41] Pp. 279–83.
[42] HMC Cowper, Coke MSS., p. 257, Sir John Coke the younger to Thomas Coke, 29 June 1640.

William Mohun and Compton Evers, were spontaneous and savage, the victims beaten to death in the streets. During the civil war, Robert Ram rationalized the excesses of Cromwellian troops by explaining, 'God hath stirred up the spirits of some honest soldiers to be His instruments . . . God hath put the sword of reformation into the soldiers' hand'.[43] Ram believed that religion was the primary force behind much of the violence amongst the soldiery in the 1640s. But as the destruction of communion rails at Kelvedon in September 1640 demonstrates, the case of John Ayly revolved more around malicious mischief than about godly religion. Further bedevilling the issue of religion was the relationship between puritanism and anti-Catholicism. Given this complication, explaining the motives for the murders of Lieutenants Mohun and Evers is no simple task. Derek Hirst suggested that the murders reflected 'political attitudes'. Conrad Russell put forth the view that 'For many soldiers, class and religious hatred were merged in assaults on Popish officers.'[44] Religion and bigotry, in the form of anti-Catholic hysteria, motivated and 'justified' these murders. Fear of popery dissolved the bonds of deference and, in these cases, suspended moral values, permitting normally unacceptable behaviour, to the degree that some of the participants might have pleaded, in modern parlance, 'justifiable homicide'. Rather than accentuating or aggravating 'class' divisions, the hysteria of anti-popery blotted out class divisions, negated deference, and in the dichotomy of good and evil, permitted excesses of behaviour that would have been unthinkable in other circumstances. No particular social stratum was immune to anti-Catholic paranoia. Buchanan Sharp has written that the

intense belief in the conspiratorial nature of Catholicism and in the threat that popery posed to the English constitution during the years 1640–42 transcended class boundaries. It was the common political currency of Englishmen. Nor is it clear that anti-Catholicism was a measure of Puritanism or any substantive religious belief system among the people. Anti-Popery was more a kind of political protestantism, an expression of English nationalism, or more accurately xenophobia, that had little connection with the sophisticated theological understanding necessary for a Calvinist faith.[45]

Lieutenant William Mohun, perhaps a veteran of the 1620s campaigns, was murdered on 17 June 1640 by the Dorsetshire soldiers going to York under the command of Captain Lewkner.[46] Mohun 'had bine very severe

---

43 Cited in C. H. Firth, *Cromwell's Army*, (third edition), p. 328. See also Aston, *England's Iconoclasts*.
44 D. Hirst, 'Parliament, Law and War in the 1620s', *The Historical Journal*, 23, no. 2 (1980) p. 461; C. Russell, 'Introduction' to *The Origins of the English Civil War* (London, 1973), p.27.
45 B. Sharp, 'The Place of the People in the English Revolution', p. 101.
46 A Lieutenant 'Moone' is listed among the officers sent to Plymouth *circa* May 1625, PRO, SP 16/2/126.

towards some of them', and was rumoured to be a papist. Hostility towards Mohun increased during the march; upon arrival at Faringdon, in Berkshire, resentment fast became mutiny. A drummer disobeyed an order and struck Mohun with his drumstick. Mohun drew his sword and nearly severed the fellow's hand at the wrist. Word of the altercation spread amongst the soldiery, the tale being told that the drummer was dead from his wounds. In retaliation, the soldiers stormed the officers' lodgings, battered down the door, and forced Mohun, Captain Lewkner, and the ensign bearer to crawl out of a second-storey window and clamber onto the beam that held the inn's sign above the street. The soldiers below, some crying, 'a Moone, a Moone', pitched debris at the hapless trio. Since Mohun was their quarry, the soldiers allowed Lewkner and the ensign bearer to escape. Declining to jump, Mohun clung desperately to the beam. A trooper appeared at the chamber window, grasping a 'greate peece of wood', reached out and struck Mohun over the head. The lieutenant toppled to the ground, 'where the souldiers beate him lamentably with their cudgells'. They dragged him 'by the haire of the head' through the streets of Faringdon, finally casting him in a ditch, left for dead.

But William Mohun had not yet expired. He regained consciousness and stumbled to a nearby house, where he received medical attention. News spread that Mohun 'was alive againe'. A mob of soldiers located the house in which Mohun lay; they were astounded to see him still breathing. Some thought his 'resurrection' to be supernatural. 'They broake into the house, and seeing him there cryed out, he was a Divill (for they thought they had killd him).' Cornered, Mohun drew a knife and swore he would stab the first to attack him. But the blade was struck from his hand by a cudgel-wielding soldier, and the men 'knockt out his brains', making certain this time that the Lieutenant was truly dead. The corpse was dragged through the town and placed in the pillory. Mohun's fellow officers retrieved the body under cover of darkness and buried it in the churchyard.[47] Neither Captain Lewkner nor the Berkshire authorities apprehended the murderers. Many deserted on the spot. Others, perhaps realizing that deserting on the day of the murder would imply guilt, simply remained in the ranks.

When the sheriff, George Purefoy, attempted to restore order his efforts were hampered by the absence of the Dorsetshire company's officers. The men had threatened to dispatch them as they had done Lieutenant Mohun, and so the officers had fled from Faringdon. Purefoy appealed to the Lord Lieutenant for assistance and summoned the trained bands from

---

[47] PRO, SP 16/457/104, f. 4, Rossingham's description of the murder, newsletter dated 23 June 1640.

Abingdon.[48] The militiamen marched through the night to Purefoy's home at Wadley. When Purefoy inspected them, he found their number insufficient to risk a confrontation with the Dorsetshire soldiers, and summoned additional trained soldiers from the next division. With their arrival, the sheriff and militiamen went to Faringdon in search of the mutineers. They arrived to find that nearly the entire force had melted away, after having rampaged through Faringdon for more than two days! Only fifty-two conscripts remained. One of the alleged murderers was apprehended; another suspect had been seized in Abingdon. Although the sheriff had done his best, the delay in assembling a sufficient number of militiamen had given the mutineers time to escape. In addition, the soldiers had committed outrages in the town for at least forty-eight hours before there was a serious attempt to extinguish the disorders. Fewer than half a dozen suspects had been captured, and a pair executed.[49]

The government responded to the murder by issuing a proclamation on 1 July. Three suspects had been apprehended. Ten others still at large were named in the proclamation. To those soldiers who witnessed Mohun's killing but were not listed in the proclamation, a pardon was extended.

those Persons, that were present at the Murder of the said Lieutenant Mohun, and assented thereunto, by the Laws of this Realm are adjudged Principal, and have thereby incurred the same Penalty of the Laws; Yet his Majesty, out of his abundant Clemency . . . [pardons] all such of those six hundred Soldiers (other than the persons before named) who were guilty of the said late Mutiny and Murder.[50]

Those seeking pardon were to surrender to the deputy lieutenants at Blandford by 13 July (for those who had deserted), or to Sir Jacob Astley at Selby by 25 July (for those who had remained with their colours). This arrangement had certain drawbacks. We do not know why the government named those particular soldiers. The guilt of the thirteen men was assumed, and also that all others would escape penalty of the law if they turned themselves in. When the authorities captured a suspect they could not actually proceed against him, since the proclamation offered a pardon to all except those named, regardless of their involvement. Sir Jacob Astley wrote from Selby on 5 August: 'I detayne still 3 of them that I apprened (apprehend) to have had ther Hande in the Murther of Leftenant Moone but the kinges proclamation fres them, else all or on [one] had died for it. I attend order

---

48 Militia that had been spared from the mobilization.
49 Huntingdonshire RO, Manchester MS. 32/5/17a, Nathaniel Fiennes newsletter, 11 July 1640; PRO, SP 16/460/56, Rossingham newsletter, 11 July 1640.
50 An original can be found in PRO, SP 45/10 and a contemporary transcription in the Corporation of London Records Office, *Journal of the Court of Common Council*, XXXIX, ff. 100v–101. It is printed in Rymer's *Foedera*, vol. XX, pp. 13–14 and Larkin (ed.), *Stuart Royal Proclamations*, vol. II, pp. 718–20.

what I shall do with them.'[51] Perhaps the Crown wished to save face by allowing the soldiers to surrender themselves, since capturing them would be exceedingly difficult, given the limitations of local government and the fact that the central government had its hands full with a war. But the Crown also sacrificed a measure of its credibility, since soldiers guilty of murder and desertion obtained the pardon relatively easily. Such a concession would do nothing to lessen lawlessness in the ranks. Astley reported from York:

> The dorsettsher men when they came to Selby they thought to do as they were wont but for disobeadientes to their officere in the feild as they wer Musteringe I was fayne to tack [take] out on [one] of them and by the Comon Vott of the Cownsell of war we Harquebussed him in the vew (view) of the Rest.[52]

The company, originally numbering 600, had dwindled to 340. The aftermath of the Mohun affair demonstrated the impotence of the government, central and local, to prevent spontaneous violence by the soldiery.

The killing of Lieutenant Compton Evers is better documented. About three weeks after the death of Mohun, Devonshire conscripts quartered at Wellington began to talk about Lieutenant Evers, who had neglected to attend church services. The soldiers 'suspected him to be a Papist, and for that cause, and noe other' beat and murdered him. Like Mohun's killing, the attack was made in public view and the corpse dragged around the vicinity for good measure.[53] A witness observed 'many blowes given him by the souldiers both with swords and staves untill they killed him'.[54] A group of soldiers had gathered outside Evers's lodgings. Three, Hannibal Pounceford (a butcher), Richard Sincklere, and an anonymous soldier entered Evers's chamber; a struggle ensued, the Lieutenant was seized, the men 'dragging him by the armes and leggs downe the staires'.[55] In the street Evers was beaten with cudgels, staves, and stabbed with his own sword, by nearly a dozen soldiers. Macklyn Locke seized Evers's 'naked sword' slashed the lieutenant, 'and broke the sword upon the streete in striking at him'. Henry Vaughan confessed to have 'stroake one blowe'. The soldiers then proceeded to rob the corpse. Hannibal Pounceford found around Evers's 'neck a Crucifixe tyed in a Riband [ribbon]' which he stole in spite of its popish nature. Another discovered in Evers's pockets a 'stiver' (a

[51] PRO, SP 16/463/4, to Conway.
[52] Ibid.
[53] PRO, SP 16/460/5, Gibson to Conway (?) 14 July 1640.
[54] PRO, SP 16/463/88, f. 4, examination of Thomas Clarke, who had been named as a suspect in the proclamation of 24 July.
[55] Vaughan confessed, even though not named in the proclamation, f. 4. See also below the examinations of John and William Toute, John Moore, William Shapcott, Thomas Clarke, John Knowle, and Thomas Badcocke.

small coin), a silver penny, a 'nutmege', and two pistol bullets. Some time after the murder, the corpse was carried to a nearby inn.[56]

On 24 July 1640, the King issued a proclamation 'for the apprehending and due punishing of the late Mutineers at Wellington'. This time there would be no pardon. The lukewarm response of the Dorsetshire soldiers who had perpetrated Mohun's murder angered Charles so much that he refused to extend a pardon to Evers's murderers. The King demanded the enforcement of the letter of the law 'as we now find that our princely Clemency, extended towards some others late Offenders in this kind, hath not produced that Conformity and Obedience in our Common Soldiers, which we expected, and that at this time, it is necessary that severe and exemplary Punishment should be inflicted on Offenders of this nature'. All 160 men were presumed guilty, and their home parishes listed along with their names. Anyone who harboured the mutineers would be prosecuted. The lieutenants and justices of the peace, as well as the mayors and sheriffs in the West Country were to raise the hue and cry. The Lord General, the Earl of Northumberland, was to see that 'Evidence be prepared and sent against the times of their trial, which we require to be respited until then, that so the Parties guilty may not, for want of Evidence, escape the just Censure and Punishment of the Law.'[57]

Although the Somerset authorities failed miserably in preventing the killing, the Devon deputy lieutenants achieved a remarkable degree of success in capturing 140 of the 160 soldiers.[58] Given the ease with which men deserted during the Bishops' Wars, the government's best chance of seizing conscripts who had fled was to seek them out in their home parishes. Enforcement could best be achieved by the authorities in the county where the men had been pressed, not in the county where the crime had taken place.

Historians have been struck not only by the brutality of Evers's murder, but also the fact that the inhabitants and authorities in Wellington did not lift a finger to halt the murder or detain the assailants. 'The population of the town and neighborhood sympathised with the perpetrators of the crime. Not a man would stir to arrest the murderers. Even the neighbouring magistrates gave no assistance':

In Somerset, at Wellington, the Devon troops turned on a Romanist lieutenant named Evers, devastated his quarters, flayed him to death with ferocious brutality, and dragged his remains through the street of the town while the constables and

---

[56] PRO, SP 16/463/88, f. 2, examinations of John Toute and William Tout; f. 3, examinations of John Moore and William Shapcott; f. 4, examinations of Thomas Clarke, Henry Vaughan, John Knowle, and John Badcocke; f. 1, examinations of Hannibal Pounceford and Robert Carpenter; f. 3, examination of John Knowle.

[57] PRO, SP 45/10/213; Larkin (ed.), *Stuart Royal Proclamations*, vol. II, pp. 722–4.

[58] PRO, SP 16/464/55, Devon deputy lieutenants to the Privy Council, 21 August 1640.

folk stood idly by. The commanding officer on sending to the nearest Somerset deputy for assistance received none.

Wellington's reluctance to become involved in this distasteful business cost them a £200 fine, 'though at the next assizes, estreat of the fine was ordered stayes'.[59]

Since the inhabitants of Wellington had been sympathetic to the soldiers' dislike of popish officers, most assuredly their neighbours and kin in Devon would be, too. The soldiers had not gone voluntarily to Wellington to seek out Evers and kill him. They had been pressed against their will to serve under Romish officers, whose popishness could be found out if they absented themselves from church or from protestant communion. The soldiers quartered in Braintree, for example, knew this. The Lord Lieutenant reported: 'I find the souldyer is very jelous in point of their Religion. They haveing often moved me That their officers might receive the Comunion with them.'[60] Troops in Worcestershire behaved in similar fashion by insisting that their officers take communion with them. Demanding greater assurances that their commanders were not papists, the men made them swear that they harboured no Roman Catholic allegiance, and that the expedition against Scotland would not be to the disadvantage of the Protestant faith.[61]

Englishmen resented forced military service and the intrusion of the press-gang or recruiting officer into their parochial existence. Pressed soldiers, not militiamen, perpetrated the great disorders of summer 1640. One should note, too, that the conductor Mohun committed the first act of violence, the laceration of the drummer, which sparked the tumult. Evers appears not to have committed an overt act of violence, but Mohun's murder served as a precedent. The Devonshire men knew that the Dorsetshire men had killed their officer and had been treated with surprising leniency. The weakness of the government's response indulged restiveness. In 1640, violence begat violence, be it murder, iconoclastic attacks on churches, or demolishing enclosures. As for 'class conflict' certainly there were those who seized the opportunity to inflict injury upon their social betters.

The success of Mohun's assailants and the government's rather flaccid response could only encourage troops some of whom regarded their commanders as subversive agents of antichrist. Evers's Catholicism was fairly certain and the soldiers' insistence that Evers take communion with them was a deliberate test of his religious affiliation. Mohun and Evers died

---

59 Gardiner, *History*, vol. IX, p. 172; Barnes, *Somerset 1625–1640*, p. 276.
60 PRO, SP 16/461/25, Warwick to Vane, 27 July 1640.
61 Huntingdonshire RO, Manchester MS. 32/5/17, Nathaniel Fiennes newsletter, 11 July 1640.

because they personified the Catholic conspiracy. The crypto-Catholic tri-umvirate of Arundel, Cottington, and Windebank advocated an aggressive military posture in 1639. The King had also been egged on by those papal agents and Catholic courtiers who surrounded his wife. As for money, the war was financed, so they said, by Catholics at home and abroad. In fact, the Queen had urged Roman Catholics to make special contributions to the war effort, and the King asked troops and loans from Rome, Madrid, and other places.[62]

In the eyes of many common soldiers, the Bishops' Wars were being waged for the benefit of the whore of Babylon, indeed Lucifer himself. The bishops, for whom ostensibly the war was to be fought, were seen as abominable relics of a superstitious past, something to be discarded, not preserved. As Sir John Wray remarked in the aftermath of the Bishops' Wars, 'we might as well meddle with bishops now as Henry VIII did with abbeys in his time'. Puffed up with 'episcopapal pride', as a pamphleteer put it, bishops were a cancerous remnant. The popish conspiracy prolifer-ated above and lay hidden from the mainstream of English life, not within it. Apart from rocking and stoning the bishops' carriages as they moved to and from the House of Lords or storming Archbishop Laud's Lambeth residence, the evil ones around the King were untouchable. The Roman Catholic officers were readily accessible. Denied opportunities to lash out against popery, and for the most part reluctant about military service in general, attacks against Romanist officers revealed long-pent up animosity as well as immediate anger over the circumstances of 1640. The popish officer personified the wicked force that was not only subverting the realm, but the entire world.

The murders were unique. English enlisted men very often disliked, sometimes despised, their captains. But the situation in 1640 encouraged destructive and mutinous behaviour far different from that of other post-Reformation English military enterprises. Men who even under more ideo-logically comprehensible circumstances would have been disagreeable about military service became dangerous when they believed they had been pressed into the service of the 'Pope of Lambeth' to fight cousin prot-estants. This was not a mutiny modelled on the Army of Flanders's sys-tematic extortion of pay and improved living conditions from the central government. These murders, like the iconoclastic attacks on churches and demolition of enclosures, were spontaneous and the soldiers appear to have gained little or no material advantage from the violence, unless one counts the crucifix that Hannibal Pounceford took from the corpse of Lieutenant Evers. The murders were desperate, vindictive, and brutal

---

[62] Hibbard, 'The Contribution of 1639', pp. 42–60.

assaults on personifications of popery. The political situation in the country loosened the bands that might have restrained this religious fanaticism. The violence of the soldiery in summer 1640 was immediately preceded by extensive rioting in London, particularly in the wake of the precipitous dissolution of the Short Parliament on 5 May. The disturbances prompted Charles's government, for the last time in English history, to resort to the rack to secure confessions as evidence[63].

The murders do raise some difficult questions, however. Was the anti-popery of the common soldier the same as that of an MP sitting in the House of Commons in late April 1640? Did an unlettered and unwashed pikeman perceive the 'popish conspiracy' in the same light as did John Pym? Popery, whatever it might be, frightened so many Englishmen that it must be reckoned as a primary motivation for the disorder of the Second Bishops' War (though the First Bishops' War may well have been different). Similar communion 'litmus test' episodes occurred, as for example at Warminster in Wiltshire. Captain Drury's company was preparing to march north in early June.

Some soldiers had heard their captain was a Roman Catholic, and ... put it to Drury that they might all receive the sacrament before they set out. Drury showed little inclination to do so, at least for his own receiving, but the soldiers pressed him so much the more to it. When he would not, they told him plainly that if he would not receive communion and pray with them, they would not fight under him. In this manner they cashiered their captain.[64]

In Brecknock one finds that among the captains conducting that county's contingent were Henry O'Brien and John Fitzgerald, presumably Irish Catholics.

Returning to Devon, the county for which we have more indentures surviving from 1640 than for any other English county (though not the north division, from which the murderers were impressed), we discover the name of young Francis Windebank, son of the famous Secretary, whose familial religious inclination was most certainly Romanist. Young Francis's fate in 1640 was strikingly different from that of Lieutenant Evers:

When I first received my men, divers of them swore desperately if they found we were Papists they would soon despatch us; but I finding their humours, upon my first day's march I desired them all to kneel down and sing psalms, and made one of my officers to read prayers, which pleased them not a little, and being very familiar with them at the first, giving them drink and stinking tobacco of sixpence a pound, gained their loves, so as they all now swear they will never leave me so long as they live, and, indeed, I have not had one man run from met yet in this nine days' march; but other captains of our regiment are so fearful of their soldiers

[63] Gardiner, *History*, vol. IX, p. 141.
[64] PRO, SP 16/456/44, 8 June 1640, Rossingham newsletter to Conway. See also p. 267 above.

having much threatened them and done much mischief ... the Puritan rascals of the country had strongly possessed the soldiers that all the commanders of our regiment were papists, so that I was forced for two or three days to sing psalms all the day I marched, for all their religion lies in a psalm.[65]

For some members of the lower orders, then, the Bishops' Wars were part of a larger struggle which was starkly simple. Either one fought for good, that is, protestantism, or evil, that is, popery. The situation was quite tidily summed up by 'Captain' Edmund Aylee, the iconoclast from Bishops Stortford, who had stated rather baldly that if Charles fought 'papists, they would fight on his side, and if the Scots fought papists, they would fight on the Scots' side'. The political situation pandered to this binary vision of the world. There is also the matter of prison attacks, where political factors do seem to have been involved, if only in the form of protecting local autonomy against incursions from the central government.

Most intriguing is the regional variation in types of violence. In Staffordshire, the enclosures were pulled down by local recruits, and attacks occurred both in 1639 and in 1640. In nearby Derbyshire, the attackers were the ubiquitous West Country men (predominantly from Somerset, Wiltshire, and Bristol), although we should keep in mind that the West Country men were allegedly incited and supported by malicious neighbours of Sir John Coke. The majority of disorders stemmed from the religious enthusiasm and bigotry which was unleashed by the political breakdown within the elite. However, the character of certain localities and the movements of the regiments from place to place, moulded and channelled the violence according to circumstance. The most markedly religious and political episodes occurred during mobilization. Protest and mutiny over pay occurred throughout the campaign, both in the recruiting localities, and in the north. If a certain population seemed prone to violence, it was most certainly the 'west country clownes', as Nathaniel Fiennes called them. Their activities spanned quite a spectrum: murder, enclosure rail burning, gaol-breaking, etc. The most spectacular attacks on churches, and on men of the cloth, occurred in the areas between Middlesex and the Wash, including Essex, Hertfordshire, the Isle of Ely, and northern Cambridgeshire. Pay became a more pronounced issue, while the religious disorders died down as summer lengthened. The violence demonstrated that the cooperation and consent that underlay English society was breaking down in response to the political stalemate created at Whitehall by the King's hand.

65 PRO, SP 16/460/46; 47.

8

Conclusion

Our survey of the mobilizations of 1639 and 1640 explains to a large degree the vulnerability of Charles I's government in autumn 1640. The weaknesses of the King's campaigns against Scotland are apparent: the difficulties in which the Council of War and the Ordnance Office found themselves, a chain of command rife with faction and ignorance, an appalling fiscal arrangement, the Crown's inability to hire mercenaries or to raise enthusiasm amongst the noblemen, and (perhaps above all) the dismal results of a decade of militia reform, which saw as its culmination disorder rather than discipline, inexperience rather than martial excellence. Can we then conclude that the military structure in England failed the King? On the contrary, it has been shown that Charles's decisions and policies brought about or aggravated these conditions. Governmental structures throughout Europe shared many of these flaws. The key to assessing English failure in the Bishops' Wars is to understand how the events of the campaigns occurred within the context of institutional limitations. The first chapter described how Charles I embarked upon and conducted the Bishops' Wars. The most striking conclusion one gleans from the narrative is that the royal strategies, and ensuing tactical moves, doomed the campaigns.

It is indeed true, as Conrad Russell has suggested, that the causes for the failure of 1640 are not necessarily the same as for 1639. But they are related, and in five critical categories Charles made the same or similar errors of judgement: strategy, officers, soldiers, supply, and tactics.

Strategy
The strategic error of threatening violence against the Covenant in 1639 was repeated by making good that threat in 1640 without the means to sustain it. The juxtaposition of these strategies undermined royal support on both sides of the border, pushing the Covenanters to increasingly militant postures and forcing the English to choose sides.

Officers

With the exception of Sir Jacob Astley, the officers of the First Bishops' War were inexpert and uninspiring. In contrast, the Covenanters selected what appear to have been able commanders. One cannot dismiss this matter by citing Scottish continental veterans as the critical factor, for such men were also available to Charles I and he did include some Scottish officers in his chain of command. More accurately, the selection for the King was determined by court connection while the kirk and committees of Scotland systematically sought out professionalism. Charles compounded his command problem in 1640 through the extraordinary turnover in officer corps personnel. Although better choice was made, many had not experienced at officer level the mobilization of 1639. Nor was the problem of the dearth of junior officers redressed. The only problem which was not ascribable to a failure of royal leadership was the coincidental illnesses of the King's foremost commanders in summer 1640, Northumberland and Strafford. Whether their vigorous leadership could have surmounted the fiscal and logistical hurdles the King had thrown in the path of victory seems doubtful. The tantalizing question remains as to whether Strafford could have won the First Bishops' War, if given the opportunity. His personality and administrative ability could better have compelled obedience in that more composed year of 1639.

Soldiers

If one mistake was repeated with devastating effect it was the substitution clause. The decision, albeit a dangerous one, not to call out the perfect militia *en masse* against the Covenant meant that the royal army would largely approximate to the riff-raff of an overseas expedition, with similar results. The ambiguous legal status of militia service might not have impeded a canny, brutal ruler such as Henry VIII or a master politician such as Elizabeth I. But the mobilizations of 1639 and 1640 were acted out in the shadow of the Petition of Right. The King's failure to recruit the right men was apparent in the disorders, especially in 1640, amongst his troops.

Supply

One cannot decide whether to pity more the Ordnance Officers or the tellers of the Exchequer of Receipt. Again, the Second Bishops' War saw the errors of the First Bishops' War repeated. Tardy and insufficient financing and procurement of supplies made the predicament of the Ordnance Office unenviable. Logistical miscalculations, which stemmed from time-tables for mobilization drafted by the King with his councillors, plagued the supply of weapons, food, and money in 1639 and 1640.

Tactics

When defeat came, it arrived with Scottish cavalry charging through the Tyne, preceded by an impressive Scottish cannonade. All the above, strategy, officer leadership, the quality of foot soldiers, and the dearth of arms, had so weakened the English forces that they crumbled at the first onslaught – the hasty retreat at Kelso in 1639 and Newburn fight in 1640. Properly prepared and deployed, the English army could have withstood the tactical reverses at Kelso and Newburn. All of this leads us back to the King.

Charles I caused the 1637 prayer book rebellion by his attempt to impose upon Scotland his policy of comprehensive uniformity. He could not enforce conformity, due to political and financial limitations which were the results of his Personal Rule: the absence of an English Parliament, and a nearly empty Exchequer. Although a Parliament would not or could not grant the entire million or so pounds necessary for a major Scottish campaign, some sort of accommodation would have demonstrated the cooperation of the ruled and made more palatable the mobilization in the localities.[1] If the parliamentary alternative was unacceptable, then a full Exchequer was an absolute necessity. As we have noted, the Exchequer on the eve of the Bishops' Wars was sometimes reduced to several hundred pounds. No wise ruler would have attacked under these circumstances.

In the years 1637–40 the King was unprepared politically, financially and administratively to enforce obedience upon Scotland. Yet he persisted, rather than alter his political agenda. He raised armies in 1639 and 1640, but failed to muster sufficient resources to keep them on a long-term footing. Worse, the strain of mobilization brought home the 'British problem' to Charles's English subjects. By choosing war in 1639 and 1640 Charles compounded his political and financial weakness because the consent of the whole realm had not been solicited, a critical consideration since the King could not absorb the cost of war from his own resources, which in turn brought into question the means by which the regime mobilized, specifically, the legal context of coat-and-conduct money and the expenses and use of the militia[2].

Hesitation and scepticism on the part of his subjects should not have surprised Charles I. The military prerogative had been questioned to its very foundation in the Parliament of 1628. The common lawyers William Hakewill and John Selden had challenged the legal basis of impressment.

---

[1] Russell, *FBM*, p. 93.
[2] Charles was the rightful ruler. However, was he living up to his responsibilities as the font of all justice and protector of the Church of England? See R. Zaller, 'Legitimation and Delegitimation in Early Modern Europe: The Case of England', *History of European Ideas*, 10, no. 6 (1989), pp. 641–65.

In his analysis of the extant statutory law, Selden argued 'in all these statutes there is not a word of any soldiers pressed or sent away by compulsion, and so the law then [prior to the reign of Elizabeth I] knew no pressing'. Selden's theory that Elizabethan innovation was distinct from medieval recruitment was pedantic and historically incorrect. As has been argued above, late Tudor and early Stuart impressment evolved from the indenture system of the Middle Ages. But for a lawyer the case is more important than the truth. The fact remained that on the floor of the Commons it had been argued, in Paul Christianson's words, that 'the Crown could not press troops legally'.[3] The subsequent dissolution of Parliament and ensuing Personal Rule only increased suspicion about the King's appreciation of the rule of law. Thus when he began the war against the Scots he was on unsound ground legally as well as institutionally. As the Council of War realized when they proposed the revocation of monopolies and patents in November 1638, the hearts and minds of Charles's subjects needed to be prepared for war.[4]

Unpreparedness was a direct result of the King's choices of strategy, timetable, and ministers. The maintenance and performance of the Exchequer, Ordnance Office, and lieutenancy were assumed to be adequate to win a Scottish war. In 1639 English success may well have been a possibility, but the King was outbluffed by the Scots. In 1640, when armed confrontation was a stronger possibility, the decision to pursue war was ill-advised, given a comparably worse financial situation and the controversy generated by a failed Parliament in spring 1640. Charles had difficulty in discerning the constraints, especially financial, under which his government functioned. The King formulated impressive plans but stumbled in carrying them through, usually due to poor judgement, mismanagement of Parliament and unrealistic demands upon governmental institutions. His conception of kingship was abstract, not grounded in the practical business of institutions.[5] Charles failed militarily because he was a failure as a politician.[6] It was the administrator that failed, not the institutions.

Charles personally chose the military option. He alone drew the sword to halt unrest in Scotland. In 1639 he wished not to have to use that sword,

[3] P. Christianson, 'Arguments on Billeting and Marital Law in the Parliament of 1628', paper presented at the 30 May 1992 conference of the Canadian Historical Association. I am grateful to Paul Christianson for allowing me to see an early draft of this work, which will be incorporated into his forthcoming book on John Selden.

[4] See above, pp. 68–70.

[5] Certainly Charles was not unique in this. See Alsop, 'Government, Finance, and the Community of the Exchequer', pp. 119–22.

[6] See J. Richards, '"His Noew Majestie" and the English Monarchy: The Kingship of Charles I before 1640', Past and Present, 113 (1986), pp. 70–96.

hoping that the Covenanters might be bullied into obedience. In 1640 he decided to fight because it seemed the only honourable course open to him and he therefore expected to have the requisite resources simply because he was the King. The Covenanters, he reasoned, would be defeated, because to rebel against one's sovereign was criminal. The rebellion was a simple matter of right or wrong. When confronted by their armed and indignant King, how could the Scots continue to use this cloak of religion as a mask for rebellion? Charles's naivete and monochromatic view of religion and politics, along with his impatience with the details of government, undermined any practical strategy against the Covenant. The triple-pronged strategy of 1639 operated on the assumption that money, supplies, and men were available at only a few months' notice. Charles made the same assumption in 1640, even after the Short Parliament had come to nought. Not all royal councillors wore blinkers. Northumberland saw the unfolding tragedy from his place at the council table:

I am yet unable to satisfye my selfe what the successe of our greate designes for the North are likely to come to, money we have not to begin this warre, [nor] to rayse an army of new and un = [trained] men wanting meanes to [maintain] them I hold no wayes councellable in these broaken times, when the kingdome in general is infinitely discontented. The conditions that .102. [the King] is in is extreemly unhappie, I could not beleeve that wise men would ever have brought us into such a straight as now we are in without being certaine of a remedie.[7]

Lack of extraordinary funds and the absence of political consensus had profound strategic and tactical ramifications which lead to defeat. The 1639 rendezvous by its nature obliged the King to coordinate skilfully the separate branches of his amalgamated army, comprised of nobles, untrained pressed men, and militia units from various shires (the latter being reconstituted due to the substitution clause). April 1639 was largely wasted in assembling and training these forces at a time when a prompt attack might have caught the Covenanters still preparing.[8] As he hoped that preparations alone might win the war (as Clarendon put it[9]) this course might have borne fruit. But Charles's methodical mobilization, plodding bureaucracy, shortage of cash, and strategy of the bluff prevented a royal lightning stroke, the only kind of strategy which would have worked in 1639. In short, Charles chose the wrong strategy. The squandering of Hamilton's force, the only army which might have been capable of delivering such a blow, through poor intelligence (so that he was denied a

[7] Centre for Kentish Studies, De L'Isle and Dudley Papers, Sydney MSS., U 1500 C2/43, f. 1, Northumberland to the Earl of Leicester, 14 May 1640. The words in brackets have been destroyed by holes worn through the paper. I have suggested the likely phraseology.
[8] Hamilton's expedition is an instructive example of Charles's failure to press home a potential advantage.
[9] See p. 37 above.

landing place) wasted valuable victuals, men and ships, exacerbating the King's weakness.[10] Waging war on a shoestring meant that logistical miscalculations could not be afforded. The same lack of judgement (and intelligence) led to the rout at Kelso and the premature negotiations of the Treaty of Berwick.[11]

The wasted opportunities of 1639 presaged worse for 1640. The political error of calling and then abruptly dissolving the Short Parliament made mobilization even more sullen and resented than before. The subsequent postponement of the mobilization until mid-June 1640 had its most fateful result in the inadequacy of English defences along the Tyne, across which the Scots came at Newburn Ford. Sir Jacob Astley refused to commit forces in Yorkshire to Tyneside because they were unpaid and mutinous, thus the limitations imposed by politics and finance upon tactics were fatal. Once again Charles failed to field his perfect militia, largely because the localities lacked enthusiasm for the war and because of the liberal use of the substitution clause. The absence of a statutory basis for the perfect militia inclined Charles to tolerate this loophole. With no firm legal foundation for militia service he had in effect created a weapon controlled by his subjects, not by himself.[12]

In deciding upon war in 1638 and 1640, the King heeded only those voices which promised victory. He trusted few unreservedly, probably only the Queen, Hamilton, Vane, and Arundel. Not even the proponents of 'thorough', Laud and Strafford, served as the innermost royal counsel. Such an attitude prevented Charles from having diverse perspectives on the realities facing him. Few in his circle suggested that perhaps he was not governing so well, or that he was alienating important constituencies within the realm.[13] This was a ruler who eschewed the ruled. He made few progresses in the shires, thwarted the gentry's petitioning by secluding himself, and trimmed the aspirations of the nobility by making the court a closed community and promoting the episcopate. He seems to have taken for granted the allegiance of his subjects, save for a favoured few, and showed little interest in the complications or imperfections of applied

---

[10] We must remember, too, that Hamilton's predicament was the result of Charles's misreading of political and religious sentiment in the north, for their supporters were unsuccessful in securing bridgeheads.

[11] 'Premature' in that once having placed his army on the border its presence might have worn down the resources of the Covenanters. Charles backed down from his bluff too soon, even if it were a dubious stratagem. Abandoning it quickly made matters worse.

[12] Russell, *FBM*, pp. 73–4; Fissel, 'Scottish War and English Money', pp. 206–8.

[13] Charles's unwillingness to listen to different points of view was illustrated nicely by Northumberland's remark that he was obeying his summons to the Council meeting 'Though my being there will be to little purpose'. Centre for Kentish Studies, De L'Isle and Dudley MSS., Sydney Papers, U 1475 C85/4, to the Earl of Leicester, 12 December 1639. See, however, pp. 68–70 above on the issues of patents and monopolies.

government. It is no surprise that he discarded the messy institution of Parliament in 1629 and spring 1640. In fact, when he summoned the Short Parliament he did so for supply only. Discussion of policy or redress of grievances were not even to be considered. The opinions and reactions of the ruled were irrelevant. Charles had succeeded in isolating himself from the political nation, but at his peril.[14] He created this arrangement; it was not forced upon him.

He was as unreasonable with institutions as with politics. The council was asked to bring off a war which the realm was at that time incapable of fighting, and the King, self-willed and myopic, chose to deal with the Covenant through military action. In 1639 Charles chose his own officers and changed commanders in 1640 on his own judgement and instincts. Many officers, from the Lord General down, did not have the misfortunes of the 1639 campaign from which to learn. Hence the one positive aspect of the expedition, its experience, was partially negated. A high percentage of new officers started from scratch.[15] Just as Charles expected miracles from his councils and officers, similarly unrealistic, and untimely, demands were imposed upon the Ordnance Office. Given the depleted state of the office and the production limitations of English arms' manufacturers (along with the unreliability of imports), Charles's expectations exceeded his institutions' capabilities. For example, considering that the King had decided to fight in 1640, the absence of cannon at Newburn Ford was inexcusable. Either cannon should have been sent to Newcastle earlier in the year, or Charles should have delayed fighting until 1641, so that the garrisons, fords, and bridges could have been made defensible. That cannon lay useless at Hull was a result of the King's erratic mobilization.[16] Similarly, the expectation that the Exchequer could put coins in the officers' pockets instantaneously is another example of Charles's inability to understand his

[14] Charles's isolation is admirably described in Donald, *An Uncounselled King*, pp. 17–42, 172–285, 320–7; Reeve, *Charles I and the Road to Personal Rule*, pp. 195–208, 293–6, especially p. 206; Lee, *The Road to Revolution*, pp. 233–44, especially the last page.

[15] See p. 89 above. Perhaps many officers declined to serve in 1640 because of their financial losses in the First Bishops' War. It was estimated by a privy councillor, the Earl of Northumberland, that in 1639 'the rayseing every trouope [of horse] stood the Captain in 6 or 800£ above the King's allowance'. Centre for Kentish Studies, De L'Isle and Dudley MSS., Sydney Papers, U 1475 C85/4, ff. 2v–3, to the Earl of Leicester, 12 December 1639.

[16] Strafford, as a voice crying in the wildnerness, admonished the leadership of the Second Bishops' War that there was insufficient ordnance at Newcastle. He specifically pointed to the bottleneck at Hull. See the case of J. Watkinson, who was unable to find land carriage by which to get powder and match to the soldiers and so had to 'hire a littell boott [boat] to Rowe up to Selbe' for the rendezvous. Stafford RO, D (w) 1778/I., i., no. 2, to William Legge, 24 June 1640. Strafford's greatest complaint was not 'institutional', but rather that court politics interfered with the mobilization. The trained bands and Lord Conway did not respond to his leadership. He accused Secretary Vane of displacing his authority. SRO, GD 406/1/1230, Strafford to Hamilton, 25 August 1640.

institutions. He chose to fight when the Exchequer was virtually empty and in the knowledge that the army's budget far exceeded his peacetime revenue. True, shortages of money plagued virtually every army in the era of the Thirty Years' War. But the Bishops' Wars were waged on English soil. What greater motivation to make certain troops were paid? Charles, though, seems not to have worried much about the plundered tradesman, despoiled farmer, or hungry trooper.

Charles I simply did not wish to see things from any point of view save his own. The King's servants were harried, unappreciated, and often despised, for they quite frequently attempted the impossible at the behest of their royal master. The King, in fact, largely left the coordination of the Bishops' Wars to his subordinates just as he frequently avoided the disagreeable duties of kingship by spurning petitioners, neglecting council meetings, and eliminating ceremonies before the unwashed multitude. This exercise of authority (or lack of it) was not accompanied by any royal willingness to re-examine policies which hindered the King's servants' efforts. He assumed that government would function smoothly, just as he took for granted the allegiance of his people. Under the circumstances, English institutions performed reasonably well; as for the ruled, they for the most part obeyed, if with grumbling and excuse-making. Even mutinous and (on occasion) murderous soldiers marched themselves into the north. Still the nation obeyed. The Bishops' Wars did force the King to contend with Parliament once again, but they did not provoke a Civil War, British or English. The institutional breakdown would come only with the Long Parliament.[17]

The most unrealistic policies of Charles's campaigns involved royal finances, whose realistic assessment should have discouraged a major expedition fought without benefit of parliamentary subsidies or a reasonable surplus in the Exchequer. The solicitation of loans and contributions would have benefited a war fought in 1639.[18] But a second campaign immediately after a failed Parliament undermined the King's political and financial credibility by demonstrating his inability to manage Parliament and his unwillingness to heed its counsels at a time of perceived crisis. It also publicly called into doubt his royal sagacity. Policies which appeared as misguided in 1639 looked illegal in 1640. The break with Parliament implied broadly that the Crown pursued policies contrary to the wishes of the country. The collection of coat-and-conduct money without reimbursement to the shires was implemented within memory of the forced loan and

---

[17] For the breakdown, see A. Fletcher, *The Outbreak of the English Civil War* (New York, 1981), and Russell, *FBM*.

[18] C. M. Hibbard argues that the clergy contribution fared well in 1639; see 'Episcopal Warriors', pp. 169–70, 173–4, especially the latter page.

with parliamentary reference to the ship money case. The deliberations of the Short Parliament provided ample constitutional grounds for resisting payment.[19] What is significant is that most continued to pay, though not enough for the Crown's needs.

As was the case with the Ordnance, Charles assumed that the Exchequer would function rapidly and efficiently in spite of a depleted treasury and the unusual political circumstances of the war (which disinclined men to pay promptly if they paid at all). In 1639 Charles's hopes were partly the fault of Juxon, a bad choice for Lord Treasurer anyway, who assured him that money would be found.[20] Money was found, but not at all quickly enough. It seems that when Charles did accept counsel it had to confirm his plans. Hence it was reinforcement, not advice, which reached the King's ear.[21] A good example of such deliberation can be found at the 5 May 1640 meeting of the Privy Council. Voices which warned of financial and logistical problems were drowned out by advocates of the policy which most pleased the King. Given the financial condition of the Crown, Charles should have postponed battle until the Exchequer was better filled. His poverty forced him to draw further upon the resources of his subjects, further delegitimizing his regime by the processes of raising money and men.

The manner in which men were called upon to fight also reflected both Charles's bare comprehension of the administrative complexities of war and his political insensitivity. Feudal summonses in 1639 and 1640 could only embarrass a nobility no longer skilled in combat and alienate the most influential stratum of English society. Charles's insistence upon *personal* service and obedience made the matter worse. As would happen at Nottingham in 1642, England's elite were forced either to endorse royal policy by hefting their swords or to disobey the King's command. No middle ground existed.

The King also had determined to create a 'perfect militia' during the Personal Rule. Charles, as was his style, had ignored the controversies over muster-masters, militia rates, and the like, and demanded compliance without considering the political situation in the localities.[22] During the

[19] Fissel, 'Scottish War and English Money', pp. 201–12.
[20] This uncharitable view should be considered along with that of Tom Mason's *Serving God and Mammon*. I am grateful for several conversations with Tom Mason regarding Juxon, though the opinion expressed here does not coincide with that developed in his book.
[21] Reeve, *Charles I and The Road to Personal Rule*, pp. 199–247, and Donald, *An Uncounselled King*, pp. 1–42, 320–7.
[22] The rift between Charles and the shires over lieutenancy and related military matters is well documented. Most influential in the formulation of this interpretation have been Barnes, *Somerset 1625–1640*, pp. 98–123, 244–80, Fletcher, *Sussex*, pp.175–227, and C. Holmes, *Seventeenth-Century Lincolnshire* (Lincoln, 1980), pp. 64–87, 104–40.

1630s he remained oblivious to the process by which the trained bands would have to be transformed. He initiated an exact militia but did not persevere and guide the programme.[23] Had Leslie's men found a couple of well-trained militia regiments, strengthened with a little artillery, defending the south bank of the Tyne, the English army might not have collapsed in September 1640. The attack might even have been repelled. But Charles never gave the militia, 'perfect' or not, a chance to prove itself. In 1639 the East Anglian militia that accompanied Hamilton were diverted to Inchcolm and Inchkeith.[24] The militia never figured in either of the Bishops' Wars, since a good many of them never marched. The substitution clause debased Charles's most prominent military force. Given the private nature of Scottish forces, it is doubtful that they would have been a match for the Caroline militia, if the trained bands had been as they were designed to be.

Pressed men Charles got, who marched the breadth of the English countryside. Better, many thought, that they should have marched on foreign soil. Anxious, propertied citizens were offended, as were the grumbling pressed troops, and all this for a pitiful collection of men, badly officered and mutinous. The abortive attempts to enlist foreign mercenaries further besmirched the King's reputation. Charles saw no hypocrisy in condemning the Scots for asking Louis XIII to intervene in making peace while he looked to Spain, Holland, Denmark, and elsewhere to help make war against his own subjects. Given the religious tensions and political uncertainties of the late 1630s, these negotiations showed clearly Charles's lack of political acumen. For all these machinations (the knight-errant nobles, the meddled-with militia. and the herded pressed men) the King never really got the kind of army he wanted. But that seems not to have mattered much, for the royal conduct of the wars of 1639 and 1640 never really pitted English arms against the Covenanters, save for Lunsford's men at Newburn Ford. Charles did, however, raise in 1639 and 1640 armies of about 20,000 men, a testament to the ability of English administration in spite of fiscal strain, religious controversy, and political dislocation.

Charles warred against his own subjects. The Tudors, in spite of the royally directed changes in ecclesiastical structure and religious practice, retained a political consensus within the realm which Charles did not achieve. Rather, he threw away the advantages he possessed, such as his peaceful accession, Anglican upbringing, and the Union of the Crowns.

---

[23] Conrad Russell makes the point that the militia, imperfect as it might have been, was the most powerful armed body in the realm ('The Scottish Party in English Parliaments', pp. 6–13). He also points out that the militia may have been 'sacrificed' to ship money in the late 1630s: *FBM*, p. 75.

[24] PRO, SP 16/419, Kentish militia indenture and pp. 5, 23, 83–4 above.

The Tudors seemed to have grasped the nature of their power more clearly, through an understanding of the institutions at their disposal, and possessed keen political insight.[25] Charles did not see things as clearly. In 1639 he bluffed when he should have fought and in 1640 plunged ahead when he should have hesitated. Charles's upbringing perhaps inclined him to think he could afford to make an error or two. His dynastic security (a peaceful accession, no rivals, no European powers capable of unseating him through invasion or the promotion of a pretender) may have fostered royal complacency.

The headstrong and insulated nature of Caroline government revealed in the Personal Rule is evident in the Bishops' Wars. The disasters of Charles's rule were largely of his own making.[26] The institutional flaws and structural weaknesses illuminated by revisionist scholarship must be placed within a more personal and political context, for it was the King's political actions based upon his personal viewpoint that determined how and when institutions functioned. According to L. J. Reeve, 'Charles's commitment to kingship as he saw it has disguised the fact that it was not a task which he could ever (or probably would ever) have embraced by choice. His real interests and abilities lay elsewhere ... Charles was not a political man.'[27] Nor was he a military man. The Tudors, often more brutal and innovative, possessed a more astute sense of government, politics, and human nature. The Tudors learned from their mistakes, but Charles did not learn from the 1620s. The failures of 1639 and 1640 were those of the King, not the realm. Thus Charles I fell from the throne; he was not pushed, if the Bishops' Wars were an indication of things to come. An inept ruler, not social forces, brought about the collapse of 1640.

Circumstances and institutions surely moulded the conditions with which the King contended. Charles's financial weakness was very much dictated by the comparatively modest means of the English Crown and the practice of soliciting extraordinary revenue through Parliament to supplement the Exchequer's regular income. But it was Charles's individual decision to rule without Parliament and, later, to enforce ecclesiastical

---

[25] Henry VIII's State Papers possess extensive documentation of the logistics of the 1544 campaign. Although one cannot argue from absence of evidence, no such kind of documents exists for the Bishops' Wars. One must wonder if late Henrician campaigns were better organized. *Letters and Papers of Henry VIII*, vol. XIX (1544), pt. 1 (London, 1903), pp.141–66, nos. 271–6. Certainly Charles had experience which he could have learned from, had he been inclined to look at the facts. The 1627 La Rochelle expedition had faltered due to lack of money (Stewart, 'Arms and Expeditions', p. 122). The Crown's poverty had a direct effect on naval construction in the 1630s (Andrew Thrush, 'Naval Finance and the Origins and Development of Ship Money', in *War and Government in Britain, 1598–1650*, ed. Fissel, pp. 135, 141).

[26] Lee, *The Road to Revolution*, p. 244.

[27] Reeve, *Charles I and The Road to Personal Rule*, pp. 3, 197.

uniformity by the sword that placed the sovereign in an untenable position. He had assumed an aggressive posture without the political consensus, religious justification, or institutional preparadness requisite for such a policy. Charles placed himself and his government in jeopardy. It was through no fault of his that the Ordnance Office was at times inefficient, cumbersome, and riddled with corruption; but if the King were to commit that institution to war, he needed to replenish its stores and personnel, making an effort to understand how well suited the institution was to meet the obligations he demanded of it. Certainly social forces were at work, particularly religious ferment. But were they any greater in magnitude than those which had wracked the 1540s and the 1590s?

Charles's failure as a warrior prince matched his failure as a monarch in general. To be precise, Charles declined to uphold tradition and custom when it suited him, willing to 'inovat and spare not' when the ends justified the means.[28] Rulers might propose new solutions to new problems, but ship money, Arminianism, and 'thorough' gave the King a reputation for upsetting a harmonious state in order to achieve goals which his subjects did not share. Likewise, as Conrad Russell noted, Charles I appeared not to play by the rules. He was not an honourable man, an allegation he proved during the procedure on the Petition of Right and finally in the Civil War. His arbitrary style of rule seemed neither rational nor legal. The forced loan and ship money certainly hampered the collection of coat-and-conduct money, his subjects believing that the King, the font of all justice, was disregarding the law. And worse, Charles in the eyes of many had betrayed his grave responsibility to foster and protect the Church of England. That he had taken up arms against Protestant Scots was proof enough. The King had betrayed the realm and the church. But no revolution occurred in 1640 in spite of the delegitimation of Charles's government. In turn, Parliament was expected to step in, purge the impurities, and restore the status quo, whatever that might be. When it did so, somewhat reluctantly and uncertainly at times, the monarchy never fully regained the authority that Charles I had claimed for it in the years leading up to and including the Bishops' Wars.

If the Bishops' Wars tell us anything about the origins of civil war in Britain it is that Charles I bears responsibility for his own fate and the sufferings of the realm. In well-known lines written only a couple of years before the birth of Charles I, an English soldier voiced sentiments which reflected the predicament of monarch and subjects in the face of an unpopular war:

---

[28] J. Malcolm, 'Charles I on Innovation: A Confidential Directive on an Explosive Issue', *BIHR*, 53, no. 128 (1980), pp. 252–5.

if the cause be not good, the King himself hath a heavy reckoning to make, when all those legs and arms and heads chopped off in a battle shall join together at the latter day, and cry all, 'We died at such a place' – some swearing, some crying for a surgeon, some upon their wives left poor behind them, some upon the debts they owe, some upon their children rawly left. I am afeard there are few die well that die in a battle, for how can they charitably dispose of anything, when blood is their argument? Now, if these men do not die well, it will be a black matter for the King that led them to it – who to disobey were against all proportion of subjection.[29]

The chaos wrought by the Bishops' Wars pales in comparison with the devastation of the ensuing civil wars. What divine judgement Charles I met in 1649 mortals do not know. But this has not dissuaded historians from judging his kingship and searching for the origins of the civil war in Britain.[30]

[29] William Shakespeare, *Henry V*, 4.1, lines 129–40. Although Shakespeare permitted King Henry to refute the soldier's argument, and certainly by no stretch of the imagination compromised the playwright's reverence for monarchy, the very nature of history plays encouraged moral judgements.

[30] Kevin Sharpe's impressive *The Personal Rule of Charles I* (New Haven, Conn., 1992) became available too late to be addressed by this work. One must agree with him that under different circumstances, such as a more timely English military intervention, Charles might have won either of the Bishops' Wars. However, it is difficult to accept without qualification assertions such as 'the rabble had become a nationalist army' by June 1639, or that in 1640 'the army was well backed by artillery and supplies' (pp. 805, 894). I have laboured to show that amalgamated royal armies in 1639 and 1640 were dominated by regional identities (for both pressed and trained soldiers) and an inchoate military obligation which worked against a 'national' (though not necessarily ethnic, i.e. English) collective sense of identity. As for artillery, arms, supplies, money, and men, speed of delivery and location were as important as availability (see above, pp. 18–19, 23, 49–52, 59–60, 77, 91–110, 131–51, 153–4, 170–1, 196, 252, 262–3).

A major thrust of this book has been that Charles I bears the brunt of responsibility for his defeat in the Bishops' Wars. Finger-pointing and the transference of blame were all too common when disaster overtook the court of Charles I. In the aftermath of Newburn, various counsellors tried to make a scapegoat of Edward Viscount Conway, and now Kevin Sharpe suggests that victory might have been salvaged save for a 'final failure of nerve on Conway's part' (p. 895). It is ironic that on the eve of the twenty-first century the field has divided between 'royalist' historians such as Kevin Sharpe, engaged in defending Caroline rule, and those sceptical about Charles I, who have aligned themselves with a descendant of the Earl of Bedford.

BIBLIOGRAPHY

MANUSCRIPT SOURCES

Alnwick Castle, Northumberland

Letters and Papers of the Earl of Northumberland, vols. XV and XVI (British Manuscripts Project microfilm 286 was used)

Arundel Castle, Sussex

Autograph Letters, 1632–1723
A. 1307, schedule of the Earl of Arundel's debts
A. 90, household, travelling, and estate accounts, 1636–44

Avon Reference Library, Bristol

B 28176, transcripts of the Smyth of Ashton Court MSS lost prior to purchase by the Bristol Record Office

Birmingham Reference Library

Coventry papers

Bodleian Library, Oxford

Additional MS. c. 259, Beaumont papers
Bankes MSS. 5/81; 18/2–3; 18/5; 27/10; 44/13; 58/1–2; 59/23; 65/53, miscellaneous papers of Attorney General Sir John Bankes, 1634–41
Carte MS. I, Irish papers (including Wandesford and Ormonde correspondence)
Carte MS. XL, Irish papers (including an account of the Irish army under Strafford, 1640)
Carte MS. XLIV, Irish papers, 1660–70 (but containing copies of letters from the period of the Bishops' Wars)
Carte MS. LXIII, Irish papers, 1634–57
Carte MS. LXVI, Irish papers (including copies of Wentworth correspondence from the 1630s)
Carte MS. LXXVII, Irish papers (including papers of the Earl of Huntingdon and Lord Wharton)

Carte MS. LXXX, papers of Philip, Lord Wharton

Carte MS. CLXXVI, Irish papers (including Strafford's commission of 12 September 1640)

Clarendon State Papers, IX-XIX, official and private correspondence from the reign of Charles I

Firth MS. c.4, a letter-book containing correspondence of deputy lieutenants and justices of the peace in Essex, 1608–1639

Radcliffe Trust MS. c.36, letter of Secretary Sir Francis Windebank to Charles I, 2 September 1640

Rawlinson MS. b.210, an anonymous account of the First Bishops' War, 1639

Tanner MS. LV, letters and papers, 1640

Tanner MS. LVII, letters and papers, 1638–39

Tanner MS. LIX, letters and papers, 1600s

Tanner MS. CLXXVII, a letter-book containing correspondence of deputy lieutenants and justices of the peace in Caroline Norfolk

Bristol Record Office

Smyth of Ashton Court MSS

British Library, London

Additional MS. 5754, original documents relating to Scotland, northern borders, garrisons, and Ireland in the sixteenth and seventeenth centuries

Additional MS. 10609, Welsh military papers, including Brecon muster rolls, 1608–37

Additional MS. 11045, Scudamore papers, vol. V, Rossingham newsletters addressed to John, first Lord Scudamore, 1639–40

Additional MS. 12093, royal autographs, including Charles I's letter to the Prince of Orange

Additional MS. 17677, transcripts from The Hague, Joachimi letters, 1637–39

Additional MS. 18979, Fairfax correspondence, 1625–88

Additional MS. 28273, John Locke memoranda, 1630–55, including Sir Ralph Hopton's Somerset muster roll for May 1639

Additional MS. 28566, John Aston's diary of the First Bishops' War

Additional MS. 34217, State Papers, letters, etc. in the time of James I–Charles II

Additional MS. 38847, Sir Edward Walker's notes, including a map of the camp at Berwick, June 1639

Additional MS. 39245, Wodehouse lieutenancy papers, including correspondence of deputy lieutenants and justices of the peace of Suffolk, 1608–1640

Additional MS. 57929, seventeenth-century papers

Coke MSS. (originally at Melbourne Hall, Derbyshire, these papers were housed temporarily at the Derbyshire Record Office, and have now been acquired by the British Library)

Egerton MS. 2533, State Papers, including military and Ireland

Harleian MS. 841, Bishop Burnet's draft of his history of the Dukes of Hamilton

Harleian MS. 2192, Imberhorne Survey, including list of lighthorse from Canterbury, 1638

Harleian MS. 2285, Hertfordshire muster book, 1640

Harleian MS. 4014, Cambridgeshire militia papers, 1626–40

Harleian MS. 4931, miscellaneous political papers, including Bishops' Wars broadsheet

Harleian MS. 6801, seventeenth century papers, including account of the Second Bishops' War

Harleian MS. 6844, military papers

Harleian MS. 6851, papers relating to the Civil War, including material of the Bishops' Wars, much of which can be found in the Public Record Office

Harleian MS. 6852, papers relating to the Civil War era

Kings MS. 265, military and historical tracts, including a manuscript copy of Norfolk lieutenancy book, similar to Tanner MS. CLXXVII in the Bodleian Library

Miscellaneous MS. 55.24, militia extracts

Sloane MS. 650, Scottish papers

Sloane MS. 1008, military papers

Sloane MS. 1467, miscellaneous political papers, including the nobles' petition of 8 August 1640 and a Rossingham newsletter

Centre for Kentish Studies, Maidstone

De L'Isle and Dudley MSS., Sydney Papers

Corporation of London Records Office, London

Journals of the Court of Common Council of the City of London, 1558–1640

City Cash Books 1638–40

City Extracts

City of London Records Office MS. 86.5

Repertories of the Court of Aldermen of the City of London, 1558–1650

Guildhall Library, London

MS. 5228, roll of vellum with seal, charter of incorporation granted under the privy seal to the London Gunmakers' Company, 14 March 1638

House of Lords Record Office, Westminster

Main Papers, April–September 1640

Huntingdonshire RO, Huntingdon

Manchester MS. 32/5/17, Nathaniel Fiennes newsletter, July 1640

Henry E. Huntington Library, San Marino, California

Ellesmere Collection, Bridgewater Papers, EL 6568–7874

Hastings Collection (including Military Box I and Parliament Box III)

Stowe Collection (including STB Boxes 64, 65, 66, Military Box I, and Personal Box IX)

Loudoun Collection

National Library of Scotland, Edinburgh
Advocates' MS. 33.4.6, Register of the Committee of Estates
Crawford MSS., the muniments of the Earl of Crawford and Balcarres
Wodrow MSS., Church and State Papers, 1618–85
MS. 9303, miscellaneous (includes some Nithisdale correspondence)

Public Record Office, London
E 101, King's Remembrancer, accounts various, bundle 67, no. 11, account concerning the pay of mercenaries, 16 May 1638
E 351/292, account of Sir William Uvedale, 'Treasurer at Wars', for the First Bishops' War, 20 March 1639–16 February 1640
E 351/293, account of Sir William Uvedale 'Treasurer at Wars', for the Second Bishops' War, 17 February 1640–10 November 1640
E 351/294, account of William Raylton, Treasurer at War in Ireland, 8 January 1640–24 July 1641
E 351/295, account of Sir Patrick Ruthven, Governor of Edinburgh Castle, 1 February 1640–31 December 1640
E 351/296, account of Sir John Lockhart, paymaster of the Scottish officers, 21 March 1640–6 November 1640
E 351/297, account of Sir John Lockhart, 21 March 1639–3 February 1640
E 351/298, account of Francis Vernon, paymaster of Hamilton's forces, 31 March 1639–30 November 1639
E 351/299, account of Francis Vernon, paymaster of Hamilton's forces, 2 June 1640–31 August 1640
E 351/579, account of L. Pinkney, for the commissary, 1 October 1638–1 May 1639
E 351/1748, account of the Marquis of Hamilton, as Master of the Horse, July 1638–November 1639
E 351/2662, account of Sir John Heydon, naval ordnance from December 1637–January 1639
E 351/2663, account of Sir John Heydon, naval ordnance from 31 December 1638–1 January 1640
E 351/2711, account of John Quarles, foreign arms purchases, 1639 E 351/2712, account of Sir Job Harby's arms purchases in Flanders, 1640
E 351/3518, account of Major Norton for the Berwick garrison, 25 December 1638–24 December 1639
E 351/3519, Major Norton's account for the Berwick garrison, 25 December 1639–16 December 1640
E 351/3520, account of Sir Alexander Davidson, 20 March 1639–16 February 1640
E 351/3521, account of George Payler, June 1639–November 1640
E 351/3598, Sir Jacob Astley's account as Governor of Plymouth Fort, 29 November 1639–30 November 1641
E 401/2342–2345, abbreviates of the Pells receipt books, 1639–40
E 401/2460–2464, auditors' receipt books, 1639–40
E 403/1752–1754, Pells issues books, 1638–41
E 403/2154, imprest certificate books, 1638–62
E 403/2198, auditors' debenture books, 1639–40
E 403/2460, auditors' patent book, 1638–43
E 403/2568, privy seals authorizing payments, 1638–40

E 403/2590, papers relating to loans on the privy seal

E 403/2813, issues and order books of the auditor of receipt, 1639–40

E 404/234, orders and warrants of the Exchequer

E 405/285, Exchequer papers

E 407/123, Exchequer papers, 1558–1820 (includes payments made during the Bishops' Wars)

IND 4225, Chancery, Patent Office docquet book, 1638–41

MPF, map collections

PC 2, Privy Council registers

SO 1/3, Signet Office docquet books (also referred to as Irish letter books), 1627–42

SP 12, State Papers Domestic, Elizabeth I

SP 14, State Papers Domestic, James I (including SP 14/178 and SP 14/179, boxes of indentures from the Mansfeld expedition 1624–5)

SP 16, State Papers Domestic, Charles I (including SP 16/28 and SP 16/396, Council of War entry books as well as SP 16/419 and SP 16/462, boxes of indentures from the First and Second Bishops' Wars respectively)

SP 17E, miscellaneous parchments of the reign of Charles I (including a list of the able-bodied men of the eastern division of Northants, along with occupational descriptions, late 1638)

SP 41/1, documents relating to the establishment of the English army, 1640

SP 45/10, royal proclamations

T 56/5 Laud's and Juxon's miscellaneous books, warrants, 1639–41

T 56/12, Laud's and Juxon's miscellaneous books, privy seals, 1637–8

T 56/13, Laud's and Juxon's miscellaneous books and letters, 1637–9

WO 49/67, Ordnance Office, bills and debentures, 1637–40

WO 49/68, Ordnance Office, bills and debentures, train of artillery, 1638–9

WO 49/69, Ordnance Office, bills and debentures, naval ordnance, February 1638–June 1640

WO 49/70, Ordnance Office, bills and debentures, 1637–41

WO 49/71, Ordnance Office, bills and debentures, August 1638–April 1640

WO 49/72, Ordnance Office, bills and debentures upon the estimate of the grand proportion, July 1638–July 1641

WO 49/73, Ordnance Office, bills and debentures, mostly naval ordnance, 14 January 1640–June 1641

WO 49/75, Ordnance Office, bills and debentures, February 1638–May 1640

WO 49/76, Ordnance Office, bills and debentures, 1639

WO 49/100, Ordnance Office, documents relating to the artillery train and the Navy, 1639

WO 54/15, Ordnance Office, Quarter Book, 1638–41

WO 55/455, Ordnance Office, warrants relating to stores 1638–42

WO 55/456, Ordnance Office, warrants relating to stores 1639–41

Scottish Record Office, Edinburgh

GD 16/50, Airlie Muniments, papers relating to the period of the Civil War

GD 16/52, Airlie Muniments, papers relating to the army, militia and police

GD 45, Dalhousie Muniments

GD 112/39, Breadalbane Muniments, mounted letters

GD 112/40/2, Breadalbane Muniments, letters, 1636–59

GD 112/43/1, Breadalbane Muniments, bundles 6 and 7, State Papers, 1545–1690

GD 406/1, Hamilton Muniments
RH 13/18, anonymous diary, April 1639–October 1640

Sheffield City Library
Strafford MSS

Somerset County Record Office, Taunton
DD/PH 220, lieutenancy book

Stafford Record Office
Dartmouth MSS
Dyott Papers
Jerningham Papers

University of Minnesota Library, Special Collections and Rare Books, Minneapolis

Phillips MS. 3863 (internal classification Z 942.06 q Su 2), the correspondence of
   Thomas Howard, first Earl of Suffolk and Theophilus Howard, second Earl
   of Suffolk, comprising lieutenancy papers, 1624–39

PRINTED PRIMARY SOURCES

A Grant of the Benevolence or Contribution to His most Excellent Majestie, by the
   Clergie of the Province of Yorke (London, 1640)
Articles Exhibited in Parliament against William Archbishop of Canterbury, 1640
   (London, 1640; facsimile, Amsterdam 1971)
Aston, John. 'Iter Boreale, Anno Salutis 1639 et Dissidae inter Anglos et Scotos
   Inchoatus 1 Aprilis, finitum 29 Junii', in J. C. Hodgson (ed.), *Six North*
   Country Diaries, Surtees society, 118 (Durham, 1910)
Atkinson, J. C. (ed.) *Quarter Sessions Records*, III–IV, North Riding Record
   Society (London, 1885–6)
Baillie, Robert. *The Letters and Journals of Robert Baillie* (Edinburgh, 1841)
Balfour, Sir James. *The Historical Works*, vol. II (Edinburgh, 1825)
Barnes, T. G. (ed.) *Somerset Assize Orders, 1629–1640*, Somerset Record Society,
   65 (Frome, 1959)
Bettey, J. H. (ed.) *Calendar of the Correspondence of the Smyth Family of Ashton*
   Court 1548–1642, Bristol Record Society, XXXV (Bristol, 1982)
Bonhote, J. (ed.) *Historical Records of the West Kent Militia* (London, 1909)
Borough, Sir John. *Notes of the treaty carried on at Ripon between King Charles I*
   and the covenanters of Scotland, A.D. 1640, ed. J. Bruce, Camden Society,
   first series C, (1869)
Bund, J.W. (ed.) *Diary of Henry Townshend of Elmley Lovett. 1640–1663*
   (London, 1915)
Calendar of State Papers, Domestic Addenda, Elizabeth I and James I, 1580–1625
   (London, 1872).
Calendar of State Papers Domestic, James I, 1603–1625, 4 vols. (London, 1857–9)
Calendar of State Papers Domestic, Charles I, 1625–1649, 23 vols. (London,
   1858–97)

Calendar of State Papers, Venetian, (1636–9) XXIV, (1640–2) XXV (London, 1923–24)

Charles I, King of England. *A Large Declaration Concerning the Late Tumults in Scotland from their first originals: together with particular deduction of the seditious practices of the Prime Leaders of the Covenanters,* (London, 1638)

His Majesties Declaration Concerning his Proceedings with his Subjects of Scotland, since the Pacification in the Camp neere Berwick (London, 1640; facsimile, Amsterdam, 1971)

Clarendon, Edward Hyde, Earl of. *History of the Rebellion and Civil Wars in England,* ed. W. D. Macray (Oxford, 1888)

Cope, E. and Coates, W. (eds.) *The Proceedings of the Short Parliament of 1640,* Camden Society (London, 1977)

Cockle, M. J. D. *A Bibliography of English Military Books up to 1642* (London, 1900)

Collins, Arthur (ed.) *Letters and Memorials of State . . .,* vol. II (London, 1746)

Conway, Viscountess Anne. *The Conway Letters, the Correspondence of Anne, Viscountess Conway, Henry More, and Their Friends,* ed. Marjorie H. Nicolson (Oxford, 1930)

Corbet, John. *An historicall relation of the military government of Gloucester, from the beginning of the Civill Warre between King and Parliament, to the removall of Colonell Massie from that government to the command of the Westerne forces* (London, 1645)

Craig, Sir Thomas. *De Unione Regnorum Britanniae Tractatus* (London, 1605)

Cruso, John. *Militarie Instructions for the Cavallrie: According to the Moderne Warr's* (Cambridge, 1632. facsimile, Amsterdam, 1968)

Cunliffe, E. S. (ed.) 'Booke concerning the Deputy Leiuetennantshipp', *Sussex Archaeological Society,* 40 (1896), pp. 1–37

Cunnington, B. H. (ed.) *Some Annals of the Borough of Devizes. Being a series of extracts from the Corporation Records, 1555 to 1791.* (Devizes, 1925)

Dalrymple, David. *Memorials and Letters Relating to the History of Britain in the Reign of Charles I* (Glasgow, 1766)

De Gheyn, Jacob. *The Exercise of Armes* (The Hague, 1612)

Dugdale, Sir William. *A Short View of the Late Troubles* (London, 1681)

DuPraissac, Lord. *The Art of Warre, or Militarie discourses,* ed. John Cruso (Cambridge, 1639)

Ellis, H. (ed.) 'Letters from a Subaltern Officer of the Earl of Essex's Army . . .', *Archaeologia,* 35 (1853), pp. 310–34

Ffarington, S.M. (ed.) 'The Farington Papers', *Remains Historical and Literary connected with the Palatine Counties of Lancaster and Chester,* Chetham Society, 39 (1856), pp. 58–73, 123–45

Gardiner, S.R. (ed.) *The Hamilton Papers,* Camden Society, new series, 28 (London, 1880)

Gordon, Patrick. *A Short Abridgement of Britane's Distemper, from the yeare of God MDCXXXIX to MDCXLIX* (Aberdeen, 1844)

Groen van Prinsterer, G. *Archives ou correspondance inédites de la Maison d'Orange-Nassau,* 2nd series, vol. III: 1625–1642 (Utrecht, 1859)

Halliwell, James (ed.) *Letters of the Kings of England,* vol. II (London, 1846)

Hamilton, James, Duke of Hamilton and Castle-Herald. *Memoires of the Lives and Action of James and William, Dukes of Hamilton and Castle-Herald,* ed. Gilbert Burnet (London, 1667)

Hardwicke, Philip, Earl of (ed.) *Hardwicke State Papers, Miscellaneous State Papers from 1501–1726*, vol. II (London, 1778)

Harland, John (ed.) *The Lancashire Lieutenancy under the Tudors and Stuarts*, part 1 (Manchester, 1859)

Harley, Lady Brilliana. *The Letters of Lady Brilliana Harley*, Camden Society, 58 (London, 1854)

Hexham, Henry. *The Principles of the Art Militarie Practised in the Warres of the United Netherlands* (London, 1637)

Heylyn, Peter. *Cyprianus Anglicus or the history of the life and death of William, by divine providence Archbishop of Canterbury* (London, 1668)

HMC Ancaster. *Report on the MSS. of the Earl of Ancaster preserved at Grimsthorpe* (Dublin, 1907), pp. 399–410

HMC Braye. *The Manuscripts of Lord Braye, at Stanford Hall, Rugby*, Tenth Report, Part VI, Appendix (London, 1887), pp. 134–8

HMC Bruce. *Additional MSS. of the Sir Hervey Juckes Lloyd Bruce*, various collections, 7 (London, 1914), pp. 416–25

HMC Buccleuch, Montagu MSS. *Report on the Manuscripts of the Duke of Buccleuch and Queensberry*, Montagu House, Whitehall, vol. I, pt. II (London, 1899), pp. 266–290; vol. III, pt. III (London, 1926), pp. 378–87

HMC Buxton. *The Manuscripts of Miss Buxton, at Shadwell Court, Norfolk*, various collections, vol. II (London, 1903), pp. 249–66

HMC City of Exeter. *Report on the Records of the City of Exeter* (Hereford, 1916), pp. 200–4

HMC Coke. *See* HMC Cowper, Coke MSS.

HMC Corporation of Bridgnorth. *The Manuscripts of the Corporation of Bridgnorth*, Tenth Report, Part IV, Appendix (London, 1885), pp. 432–4

HMC Cowper, Coke MSS. *The Manuscripts of the Coke Family, of Melbourne, Co. Derby, Belonging to the Earl Cowper, K. G., preserved at Melbourne Hall*, Twelfth Report, Part II, Appendix, II (London, 1888), pp. 171–261

HMC De La Warr. *The Manuscripts of the Right Honourable the Earl of de la Warr (Baron Buckhurst) at Knole Park, Co. Kent*, Fourth Report (London, 1874), pp. 276–317

HMC De L'Isle and Dudley, Sydney MSS. *Report on the Manuscripts of Viscount De L'Isle preserved at Penshurst Place, Kent*, VI (London, 1966), pp. 76–338

HMC Denbigh. *Report on the Manuscripts of the Earl of Denbigh preserved at Newnham Paddox, Warwickshire*, V, Part I (Hereford, 1911), p. 47–73

HMC Devonshire. *The Manuscripts of His Grace the Duke of Devonshire at Bolton Abbey, Co. York*, Fourth Report, Appendix (London, 1872), pp. 36–45

HMC Egmont. *Report on the Manuscripts of the Earl of Egmont*, I, Part I (London, 1905), pp. 101–22

HMC Gawdy. *Report on the Manuscripts of the Family of Gawdy, formerly of Norfolk* (London, 1885), pp. 172–5

HMC Hamilton. *Report on the Manuscripts of the Duke of Hamilton* (London, 1887)

HMC Hamilton supplementary. *Supplementary Report on the Manuscripts of the Duke of Hamilton at the Register House* (Edinburgh, 1932), pp. 38–61

HMC Hastings. *Report on the Manuscripts of the Late Reginald Rawden Hastings, Esq., of the Manor House, Ashby-de la-Zouche*, vol. II (London 1930), pp. 80–2; vol. IV, (London, 1947), pp. 73–92

HMC House of Lords. *Calendar of House of Lords Manuscripts*, Fourth Report, Part I (London, 1874), pp. 2–27

HMC House of Lords. *State Trials: Record of the Trial of Archbishop Laud* (Braye MS. 3641), new series, XI, Addenda 1514–1714 (London, 1962), pp. 364–467

HMC Lothian. *Report on the Manuscripts of the Marquess of Lothian preserved at Blickling Hall, Norfolk* (London, 1905), pp. 85–6

HMC Mar and Kellie. *Report on the MSS. of the Earl of Mar and Kellie at Alloa House, Clackmannanshire* (London, 1904), pp. 195–8

HMC Middleton. *Report on the manuscripts of Lord Middleton, preserved at Wollaton Hall, Nottinghamshire* (Hereford, 1911), pp. 193–4

HMC Morrison. *The MSS. of Alfred Morrison, Esq., of Fonthill House, Hindon, Wilts, and Carlton House Terrace, London*, Ninth Report, Part II. (London, 1884), pp. 430–4

HMC Muncaster. *The Manuscripts of Lord Muncaster, M.P., Muncaster Castle*, Tenth Report, Part IV, Appendix (London, 1885), pp. 273–97

HMC Northumberland. *The Manuscripts of His Grace the Duke of Northumberland at Alnwick Castle*, XIV, Letters and Papers 1636–39, pp. 71–80; XV, Letters and Papers 1640–41, pp. 80–4. Third Report, Appendix (London, 1872), pp. 71–84

HMC Poll-Gell. *The MSS. of Henry Chandos-Poll-Gell, Esq., Hopton Hall, Co. Derby*, Ninth Report, Part II. (London, 1884) pp. 384–403

HMC Portland. *The Manuscripts of His Grace the Duke of Portland, preserved at Welbeck Abbey*, Thirteenth Report, Part I, Appendix I (London, 1891), pp. 2–7

HMC Rinuccini. *The Rinuccini MS., styled 'The Nuncio's Memoirs', Collection of the Right Honourable the Earl of Leicester, Holkham, Norfolk*, Ninth Report, Part II (London, 1884), pp. 340–57

HMC Russell-Astley. *Report on the Manuscripts of Mrs. Frankland-Russell-Astley, of Chequers Court, Bucks* (London, 1900), pp. 18–21

HMC Rutland. *The Manuscripts of His Grace the Duke of Rutland, G.C.B., preserved at Belvoir Castle*, Twelfth Report, Part IV, Appendix (London, 1888), pp. 498–525

HMC Rye. *The Manuscripts of the Corporation of Rye*, Thirteenth report, Part IV, Appendix (London, 1892), pp. 205–13

HMC Salisbury, Cecil MSS. *Report on the Manuscripts of the Marquis of Salisbury, Hatfield House, Hertfordshire*, XXII (London, 1971), pp. 292–360

HMC Traquair. *Report on the Muniments of the Honourable Henry Constable Maxwell Stuart of Traquair at Traquair House in the County of Peebles*, Ninth Report, Part II (London, 1884), pp. 241–62

HMC Wilts QS. *Records of the Quarter Sessions in the County of Wilts*, Various Collections, I (London, 1901), pp. 65–176

HMC Wodehouse. *Report on Muniments in the possession of Edmond R. Wodehouse, Esq., M.P.*, Thirteenth Report, Part IV, Appendix (London, 1892), pp. 433–63

HMC Woodford. *The Manuscripts of the late Reverend W. Pyne, of Charlton Mackerel, and of Pitney, Somerset, and of the Reverend A. J. Woodforde, of Ansford, Somerset*, Ninth report, Part II, 'The Diary of Robert Woodford, Steward of Northampton' (London, 1883), pp. 496–9

Hitchcock, Robert. 'The English Army Rations in the time of Elizabeth', *An English Garner. Social England Illustrated* (New York, 1964), pp. 115–32.

Hobbes, Thomas. *Leviathan*, ed. H. Schneider (Indianapolis, 1958)

Hope, Sir Thomas. *A Diary of the Public Correspondence of Sir Thomas Hope of Craighall, Bart. 1633–1645* (Edinburgh, 1843)

Kenyon, J.P. (ed.) *The Stuart Constitution, Documents and Commentary* (Cambridge, 1973)

Knowler, William (ed.) *The Earl of Strafforde's Letters and Dispatches* (2 vols.) (London, 1739)

Larkin, J. F. (ed.) *Stuart Royal Proclamations*, vol. II (Oxford, 1983)

Lawes and Ordinances of Warre, Established for the better conduct of the Service in the Northern parts ... (London, 1640)

Lawes and Ordinances of Warre, for the better Government of His Majesties Army Royall ... (Newcastle, 1639)

Leslie, J. H. (ed.) 'Statutes and Acts of Parliament – Army – From 1225 to 1761', *JSAHR*, 11, no. 44 (October 1932), pp. 216–24

Letters and Papers, Foreign and Domestic, of the Reign of Henry VIII (1542) XVII (London, 1900), and (1544) XIX (London, 1903)

Lister, J. (ed.) *West Riding Sessions Records*, II, The *Yorkshire Archaeological Society Journal*, (Leeds, 1915)

Loomie, A. J. (ed.) *Ceremonies of Charles I. The Note Books of John Finet, Master of Ceremonies, 1628–1641* (New York, 1987)

Maltby, Judith (ed.) *The Short Parliament (1640) Diary of Sir Thomas Aston* (London, 1988)

Markham, Gervase. *The Muster Master*, ed. Charles L. Hamilton in *Camden Miscellany*, XXVI, fourth series, 14, Royal Historical Society (London, 1975), pp. 49–76

Maseres, Francis (ed.) *Select Tracts Relating to the Civil Wars in England* (London, 1815)

Murphy, W. P. D. (ed.) *The Earl of Hertford's Lieutenancy Papers 1603–1612* (Devizes, 1969)

Myers, A.R. (ed.) *English Historical Documents 1327–1485*, vol. IV (New York, 1969)

Newcastle, Margaret Cavendish, Duchess of. *The Life of* ... *William Cavendish, duke of* ... *Newcastle*, ed. C. H. Firth (London, 1886)

Nicholson, J. (ed.) *Minute Book kept by the War Committee of the Covenanters in the Stewartry of Kirkcudbright in 1640 and 1641* (Kirkcudbright, 1855)

Ogle, O. and Bliss, W. H. (eds.) *Calendar of the Clarendon State Papers Preserved in the Bodleian Library* (Oxford, 1872)

Oxinden, Henry. *The Oxinden Letters 1607–1642 being the Correspondence of Henry Oxinden of Barham and His Circle*, ed. Dorothy Gardiner (London, 1933)

Patten, Sir William. *The Expedicion into Scotlande, 1548 [1547]*, *Tudor Tracts, 1532–1588*, ed. A. F. Pollard (New York, 1964), pp. 53–157

Peacock, Edward (ed.) *The Army Lists of the Roundheads and Cavaliers* (London, 1983)

Petrie, Charles (ed.) *The Letters, Speeches and Proclamations of King Charles I* (New York, 1968)

Pollard, A.F. (ed.) *The Late Expedicion into Scotlande* ... *1544* (London, 1544), *Tudor Tracts 1532–1588* (New York, 1964), pp. 37–51

Raine, James. *The History and Antiquities of North Durham* ... . (London, 1852)

Rushworth, John. *Historical Collections*, vol. III (London, 1722)

Rutherford, Samuel. *Letters* (Aylesbury, Bucks., 1973)

Ruthven, Patrick. *Ruthven Correspondence. Letters and Papers of Patrick*

Ruthven, *Earl of Forth and Brentford, and of his family: A.D. 1615 – A.D. 1662,* ed. W. D. Macroy (London, 1868)

Rous, John. *Diary of John Rous, incumbent of Santon Downham, Suffolk from 1625 to 1642,* ed. M. A. E. Green, Camden Society, first series (London, 1856)

Rymer, Thomas (ed.). *'Foedera', Conventiones Literae, et cujuscunque generis acta publica, inter reges angliae* (The Hague, 1744)

Sanderson, William. *A Compleat History of the Life and Reign of Charles I from Cradle to Grave* (London, 1658)

Scrope, R. and Monkhouse, T. (eds.) *Clarendon State Papers,* 3 volumes (Oxford, 1767–86)

Shakespeare, William. *Henry V,* ed. Gary Taylor (Oxford, 1982).

Smith, John. *The Names and Surnames of all the Able and Sufficient Men in Body fit for His Majesty's Service in the Wars, within the County of Gloucester Viewed by the Right Hon. Henry, Lord Berkeley, Lord Lieutenant of the said County by Direction from His Majesty, in the Month of August, 1608, in the Sixty Year of the Reign of James the First, Compiled by John Smith of North Nibley, in Gloucestershire* (London, 1902; facsimile Ann Arbor, Mich., 1972)

Smythe, Sir John. *Certain Discourses Military . . .,* ed. J. R. Hale (Ithaca, N.Y., 1964)

Instructions, Observations, and Orders Military . . . (London, 1595)

Spalding, John. *The History of the Troubles and Memorable Transactions in Scotland in the Reign of Charles I* (Aberdeen, 1829)

Spaulding, Thomas M. and Karpinski, Louis C. *Early Military Books in the University of Michigan Libraries* (Ann Arbor, Michigan, 1941)

Squibb, G. D. (ed.) *Reports of Heraldic Cases in the Court of Chivalry, 1623–1732,* Harleian Society (London, 1956)

Squibb, L. *A Book of all the Several Officers of the Court of Exchequer . . .,* W. Bryson (ed.), *The Camden Miscellany v. 26,* Camden Society, fourth series, 14 (London, 1975), pp. 118–24

Taylor, Jeremy. *A Sermon Preached in Saint Maries Church of Oxford* (Oxford, 1638; facsimile, Amsterdam, 1971)

Thomson, G.S. (ed.) *The Twysden Lieutenancy Papers, 1583–1668* (Ashford, Kent, 1926)

Thornborough, John. *A Discourse Plainely Proving the Evident utilitie and urgent neccessitie of the desired happie Union of the two famous Kingdomes of England and Scotland* (Oxford, 1604)

Ioiefull and Blessed Reuniting of two mighty and famous kingdomes, England and Scotland into Their Ancient Name of Great Brittaine (Oxford, 1604)

Valentine, Henry. *God Save the King* (London, 1639)

Verney, Frances. *Letters and papers of the Verney Family,* ed. J. Bruce, Camden Society, 56 (London, 1853)

(ed.) *Memoirs of the Verney Family . . .* (London, 1892)

Wake, Joan. (ed.) *The Montagu Musters Books, A.D. 1602–1623,* Northampton Record Society, 7 (Peterborough, 1935)

(ed.) *A Copy of Papers Relating to Musters, Beacons, Subsidies, etc., in the County of Northampton A.D. 1586–1623,* Northampton Record Society, 3 (Kettering, 1926)

Ward, Robert. *Anima'dversions of Warre . . .* (London, 1639)

The Winthrop Papers, vol. II, Massachusetts Historical Society (1929)

Wrottesley, G. (ed.) 'The Staffordshire Muster of A.D. 1640', *Proceedings of the William Salt Archaeological Society,* 15 (1894), pp. 201–31

SECONDARY SOURCES

Adair, E. R. 'The Privy Council Registers', *EHR*, 38, no. 151 (July 1923), pp. 410–22

Albion, Gordon. *Charles I and the Court of Rome, A Study in 17th Century Diplomacy* (London, 1935)

Alsop, J.D. 'The Exchequer in late Medieval Government, c1485–1530', *Aspects of Late Medieval Government and Society*, ed. J. G. Rowe (Toronto, 1986), pp. 179–212

'Exchequer Office-Holders in the House of Commons, 1559–1601', *Parliamentary History*, 8, pt. II (1989), pp. 240–74

'Government, Finance and the Community of the Exchequer', *The Reign of Elizabeth I*, ed. C. Haigh (Athens, Ga, 1985), pp. 101–23, 273–5.

Aston, Margaret. *England's Iconoclasts* (Oxford, 1988)

'Iconoclasm at Rickmansworth, 1522: Troubles of Church Wardens', *Journal of Ecclesiastical History*, 40, no. 4 (October 1989), pp. 24–52

Ashton, Robert. *The City and The Court 1603–1643*, (Cambridge, 1979)

The Crown and The Money Market (Oxford, 1963)

Aylmer, Gerald. 'Attempts at Administrative Reform, 1625–40', *EHR*, 72, no. 283 (April 1957), pp. 229–59

'Charles I's Commission on Fees, 1627–40', *BIHR*, 31 (May 1958), pp. 58–67

The King's Servants: The Civil Service of Charles I 1625–1642 (New York, 1961)

'The Officers of the Exchequer, 1625–1642', in *Essays in the Economic and social History of Tudor and Stuart England, in Honour of R.H. Tawney*, ed. F. J. Fisher (Cambridge, 1961), pp. 164–81

Barnes, T. G. 'Deputies not Principals, Lieutenants not Captains: The Institutional Failure of Lieutenancy in the 1620s' in *War and Government in Britain*, ed. M. Fissel (Manchester, 1991), pp. 58–86

Somerset 1625–1640: A County's Government During the Personal Rule (Cambridge, Mass., 1961)

Bartlett, I. R. 'Scottish Mercenaries in Europe, 1570–1640: A Study in Attitudes and Policies', *The Scottish Tradition*, 13 (1986), pp. 15–24

Beatty, J. L. *Warwick and Holland, being the Lives of Robert and Henry Rich* (Denver, 1965)

Benbow, R. M. 'The Court of Aldermen and the Assizes: The Policy of Price Control in Elizabethan England', *Guildhall Studies in London History*, 4, no. 3 (October 1980), pp. 93–118

Bernard, G. W. *War, Taxation and Rebellion in Early Tudor England. Henry VIII, Wolsey and the Amicable Grant of 1525* (Brighton, Sussex, 1986)

Bettey J. H. *The Rise of a Gentry Family: The Smyths of Ashton Court ca. 1500–1642* (Bristol, 1978)

Billington, Sandra. 'An Horation Ode – Charles I and the Army as Actors', *Notes and Queries*, new series, 25, no. 6, (December 1978), pp. 512–13

Bindoff, S. T. 'The Stuarts and Their Style', *EHR*, 60, no. 237 (May 1945), pp. 192–216

Black, Jeremy. *A Military Revolution? Military Change and European Society 1550–1880* (Atlantic Highlands, N.J., 1991)

Blackwood, B. G. *The Lancashire Gentry and the Great Rebellion 1640–60*, Chetham Society, series 3, XXV (Manchester, 1978)

Blair, Claude. 'Further Notes on the Origins of the Wheellock', *Arms and Armour Annual*, 1 (1973), pp. 28–47

Bonney, Richard. *The King's Debts. Finance and Politics in France 1589–1661* (Oxford, 1981)

Boynton, Lindsay. 'Billeting – The Example of the Isle of Wight', *EHR*, 74, no. 290 (January 1959), pp. 23–40

The Elizabethan Militia 1558–1638 (London, 1967)

'Martial Law and The Petition of Right', *EHR*, 79, no. 311 (April 1964), pp. 255–84

'The Tudor Provost Marshal', *EHR*, 77, no. 304 (July 1962), pp. 347–455

Brooke, G. *English Coins* (London, 1932)

Brown, K. B. 'Aristocratic finances and the origins of the Scottish Revolution', *EHR*, 104, no. 410 (January 1989), pp. 46–87

Brunton, D. and Pennington, D. H. *Members of the Long Parliament* (London, 1954)

Bush, M. L. *The Government Policy of Protector Somerset* (Montreal, 1975)

Carlton, Charles. *Archbishop William Laud* (London, 1987)

Carter, D. P. 'The "Exact Militia" in Lancashire, 1625–1640', *Northern History*, 11 (1976 for 1975), pp. 85–106

Christianson, Paul. 'Arguments on Billeting and Marital Law in the Parliament of 1628', paper presented at the 30 May 1992 conference of the Canadian Historical Association

'The Causes of the English Revolution: A Reappraisal', *JBS*, 15, no. 2 (spring 1976), pp. 40–75

Cipolla, C. M. *Guns, Sails, and Empires: Technological Innovation and the Early Phases of European Expansion 1400-1700* (New York, 1965)

Clark, Andrew. 'A Lieutenancy Book for Essex, 1608 to 1631, and 1637 to 1639', *The Essex Review*, 17, no. 67 (July 1908), pp. 157–69

'The Essex Territorial Force in 1608', *The Essex Review*, 17, no. 66 (April 1908), pp. 98–115

'The Essex Territorial Force, 1625–1638', *The Essex Review*, 18, no. 70 (April 1909), pp. 65–74

Clark, Peter. 'Popular Protest and Disturbance in Kent, 1558–1640', *EconHR*, second series, 29, no. 3 (August 1976), pp. 365–81

English Provincial Society from the Reformation to the Revolution: Religion, Politics and Society in Kent 1500–1640 (Hassocks, Sussex, 1977)

Clarke, Aidan. 'The Earl of Antrim and the First Bishops' War', *Irish Sword*, 6, no. 23 (winter 1963), pp. 108–15

Clay, C. G. A. *Economic Expansion and Social Change: England 1500–1700, II, Industry, Trade and Government* (Cambridge, 1984)

Cliffe, J. T. *The Yorkshire Gentry from the Reformation to the Civil War* (London, 1969)

Clifford, C. A. 'Ship Money in Hampshire: Collection and Collapse', *Southern History*, 4 (1982), pp. 91–106

Clifton, Robin. 'Fear of Popery', in *The Origins of the English Civil War*, ed. C. Russell (New York, 1973), pp. 144–67

Clode, Charles M. *The Administration of Justice under Military and Marital Law* (London, 1872)

The Military Forces of the Crown; Their Administration and Government, vol. I (London, 1869)

Colket, Meredith B. 'The Jenks Family of England', *The New England Historical and Genealogical Register*, 110 (January 1956), pp. 9–20; (April 1956), pp. 80–93; (July 1956), pp. 160–72; (October 1956), pp. 244–56

Colvin, H., Ransome, O. and Summerson, J. *The History of the King's Works*, vols. III–IV (London, 1975)

Cooper, J. P. *Land, Men and Belief: Studies in Early Modern History* (London, 1983)

Cope, Esther S. 'The Bishops and Parliamentary Politics in Early Stuart England', *Parliamentary History*, 9, pt.1 (1990), pp. 1–13

'The Earl of Bedford's Notes of the Short Parliament of 1640', *BIHR*, 53, no. 128 (November 1980), pp. 255–8

The Life of a Public Man, Edward First Baron Montagu of Boughton, 1562–1644, *Memoirs of the American Philosophical Society*, 142 (Philadelphia, 1981), pp. 158–70

'Compromise in Early Stuart Parliaments: The Case of the Short Parliament of 1640', *Albion*, 9 (1977), pp. 135–45

Politics Without Parliaments 1629–1640 (London, 1987)

'Public Images of Parliament During its Absence', *Legislative Studies Quarterly*, 7, no. 2 (May 1982), pp. 221–34

'The Short Parliament of 1640 and Convocation', *Journal of Ecclesiastical History*, 25, no. 2 (April 1974), pp. 167–84

Craig, J. *The Mint* (Cambridge, 1953)

Cruickshank, C. G. *Elizabeth's Army* (second edn) (Oxford, 1966)

Cust, Richard. *The Forced Loan and English Politics* (Oxford, 1987)

Cust, Richard and Hughes, Ann (eds.) *Conflict in Early Stuart England. Studies in Religion and Politics* (London, 1989)

Davies, C. S. L. 'Provisions for Armies, 1509–50; A Study in the Effectiveness of Early Tudor Government', *EconHR*, second series, 17, no. 2 (December 1964), pp. 234–48

Dietz, F. C. *English Public Finance, 1558–1641* (New York, 1932)

'The Receipts and Issues of the Exchequer during the Reigns of James I and Charles I', *Smith College Studies in History*, 13, no. 4 (July 1928), pp. 117–71

Dodd, A. H. 'Wales and the Second Bishops' War (1640)', *The Bulletin of the Board of Celtic Studies*, 12, part 4 (May 1948), pp. 92–6

'Welsh Opposition Lawyers in The Short Parliament', *The Bulletin of the Board of Celtic Studies*, 12 (1948), pp. 106–7

Donagan, Barbara. 'Codes and Conduct in the English Civil War', *Past and Present*, 118 (February 1988), pp. 65–95

Donald, P. H. *An Uncounselled King: Charles I and the Scottish Troubles (1637–1644)* (Cambridge, 1990)

'New Light on the Anglo-Scottish Contacts of 1640', *Historical Research*, 62, no. 148 (1989), pp. 221–9

'The Scottish National Covenant and British Politics, 1638–1640', in *The Scottish National Covenant in its British Context, 1638–1651*, ed. J. Morrill (Edinburgh, 1990), pp. 90–105

Downing, Brian. *The Military Revolution and Political Change. Origins of Democracy and Autocracy in Early Modern Europe* (Princeton, N.J., 1992)

Elliot, J. H. *Richelieu and Olivares* (Oxford, 1987)

'The Year of Three Ambassadors', in *History and Imagination: Essays in Honour of H. R. Trevor-Roper*, ed. H. Lloyd-Jones, V. Pearl, and B. Worden (London, 1981), pp. 165–81

Elton, G. R., 'Taxation for War and Peace in early Tudor England', in *War and Economic Development*, ed. J. M. Winter (Cambridge, 1975), pp. 33–48

Evans, John T. *Seventeenth Century Norwich: Politics, Religion, and Government, 1620–1690* (Oxford, 1979)

Everitt, Alan. *The Community of Kent and the Great Rebellion, 1640–60* (Leicester, 1966)

Falls, Cyril. *Elizabeth's Irish Wars* (New York, 1970)

Feld, M. D. 'Middle-Class Society and the Rise of Military Professionalism, the Dutch Army 1589–1609', *Armed Forces and Society*, 1, no. 4 (August 1975), pp. 419–42

Firth, C. H. 'A Ballad Illustrating the Bishops' Wars', *Scottish Historical Review*, 9, no. 36 (July 1912), pp. 363–5

'Ballads on the Bishops' Wars, 1638–40', *Scottish Historical Review*, 3, no. 11 (April 1906), pp. 257–73

Cromwell's Army. A History of the English Soldier during the Civil Wars, the Commonwealth and the Protectorate (third edn) (London, 1962)

Fissel, Mark C. *'Bellum Episcopale': The Bishops' Wars and the End of the 'Personal Rule' in England, 1638–1640*, Ph.D. dissertation, University of California, (Berkeley, 1983)

'The Identity of John Bishop, Gunner, 1625', *JSAHR*, 68, no. 274 (summer 1990), pp. 138–9

'Scottish War and English Money: The Short Parliament of 1640', in *War and Government in Britain, 1598–1650*, ed. M. Fissel (Manchester, 1991) pp. 193–223

'Tradition and Invention in the Early Stuart Art of War', *JSAHR*, 65, no. 263 (autumn 1987), pp. 133–47

(ed.) *War and Government in Britain, 1598–1650* (Manchester, 1991)

Fletcher, Anthony J. *A County Community in Peace and War: Sussex 1600–1660* (London, 1975)

Reform in the Provinces. The Government of Stuart England (New Haven, Conn., 1986)

The Outbreak of the English Civil War (New York, 1981)

Foster, E. R. 'The Procedure of the House of Commons against Patents and Monopolies, 1621–1624', in *Conflict in Stuart England. Essays in Honour of Wallace Notestein*, ed. W. Aiken and B. Henning (New York, 1960), pp. 59–85

Fraser, G. M. *The Steel Bonnets* (London, 1971)

Furgol, E. M. 'Scotland Turned Sweden: The Scottish Covenanters and the Military Revolution, 1638–1651', *The Scottish National Covenant in its British Context, 1638–51*, ed. J. S. Morrill (Edinburgh, 1990), pp. 134–54

A Regimental History of the Covenanting Armies 1639–1651 (Edinburgh, 1990)

The Religious Aspects of the Scottish Covenanting Armies, 1639–1651 (D.Phil thesis, University of Oxford, 1982)

Fyers, Evan. 'Notes on Class Catalogue, No. 50 (military) in the Department of Manuscripts, British Museum'. *JSAHR*, 4, no. 15 (January–March 1925), pp. 38–47

Gainsford, B. 'The English Expedition into Scotland in 1542', *Archaeologia Aeliana*, third series, 3 (1907), pp. 191–212

Gardiner, Samuel Rawson. *History of England from the Accession of James I to the Outbreak of the Civil War 1603–1642*, vols. VIII–IX (London, 1884)

George, M. Dorothy. 'Notes on the Origin of the Declared Account', *EHR*, 21 (January 1916), pp. 41–58

Gibson, Jeremy, and Dell, Alan. *Tudor and Stuart Muster Rolls* (Birmingham, 1991)

Gillett, E. and MacMahon, K. *A History of Hull* (London, 1980)

Gould, J. 'The Royal Mint in the Early Seventeenth Century', *EconHR*, second series, 5, no. 1 (1952), pp. 240–8

Goring, J. J. 'The General Proscription of 1522', *EHR*, 86 (1971), pp. 681–705
'Social Change and Military Decline in Mid-Tudor England', *History*, 60, no. 199 (June 1975), pp. 185–97

Groome, A. N. 'Higham Ferrers Elections in 1640. A Midland Market Town on the Eve of Civil War', *Northamptonshire Past and Present*, 2, no. 5 (1958), pp. 243–51

Gruenfelder, John K. *Influence in Early Stuart Elections 1604-1640* (Columbus, Ohio, 1981)
'The Election for Knights of the Shire for Essex in the Spring, 1640', *Transactions of the Essex Archeological Society*, third series, 2, part 2 (1968), pp. 143–6
'The Elections to the Short Parliament, 1640' in *Early Stuart Studies. Essays in Honour of David Harris Willson*, ed. H. Reinmuth (Minneapolis, 1970), pp. 180–230
'The Spring Parliamentary Election at Hastings, 1640', *Sussex Archaeological Collections*, 105 (1967), pp. 47–55

Guizot, F. *History of the English Revolution of 1640* (London, 1846)

Gutmann, Myron P. *War and Rural Life in the Early Modern Low Countries* (Princeton, N.J., 1980)

Guy, J. A. *Tudor England* (Oxford, 1988)

Hale, John R. *War and Society in Renaissance Europe 1450–1620* (London, 1985)
(ed.) *The Art of War and Renaissance England.* (Washington, D.C., 1961)

Hardacre, P. H. 'Patronage and Purchase in the Irish Standing Army under Thomas Wentworth, Earl of Strafford, 1632–1640', *JSAHR* 67, no. 269, (spring 1989) pp. 40–5, and 68, no. 270, (summer 1989) pp. 94–104.

Harriss, G. L. *King, Parliament, and Public Finance in Medieval England to 1369* (Oxford, 1975)
'Aids, Loans and Benevolences', *Historical Journal*, 6 (1963), pp. 1–19
'Marmaduke Lumley and the Exchequer Crisis of 1446–9', in *Aspects of Late Medieval Government and Society*, ed. J. G. Rowe (Toronto, 1986), pp. 143–78
'Medieval Doctrines in the Debates on Supply', in *Faction and Parliament*, ed. Kevin Sharpe (Oxford, 1978), pp. 73–103

Hassell-Smith, A. 'Militia Rates and Militia Statutes, 1558–1663', in *The English Commonwealth, 1547–1640, Essays in Politics and Society presented to Joel Hurstfield*, ed. P. Clark, A. Smith, and N. Tyacke (Leicester, 1979), pp. 93–110

Havran, Martin J. *Caroline Courtier: The Life of Lord Cottington* (London, 1973)
'The Character and Principles of an English King: The Case of Charles I', *The Catholic History Review*, 69, no. 2 (April 1983), pp. 169–208

Hay, G. J. *An Epitomized History of the Militia* (London, 1906)

Hayward, J. F. 'English Swords 1600–1650', in *Arms and Armour Annual*, ed, R. Held, I (Northfield, Ill., 1973), pp. 142–61

Hervey, Mary. *The Life of Thomas Howard, Earl of Arundel* (Cambridge, 1921)

Hewitt, H. J. *The Organization of War under Edward III* (Manchester, 1966)

Hibbard, Caroline M. 'The Contribution of 1639: Court and Country Catholicism', *Recusant History*, 16 (1982), pp. 42–60

Charles I and the Popish Plot (Chapel Hill, N.C., 1983)

'Early Stuart Catholics: Revisions and Re-revisions', *Journal of Modern History*, 52 (March 1980), pp. 1–34

'Episcopal Warriors in the British Wars of Religion', in *War and Government in Britain, 1598–1650*, ed. M. Fissel (Manchester, 1991), pp. 164–92

Hill, Christopher. 'Parliament and People in Seventeenth Century England', *Past and Present*, no. 92 (August 1981), pp. 100–24

The Economic Problems of the Church (Oxford, 1956)

Hill, J. F. W. *Tudor and Stuart Lincoln* (Cambridge, 1956)

Hirst, Derek. 'Revisionism Revised: Two Perspectives on Early Stuart Parliamentary History – The Place of Principle', *Past and Present*, 92 (August 1981), pp. 79–99

'The Privy Council and Problems of Enforcement in the 1620's', *JBS*, 18, no. 1 (autumn 1978), pp. 46–66

The Representative of the People? Voters and Voting in England Under the Early Stuarts (Cambridge, 1975)

'Parliament, Law and War in the 1620s', (review of C. S. R. Russell's *Parliaments and English Politics*), *The Historical Journal*, 23, no. 2 (1980), pp. 455–61

'The Seventeenth Century Freeholder and the Statistician: A Case of Terminological Confusion', *EconHR*, second series, 9, no. 2 (May 1976), pp. 306–10

Hirst, Joseph. 'The Castle of Kingston-upon-Hull', *East Riding Antiquarian Society*, 3 (1895), pp. 24–39

Hockey, S.F. 'The Transport of Isle of Wight Corn to feed Edward I's Army in Scotland', *EHR*, 77, no. 305 (October 1962), pp. 703–5

Holmes, Clive. *Seventeenth-Century Lincolnshire* (Lincoln, 1980)

'The County Community in Stuart Historiography', *JBS* (1980), pp. 54–73

Holmes, Martin R. *Arms and Armour in Tudor and Stuart London* (London, 1970)

Howell, Roger, Jr. *Newcastle upon Tyne and the Puritan Revolution: A Study of the Civil War in North England* (Oxford, 1967)

Hudson, W. 'Norwich Militia in the 14th Century', *Norfolk Archaeology*, 14 (1901), pp. 263–95

Hughes, Ann. *The Causes of the English Civil War* (New York, 1990)

Hurstfield, Joel. *The Illusion of Power in Tudor Politics* (London, 1979)

Hutchinson, J. R. *The Press Gang Afloat and Ashore* (London, 1918)

Hutton, Ronald. 'An Armistice in Civil War Studies', review, in *The Historical Journal*, 23, no. 3 (1980), pp. 729–36

Huxley, Gervase. *Endymion Porter, The Life of a Courtier 1587–1649* (London, 1959)

Jones, W. R. 'Purveyance for War and the Community of the Realm in Late Medieval England', *Albion*, 7, no. 4 (winter 1975), pp. 300–16

Kaeuper, R. W. *War, Justice and Public Order* (Oxford, 1988)

Kearney, Hugh. *Strafford in Ireland, 1633–41. A Study in Absolutism* (Cambridge, 1989)

Keegan, John. *The Face of Battle: A Study of Agincourt, Waterloo and the Somme* (New York, 1977)

Keeler, M. F. *Members of the Long Parliament* (Philadelphia, 1954)

Kenyon, J. P. *The Stuarts, A Study in English Kingship* (London, 1972)

Ketton-Cremer, R. W. *Norfolk in the Civil War* (London, 1969)
Kiernan, V. G. 'Foreign Mercenaries and Absolute Monarchy', *Past and Present*, no. 11 (1957); reprinted in *Crisis In Europe: 1560–1660*, ed. Trevor Aston (New York, 1967), pp. 124–49
Kishlansky, M. *Parliamentary Selection. Social and Political Choice in Early Modern England* (Cambridge, 1986)
Kist, J. B. *Jacob De Gheyn, 'The Exercise of Arms': A Commentary* (New York, 1971)
Koenigsberger, Helmut. 'Dominium regale or dominium politicum et regale? Monarchies and Parliaments in Early Modern Europe', in *Der moderne Parlamentarismus und seine in der ständischen Repräsentation* (Berlin, 1976), pp. 43–68
Lachmann, Robert. *From Manor to Market: Structural Change in England, 1536–1640* (Madison, Wisc., 1987)
Lake, Peter. 'The Collection of Ship Money in Cheshire during the Sixteen Thirties: A Case Study of Relations between Central and Local Government', *Northern History*, 17 (1981), pp. 44–71
Lapsley, Gaillard Thomas. *The County Palatine of Durham: A Study in Constitutional History* (London, 1900)
Lee, Maurice, Jr. *The Road to Revolution. Scotland under Charles I, 1625–1637* (Urbana, Ill., 1985)
Leonard, H. H. 'Distraint of Knighthood: The Last Phase, 1625-41', *History*, 63, no. 207 (February 1978), pp. 23–37
Leslie, J. H. (ed.) 'A Survey, or Muster of the Armed and Trained Companies in London, 1558 and 1559', *JSAHR*, 4, no. 1 (April–June 1925), pp. 62–71
Levy, F. J. 'How information spread among the Gentry, 1540–1640' *JBS*, 21, no. 2 (spring 1982), pp. 11–34
Lewis, N. B. 'An Early Indenture of Military Service, 27 July 1287', *BIHR*, 13 (1935), pp. 85–9
   'The Organization of Indentured Retinues in Fourteenth Century England', *TRHS*, fourth series, 27 (1945), pp. 29–39
   'The Recruitment and Organization of a Contract Army, May to November 1337', *BIHR*, 37, no. 95 (May 1964), pp. 1–19
Loomie, A. J. 'Gondomar's Selection of English Officers in 1622', *EHR*, 88, no. 348 (July 1973), pp. 574–81
   'The Spanish Faction at the Court of Charles I, 1630-8', *BIHR*, 59, no. 139 (May 1986), pp. 37–49
Lydon, J. F. 'An Irish Army in Scotland, 1296', *Irish Sword*, 5 (1962), pp. 184–90
McGurk, J. N. 'Armada Preparations in Kent and Arrangements Made after the Defeat (1587–1589)', *Archeologia Cantiana*, 85 (1970), pp. 71–93
   'The Clergy and the Militia, 1580–1610', *History*, 60, no. 199 (June 1975), pp. 198–210
Macinnes, Allan. *Charles I and the Making of the Covenanting Movement 1625–1641* (Edinburgh, 1991)
   'The Scottish Constitution, 1638–1651. The Rise and Fall of Oligarchic Centralism', in *The Scottish National Covenant in its British Context, 1638–1651*, ed. J. Morrill (Edinburgh, 1990), pp. 106–33
MacIvor, I. 'The Elizabethan Fortifications of Berwick-upon-Tweed', *Antiquaries Journal*, 45 (1965), pp. 64–96

Malcolm, Joyce. 'A King in Search of Soldiers', *The Historical Journal*, 21 (June 1978), pp. 251–73
'Charles I on Innovation: A Confidential Directive on an Explosive Issue', *BIHR*, 53, no. 127 (1980) pp. 252–5
Mason, Thomas A. *Serving God and Mammon: William Juxon, 1582–1663* (Newark, Delaware, 1985)
Mathew, David. *Scotland Under Charles I* (London, 1955)
Meyer, Arnold Oscar. 'Charles I and Rome', *American Historical Review*, 19 (October 1913), pp. 13–26
Millar, Gilbert J. *Tudor Mercenaries and Auxiliaries 1548–1547* (Charlottesville, N.C., 1980)
Milward, Clement. 'English Signed Swords in the London Museums', *Apollo*, 29 (March 1939), pp. 125–9
'Notes on London and Hounslow Swordsmiths', *Apollo*, 30 (April 1940), pp. 93–5
Morrill, John S. *Cheshire 1630–1660: County Government and Society During the English Revolution* (Oxford, 1974)
(ed.), *The Impact of the English Civil War* (London, 1991)
'The Religious Context of the English Civil War', *TRHS*, fifth series, 24, pp. 155–78
The Revolt of the Provinces: Conservatives and Radicals in the English Civil War 1630–1650 (London, 1976)
(ed.), *The Scottish National Covenant in its British Context 1638–1651* (Edinburgh, 1990)
Morris, J. E. 'Mounted Infantry in Mediaeval Warfare', *TRHS*, third series, 8 (1914), pp. 77–102.
The Welsh Wars of Edward I (Oxford, 1901)
Newman, P. R. *Royalist Officers in England and Wales, 1642–1660* (New York, 1981)
Nicholas, Donald. *Mr. Secretary Nicholas (1593–1669), His Life and Letters* (London, 1955)
Nicholson, R. *Edward III and the Scots* (Oxford, 1965)
Nolan, John S. 'The Muster of 1588', *Albion*, 23, no. 3 (autumn 1991), pp. 387–407
Noyes, Arthur H. *The Military Obligation in Mediaeval England, with Especial Reference to Commissions of Array* (Columbus, Ohio, 1930)
Ogilvie, J. D. 'A Bibliography of the Bishops' Wars, 1639–40', *Records of the Glasgow Bibliographical Society*, 12 (1936), pp. 21–40
Ohlmeyer, J. H. *Civil War and Restoration in Three Stuart Kingdoms. The Career of Randal MacDonnell, the Marquis of Antrim, 1609–1683* (Cambridge, 1993)
Ollard, Richard. *The Image of the King, Charles I and Charles II* (London, 1979)
Orgel, Stephen. *The Illusion of Power, Political Theater in the English Renaissance* (Berkeley, Calif., 1975)
Parker, Geoffrey. *The Army of Flanders and the Spanish Road, 1567–1659. The Logistics of Spanish Victory and Defeat in the Low Countries' War* (Cambridge, 1972)
Europe in Crisis 1598–1648 (New York, 1979)
'If the Armada had Landed', *History*, 61 (1976), pp. 358–68
The Military Revolution: Military Innovation and the Rise of the West, 1500–1800 (Oxford, 1990)

'War and Economic Change: the Economic Costs of the Dutch Revolt', in *War and Economic Development*, ed. J. M. Winter (Cambridge, 1975), pp. 49–71

Parry, Graham. *The Golden Age Restor'd. The Culture of the Stuart Court, 1603–42* (Manchester, 1985)

Pearce, Brian. 'Elizabethan Food Policy and the Armed Forces', *EconHR*, 12, no. 1 (1942), pp. 39–46

Pearl, Valerie. *London and the Outbreak of the Puritan Revolution: City Government and National Politics, 1625–43* (Oxford, 1961)

Pearse, Richard. 'The Use of the Matchlock When Mounted', *JSAHR*, 44. no. 180 (December 1966), pp. 201–4

Peck, Linda L. *Northampton: Patronage and Policy at the Court of James I* (London, 1982)

Perceval-Maxwell, Michael. 'Ireland and the Monarchy in the Early Stuart Multiple Kingdom', *The Historical Journal*, 34, no. 1 (March 1991), pp. 279–95

'Ireland and Scotland 1638–1648', in *The Scottish National Covenant in its British Context, 1638–1651*, ed. J. Morrill (Edinburgh, 1990), pp. 193–211

Phelps, W. H. 'The Second Night of Davenant's "Salmacida Spolia"', *Notes and Queries*, new series, 26, no. 6 (December 1979), pp. 512–13

Phillips, John. *The Reformation of Images: Destruction of Art in England, 1535–1660* (Berkeley, Calif., 1973)

Powicke, F.M. *The Thirteenth Century, 1216–1307* (Oxford, 1962)

Powicke, Michael. *The Military Obligation in Medieval England; A Study in Liberty and Duty* (Oxford, 1962)

Prestwich, Menna. *Cranfield: Politics and Profits under the Early Stuarts. The Career of Lionel Cranfield, Earl of Middlesex* (Oxford, 1966)

Prestwich, Michael. 'Victualling Estimates for English Garrisons in Scotland during the Early Fourteenth Century', *EHR*, 82, no. 324 (July 1967), pp. 536–41

War, Politics and Finance Under Edward I (London, 1972)

Price, W. H. *The English Patents of Monopoly* (Cambridge, Mass., 1906; reprinted New York, 1978)

Prince, Albert E. 'The Army and the Navy' in *The English Government at Work, 1327–36*, ed. J. Willard and W. Morris, vol. I (Cambridge, Mass., 1940), pp. 332–93

Public Record Office. 'Militia Muster Rolls 1522–1640', Public Record Office Leaflet 10 (London, October 1977)

Quintrell, Brian. 'Government in Perspective: Lancashire and the Privy Council, 1570–1640', *Transactions of the Historic Society of Lancashire and Cheshire*, 131 (1982), pp. 35–63

'The Government of the County of Essex 1603–1642' (Ph.D. thesis, University of London, 1965)

'The Making of Charles I's *Book of Orders*', *EHR*, 95, no. 376 (July 1980), pp. 553–72

Rabb, Theodore K. 'Revisionism Revised: Two Perspectives on Early Stuart Parliamentary History – The Role of the Commons', *Past and Present*, 92 (August 1981), pp. 55–78

Reeve, L. J. *Charles I and the Road to Personal Rule* (Cambridge, 1989)

Reid, S. *Scots Armies of the Civil War 1639–1651* (Leigh-on-Sea, Essex, 1982)

Revill, Philippa and F. W. Steer. 'George Gage I and George Gage II', *BIHR*, 31 (1958), pp. 141–58

Richards, J. '"His Noew Majestie" and the English Monarchy: The Kingship of Charles I before 1640', *Past and Present*, 113 (1986), pp. 70–96

Ricketts, Howard. *Firearms* (London, 1964)

Robertson, James C. 'Caroline Culture: Bridging Court and Country?', *History*, 75, no. 245 (October, 1990), pp. 388–416

Roy, Ian. 'The English Civil War and English Society', in *War and Society: A Yearbook of Military History*, ed. Brian Bond and Ian Roy (London, 1977), pp.24–43

Rubinstein, H. L. *Captain Luckless: James First Duke of Hamilton, 1606–1649* (Edinburgh, 1975)

Russell, Conrad. 'Arguments for Religious Unity: 1530–1650', *Journal of Ecclesiastical History*, 18, no. 2 (October 1967), pp. 201–26

'The British Problem and the English Civil War', *History*, 72 (1987), pp. 395–415

The Causes of the English Civil War (Oxford, 1990)

'Charles I's Financial Estimates for 1642', *BIHR*, 58, no. 137 (May 1985), pp. 109–120

The Crisis of Parliaments: English History 1509–1660 (Oxford, 1971)

The Fall of the British Monarchies, 1637–1642 (Oxford, 1991)

'Monarchies, Wars, and Estates in England, France, and Spain, c.1580–c.1640', *Legislative Studies Quarterly*, 7, no. 2 (May 1982), pp. 205–20

'The Nature of a Parliament in Early Stuart England', in *Before the English Civil War*, ed. H. Tomlinson (New York, 1984), pp. 23–50, 202–6

(ed.). *The Origins of the English Civil War* (London, 1973)

'Parliament and the King's Finances', in *The Origins of the English Civil War*, ed. C. Russell (London, 1973), pp. 91–116, 268–70

Parliaments and English Politics 1621–1629 (Oxford, 1979)

Review of Lawrence Stone's *The Cause of the English Revolution, 1529–1642*, *EHR*, 88, no. 349 (October 1973), pp. 856–61

'The Scottish Party in English Parliaments 1640–1642 or the Myth of the English Revolution', Inaugural Lecture in the Department of History, King's College London, 29 January, 1991

Unrevolutionary England 1603–1642 (London, 1990)

'Why did Charles I Summon the Long Parliament?', *History*, 69, no. 227 (October 1984), pp. 375–83

Sainty, J. C. 'Lieutenants of Counties, 1585–1642', *BIHR*, special supplement no. 8 (May 1970)

Schwarz, Marc L. 'Viscount Saye and Sele, Lord Brooke and Aristocratic Protest to the First Bishops' War', *Canadian Journal of History*, 7, no. 1 (April 1972), pp. 1–36

Schwoerer, Lois. '"The Fittest Subject for a King's Quarrel": An Essay on the Militia Controversy 1641–1642', *JBS*, 7, no. 1 (1971), pp. 45–76

Scott, Jonathan. 'Revising Stuart Britain: Towards a New Synthesis', review essay, *Historical Journal*, 31, no. 2 (June 1988), pp. 443–67

Seaver, Paul S. *The Puritan Lectureships: The Politics of Religious Dissent, 1560–1662* (Stanford, 1970)

Seddon, P. R. 'The Nottinghamshire Elections for the Short Parliament of 1640', *Transactions of the Thoroton Society of Nottinghamshire*, 80 (1976), pp. 63–8

Sharp, Buchanan. 'Common Rights, Charities and the Disorderly Poor', in *Reviving the English Revolution*, ed. Geoff Eley and William Hunt (London, 1988), pp. 107–37

In Contempt of All Authority: Rural Artisans and Riot in the West of England 1586–1660 (Berkeley, Calif., 1980)

'The Place of the People in the English Revolution', *Theory and Society*, 13 (1984), pp. 93–110

Sharpe, J. A. 'Crime and Delinquency in an Essex Parish 1600–1640', in *Crime in England 1550–1800*, ed. J. S. Cockburn (London, 1977), pp. 90–109, 316–21

Sharpe, Kevin. 'Crown, Parliament and Locality: Government and Communication in early Stuart England', *EHR*, 101, centenary number (January 1986), pp. 321–50

(ed.) *Faction and Parliament: Essays on Early Stuart History* (Oxford, 1978)

The Personal Rule of Charles I (New Haven, Conn., 1992)

Sharpe, Reginald. *London and the Kingdom*, vol. II (London, 1894)

Shelby, L. R. *John Rogers, Tudor Military Engineer* (Oxford, 1967)

Sinclair, G. E. 'Scotsmen Serving the Swede', *Scottish Historical Review*, 9, no. 33 (October 1911), pp. 37–51

Slack, Paul. 'An Election to the Short Parliament', *BIHR*, 46, (1973), pp. 108–14

'Books of Orders: The Making of English Social Policy, 1577–1631', *TRHS*, fifth series, 30 (1980), pp. 1–22

Smuts, R. M. 'The Puritan Followers of Henrietta Maria in the 1630's', *EHR*, 93 (January 1978), pp. 26–47

Snow, Vernon F. *Essex The Rebel The Life of Robert Devereux, The Third Earl of Essex, 1591–1646* (Lincoln, Nebraska, 1970)

Solt, Leo F. *Saints in Arms: Puritanism and Democracy in Cromwell's Army* (Stanford, 1959)

Sommerville, J. P. *Politics and Ideology in England 1603–1640* (London, 1986)

Spence, R. T. 'The Pacification of the Cumberland borders, 1593–1628', *Northern History*, 13 (1977), pp. 59–160

Stater, V. 'The Lord Lieutenancy on the Eve of the Civil Wars: The Impressment of George Plowright', *The Historical Journal*, 29, no. 2 (1986), pp. 279–96

'War and the Structure of Politics, Lieutenancy and the Campaign of 1628', *War and Government in Britain, 1598–1650*, ed. M. Fissel (Manchester, 1991), pp. 87–109

Stearns, Stephen J. 'Conscription and English Society in the 1620's', *Journal of British Studies*, 11, no. 2 (May 1972), pp. 1–23

'Caroline Military Organization: The Expeditions to Cadiz and Rhé 1625–7' (Ph.D. dissertation, University of California, Berkeley, 1967)

Steel, Anthony. *The Receipt of the Exchequer 1337–1485* (Cambridge, 1954)

Stevenson, David. 'The Financing of the Cause of the Covenants, 1638–51', *The Scottish Historical Review*, 51:2, no. 152 (October 1972), pp. 89–100

(ed.) *The Government of Scotland under the Covenanters, 1637–1651* (Edinburgh, 1982)

Scottish Covenanters and Irish Confederates. Scottish-Irish Relations in the Mid-Seventeenth Century (Belfast, 1981)

The Scottish Revolution 1637–44: The Triumph of the Covenanters (Newton Abbot, 1973)

Stewart, Richard. 'Arms Accountability in Early Stuart Militia', *BIHR*, 57, no. 135 (May 1984), pp. 113–17

'Arms and Expeditions: The Ordnance Office and the Assaults on Cadiz (1625) and the Isle of Rhé (1627)', in *War and Government in Britain, 1598–1650*, ed. M. Fissel (Manchester, 1991), pp. 112–32

'The "Irish Road": Military Supply and Arms for Elizabeth's Army during the O'Neill Rebellion, 1598–1601', in *War and Government in Britain, 1598–1650*, ed. M. Fissel (Manchester, 1991), pp. 16–37

Stone, Lawrence. *The Crisis of the Aristocracy* (Oxford, 1965)

Stones, E. 'The Folvilles of Ashby-Folville, Leicestershire, and Their Associates in Crime, 1326–1347', *TRHS*, fifth series, 7 (1957) pp. 117–36

Storey, R. L. 'The North of England', in *Fifteenth Century England*, ed. S. B. Chrimes, C. D. Ross, and B. A. Griffith (Manchester, 1972), pp. 129–144

Strong, Roy. *Van Dyck: Charles I on Horseback* (New York, 1972)

Supple, B. E. *Commercial Crisis and Change in England 1600–1642* (Cambridge, 1959)

Tawney, A. J. and Tawney, R. H. 'An Occupational Census of the Seventeenth Century', *EconHR*, 5, no. 1 (October 1934), pp. 25–64

Terry, C. S. *The Life and Campaigns of Alexander Leslie, First Earl of Leven* (London, 1899)

Thomas, David. 'Financial and Administrative Developments', in *Before the English Civil War*, ed. H. Tomlinson (New York, 1984), pp. 103–22, 200–2

Thomas, Keith. *Religion and the Decline of Magic: Studies in Popular Beliefs in Sixteenth and Seventeenth Century England* (London, 1971)

Thomas, P. W. 'Two Cultures? Court and Country under Charles I', in *The Origins of the English Civil War*, ed. C. Russell (New York, 1973), pp. 168–93

Thompson, I. A. A. 'The Impact of War' in *The European Crisis of the 1590s*, ed. P. Clark (London, 1985), pp. 261–84

Thomson, Gladys S. 'The Bishops of Durham and the Office of Lord Lieutenant in the Seventeenth Century', *EHR*, 40 (July 1925), pp. 351–74

'The Origin and Growth of the Office of Deputy Lieutenant', *TRHS*, fourth series, 5 (1922), pp. 150–67

Thrush, Andrew. 'Naval Finance and the Origins and Development of Ship Money', *War and Government in Britain, 1598–1650* ed. M. Fissel (Manchester, 1991), pp. 133–62

'The Ordnance Office and the Navy, 1625–40', *The Mariner's Mirror*, 77, no. 4 (November 1991), pp. 339-54

Tough, D. L. *The Last Years of a Frontier; A history of the borders during the reign of Elizabeth* (Oxford, 1928)

Trevor-Roper, H. R. 'Scotland and the Puritan Revolution', in *Historical Essays 1600–1750 presented to David Ogg*, ed. H. E. Bell and R. L. Ollard (New York, 1973), pp. 78–130

Tuck, J. A. 'War and Society in the Medieval North', *Northern History*, 21 (1985), pp. 33–52

Tyacke, Nicholas. *Anti-Calvinists. The Rise of English Arminianism c. 1590–1640* (Oxford, 1987)

Ullmann, Walter. '"This Realm of England is an Empire"', *Journal of Ecclesiastical History*, 30, no. 2 (April 1979), pp. 175-203

Ward, Marjorie. *The Blessed Trade* (London, 1971)

Watts, S. J. *From border to Middle Shire. Northumberland 1586–1625* (Leicester, 1975)

Way, L. V. 'The Smyths of Ashton Court', *Transactions of the Bristol and Gloucestershire Archaeological Society*, 31, Part II (1908), pp. 244–60

Webb, Henry J. *Elizabethan Military Science, the Books and the Practice* (London, 1965)

Wedgwood, C. V. *The King's Peace 1637–1641* (New York, 1969)

Welch, Charles. *History of the Cutlers' Company* (London, 1922)

Wernham, R. B. *After the Armada. Elizabethan England and the Struggle for Western Europe 1588–1595* (Oxford, 1984)

'Elizabethan War Aims and Strategy', in *Elizabethan Government and Society: Essays presented to Sir John Neale*, ed. S. Bindoff, J. Hurstfield, and C. Williams (London, 1961), pp. 340–68

Whiting, Robert. 'Abominable Idols: Images and Image-breaking under Henry VIII', *Journal of Ecclesiastical History*, 33, no. 1 (January 1982), pp. 30–47

Williams, Penry. 'The Northern borderland under the Early Stuarts', in *Historical Essays 1600–1750 presented to David Ogg*, ed. H. E. Bell and R. L. Ollard (New York, 1973), pp. 1–17

Willcox, William B. *Gloucestershire 1540–1640, A Study in Local Government* (New Haven, Conn., 1940)

Woolrych, Austin. 'Court, County, and City Revisited', review essay, *History*, 65, no. 214 (June 1980), pp. 236–45

Wrightson, Keith. *English Society, 1580–1680* (New Brunswick, N.J., 1982)

'Two Concepts of Order: Justices, Constables, and Jurymen in Seventeenth Century England', in *An Ungovernable People, The English and their Law in the Seventeenth and Eighteenth Centuries*, ed. John Brewer and John Styles (London, 1980), pp. 21–46

Young, Michael B., 'Charles I and the Erosion of Trust, 1625–8', *Albion*, 22 (summer 1990), no. 2, pp. 217–35

'Illusions of Grandeur and Reform at the Jacobean Court: Cranfield and the Ordnance', *Historical Journal*, 22, no. 1 (1979), pp. 53–73

'Revisionism and the Council of War', *Parliamentary History*, 8, pt. 1 (1989), pp. 1–27

Servility and Service. The Life and Work of Sir John Coke (Woodbridge, Suffolk, 1986)

Zaller, R. 'Legitimation and Delegitimation in Early Modern Europe: The Case of England', *History of European Ideas*, 10, no. 6 (1989), pp. 641–65.

INDEX

Cambridge Studies in Early Modern British History

Titles in the series